Please return to Robbie Roberts
403-938-5074.

SAFARI 04/18 -24/2010

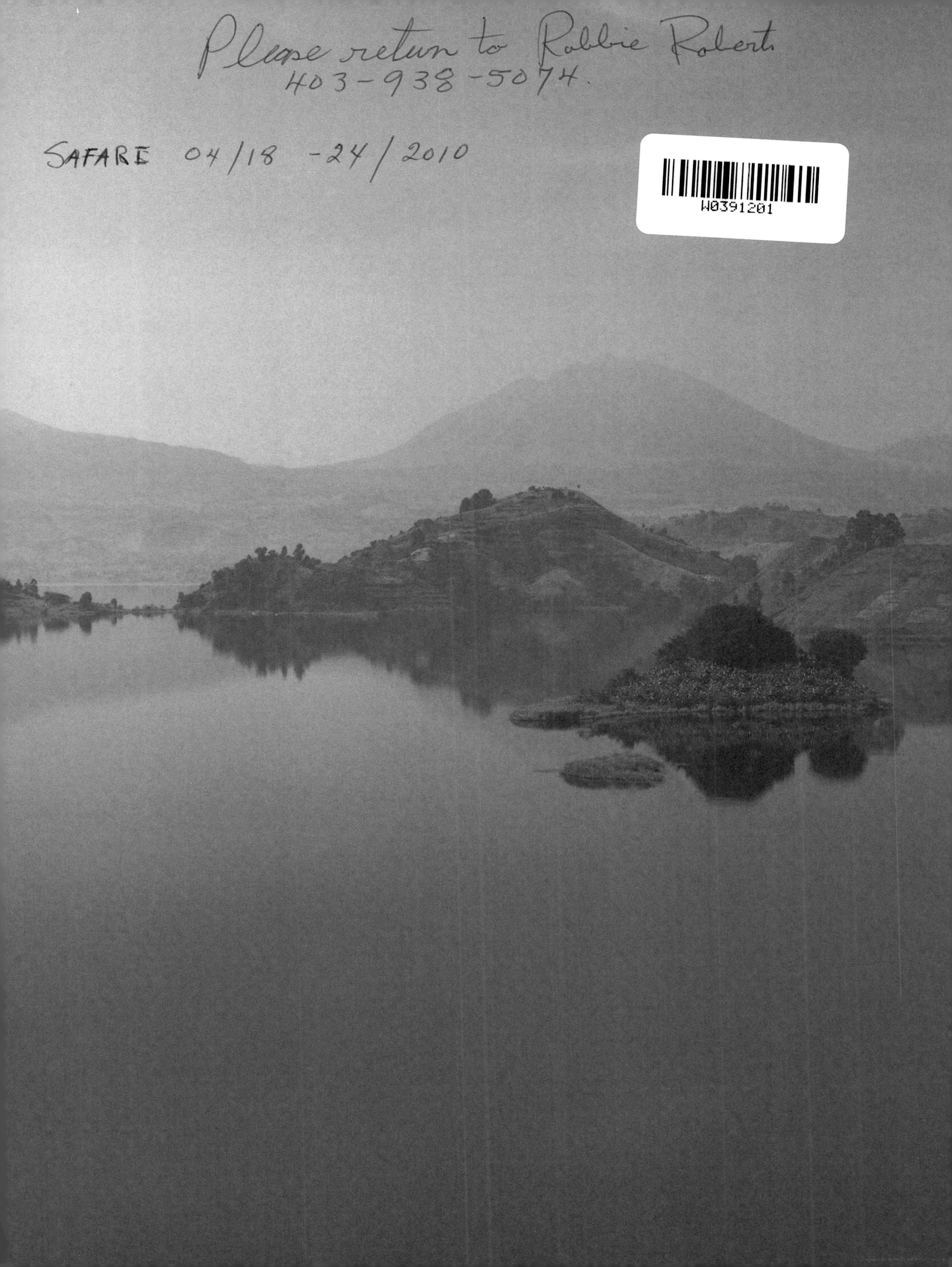

▪ JOURNEY THROUGH ▪
UGANDA

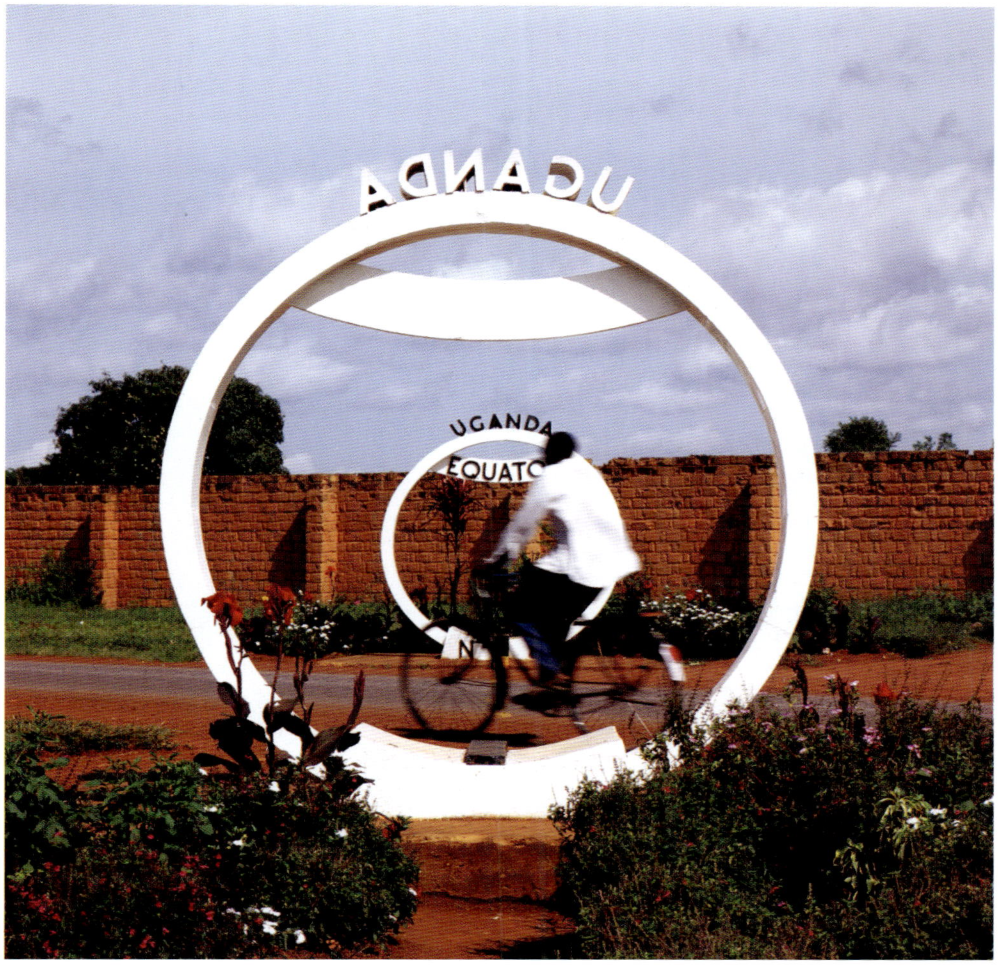

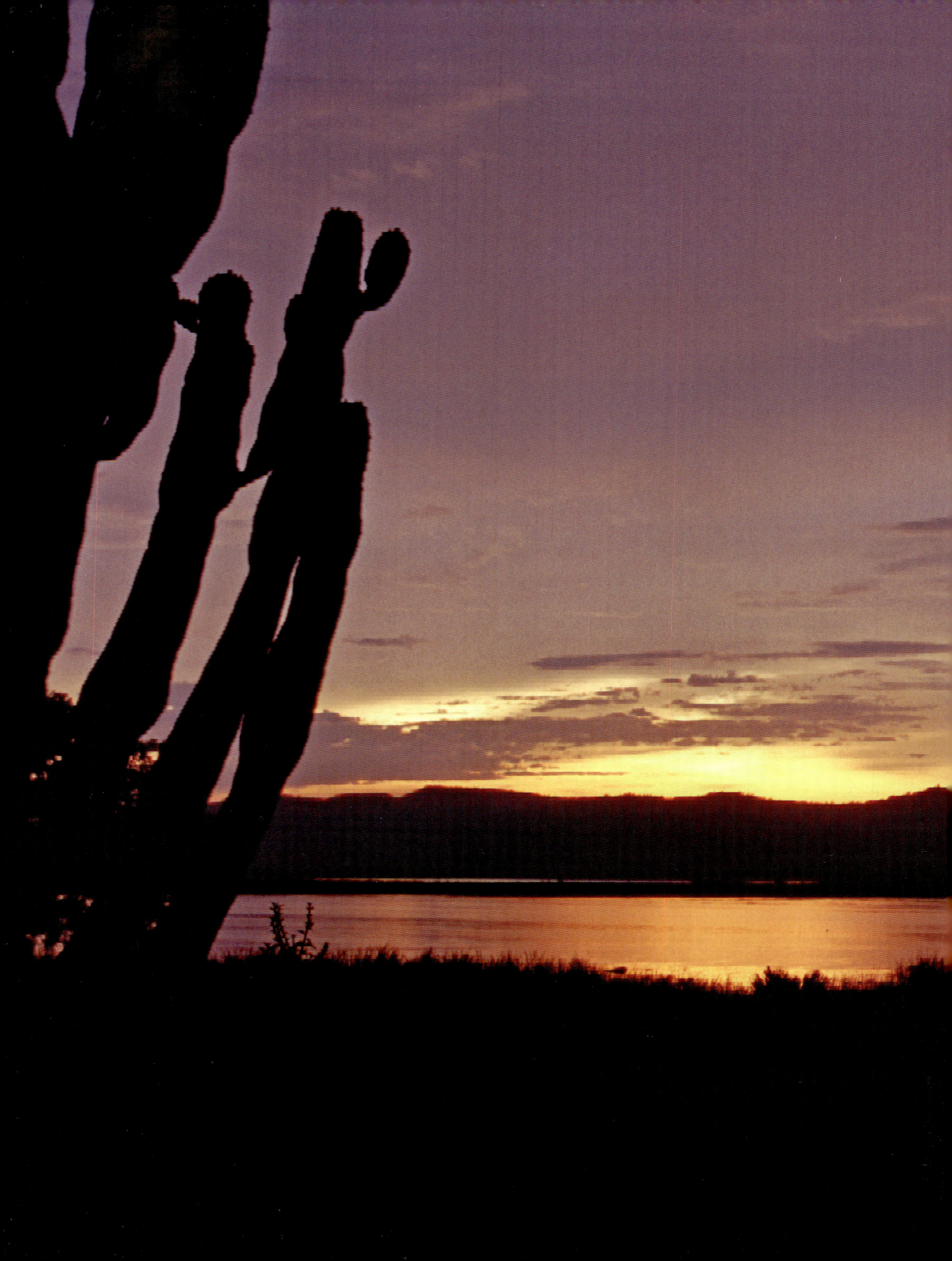

JOURNEY THROUGH
UGANDA

DAVID PLUTH • PHILIP BRIGGS

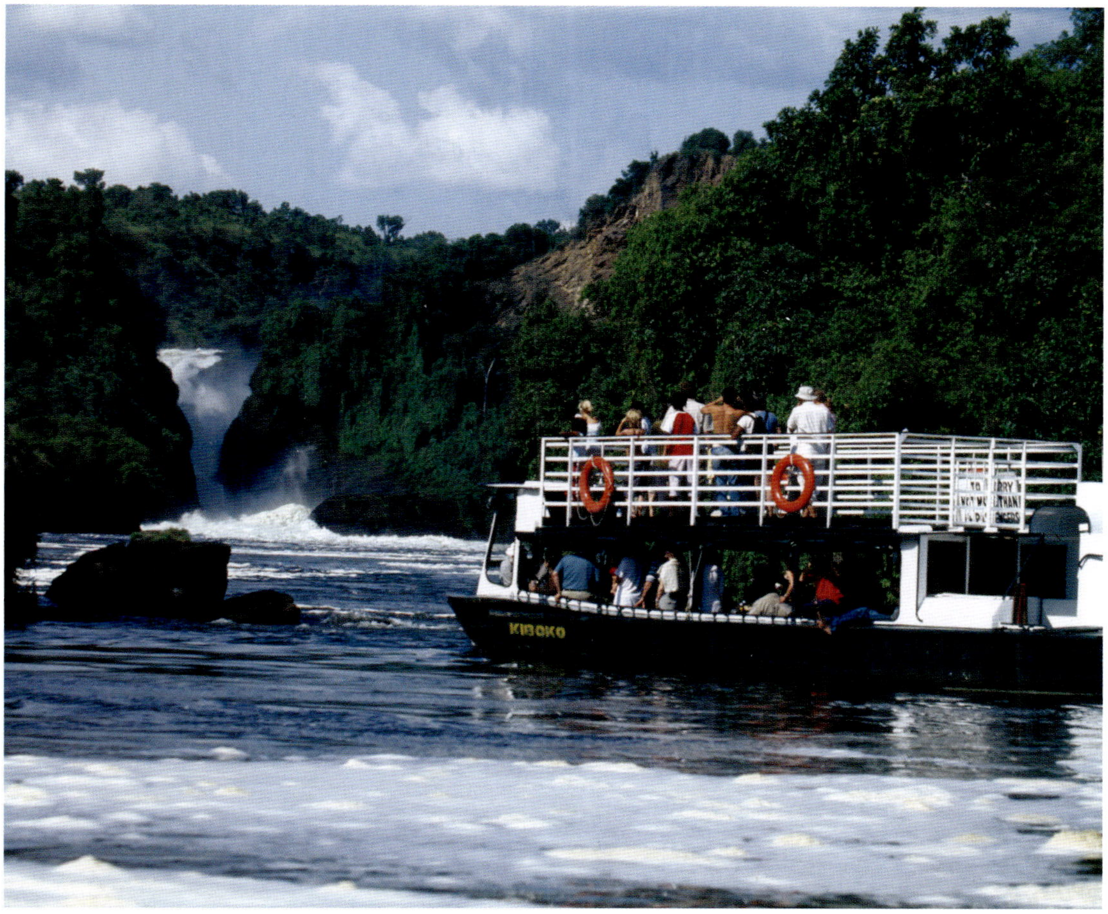

CAMERAPIX
PUBLISHERS INTERNATIONAL

This book was designed and produced by
Camerapix Publishers International
PO Box 45048, 00100 GPO
Nairobi, Kenya

ISBN: 978-1-904722-30-4

Production Director: Rukhsana Haq
Edited by: Philip Briggs and Roger Barnard
Design: Sam Kimani and Rachel Musyimi

Printed in Singapore.

All pictures by **David Pluth.**

Half-title: Crossing the Equator is a regular occurrence for many Ugandans.

Page 2: Uganda can boast of some of the most spectacular sunsets in the world; on the Nile, near Adjumani.

Title page: The boat trip to the foot of Murchison Falls, in western Uganda, is a never-to-be-forgotten experience for thousands of visitors every year.

Contents: Uganda is home to a remarkable 13 primate species, including the chimpanzee.

CONTENTS

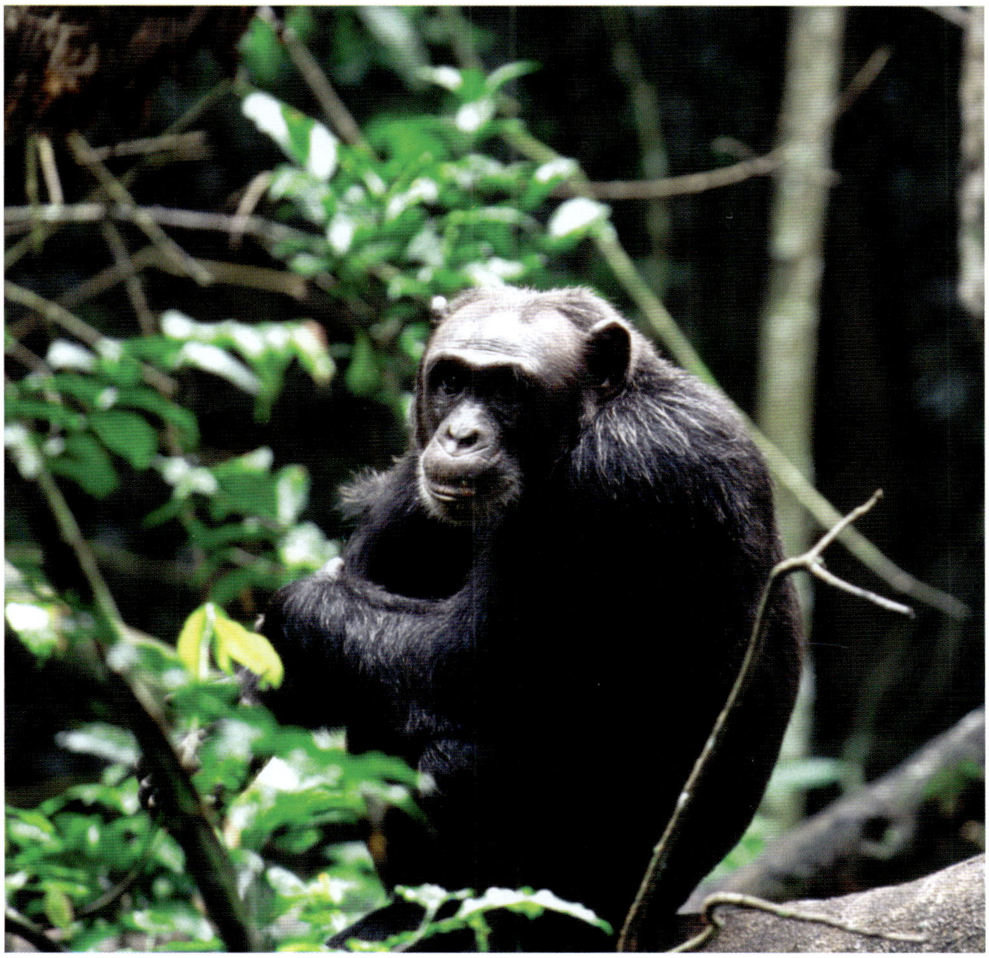

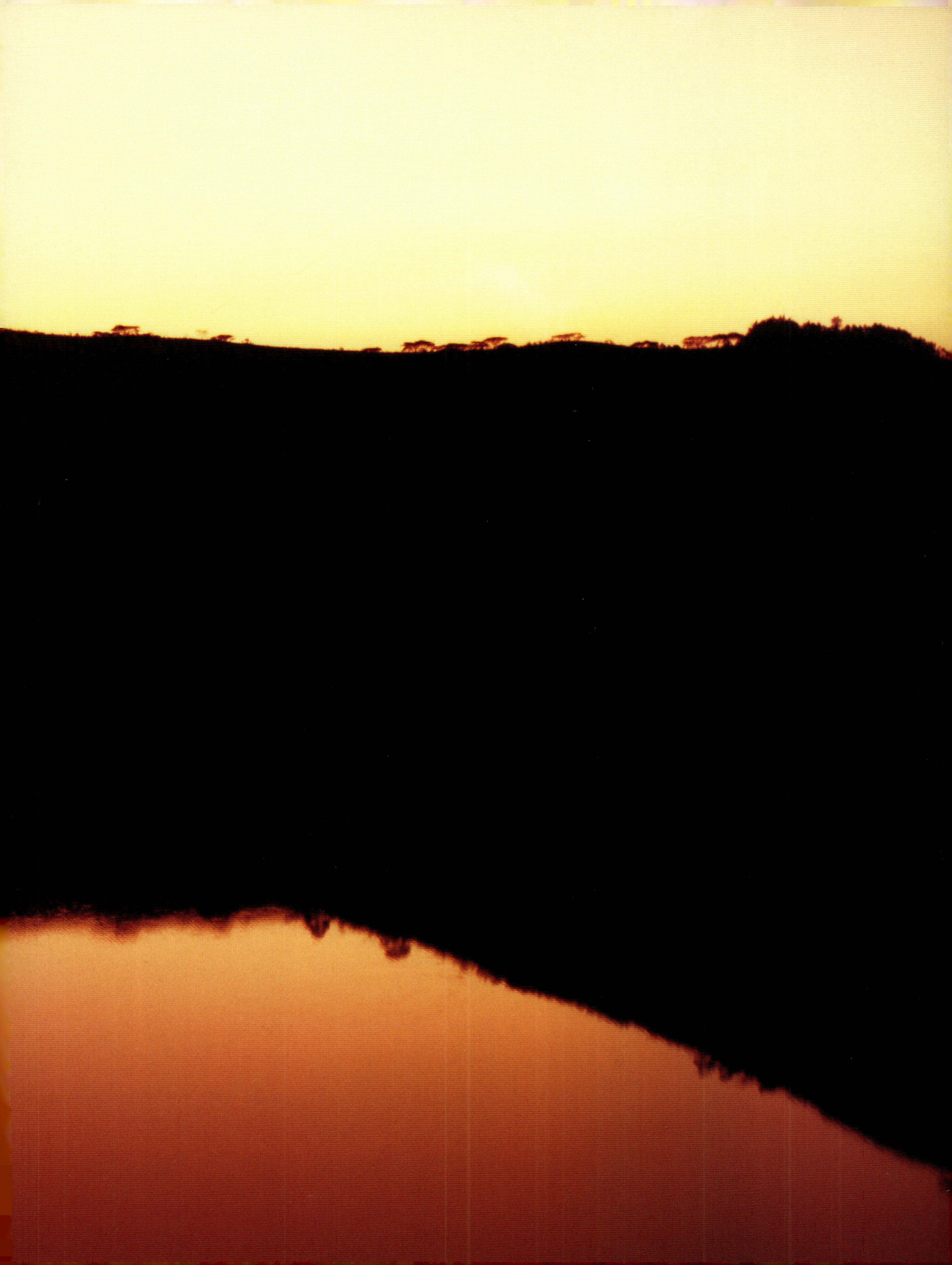

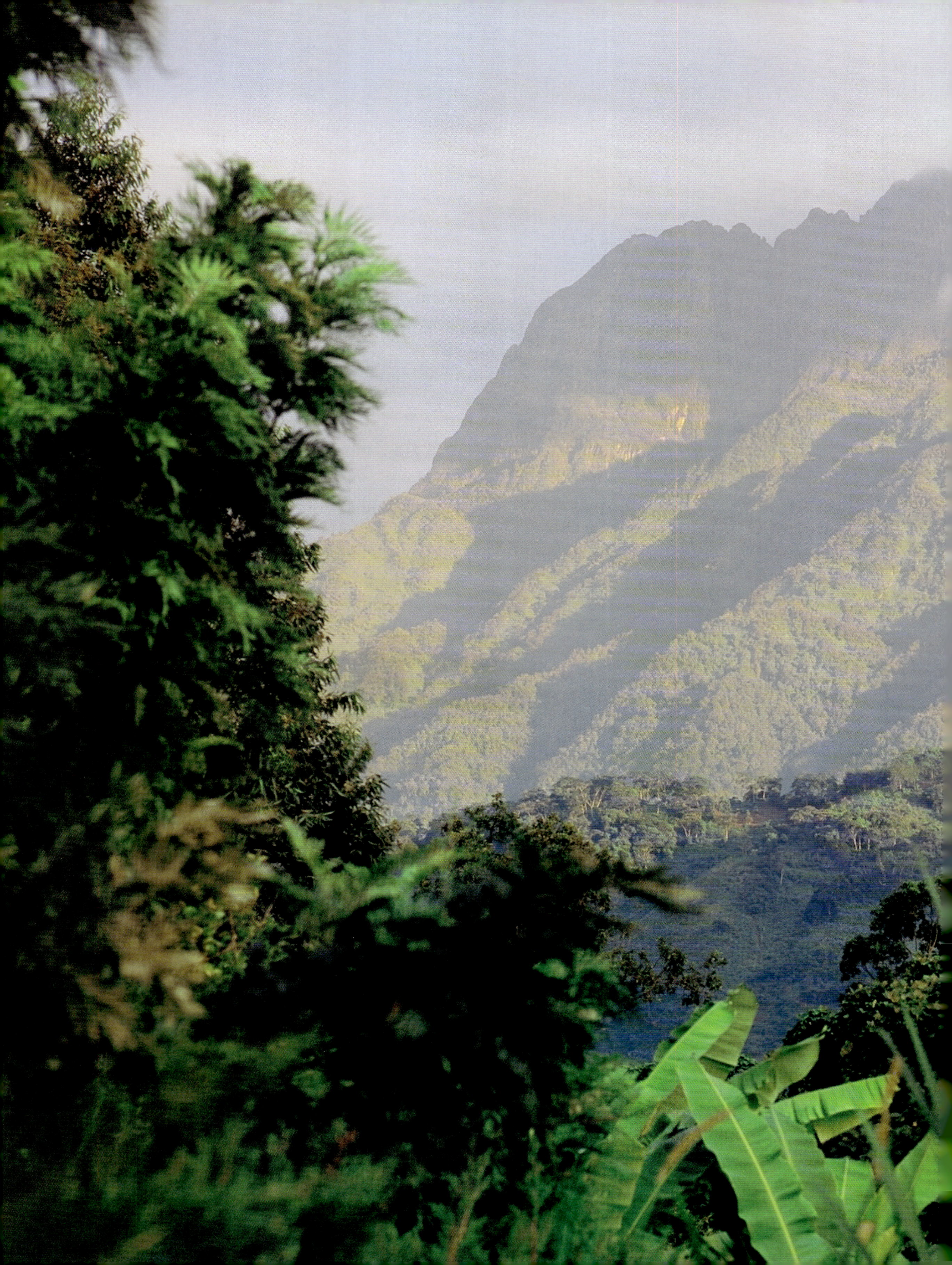

1. Introduction

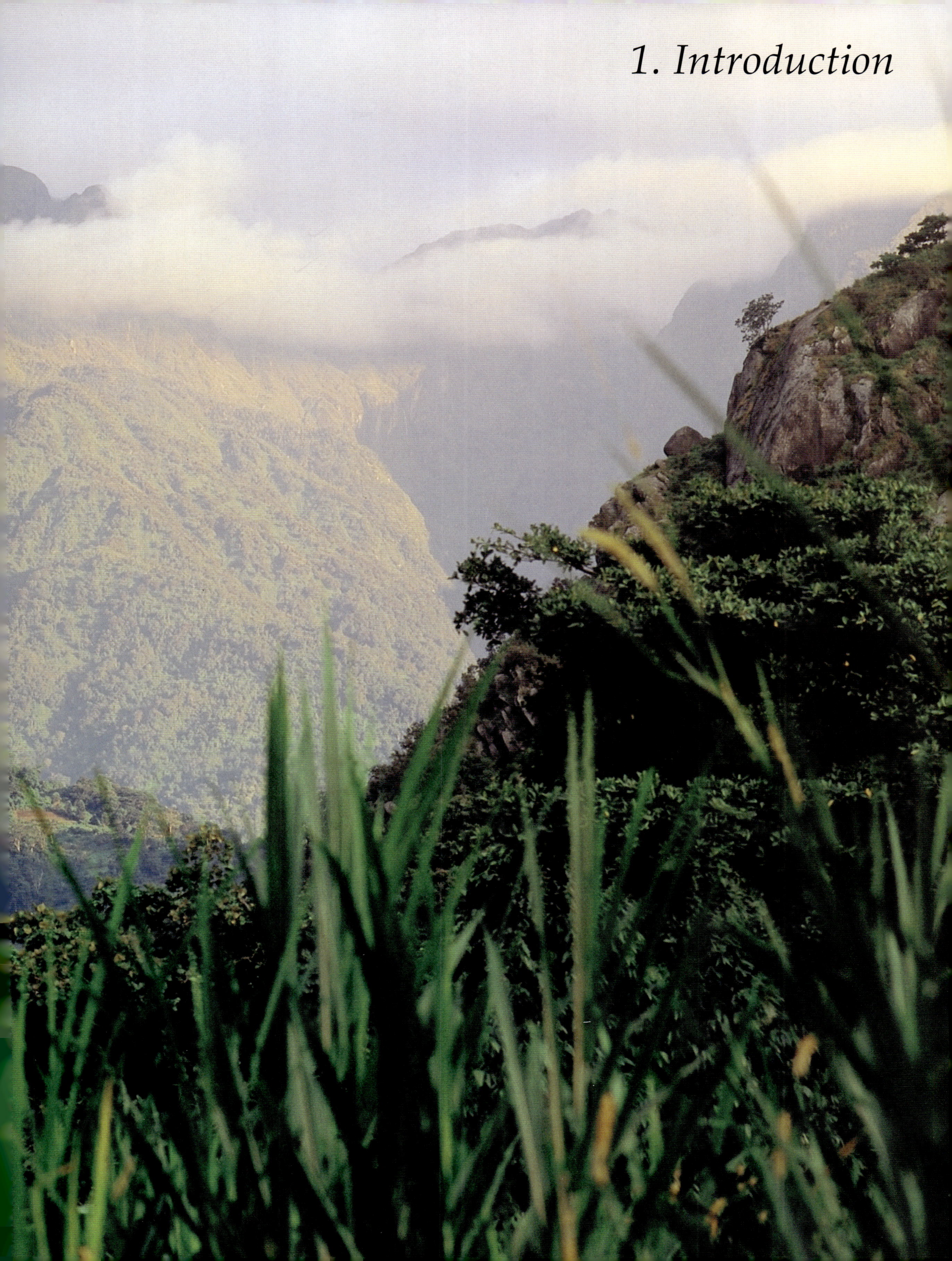

Previous pages: Spectacular sunset over Nyambuga Crater Lake; Magnificent peaks of the Rwenzoris – the fable 'Mountains of the Moon'.

Right: The source of the Nile, once the quest of explorers, can now readily be seen by any visitor to Uganda.

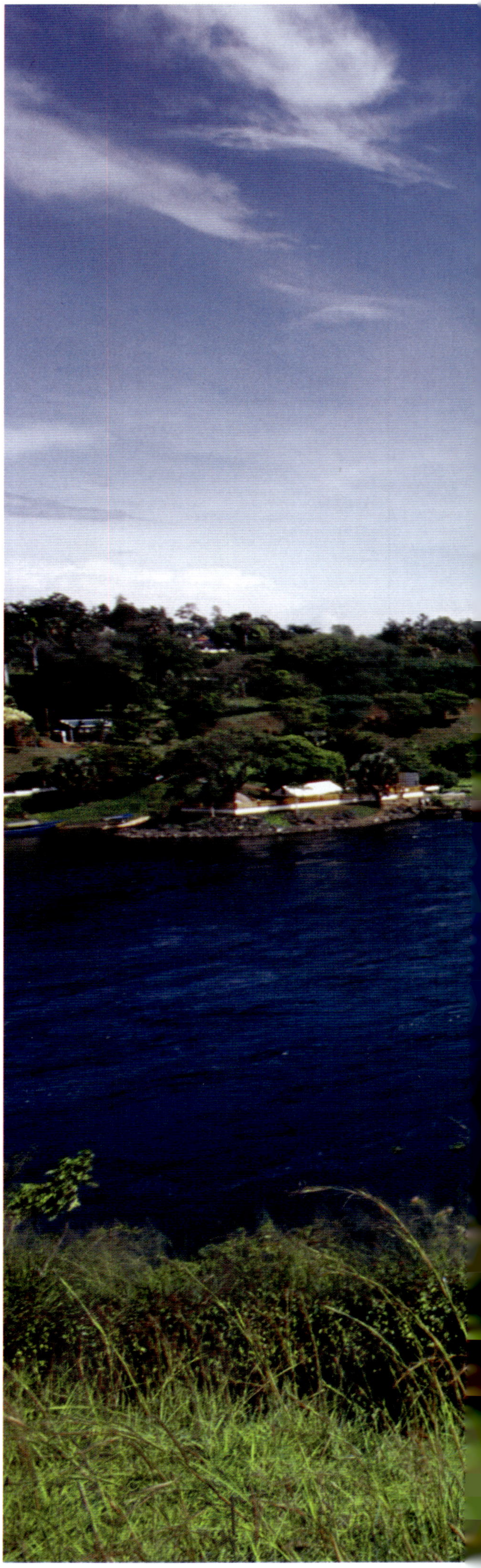

Landlocked Uganda lies on a beautiful, green plateau that straddles the Equator between the eastern and western branches of the Great Rift Valley. Nature has endowed this East African country with one of the most pleasant climates in the world – actually, a variety of different local climates – and if you don't like one, you won't travel far to find another that's more to your liking. Featuring a dramatic combination of mountains, semi-desert, rainforest, savannah, lakes and rivers, the country supports also a splendid array of fauna and flora, ranging from mountain gorillas and lions to the enigmatic shoebill stork and weird giant lobelia.

Uganda is a compact country, covering 241,550 square kilometres (91,344 square miles) – roughly the size of Great Britain or the state of Oregon. The central plateau averages 1,050 metres (3,450 feet) above sea level. The country is unusually moist and fertile by African standards: roughly one-quarter of its surface area is comprised of wetlands, including the world's second-largest freshwater body, Lake Victoria, and the legendary Nile River. Some 100 years ago Winston Churchill famously described Uganda as the 'Pearl of Africa'. Much water has flown through the Nile since then, but the pearl still shines strongly.

Along the borders, several mountain masses protrude from the plateau. The largest and tallest of these is the Rwenzoris range, which runs along the Congolese border for 120 kilometres (72 miles) and whose glacial peaks tower to 5,109 metres (16,762 feet), the third highest point in Africa. The range is also known as the Mountains of the Moon, an evocative name that dates back to the 2nd century AD, when it was identified as the source of the Nile by the Roman geographer Ptolemy. Possessed of great physical beauty, the Rwenzoris is the highest non-volcanic mountain range in Africa, having formed as a result of the same tectonic shifts that created the Rift Valley, and the rocky upper slopes support the unusual phenomenon of equatorial snowfields. At the southern base of the Rwenzoris are salt lakes and the renowned Queen Elizabeth National Park, while the northern slopes descend to the shores of Lake Albert, which also lies along the Congolese border.

In eastern Uganda looms Mount Elgon, an extinct volcano that rises to 4,324 metres (14,186 feet) from its immense base along the boundary with Kenya. North of Mount Elgon are four smaller volcanic mountains running up towards the border with Sudan. Meanwhile, in the extreme southwest, a trio of recently extinct volcanoes – Sabinyo, Muhavura and Gahinga – form part of the spectacular Virunga Range, a group of seven freestanding volcanic massifs that extends southwest into Rwanda and The Democratic Republic of Congo, and whose forested slopes are renowned as the home of the mountain gorilla. The dissected plateau to the northeast of these volcanic mountains resembles the Scottish or

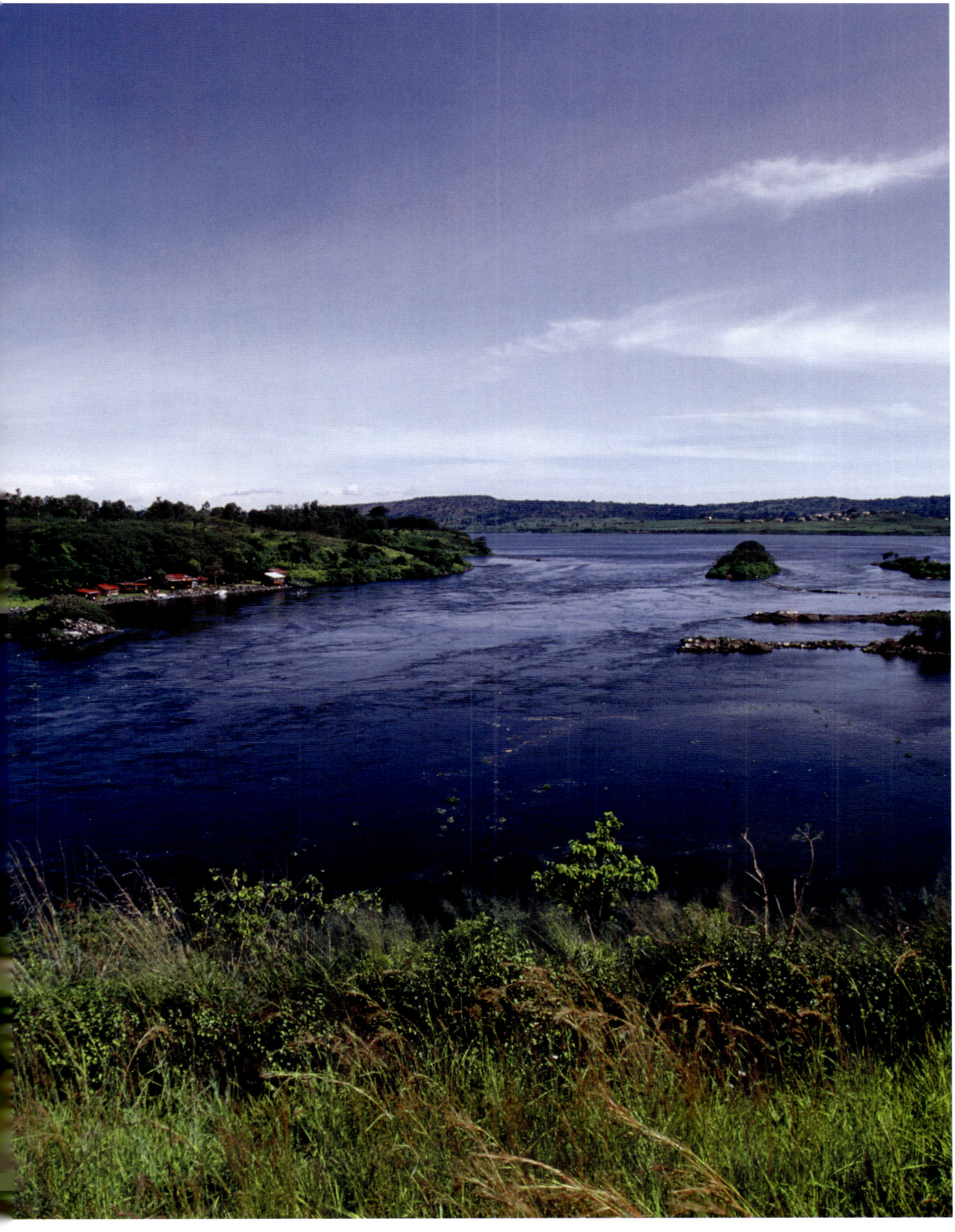

Uganda

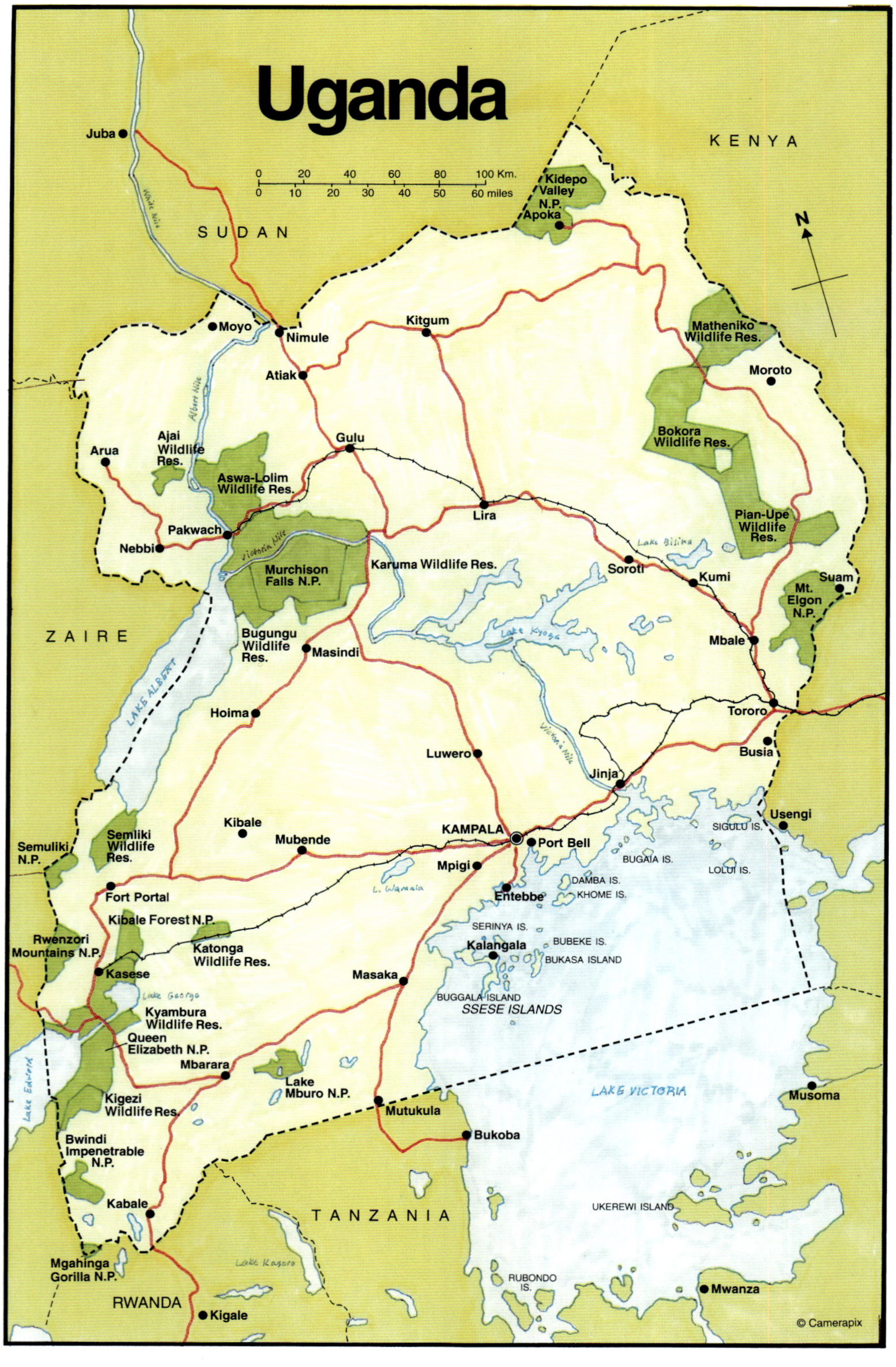

Uganda
0 20 40 60 80 100 Km.
0 10 20 30 40 50 60 miles
N
Juba
SUDAN
KENYA
Kidepo Valley N.P.
Apoka
Moyo
Nimule
Kitgum
Atiak
Matheniko Wildlife Res.
Moroto
Arua
Ajai Wildlife Res.
Gulu
Bokora Wildlife Res.
Aswa-Lolim Wildlife Res.
Lira
Pakwach
Nebbi
Pian-Upe Wildlife Res.
Murchison Falls N.P.
Karuma Wildlife Res.
Soroti
Kumi
Suam
Mt. Elgon N.P.
ZAIRE
Bugungu Wildlife Res.
Masindi
Mbale
Hoima
Tororo
Busia
Luwero
Jinja
Kibale
Usengi
Semuliki N.P.
Semliki Wildlife Res.
Mubende
KAMPALA
Port Bell
SIGULU IS.
BUGAIA IS.
LOLUI IS.
Mpigi
Fort Portal
DAMBA IS.
Entebbe
KHOME IS.
Kibale Forest N.P.
SERINYA IS.
Rwenzori Mountains N.P.
Katonga Wildlife Res.
Kalangala
BUBEKE IS.
BUKASA ISLAND
Kasese
Masaka
BUGGALA ISLAND
SSESE ISLANDS
Kyambura Wildlife Res.
Queen Elizabeth N.P.
Mbarara
Lake Mburo N.P.
Kigezi Wildlife Res.
Mutukula
Musoma
Bukoba
Bwindi Impenetrable N.P.
Kabale
TANZANIA
UKEREWI ISLAND
Mgahinga Gorilla N.P.
RUBONDO IS.
Mwanza
RWANDA
Kigale
© Camerapix

Swiss mountains, but on a grander scale, and has been described as the 'Switzerland of Africa'.

The south-central region of Uganda is dominated by the saucer-like depression of Lake Victoria, an immense inland sea wherein the boundaries of Uganda, Tanzania, and Kenya converge. Alongside the lakeside port of Jinja is the source of the Nile River, which emerges from the lake at an altitude of 1,240 metres (4,070 feet). Almost as soon as the river commences its long journey it flows through the Owen Falls Dam, which was constructed in the early 1950s to provide hydroelectric power to Uganda, Kenya and northern Tanzania. Another dam is being constructed nearby to generate more hydroelectric power for the ever-growing demand for energy in the region.

From Jinja, the great Nile flows northwards, traversing the Buganda region to flow through the swampy valley of Lake Kyoga, where it captures several tributaries from the eastern plateau. From Lake Kyoga the river flows towards the northern tip of Lake Albert, which it reaches after crossing the Karuma Falls, then funnelling into a cleft less than seven metres (23 feet) wide at the spectacular Murchison Falls, centrepiece of the country's largest national park. The river then flows out of Lake Albert in a northerly direction, reaching the Sudanese border at Nimule, joining with the Blue Nile (which rises in Ethiopia) at Khartoum, and then coursing the desert wastes of northern Sudan and Egypt. The world's longest river, the Nile traverses some 6,750 kilometres (4,050 miles) en route to the Mediterranean from its most remote source, which was thought to be in Burundi until a more distant candidate was located in Rwanda's Nyungwe Forest in 2006.

To the north of Lake Kyoga is a generally flat area through which the Aswa River follows an old fault line to join the Nile River just beyond the border of Uganda and Sudan after Nimule. The north-western part of Uganda forms the West Nile Plateau – an uplifted block lying on the western side of the Rift – which forms the boundary between Uganda and the DRC.

A variety of mineral deposits exist in Uganda, some of which have been mined for centuries, although the economic potential of most has yet to be exploited. These include industrial minerals such as graphite, talc, asbestos, garnet, magnetite, vermiculite, dolomite and limestone, as well as chromite, gold and copper, which are concentrated in Karamoja, with minor gold centres in the east, west and south-west. Until the 1960s, copper was of great importance in the Rwenzoris region. Tin, tungsten (wolfram) and beryllium have been mined in small quantities in southern Uganda, and several million tonnes of high-quality iron ore occurs around Kisoro and Kabale. Local salt extraction has gone on for a long time in

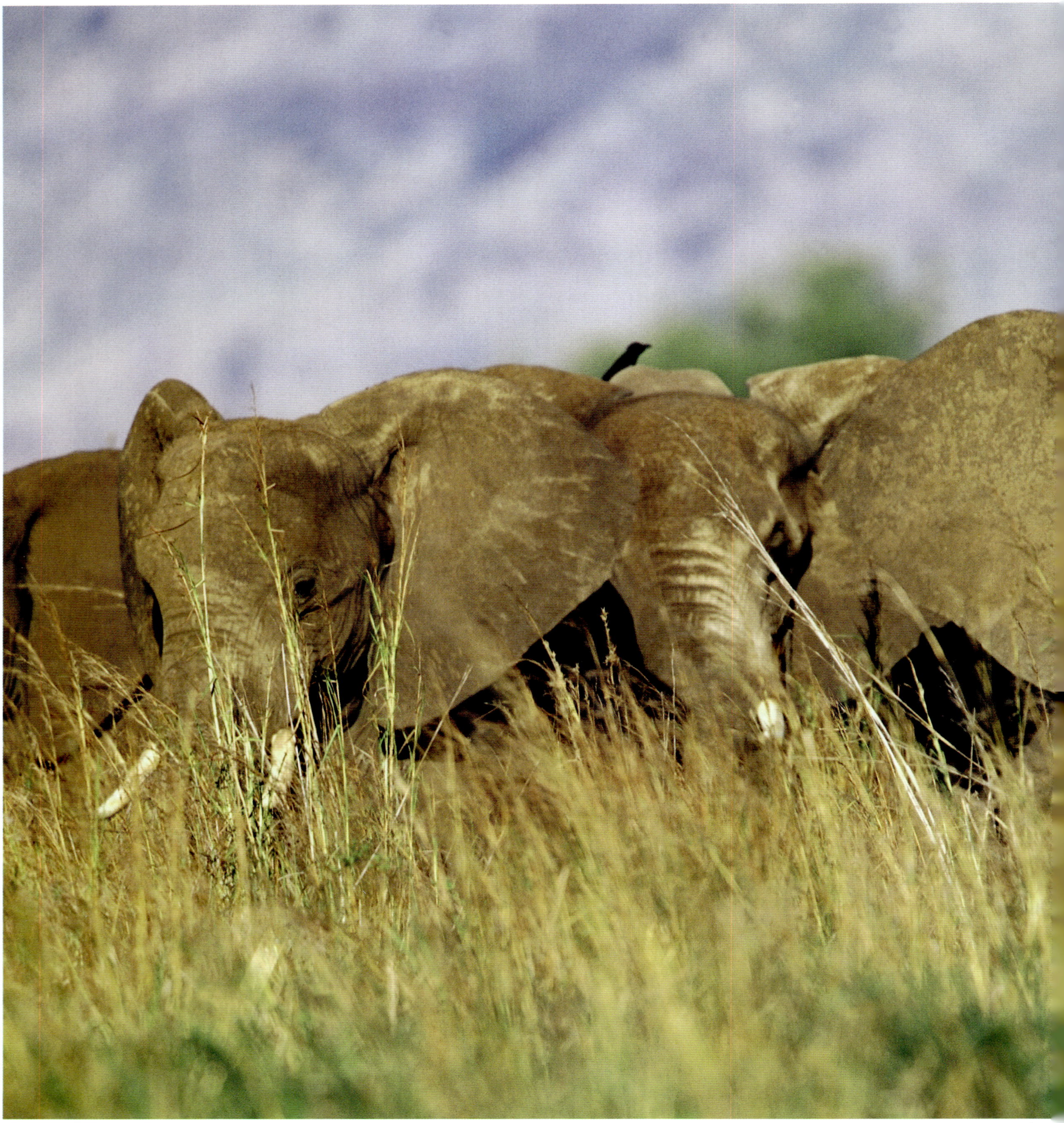

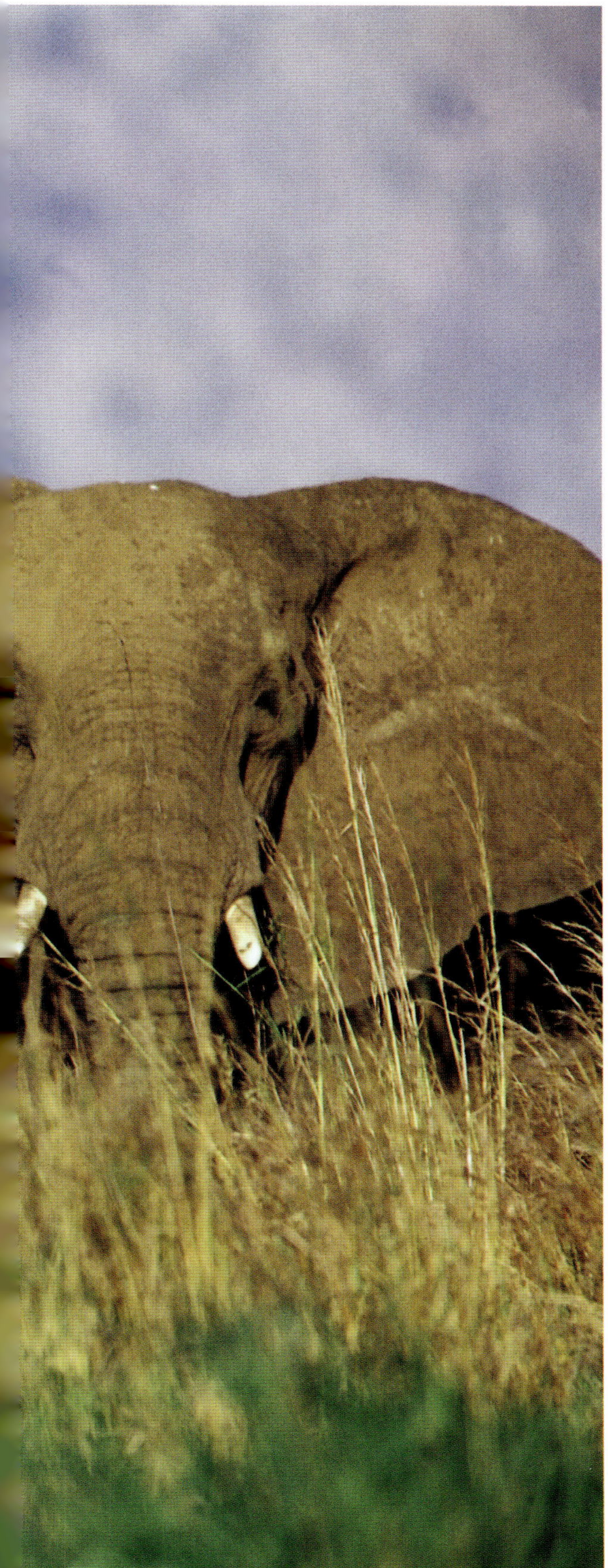

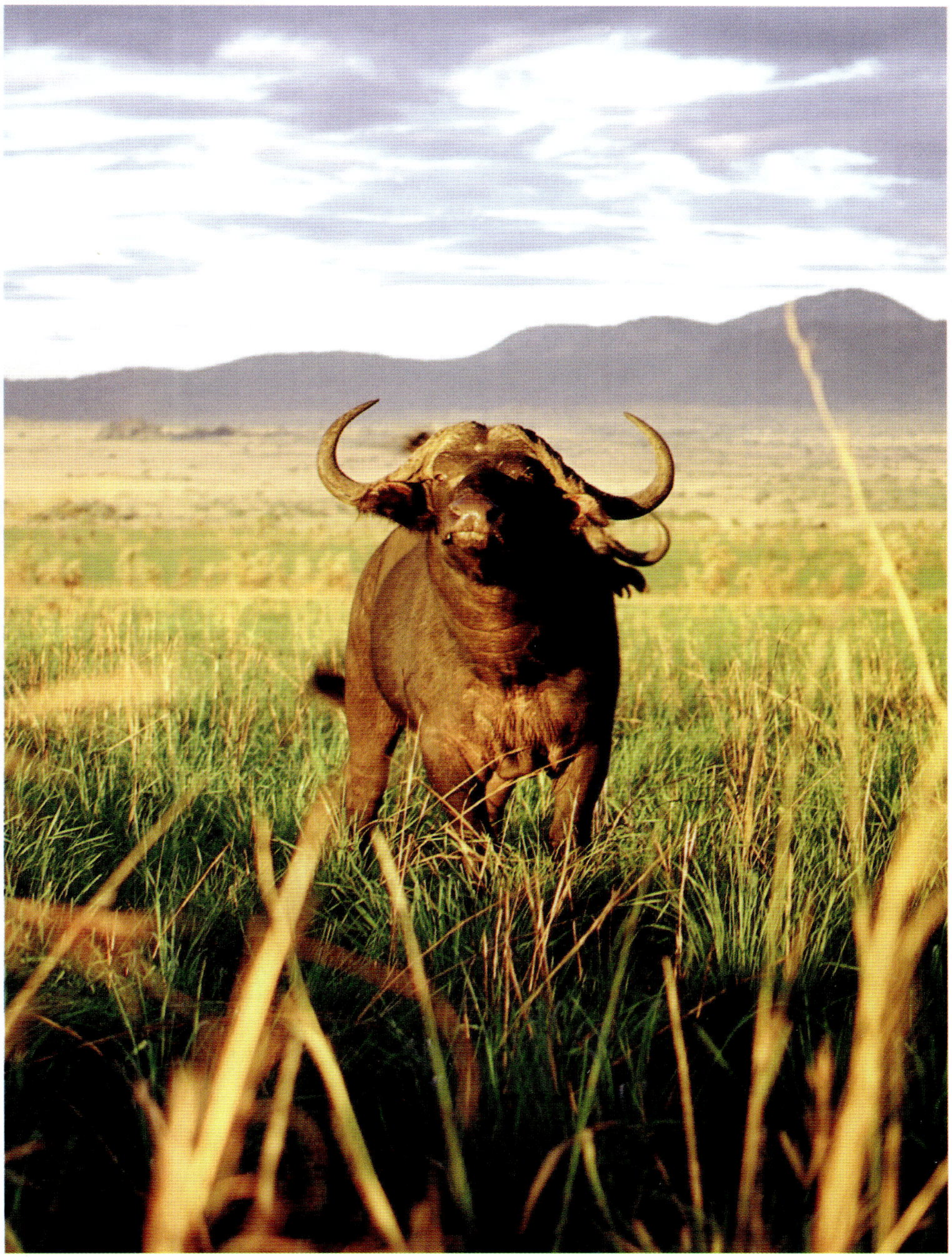

Above: Magnificent, but unpredictable, African Buffalo in Kidepo National Park.

Left: Uganda's elephant herds are now returning to their former numbers.

Below: Traditional boats on Lake Bisina, one of Uganda's many lakes.

Following pages: Casting net for fishing on Lake Victoria.

Katwe and Kibiro, while glass sands of high quality are available from the Lake Victoria region. Oil has recently been discovered at several sites in the vicinity of Lake Albert.

Much of Uganda receives in excess of 1,500mm of rain annually. There are distinct wet and dry seasons, but these tend not to be as marked as elsewhere in East Africa, with most regions receiving an average monthly precipitation of 50-100mm even in the relatively dry season. In the south, the wettest months are March-May and September-November, but these merge to form one extended rainy season in the northwest. The northeast is much drier than the rest of the country, partly as a result of the influence of the dry winds blowing across from Somalia, with a rainy season that runs from April to August, peaking from May to July. In most of Uganda rain most commonly falls in the afternoons, often in the form of dramatic thunderstorms, and severe hailstorms are frequent in the west, damaging crops and soil cover.

Uganda is blessed with fertile soils that support a wide variety of vegetation. There's Afro-alpine moorland and heath on the mountaintops, a habitat characterized by patches of ferns, reeds and sedges, as well as tree heathers, mosses, liverworts and pretty everlasting flowers. Forests abound in the mountains, valleys, and plateaux. Montane forests blanket the middle slopes of Elgon and Rwenzoris, interspersed with stands of pure bamboo towering up to 20 metres (65 feet) high, while evergreen lowland forest is to be found in well-watered areas along the Lake Victoria littoral, and in the east and west. Wooded savannahs are scattered throughout the high grassland areas of most of Uganda, whereas swamps are a common feature of central Uganda. Elsewhere, the combination of clearing, cultivation and burning has created a forest-savannah mosaic dominated by tall elephant grass.

This varied flora is reflected in an equally diverse fauna. In the forests of the west there are mountain gorillas, chimpanzees and a multitude of monkeys, while grazers such as elephant, buffalo, zebra, hartebeest, topi, Uganda kob and hippo thrive in more open habitats, where they are preyed upon by lion, leopard and spotted hyena. In low rainfall areas of the northeast, dry-country wildlife includes oryx, gazelle, kudu and cheetah. Overall, the country's mammalian fauna totals 342 species, including at least 13 primates, 38 carnivores, 29 antelope and several other large ungulates, with species typical of both the eastern savannah and western forest biomes being well represented. This rich natural heritage is safeguarded in an impressive network of national parks, wildlife reserves and forest reserves, most of which are managed by the Uganda Wildlife Authority (UWA), and laws regarding the preservation of natural habitats, wildlife and historical sites are strictly enforced.

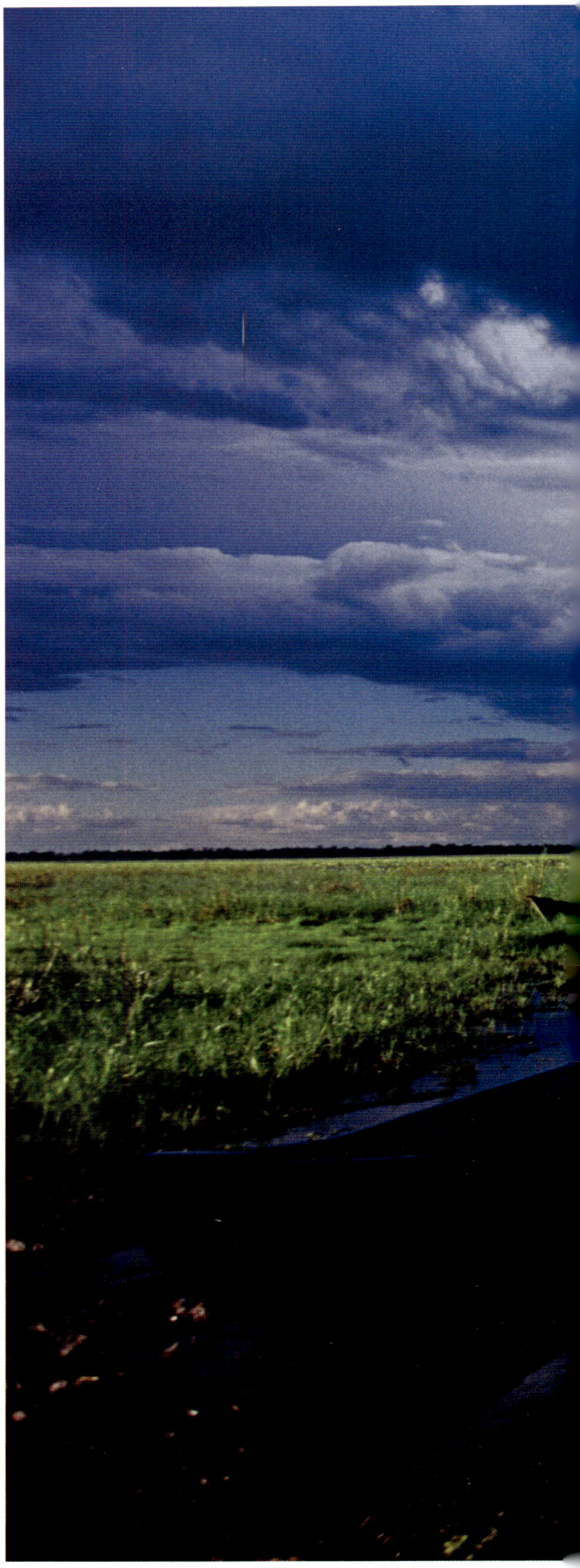

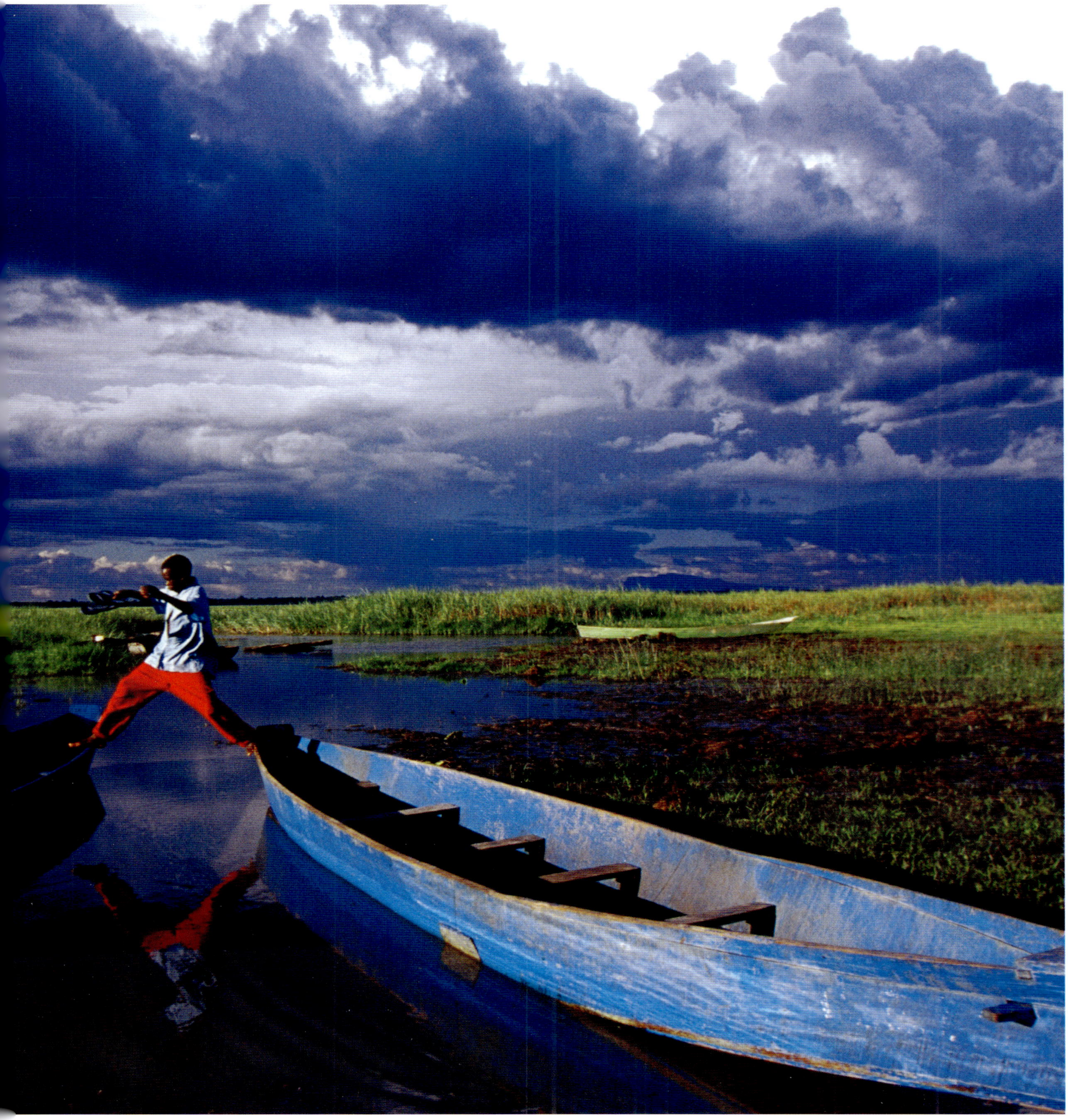

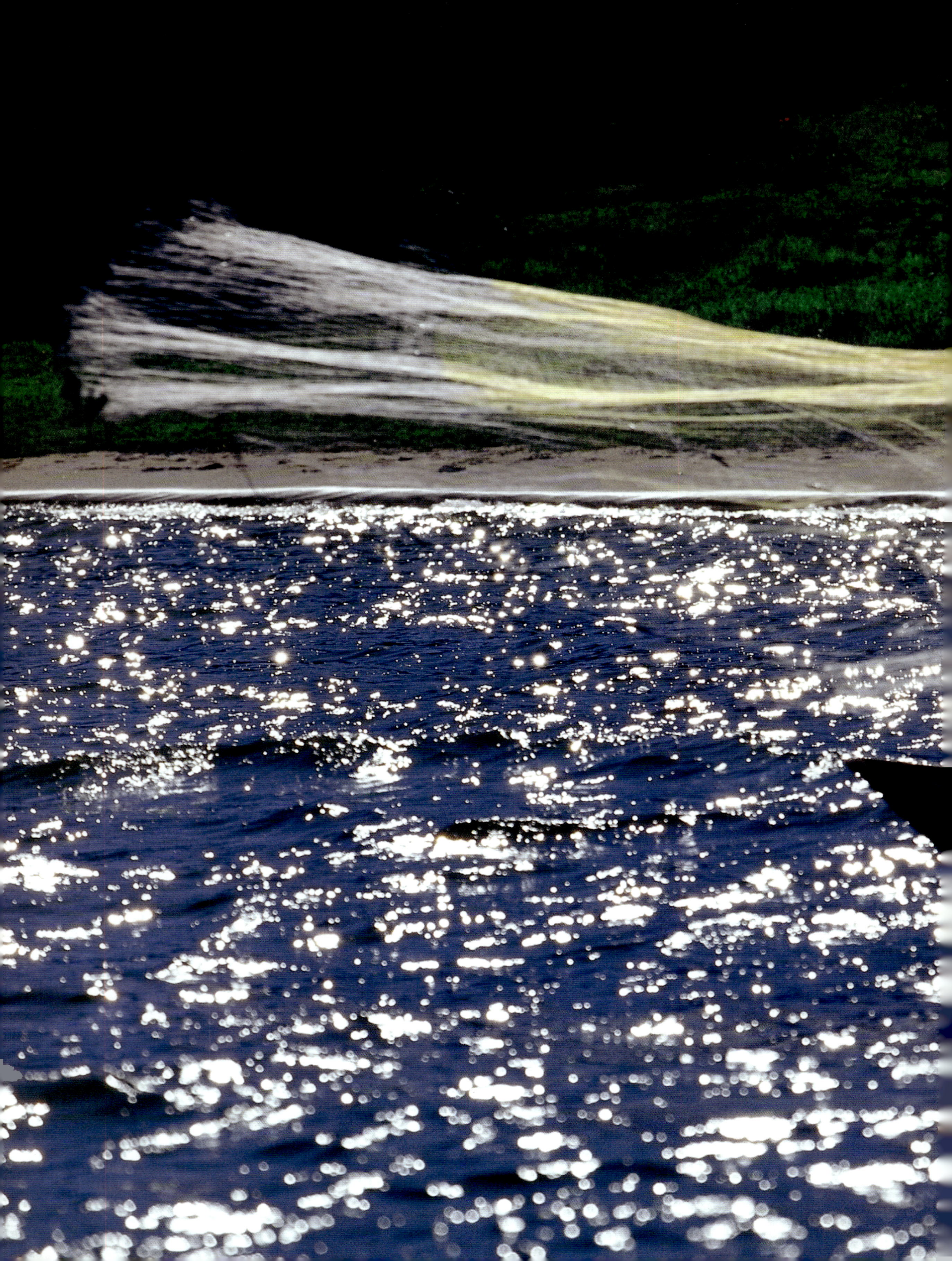

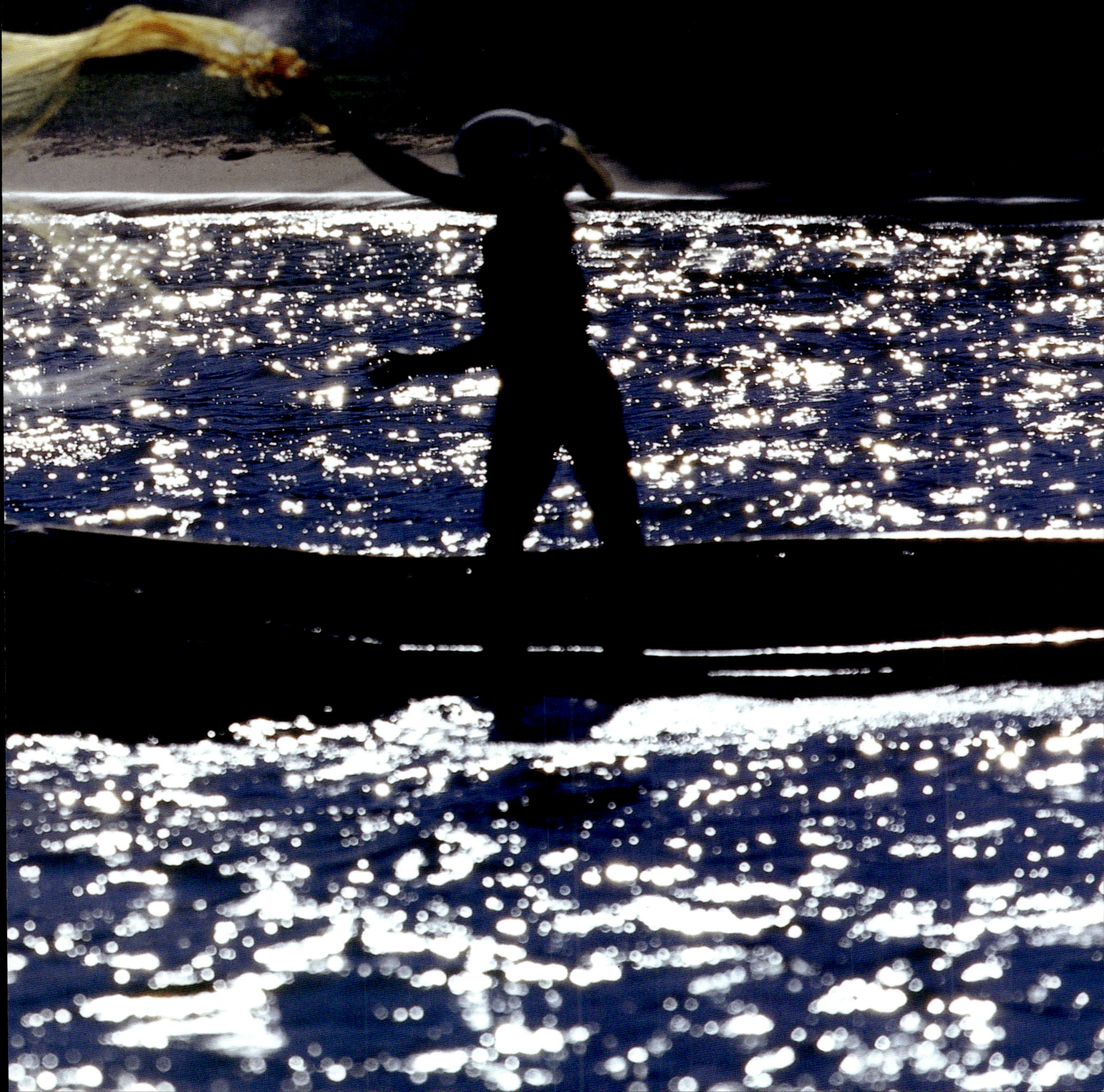

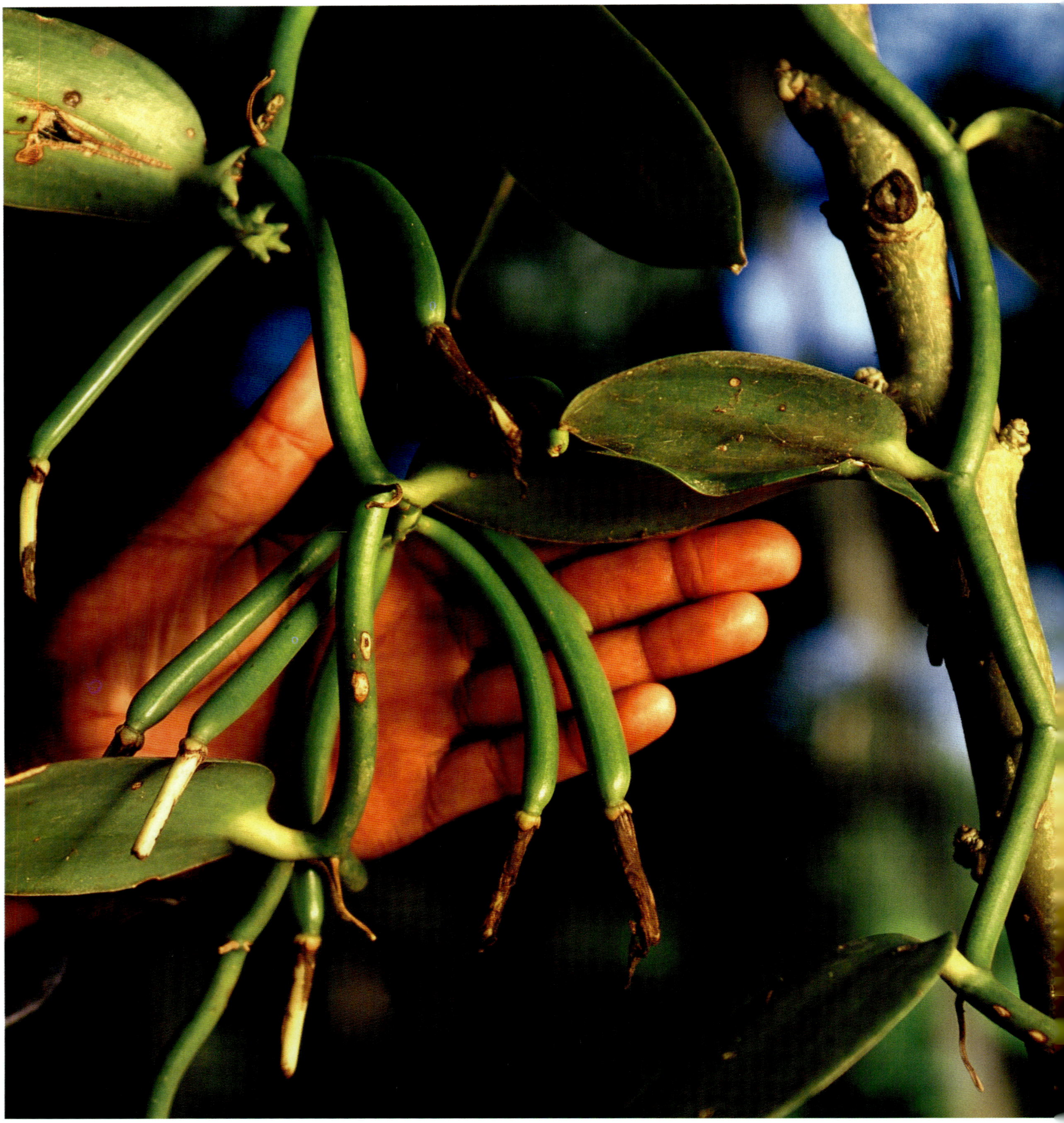

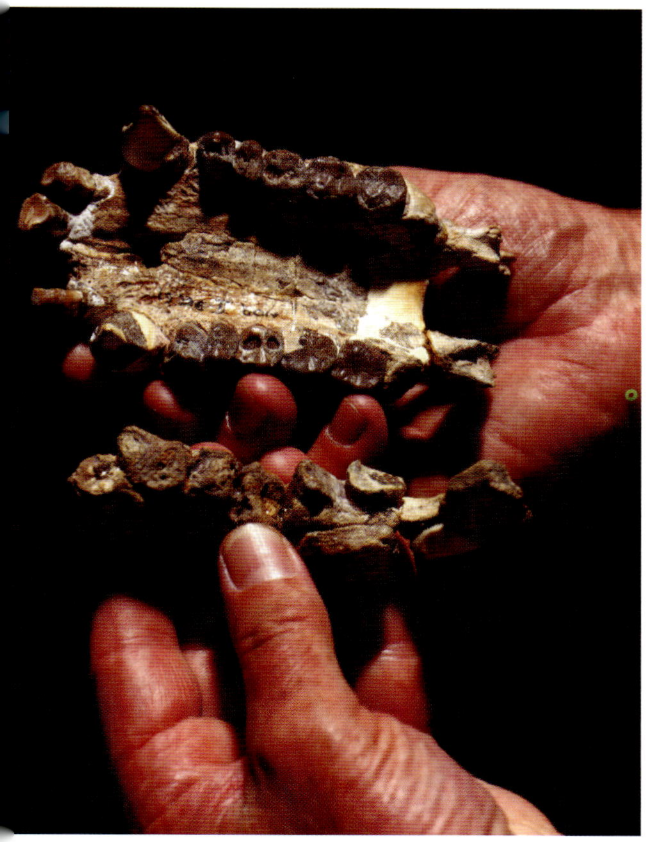

Above: The ape's enigmatic fossils were first discovered n the 1960s near the village of Moroto. They consists of a utting jaw and primitive teeth that resemble those of other early apes.

Opposite: Very few countries have the right ecological conditions to grow vanilla and Uganda is one of them.

For tourists, a typical Uganda safari combines tracking gorillas and chimpanzees in the lush forests of Bwindi Impenetrable, Kibale Forest or Mgahinga Gorilla National Parks with game drives in the more open savannah of Queen Elizabeth, Murchison Falls, Kidepo Valley or Lake Mburo. Other popular natural sites include hilly Lake Bunyonyi, the Ssese Islands on Lake Victoria, and Sipi Falls on the footslopes of Mount Elgon, while Bujagali Falls downstream of the source of the Nile is the country's adrenalin capital, offering some of the most exciting commercial white-water rafting in the world. More specialised endeavours include hiking and mountaineering expeditions into the upper Rwenzoris, as well as hikes on the less demanding slopes of Mount Elgon.

Uganda's fertile soils support a wide variety of food and export crops, both annual and perennial. Agriculture is the dominant economic sector, accounting for 70 percent of the gross domestic product and providing a livelihood to 90 percent of the population. Smallholders account for more than 90 percent of the country's agricultural output. The major traditional exports are coffee, cotton, tea, tobacco and sugarcane, while groundnuts, maize, beans, sorghum, and millet have emerged in recent years as cash crops. Cereals, legumes, tubers and plantains (matoke) are important staple foodstuffs. A variety of tropical fruit trees are grown in the lower plateau areas, while the upland areas grow a range of temperate crops, such as Irish potatoes, wheat and barley. Most of the livestock is kept by smallholder farmers, although the Karimojong in the north-east and the Bahima in the south-west are important traditional cattle keepers.

East Africa has been shown to be the 'cradle of mankind' and while Uganda has not as yet revealed human fossils of comparable antiquity to those unearthed in Ethiopia, Kenya and Tanzania, it is reasonable to assume that human-like beings have inhabited the country for millions of years. Fossils on the floor of the western Rift Valley confirm the definite presence of early humans around 500,000 years ago. By 50,000 years ago, the people living in present-day Uganda had mastered the use of fire, which enabled them to move into the more forested areas around the margins of Lake Victoria. Some 40,000 years later they had conquered most of the regions of Uganda and were living throughout the land, from the Rwenzori Mountains to Mount Elgon and from the Lake Victoria Basin to Karamoja. Up until around 500 BC it is impossible to put a name to the communities that lived in Uganda, but we do know that they practised a hunter-gatherer lifestyle, and their ethnic and linguistic affiliations are probably closer to those of modern-day Pygmies or the Southern African Khoisan than to other modern-day Ugandans.

Most Ugandans today speak a Bantu language, a linguistic group that has its roots in west-central Africa but is now spoken throughout eastern and southern Africa. Literally hundreds of Bantu languages are recognized throughout this region, with at least 17 being spoken in Uganda alone, but they are all quite closely related and many are mutually intelligible. The arrival of Bantu-speakers in Uganda is associated with the introduction of agriculture and iron working. By AD 1000, the agricultural Bantu were well established in western and southern Uganda and were organized in small political units, of which the clan was the norm.

More recent arrivals to the grasslands of western and southern Uganda were the Cushitic-speaking pastoralists who brought with them the founding stock of Ankole (or Sanga) cattle. Like their Ethiopian precursors, the Ankole cattle are known for their large humps and long horns, but the latter feature is taken to uniquely outsized dimensions in southwest Uganda and Rwanda, almost certainly as a result of selective breeding since they were imported to the region in mediaeval times. These pastoralists probably adopted local Bantu languages after they settled in the region, and the emergence of mediaeval pastoral aristocracies in modern-day Uganda, Rwanda and Burundi is almost certainly linked to their cultural fusion with Bantu-speaking agriculturalists. Another element in Uganda's linguistic and cultural fabric is the Nilotic-speaking Luo, whose precursors arrived from the north and migrated as far south as the northeastern shore of Lake Victoria in the 15th century.

Local oral traditions, supported by archaeological evidence, suggest that the earliest centralised state in Uganda was founded in the 11th century. Known as Bunyoro-Kitara, this kingdom was probably centred on Ntusi, to the north of present-day Masaka. The origin of the ruling Batembuzi dynasty is obscured by legend, which states that it was founded by Ruhanga, King of the Underworld, and that its rulers were semi-deities with supernatural powers. Local traditions list up to 22 Batembuzi kings prior to the 14th century upheavals that led to the foundation of the Bacwezi dynasty by one Ndahura (the Uprooter). Almost certainly a genuine historical figure, Ndahura is traditionally accredited with having introduced Ankole cattle and coffee cultivation to Bunyoro-Kitara, suggesting a possible Ethiopian origin. The Bacwezi dynasty still looms large in local legend, despite having endured for only two generations, and it left behind several impressive physical edifices, notably the extensive earthworks at Bigo bya Mugenyi and Munsa. The spirit of Ndahura is said to reside in the Nakaima Tree on Mubende Hill, which remains a focal point of Bacwezi cults to this day.

The 15th century saw the emergence of the kingdoms that dominated regional politics ever since. These are Bunyoro, Buganda and Ankole, respectively centred on western, central and southwestern Uganda, as well as Rwanda, Burundi and Karagwe kingdom (the latter in northwest

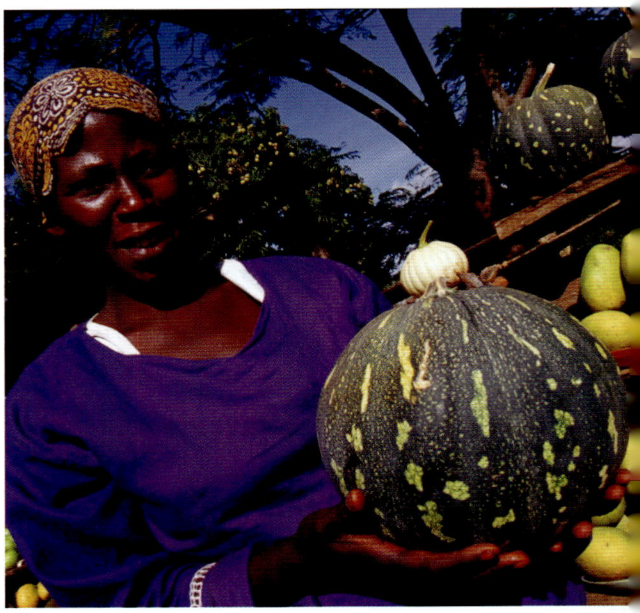

Above and opposite: A typical market scene. The bountiful climate produces a wealth of high-quality fruit and vegetables.

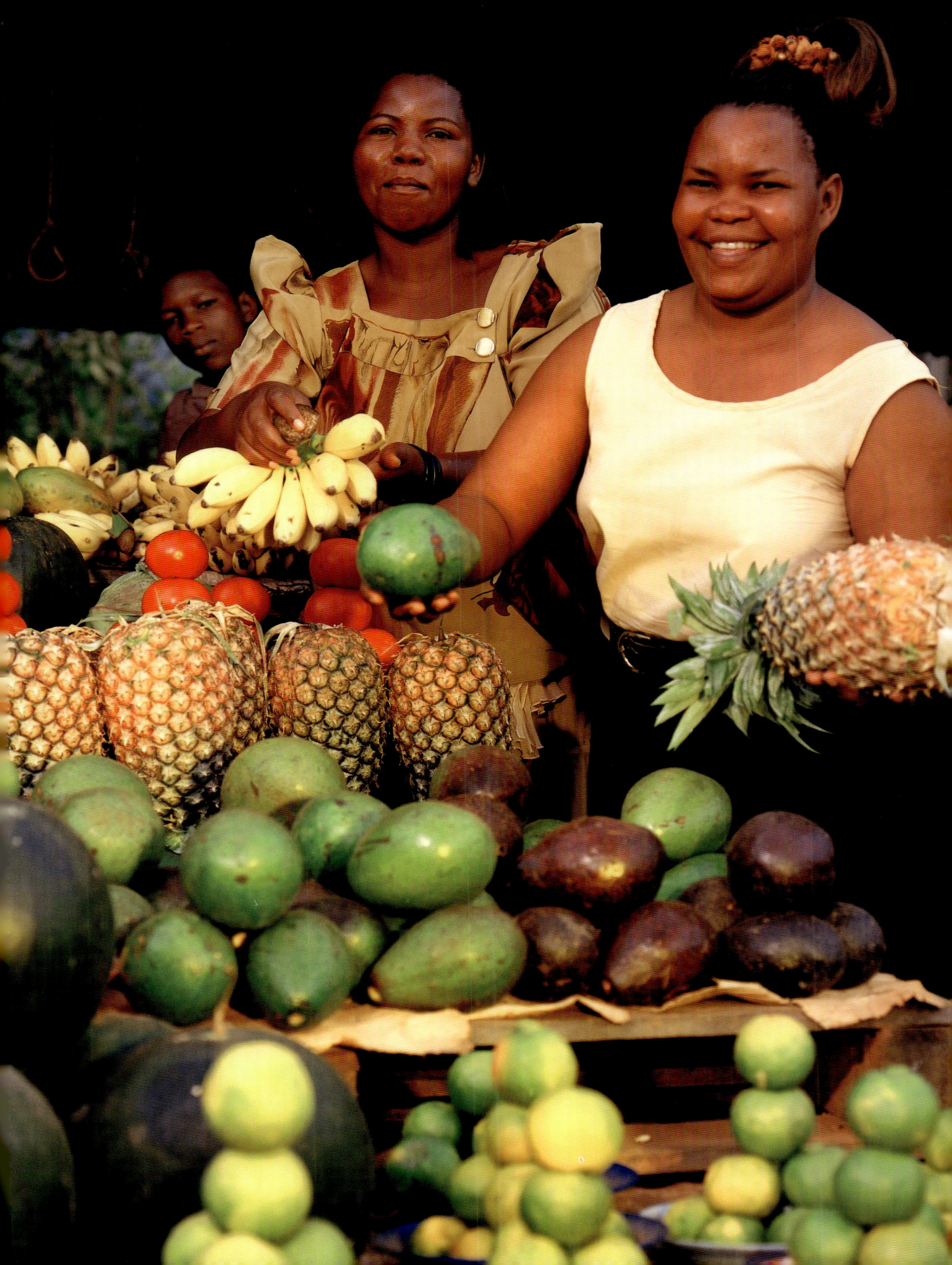

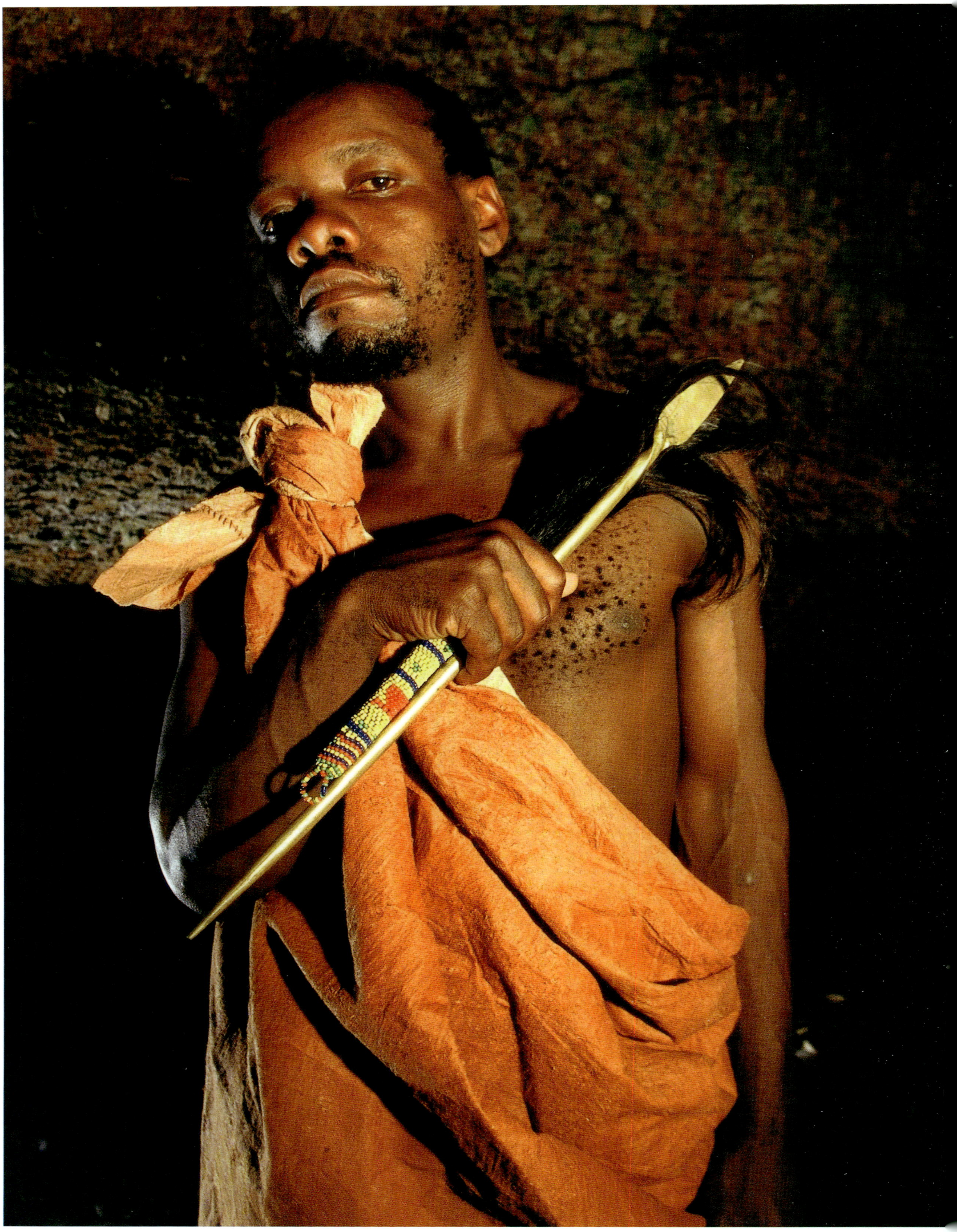

Opposite: Baganda elder in traditional attire.

Right: Karamajong warrior, displays his carefully pleated hairstyle. The lines of scars on his chest signify his success in raiding and battle.

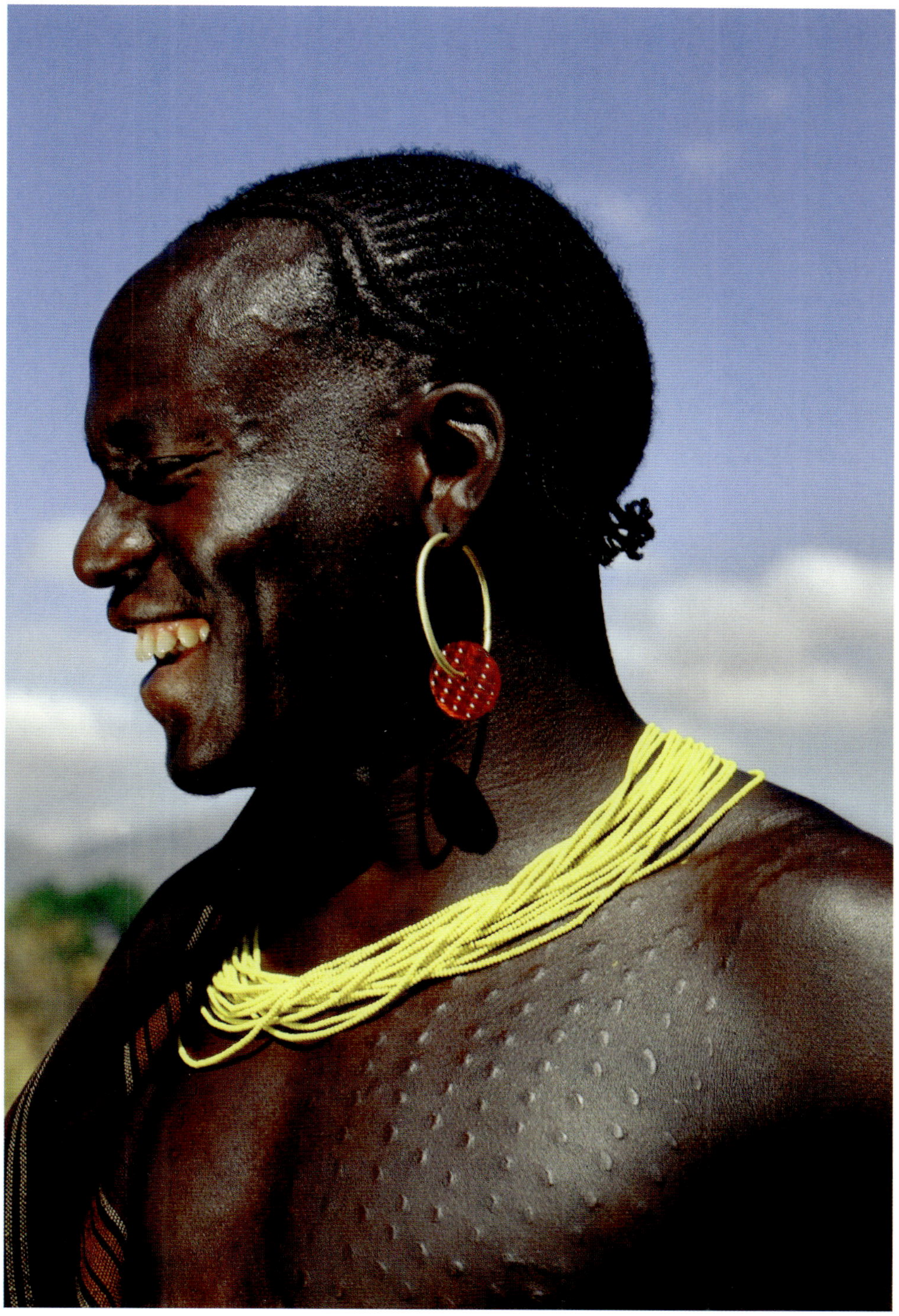

Tanzania). Oral tradition states that they all share a Bacwezi heritage, having been founded by sons or other descendents of Ndahura. Bunyoro was initially the largest kingdom, extending over 80,000 square kilometres, with exclusive control of the region's salt mines. Buganda, the most fertile of the kingdoms, had a more agricultural economy, while Ankole was stratified into two classes, the cattle-owning Bahima and the agriculturist Bairu. By the mid-19th century, however, Bunyoro had been reduced to a fraction of its former area and the dominant regional power was Buganda, which by then was centred on the Kampala area, and stretching east to the Victoria Nile, west to Mubende, and south to the present-day Tanzania border.

In the late 18th century the Nyamwezi traders of modern Tanzania reached Buganda and exchanged cloth and domestic utensils for ivory and slaves. They were followed, in the 1840s, by the Arabs who introduced guns and Islam, among other things. It was the well-beaten paths of these traders that the British explorers, Grant and Speke, followed in the 1860s

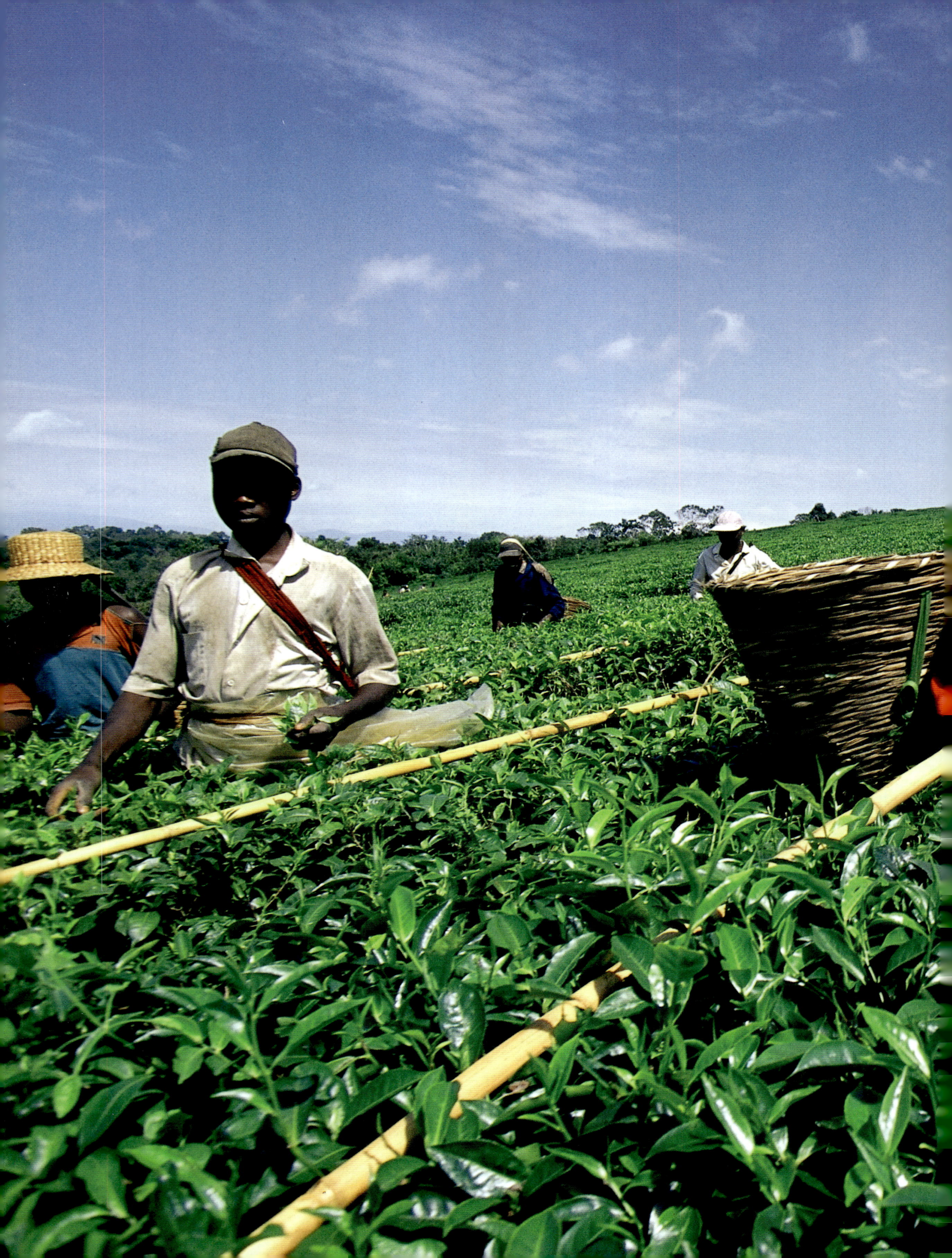

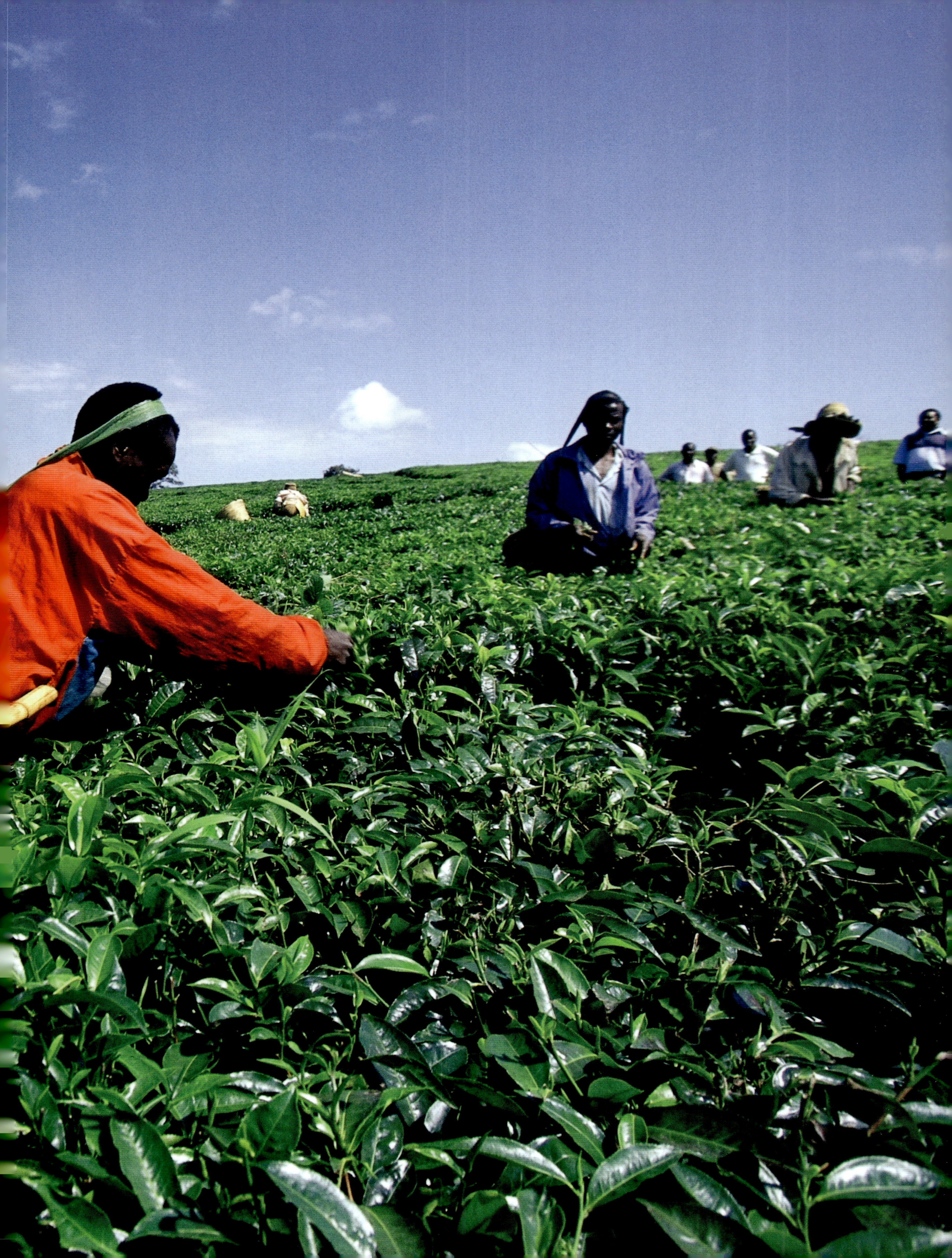

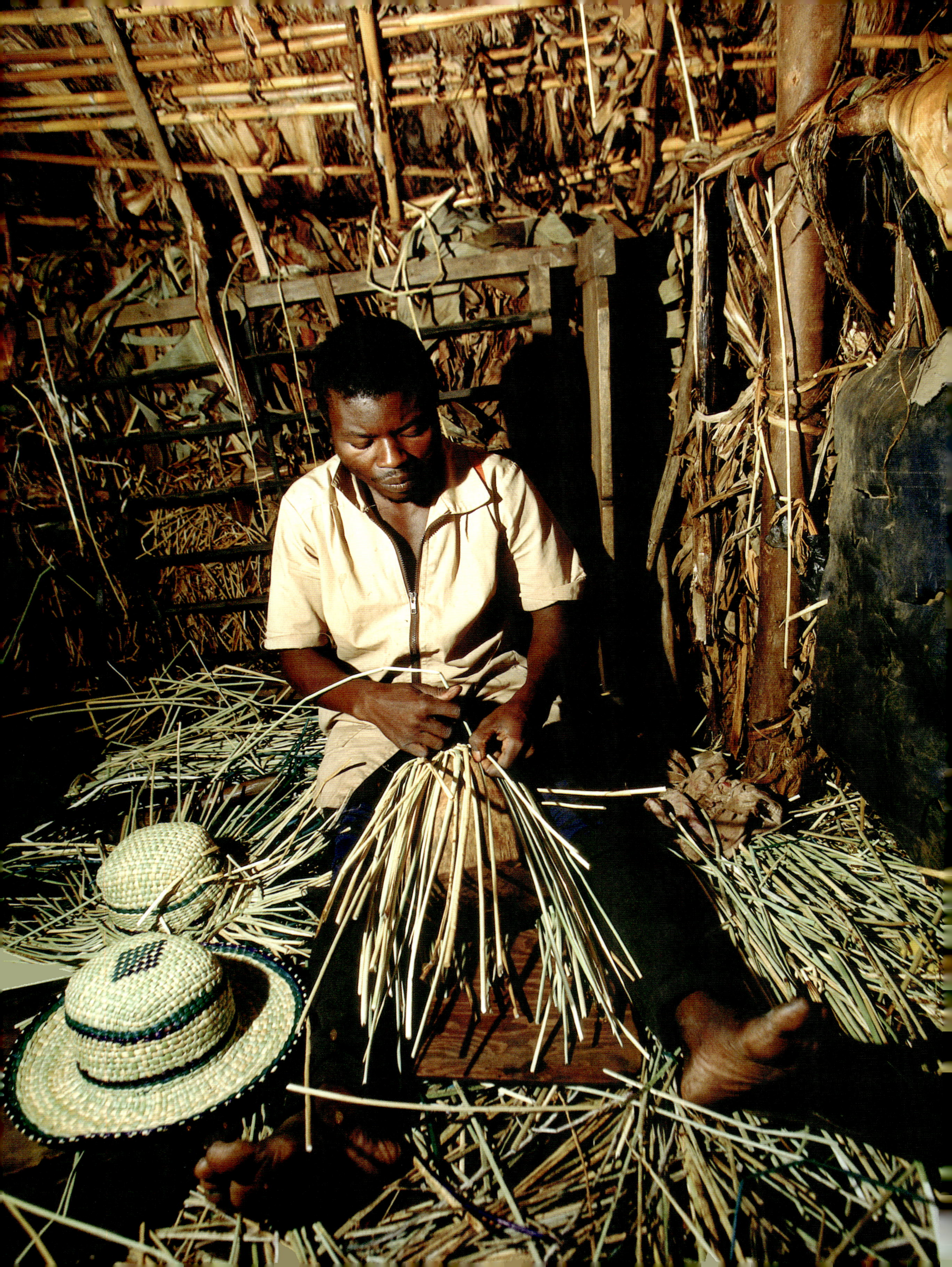

Previous pages: Harvesting tea at a lush plantation.

Opposite and right: The arts and crafts of Uganda are found everywhere and have religious, cultural, and psychological significance – as well as practical use.

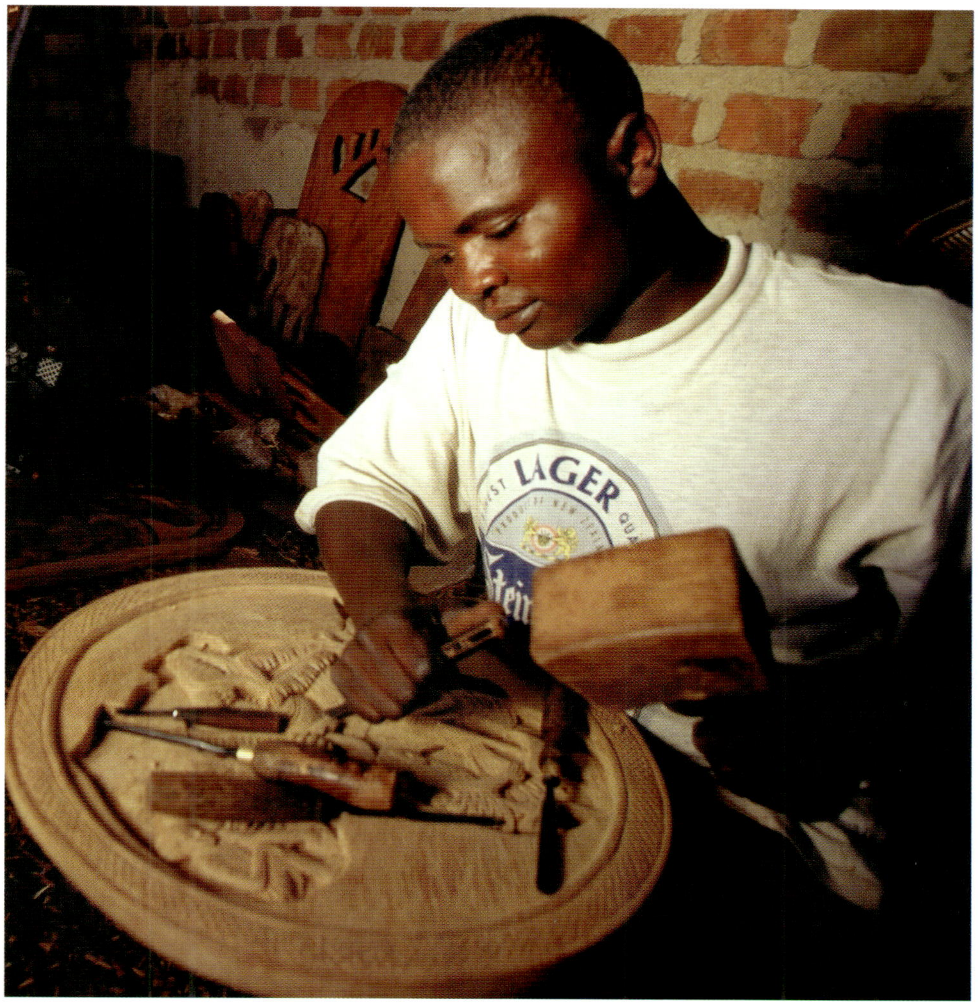

in their search for the source if the Nile, to be followed in the 1870s by Anglican missionaries of the Church Missionary Society and Catholic missionaries of the White Fathers. It was the same trade route, too, that various other adventurers and colonialists followed in the 1880s and 1890s, leading to the official declaration of the Uganda Protectorate in 1894 by Britain.

Because the British administration was understaffed and was not provided with sufficient money to run the protectorate centrally, they resorted to indirect rule – governing through the prevailing indigenous authorities. This was a relatively easy task in those parts of Uganda where authority was traditionally centralized, such as in the kingdoms of Buganda, Bunyoro, Ankole and Toro. Where there was no central or recognized authority, Baganda chiefs were used as agents and local chiefs were created. The agency system caused much resentment outside Buganda and the iniquities of the Baganda agents were neither forgotten nor forgiven in the post-colonial era – the root of many of Uganda's modern political problems.

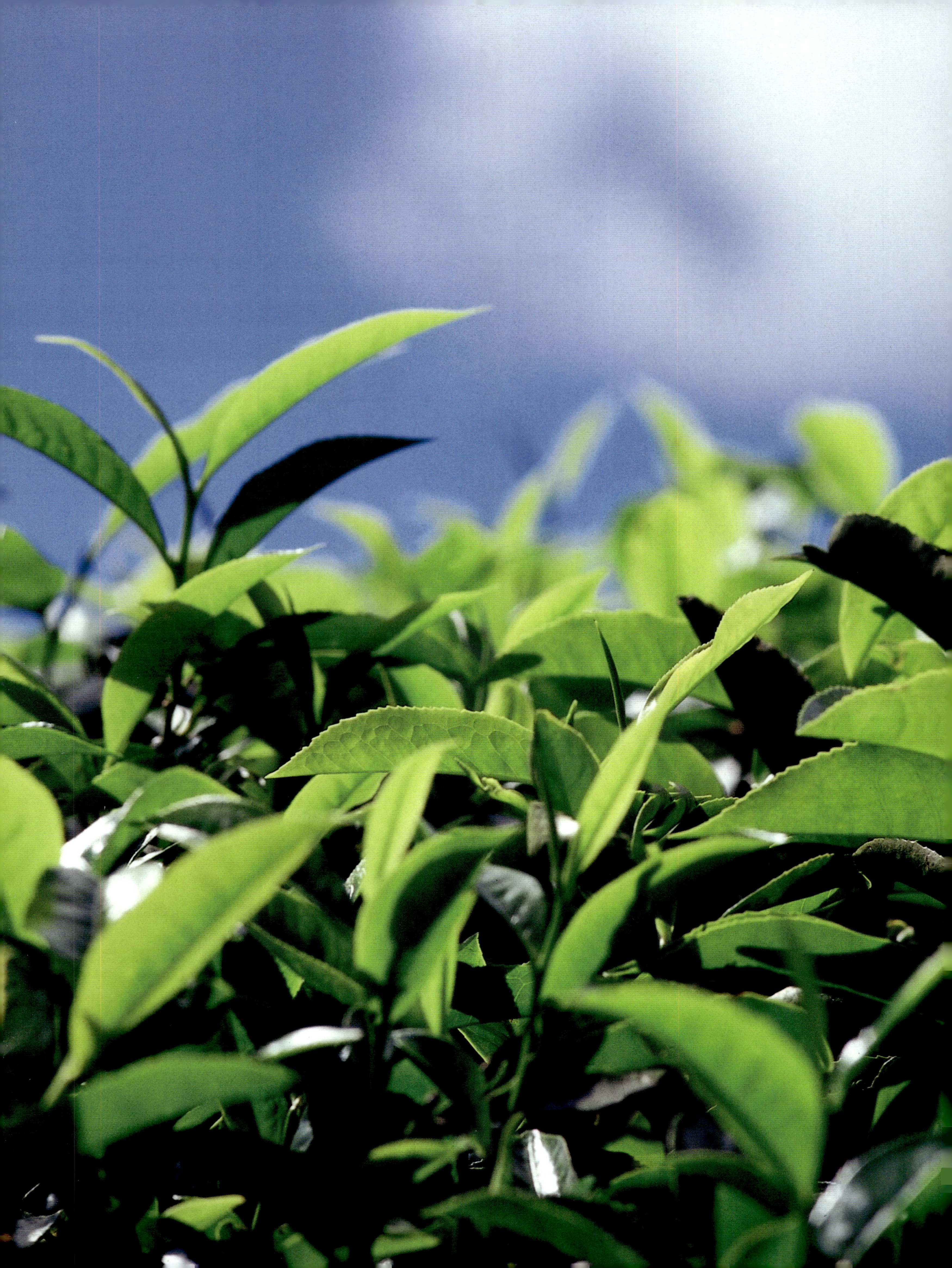

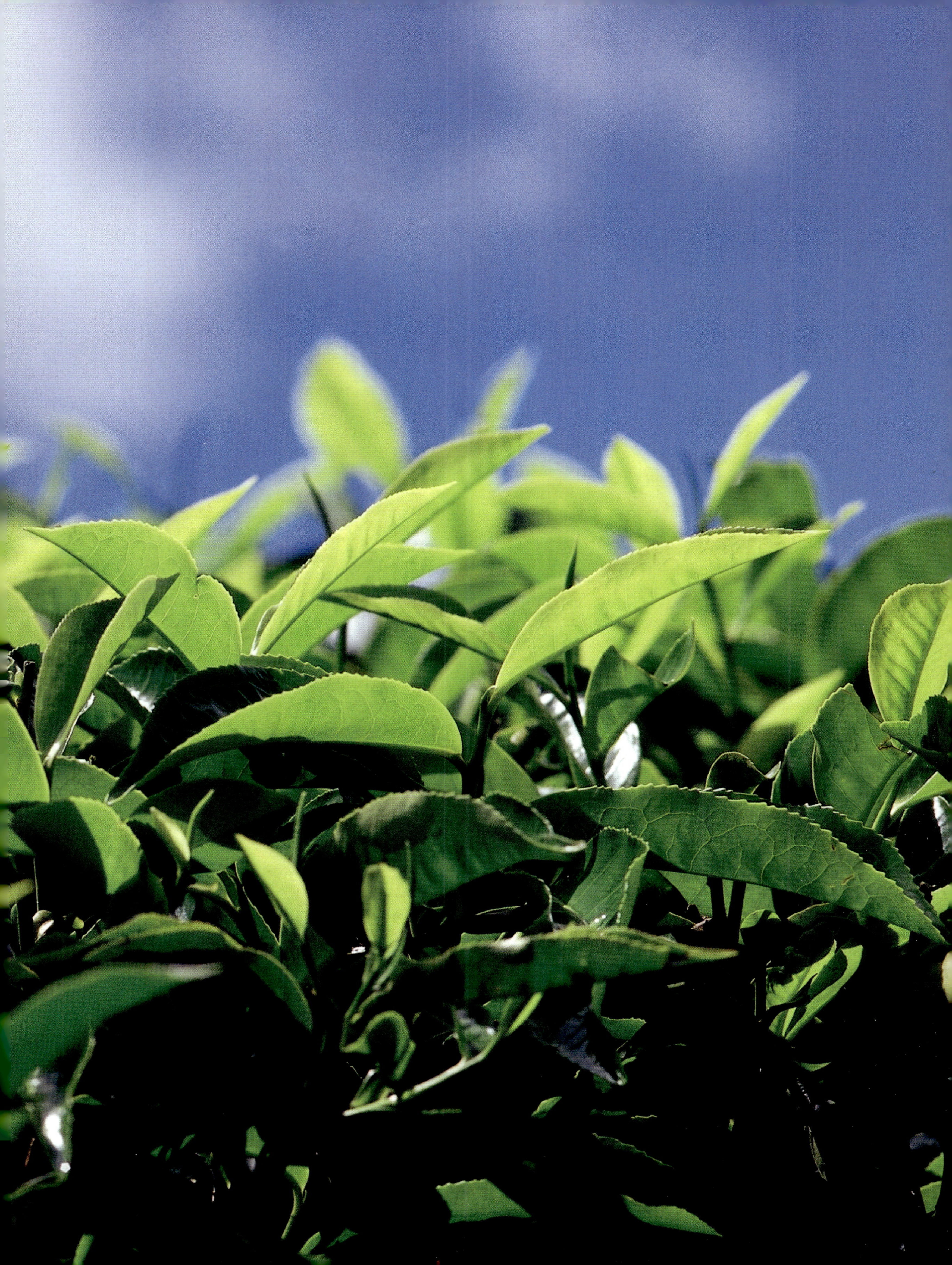

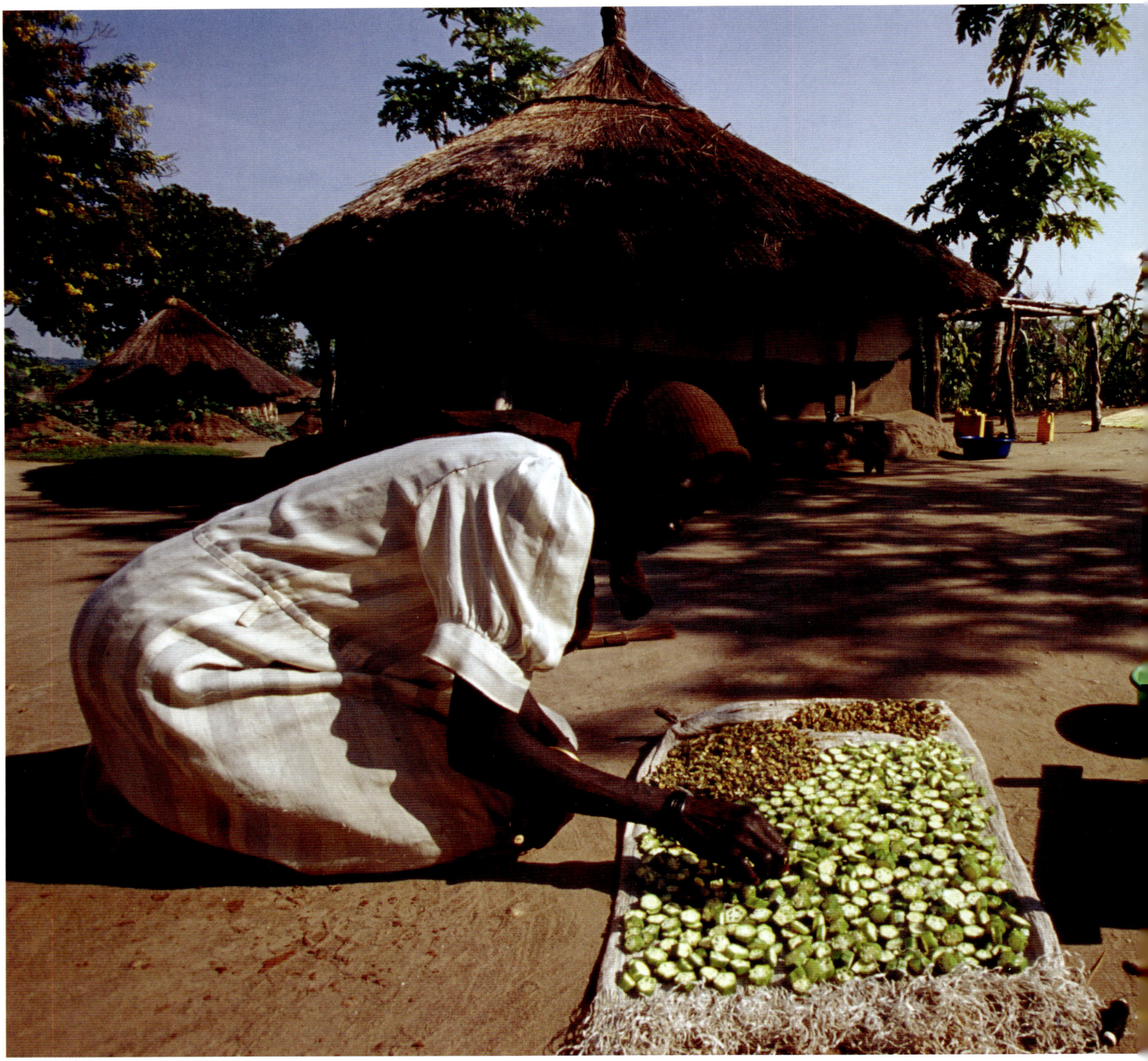

The main political developments in the 1950s were the approval of a new agreement (constitution) to Buganda in 1955 and the participation of Africans in the legislative and even executive arms of the colonial government. National political parties were also founded during this period, leading to independence from colonial rule, a process that was not without birth pangs. Indeed, until the independence flag was hoisted at midnight on 9 October 1962, it had been uncertain which of the country's various ethnic groups would agree to come together and forge a new nation. In retrospect, it is not surprising that the Independence Constitution lasted no more than three years. For the first two years of independence, the elected Prime Minister, Milton Obote, presided over a government that quarrelled incessantly with the government of Buganda, whose King Mutesa II had been appointed as State President of Uganda to appease Baganda traditionalists.

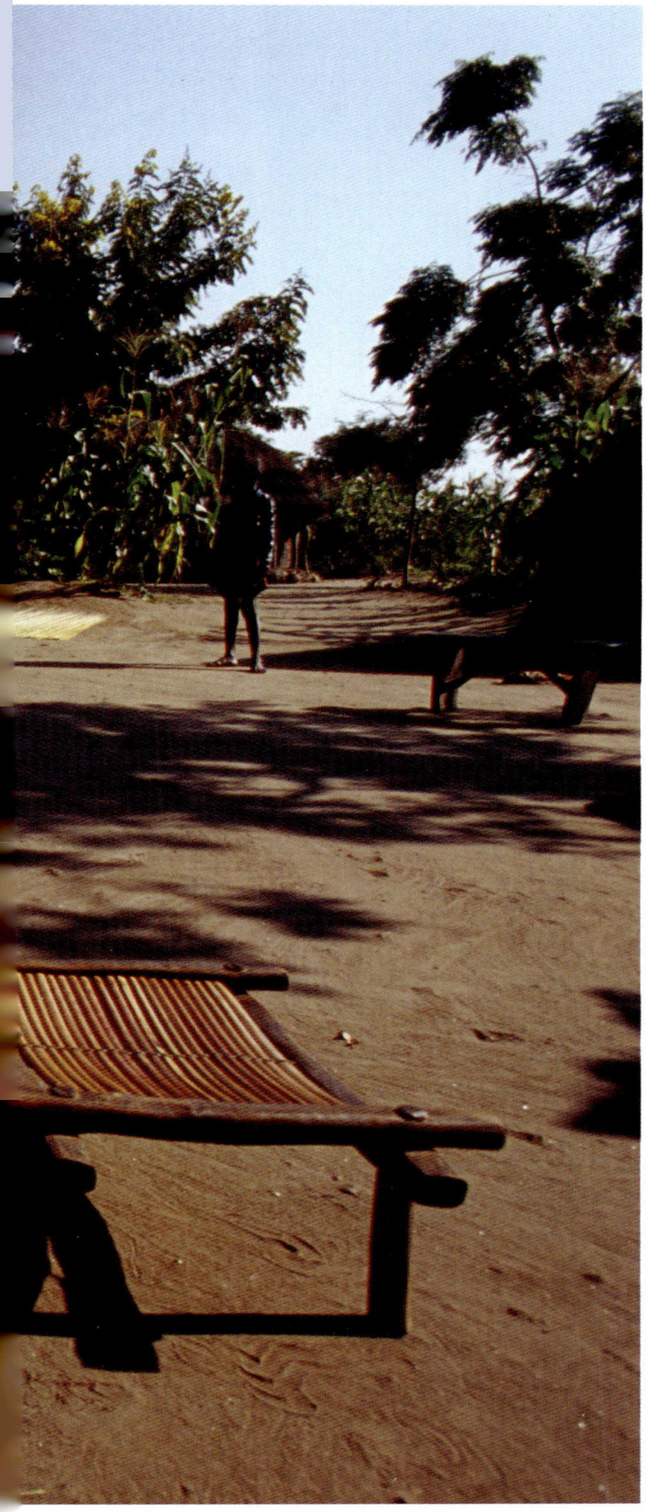

Previous pages: Tea plantations, mainly located in the Fort Portal area, provide an important export crop.

Left: Okra in Moyo village.

These and other factors formed the background to the Constitutional Crises of 1966-7, which saw Obote progressively sweep away all opposition, first by stripping Mutesa of the presidency and forcing him into exile, then by declaring himself President for Life, and then finally abolishing all the kingdoms and their traditional rulers and carving the country up into four districts. Faced with the smouldering resentment of the powerful Baganda elite, Obote became increasingly dependent on the army to prop up his unpopular and dictatorial regime, paving the way for another important entrant onto the political scene, his military commander Major General Idi Amin. Obote and Amin cooperated closely for the five years until January 1971 when Amin overthrew Obote while the latter was out of the country on state business.

Initially, Amin received support from Britain, Israel and other Western powers. However, it was not long before the Israelis and Asians were expelled by Amin. This, together with the general appropriation of Asian property and mostly British firms, led to what Amin described as an 'economic war'. Eight years of increasingly autocratic and murderous rule followed, with Amin finally being swept out of power by the combined forces of the Tanzania People's Defence Forces and various Ugandan exiles in March 1979. Sadly, however, the removal of Amin plunged Uganda ever deeper into a cycle of coup, counter-coup and civil war.

Stability was restored in 1986, when Yoweri Museveni seized power. The reforms enacted by President Museveni, backed by the IMF, World Bank, UNDP and other development partners, have subsequently turned things around – indeed, Uganda achieved the highest sustained economic growth rate in Africa over the 1990s, one equivalent to the best in Asia. Today, most of Uganda enjoys peace and security, the main exception being the far northwest, which has suffered greatly at the hands of the Lord's Resistance Army, a quasi-religious guerrilla army whose brutal attacks on civilian targets have resulted in the death, displacement and abduction of tens of thousands of innocent villagers.

Nevertheless, almost 20 years into the Museveni era, Uganda was described in a respected Oxfam publication as "an inspirational economic success story, and a symbol of a more vibrant, successful Africa".

The economic transformation wrought by Museveni has been mirrored by a steady realisation of Uganda's vast potential as one of Africa's most exciting ecotourism and adventure travel destinations. A pivotal step in this rehabilitation was the issuing of the first gorilla-tracking permits for Bwindi and Mgahinga National Parks in 1993. This, arguably, is the most exciting wildlife encounter Africa has to offer – though it is run a close second by the heart-stopping pant-hoot chorusing of Kibale and Budongo's habituated chimpanzees. Another important development, in

Right: Boys taking a dip in one of Uganda's many lakes.

Following pages: Tea Shamba acrobat.

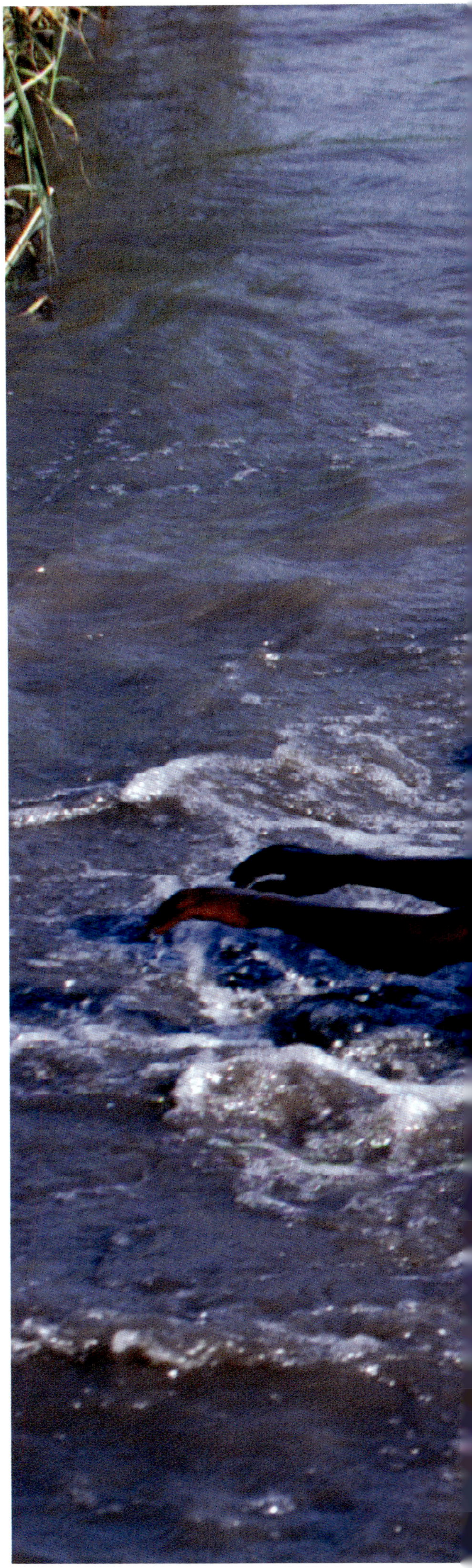

dramatic contrast to the situation 20 years ago, is that practically every major attraction in the country is now serviced by at least one world-class accommodation option – and many such places offer a varied selection of upmarket lodges, midrange camps and budget digs.

This notable improvement in tourist facilities has been matched by the staggering recovery of the country's premier savannah reserves, where visitors can now be almost certain of encountering lion, elephant, buffalo, giraffe and various antelope. Then there are the Rwenzoris and Mount Elgon, where one can explore East Africa's bizarre montane vegetation without the goal-oriented approach associated with ascents of mounts Kilimanjaro or Kenya. There is the serene Kazinga Channel, where hippos grunt in the long shadow of the Rwenzoris, and further north, along the Nile, there is the roaring, spraying sensory overload of Murchison Falls. Meanwhile, below the Nile's source at Jinja, a succession of thrilling grade-five rapids have earned Bujagali Falls the reputation of East Africa's answer to that more southerly 'adrenalin capital' Victoria Falls.

The Uganda travel experience is encapsulated by the prospect of staring deep into the eyes of a mountain gorilla one day, and watching lions laze in the wide boughs of Ishasha the next. But many wildlife enthusiasts are just as enthralled by the so-called small stuff. Primates are exceptionally well represented, ranging from the troops of spindly patas monkey that forage on the northern plains of MFNP to the dozen forest species resident in Kibale Forest. And Uganda is by far the smallest of those four African countries whose bird checklist tops the thousand species mark – dedicated ornithological tours routinely notch up 400-plus species over a fortnight, including a wide range of rainforest inhabitants otherwise restricted to inaccessible parts of west-central Africa. Uganda, in an ecological nutshell, is where the eastern savannah meets the West African jungle, and it really does offer visitors the best of both these fantastic worlds!

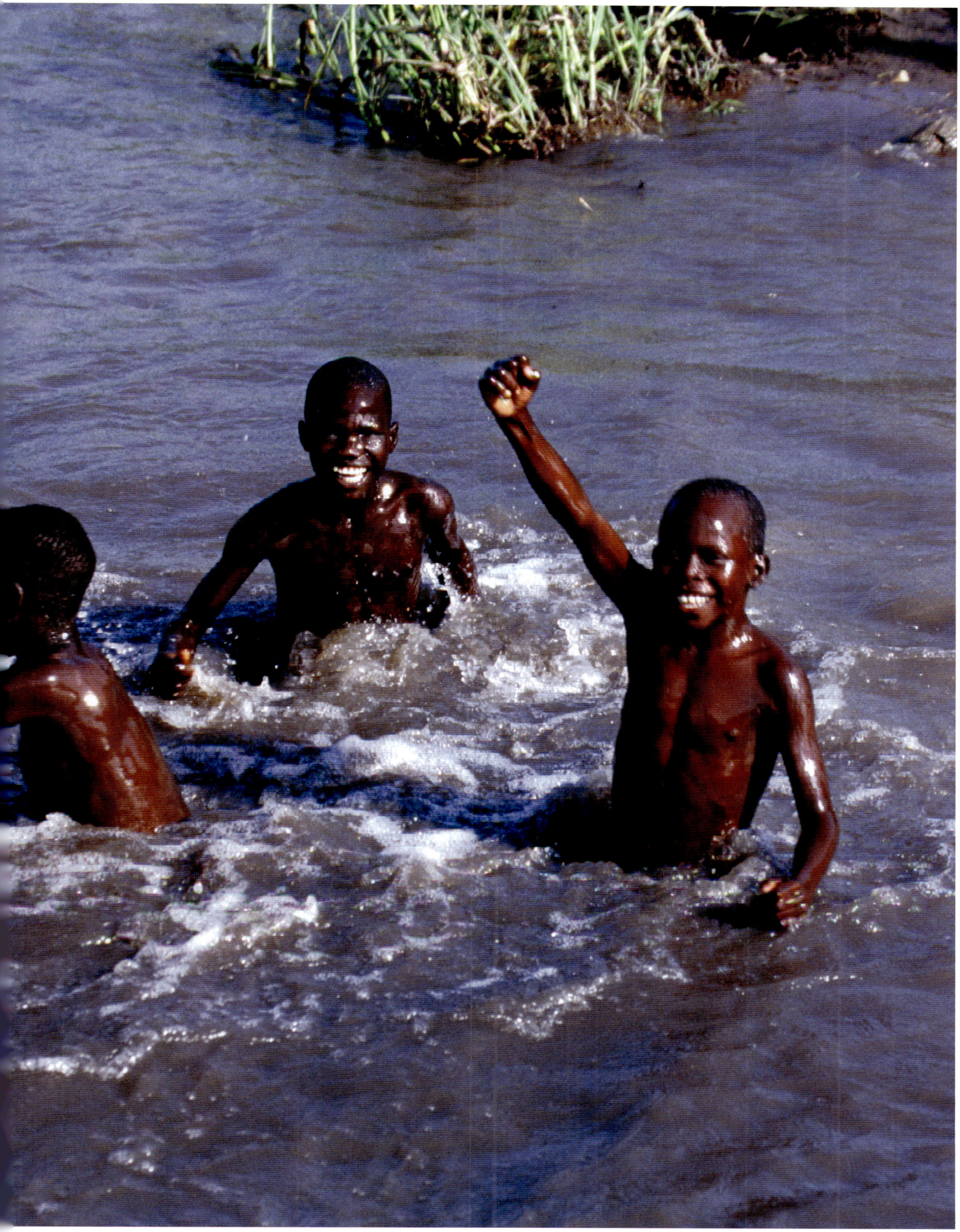

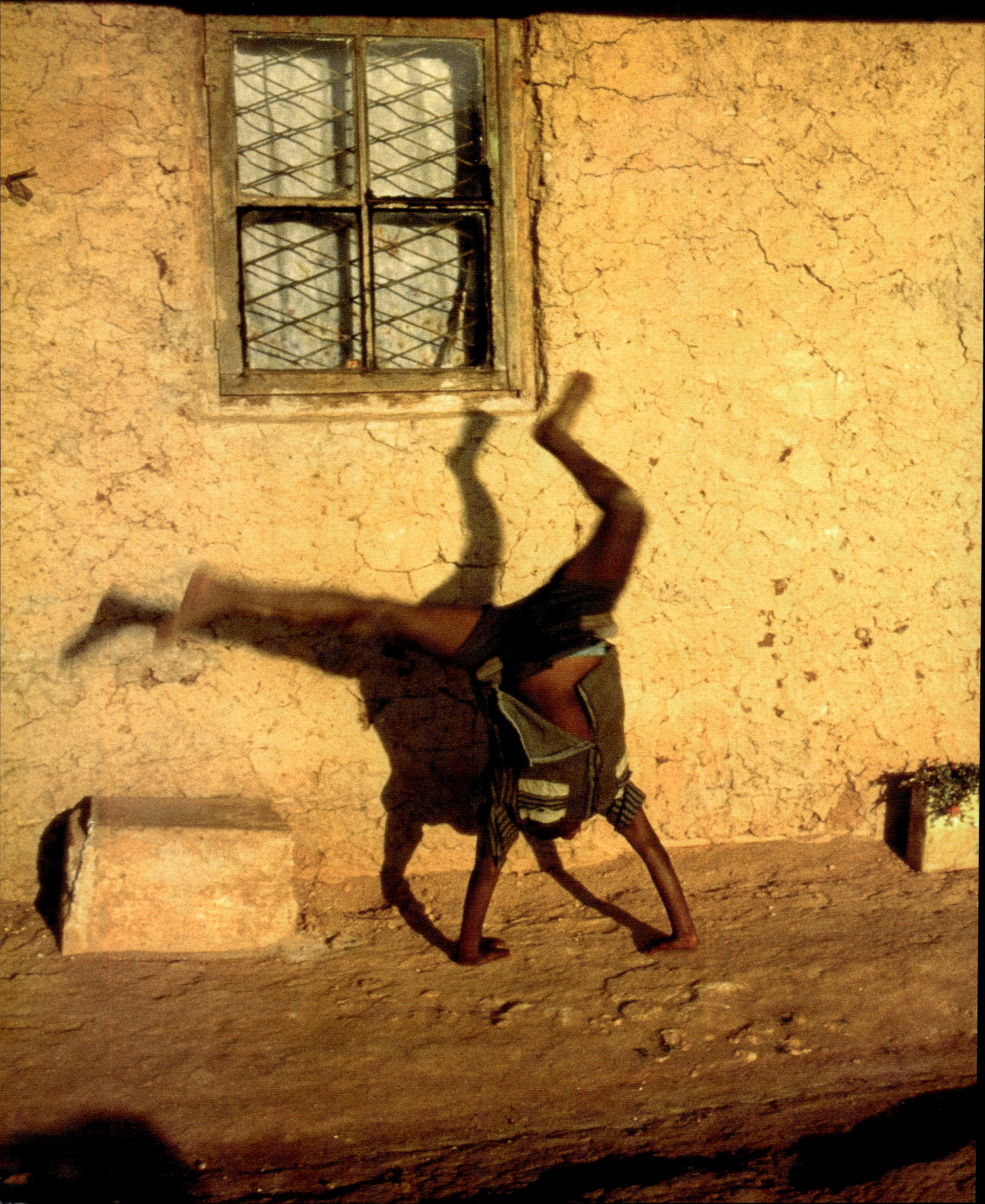

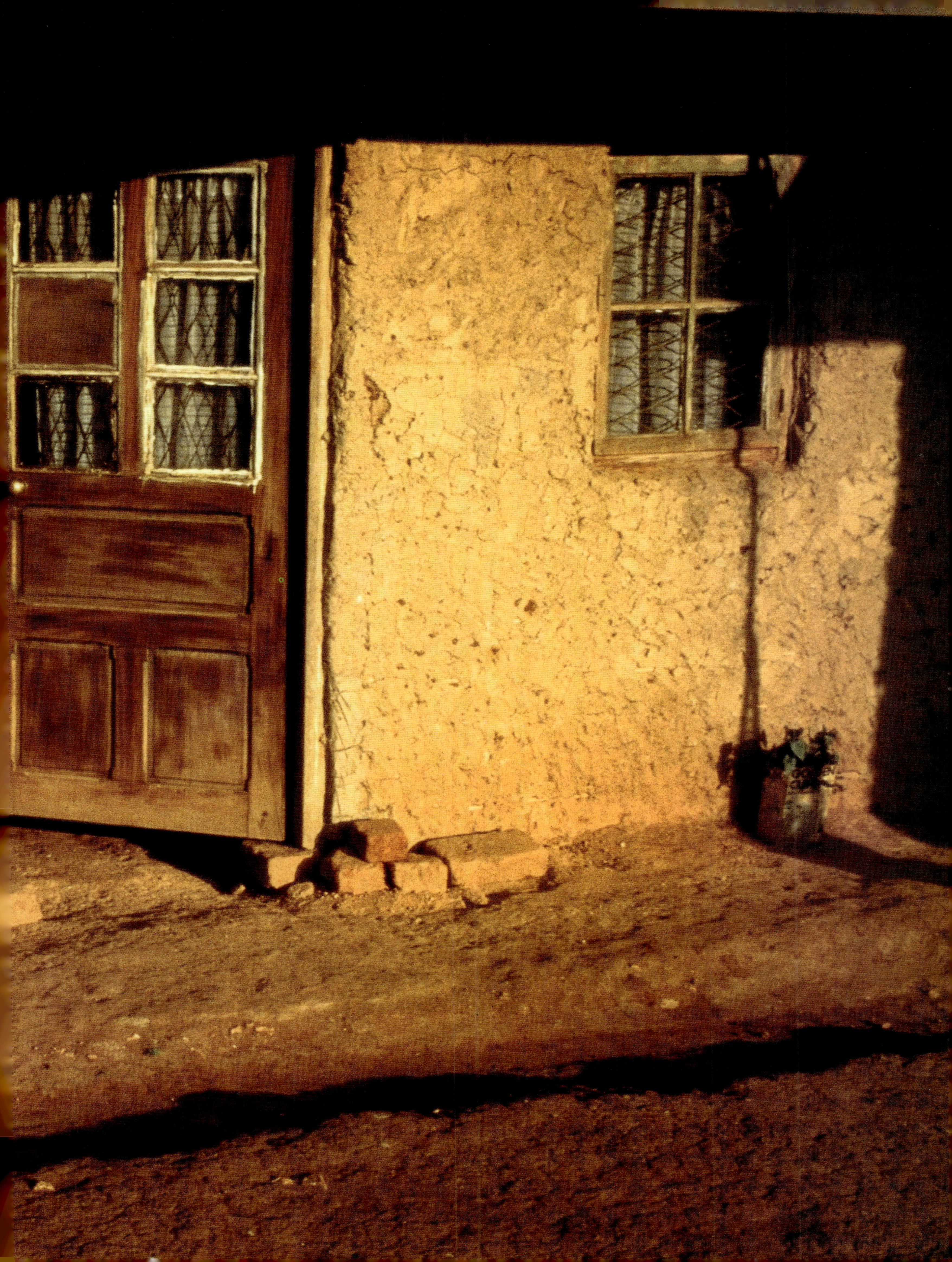

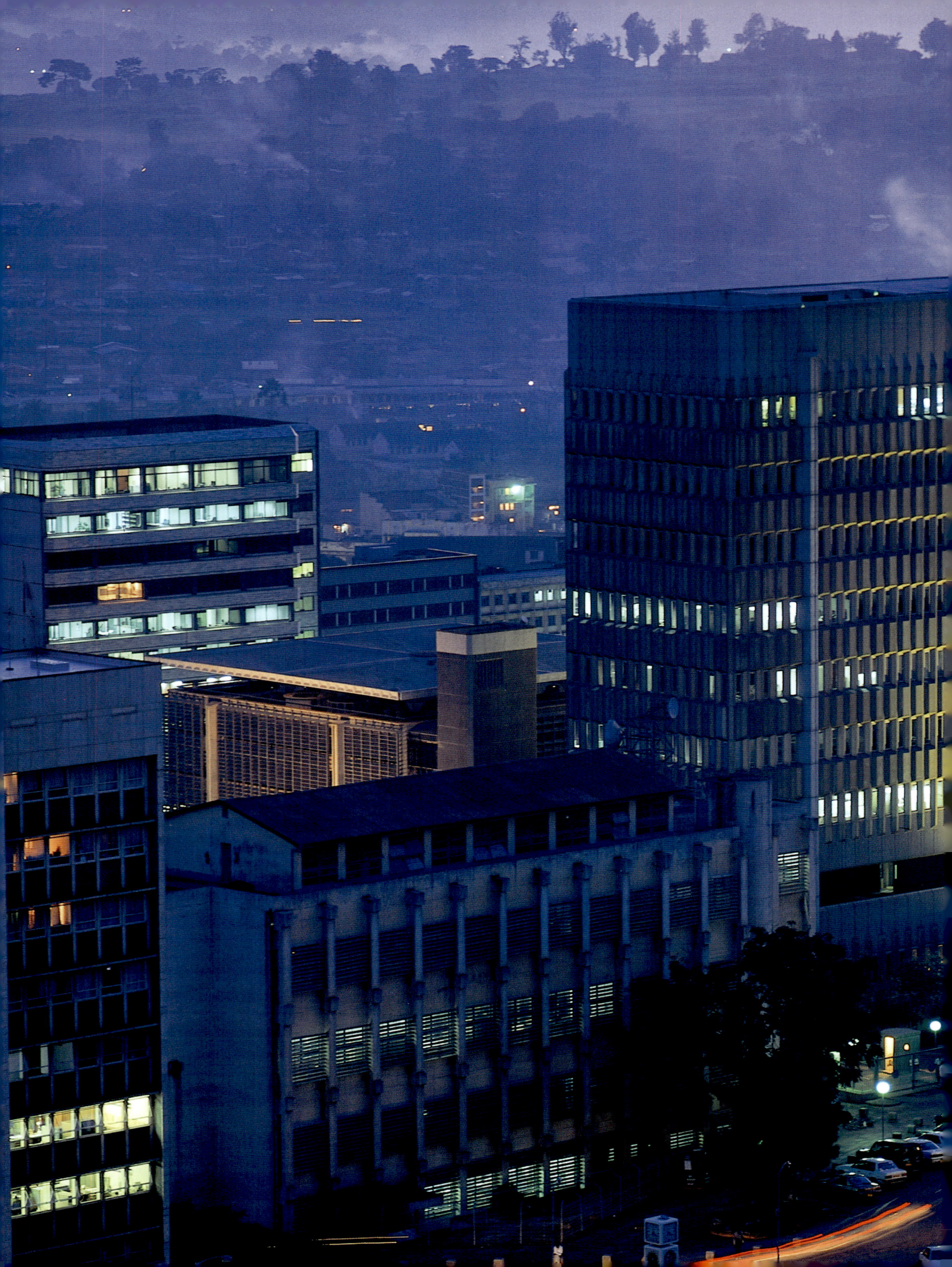

2. *Kampala and Environs*

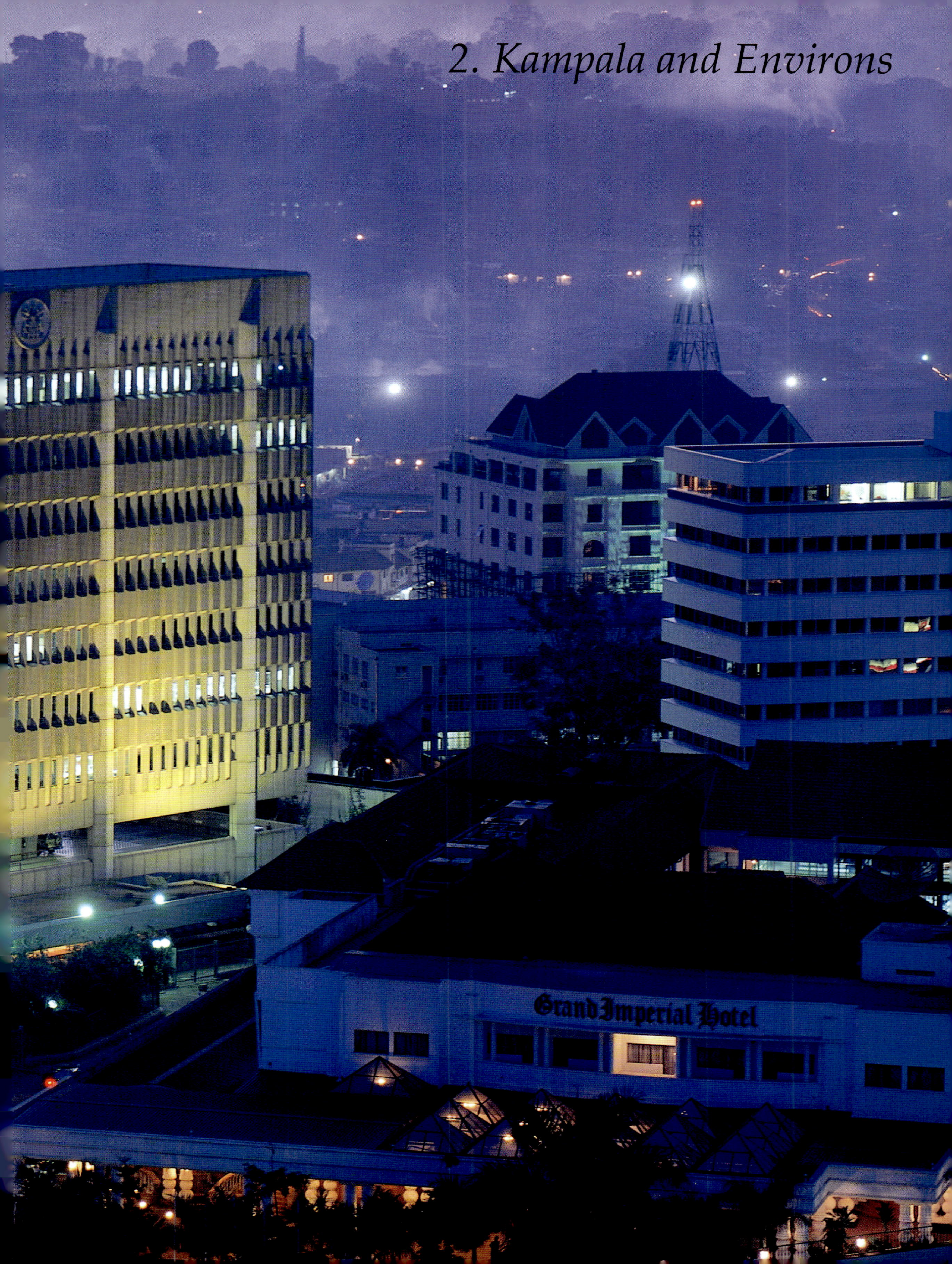

Previous page: Kampala by night. The city was founded on seven hills.

Opposite: Captain's Lugard's old house in Kampala.

Situated a mere 35 kilometres apart on the verdant hinterland of Lake Victoria, Uganda's present-day capital Kampala and its colonial-era forbear Entebbe represent wildly contrasting faces of modern Africa. Kampala, with a population approaching 1.5 million, is Uganda's largest city and most significant economic and cultural hub, sprawling outward from a compact high-rise city centre that bustles with recklessly honking minibus-taxis, kamikaze motor scooters, and a vibrant mixture of urban humanity, ranging from earnest and harried-looking office workers to cheerful street vendors and hawkers. Entebbe, carved haphazardly into the tropical lakeshore jungle, is by contrast a remarkably unfocused and sedate little town, and quite possibly the only African capital past or present whose golf course is more expansive than its main built-up area.

Kampala derives its name from the Luganda phrase *Kasozi ka Impala* (Hill of Antelopes), a reference to the impala herd that the 19th century kabakas (kings) of Buganda allowed to graze on the slopes of a hill near Mengo Palace. The area had long been a centre of Baganda activity, with Kabaka Mutesa having his capital at Kasubi Hill and Kabaka Mwanga establishing his at nearby Mengo Hill. The name Kasozi ka Impala was given specifically to the hill on which a British explorer and adventurer, Captain Fredrick Lord Lugard, established a fort and administrative post in December 1890. Here, Lugard hoisted the flag of the Imperial British East Africa Company, which was to be replaced by the Union flag three years later. The fort, which stood on what is now known as Old Kampala Hill, attracted hundreds of people, who formed the small township from which the modern city developed.

Like Rome, Kampala was originally built on seven hills, Lubaga, Namirembe (Mengo), Makerere, Kololo, Kibuli, Kampala (Old Kampala), and Mulago, around which was an appealing mixture of delightful valleys, green swamplands and flowing streams. Soon traders erected shops at the foot of the hill by the fort. By 1909 the confines of the fort had become too small for administrative purposes, and it was decided to move the colonial offices and government residences to the nearby Nakasero Hill. The shops and other commercial premises followed suit.

Kampala's hills all developed their own identities in the ensuing years. Lubaga, Namirembe, and Kibuli became the headquarters of Uganda's three main religious groups: the Roman Catholic Order of the White Fathers, the Protestants of the British Church Missionary Society, and the Muslims. Nakasero and Kololo became prime sites for administrative offices and residential areas for senior government civil service staff. Makerere (much later) evolved into a university campus, and Mulago developed into a site for health institutions. Kampala Hill remained a fort, with a small administrative centre. Now, years later, the hills all still have

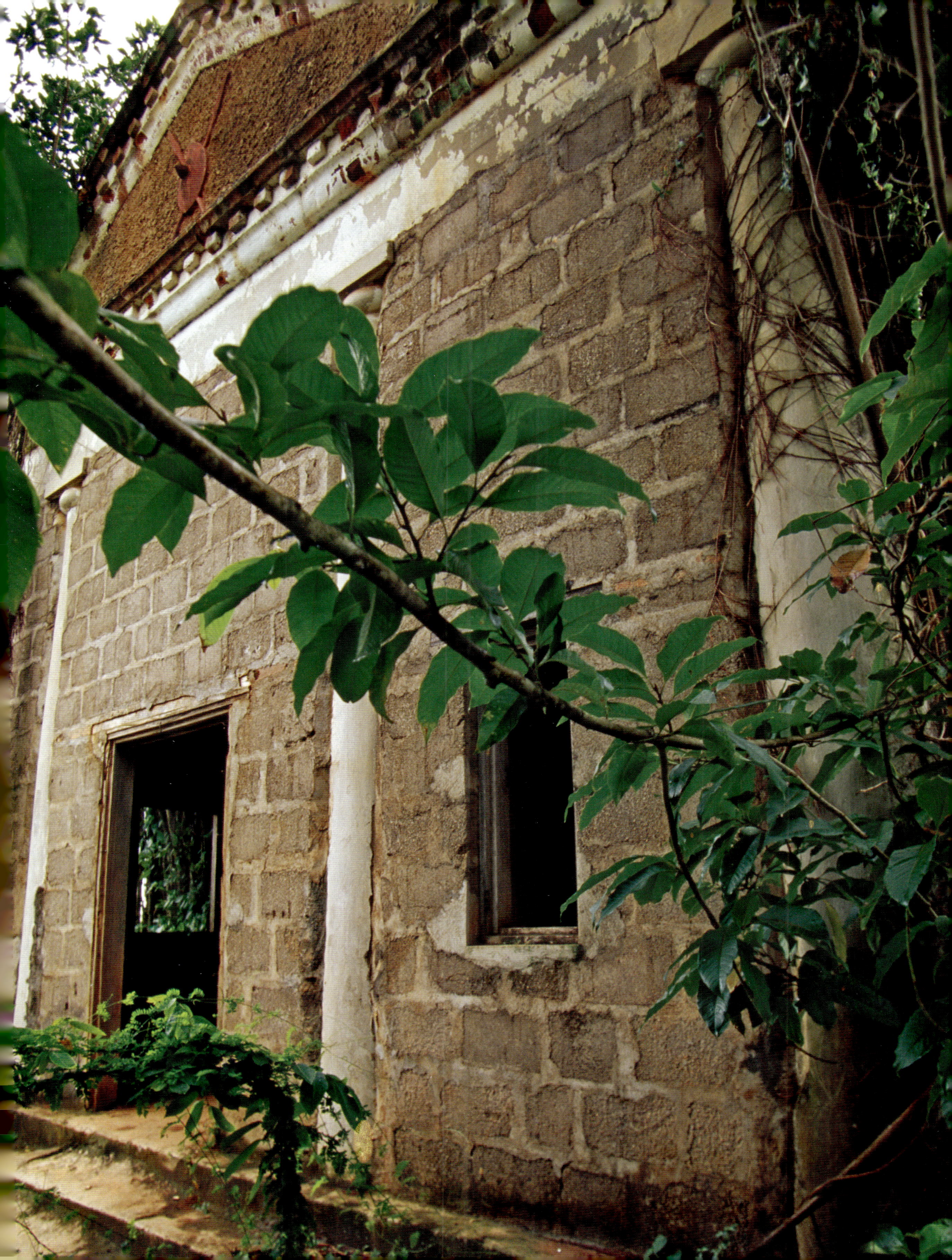

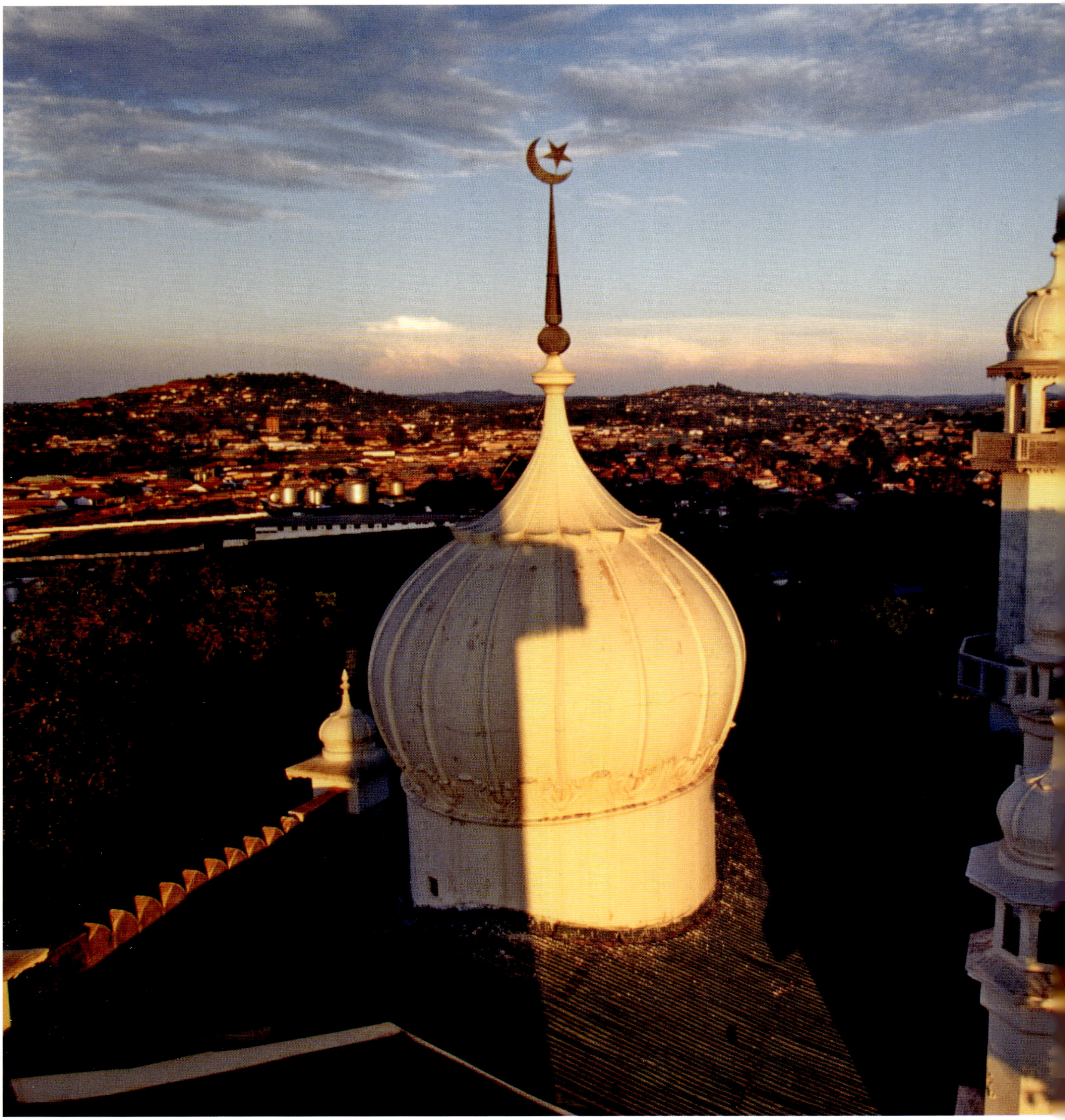

Below: Kibuli Mosque overlooking Kampala's urban sprawl.

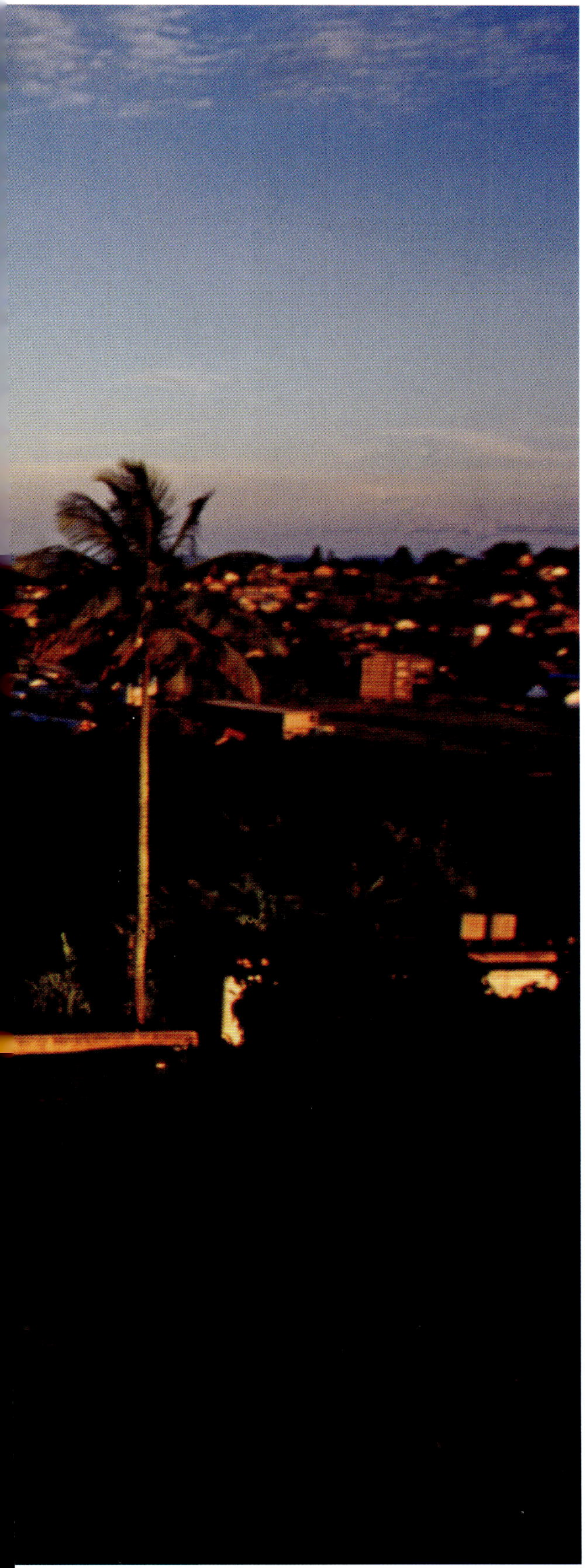

those same basic identities. Mengo Hill – where the palace (lubiri) of the king (kabaka) of Buganda was situated – remained separate as the capital of the Buganda kingdom. White missionaries, before proceeding to their respective hills, were first required to report at Mengo.

Visitors standing for the first time on any of the original seven hills, at an altitude of 1,200 metres (3,800 feet), are often surprised by the greenness of the capital, which is broken by red-tiled villas, green-roofed bungalows and their whitewashed walls, and the modern high-rise buildings of the city centre. Kampala still retains its charm and remains one of the greenest cities in Africa, with a beauty giving way to a still more attractive countryside. The city is traversed by streams and small rivers, features a small lake (the Kabaka's Lake), and lies in the fertile Lake Victoria Basin region, all of which assure Kampala of abundant fresh water for both industrial and domestic use.

As it has grown, Kampala has extended to cover more than 20 green, gently rounded hills in the area. The city's pleasant climate and temperatures – which are improved by the night breezes from Lake Victoria – have attracted thousands of people to work, build, and settle in the city. In the 2002 census, Kampala's official population was given as 1.2 million (up from 774,261 in 1991), and it is probably closer to 1.5 million today. About 90% of the population is of indigenous African descent, with the remainder comprising a cosmopolitan mixture of Asians, Europeans and mixed race 'chotaras'. The city – one of the fastest growing districts in the country – now covers more than 300 square kilometres (116 square miles).

By the early 1970s Kampala was well-known as a beautiful city and major rendezvous, and was frequently chosen to host international conferences and meetings. That all changed on 26 January 1971, when a military coup ushered in the changes that would lead the country and its capital into a steep decline from which some feared they would never recover. However, after the restoration of peace and stability in most parts of the country, including the capital, in 1986, Kampala has risen phoenix-like from the ashes of war to regain much of its former glory – a process that moved slowly at first, but has progressed more rapidly as the city grew in self-confidence.

Under the new regime, around 10,000 Asians and other foreign investors expelled by Amin were persuaded to return to reclaim their property, shops, factories, and other estates. Some of the returned exiles rehabilitated, renovated, and put on new coats of paint; others pulled their old buildings down and started from scratch, adding a taste of new and modern architecture to the city's skyline. Over the 1990s, Kampala developed with remarkable speed, with the building industry one of the

Right: Makerere University has an Africa-wide reputation for excellence.

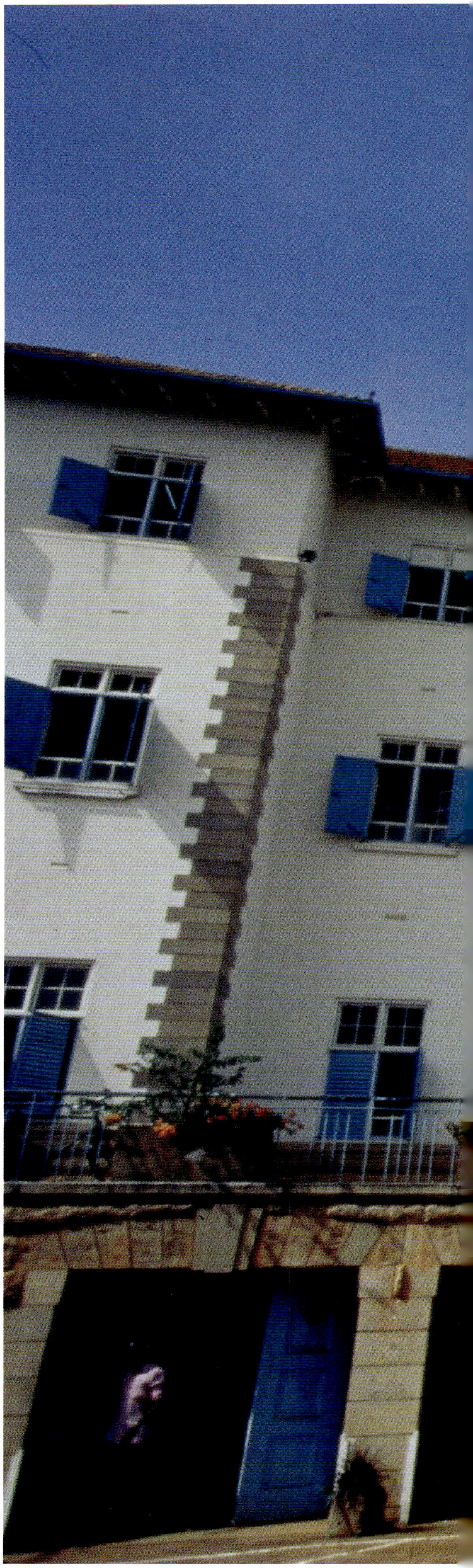

fastest growing enterprises in the city. Places of worship replaced old, rundown cinema halls. New restaurants and 'take-away' establishments popped up on every street corner. Much of the new building was being done by foreign investors, but residents, too, played their part in the rebuilding of Kampala. The rapid development of Kampala has continued into the 21st century and the city is now a pleasant and intriguing place to explore. Attractive, green and overwhelmingly friendly, this is one African city that's generally safe to walk around at any time of day or night.

Symbols of the new Kampala include sprawling suburbs with large trading centres, multiplex cinemas, a wealth of theatres featuring local music and dance, and many entertaining nightspots. The city's shops are full of the latest local – as well as imported – goods, and bargaining is all part of the shopping experience. For the sports-minded, football is the favourite sport, with matches played at the City Centre Nakivubo Stadium, and the Mandela Sports Stadium. A wide range of sports is available to visitors, along with health clubs and gyms. In addition to an ever-expanding range of excellent hotels, the city boasts many restaurants, offering an international, as well as Ugandan cuisine.

The famous Makerere University, once the foremost seat of learning in East Africa, is doing well again. The public is often invited to lectures in the Main Hall of the imposing university administrative block, with its so-called ivory tower. In addition, the School of Fine Arts on the campus features the modern Margaret Trowell Art Gallery, named after the school's founder and mentor. The public is welcome to view the many fine paintings, sculptures, and other works of art on display in this gallery, some of which are for sale.

The Uganda National Museum has displays on the Nakaima Tree, Ntusi, Bigo Bya Mugenyi, and many other aspects of Ugandan history. There are also good ethnological exhibits covering hunting, agriculture, war, religion, and witchcraft, as well as natural history displays. One of the museum's most enjoyable features is its collection of traditional musical instruments.

Uganda's National Theatre has a regular programme of events and offers performances in English as well as vernacular languages. One of the more popular groups performing there regularly is the Ndere Troupe, a company composed of members of Uganda's many ethnic groups, who have gained worldwide acclaim for their excellent traditional dance, music, and drama shows. Work of local artists is often displayed on the walls of the National Theatre. In addition, in the museum grounds is an artists' village, where Ugandan arts and crafts of all types are for sale in a number of colourful kiosks.

The impressive-looking white Parliament Buildings are a link in

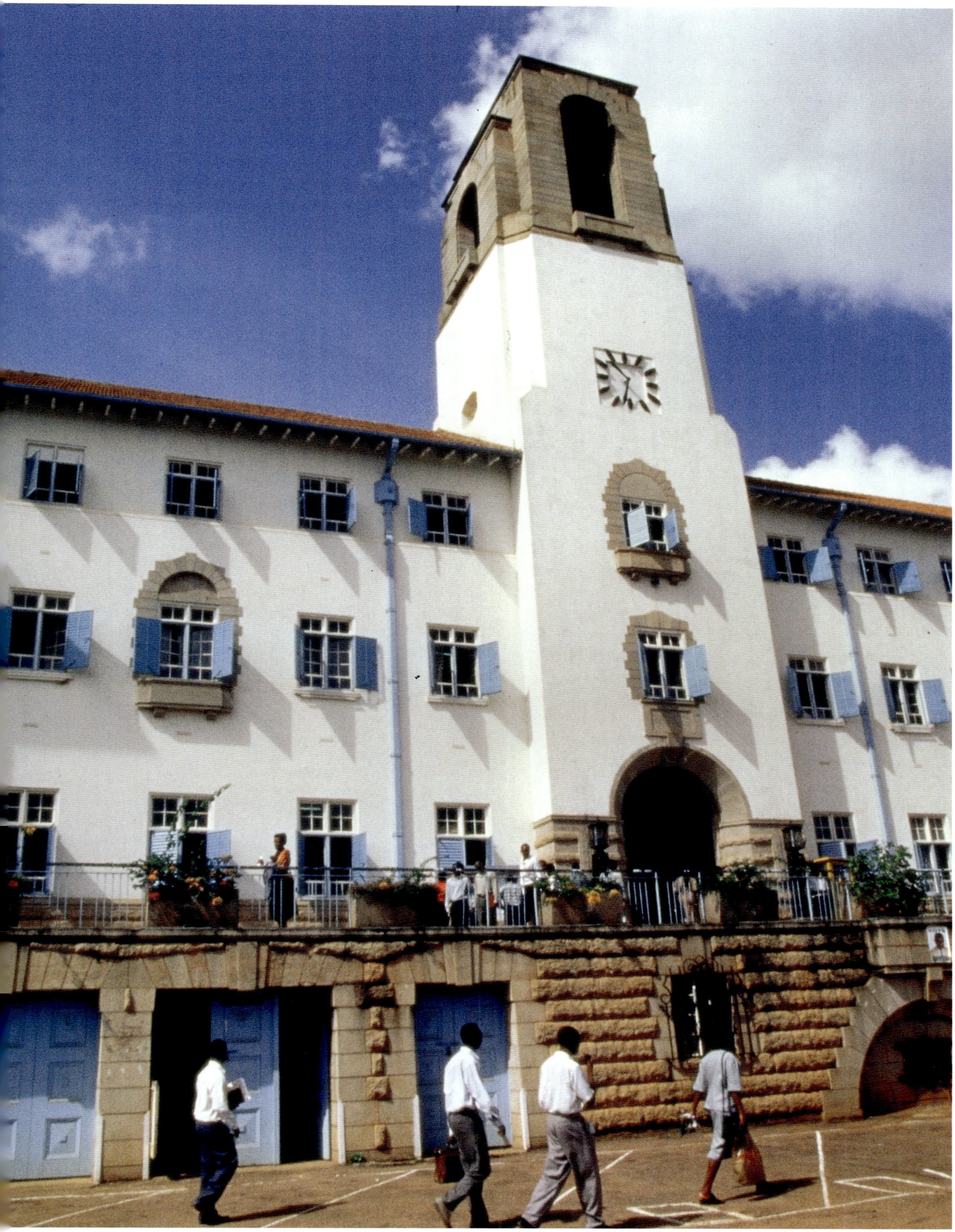

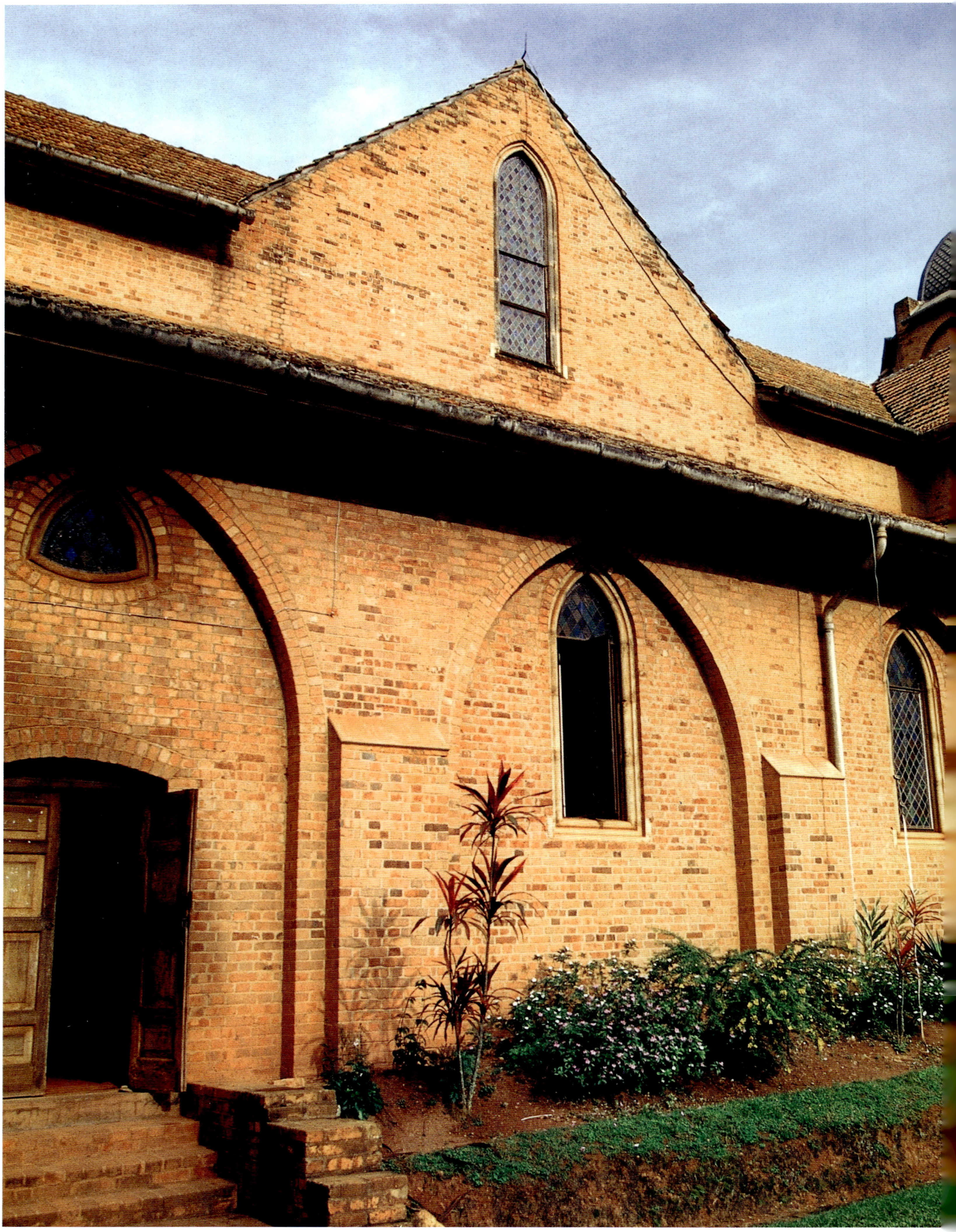

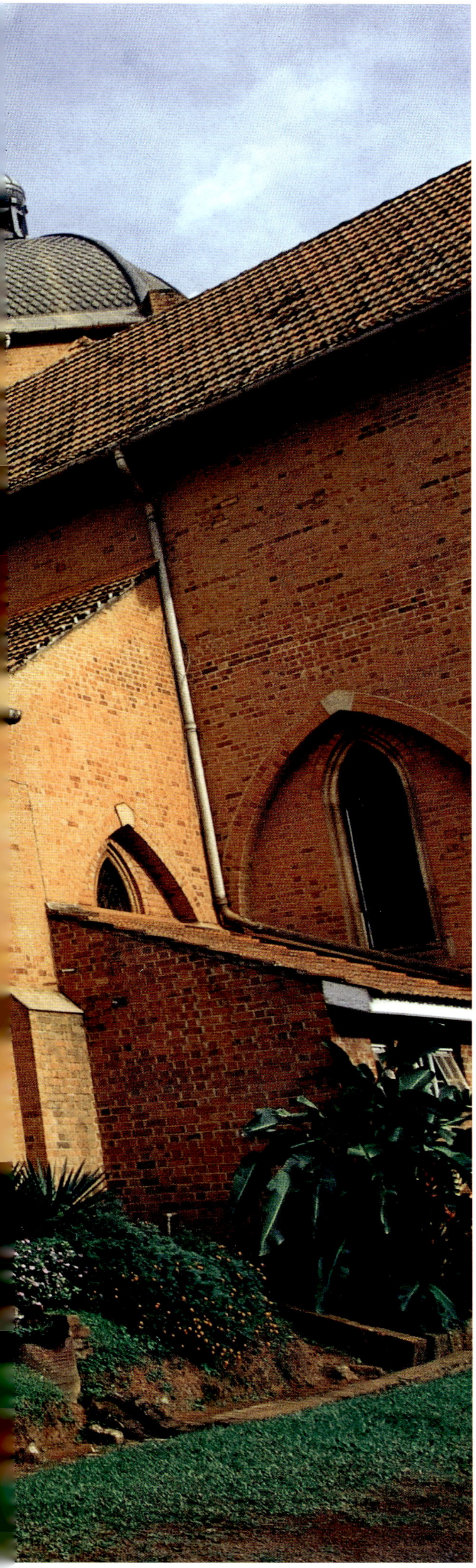

Left: Namirembe Cathedral, also known as St. Paul's, is Uganda's oldest cathedral, built by the Protestant Church Missionary Society in 1890.

the historical chain of Uganda's colonization dating from the 1880s up to today. Close to the Parliament Buildings is the Uganda International Conference Centre, now having regained its status as a premier meeting place.

On the top of Nakasero Hill is All Saints Cathedral, the cathedral of the Anglican Church of Uganda. Until independence in October 1962 it was a small parish church used by the white expatriates residing in the Nakasero Hill area, but after independence, when the white community dwindled, the well-to-do Ugandan Christians took over the church.

However, when the Baganda Christians refused to let a non-Muganda archbishop turn nearby Namirembe Cathedral into the church headquarters, Nakasero church was expanded physically and was promoted to cathedral status and the seat of the Uganda archbishop. All Saints is open daily, but the big day, of course, is Sunday when there are four or more services – all of which are filled to capacity, with many people spilling out onto the lawns and listening to the proceedings via outside loudspeakers.

A number of Kampala's most interesting attractions to visitors are located in its suburbs. The most impressive of these are the Kasubi Tombs, relics of the ancient Buganda kingdom, located on Kasubi Hill off the main Hoima Road. Constructed in traditional fashion, with thatch, poles and reeds, the tombs are housed in a huge domed structure that holds the remains of four former kings of Buganda, namely Mutesa I, Mwanga II, Daudi Chwa II, and Edward Mutesa II. Maintained and guarded by Baganda tribespeople, the tombs also hold a variety of artefacts that belonged to the kings, including musical instruments (such as drums), weapons, fetishes – and a stuffed leopard once kept as a pet by Mutesa I.

En route to Kasubi, Namirembe Cathedral – also known as St Paul's – is Uganda's oldest. The representatives of the Church Missionary Society who arrived in Uganda in 1877 at the invitation of Kabaka Mutesa erected the first church building on Namirembe Hill in March 1890. Namirembe, the name by which both the hill and the cathedral have come to be known, means 'the mother of peace and tranquillity' in the Luganda language.

When this first grass-thatched church was completed, it coincided with the murder of Bishop Hannington in Busoga, allegedly carried out in error when the kabaka's orders, given in Luganda, were misinterpreted. The kabaka had ordered that the bishop be freed – *mute* in Luganda – but his overzealous aides understood it to mean kill – *mutte* – him. During the same year, hundreds of Christian converts were burnt to death. Despite such setbacks, only four years after these terrible events, some 1,000 worshippers thronged the new Namirembe church at Christmas in defiance.

Opposite: Buganda Parliament and statue of the King.

Below: Kampala's old Market has been a focus for traders and buyers for 80 years.

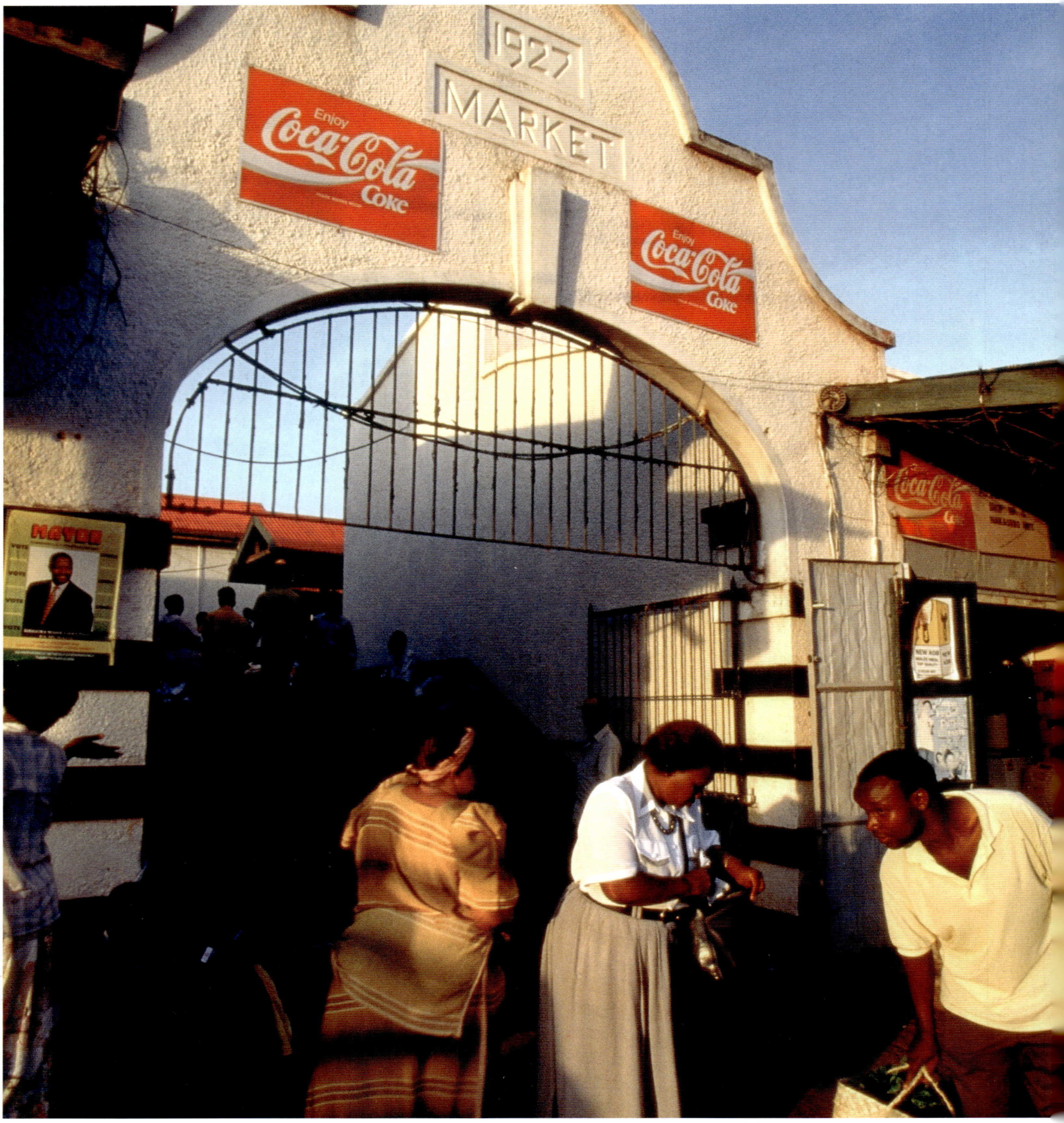

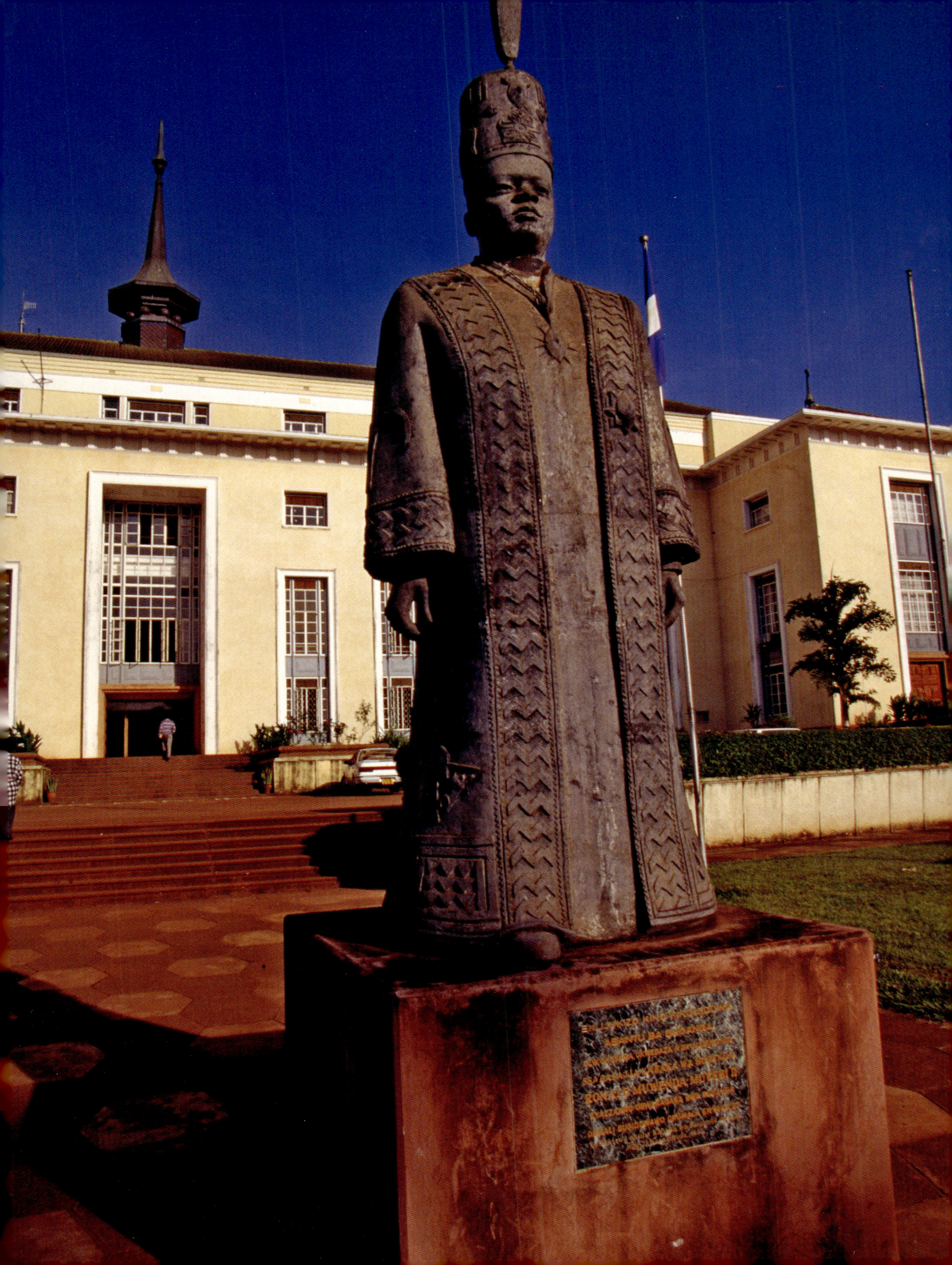

Namirembe Cathedral, like the countryside around it, has undergone tremendous changes over the years. Now a huge, impressive edifice with fine views of the city from its grounds, the cathedral betrays no outward signs of its chequered history. The congregation continues to flock to its services, called to worship by the beating of drums.

Another important religious and historical site related to the Buganda kingdom is the Namugongo Martyrs' Shrine. This marks the spot where in 1886 more than 20 newly converted Ugandan Christians were burnt alive by command of Kabaka Mwanga II, who had ordered them to renounce the white man's religion. A beautiful steel structure, in traditional style, stands at the scene of the atrocity. Artistic work depicting the scenes of this historic Christian episode grace the interior wall of the circular church that stands on the site. In the centre of the church, preserved in glass, are some remains of one of the Roman Catholic Martyrs, Kaloli Lwanga. The shrine was visited and consecrated by Pope Paul V during his first visit to Uganda in 1969. Anglicans, as well as Catholics, were among the martyrs and, to commemorate their suffering, the Anglican Church of Uganda has built a seminary at the spot. Every year, on 3 June, the country observes Martyrs Day as a public holiday. During the day, thousands of the faithful make a religious pilgrimage to Namugongo in remembrance of the martyrs.

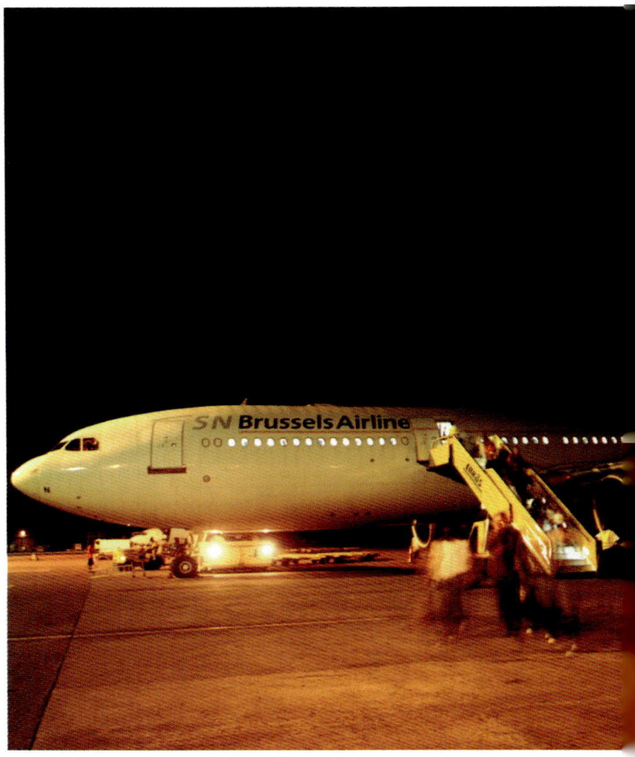

Above and opposite: Many international airlines fly in and out of Entebbe International Airport.

In colonial times, Entebbe, on the lakeshore south of Kampala, served as the administrative capital of Uganda. In 1962, the rapidly-growing business centre of Kampala was chosen as the capital city of the newly independent country, but the leafy backroads of Entebbe are still studded with elegantly faded government buildings betraying its colonial past. Indeed, much of Uganda's history was forged at Entebbe's State House, where colonial governors and independent Uganda rulers conferred with local and foreign leaders on matters of international importance. The building is now the official residence of the head of state, and the site of weekly cabinet meetings away from the hustle and bustle of the capital city.

Entebbe means 'chair' in the Luganda language, and the town derives its name from a legend about Mugula, head of the local Mamba (lungfish) clan, who legendarily commanded his dominion from a rock-hewn chair in a royal enclosure close to present-day Entebbe International Airport. Eventually, the seat was submerged in the waters of Lake Victoria, but the legend lived on when the colonial town nearby was named Entebbe.

Sitting 1,158 metres (3,800 feet) above sea level and almost entirely surrounded by the cool waters of Lake Victoria, Entebbe has a comfortable climate throughout the year – so much so that some choose to live in old colonial residences there and commute every weekday to and from

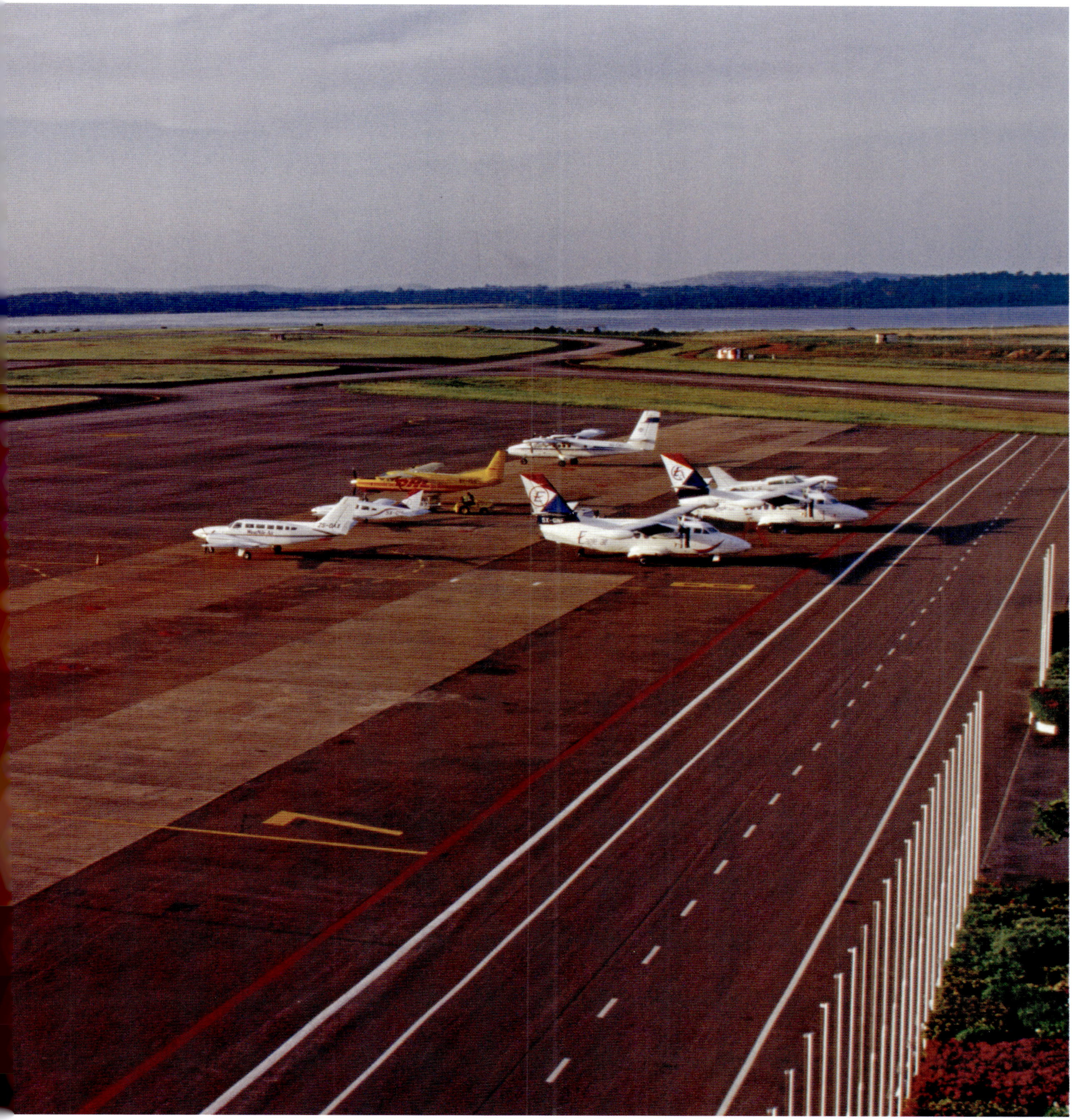

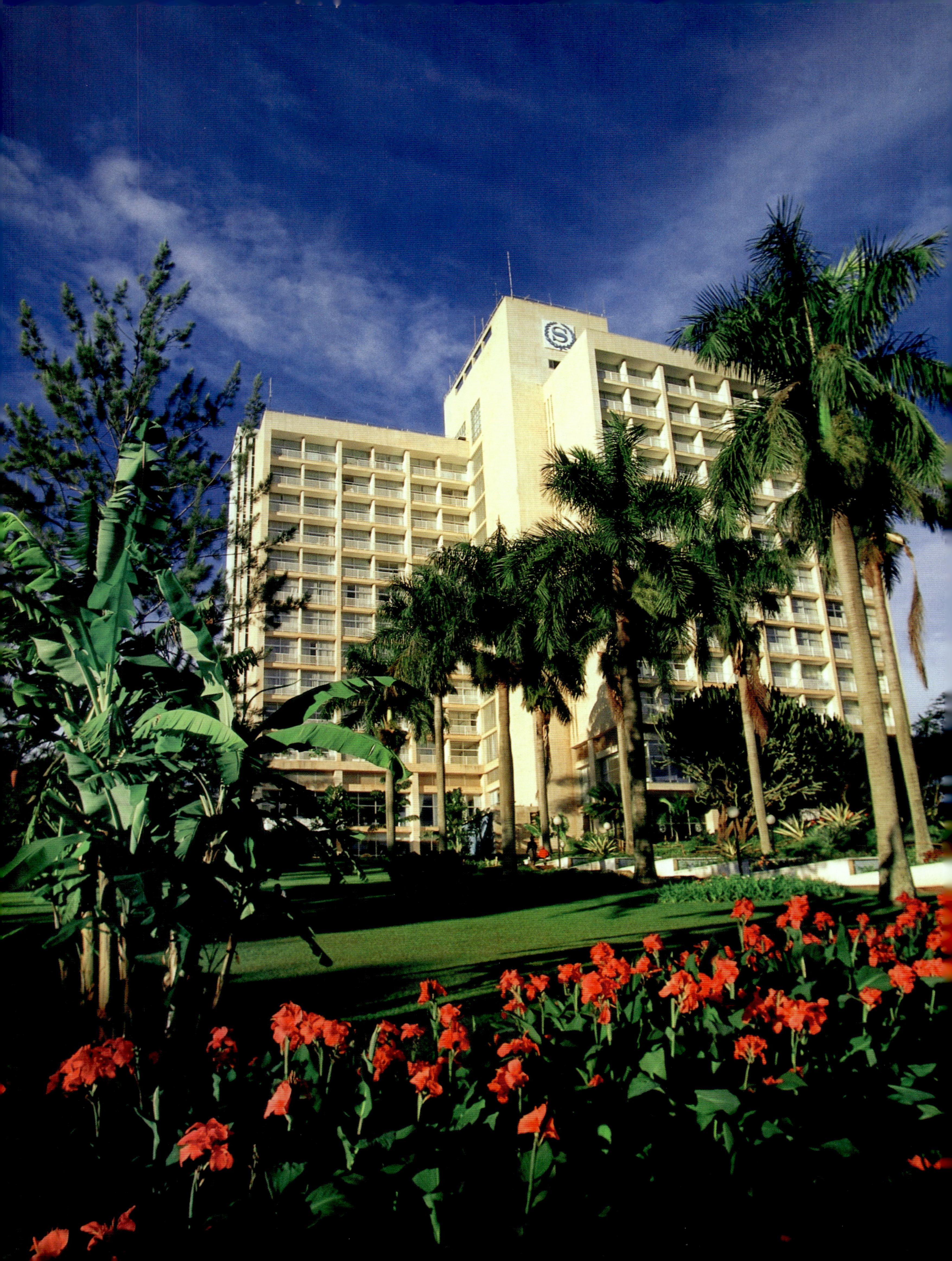

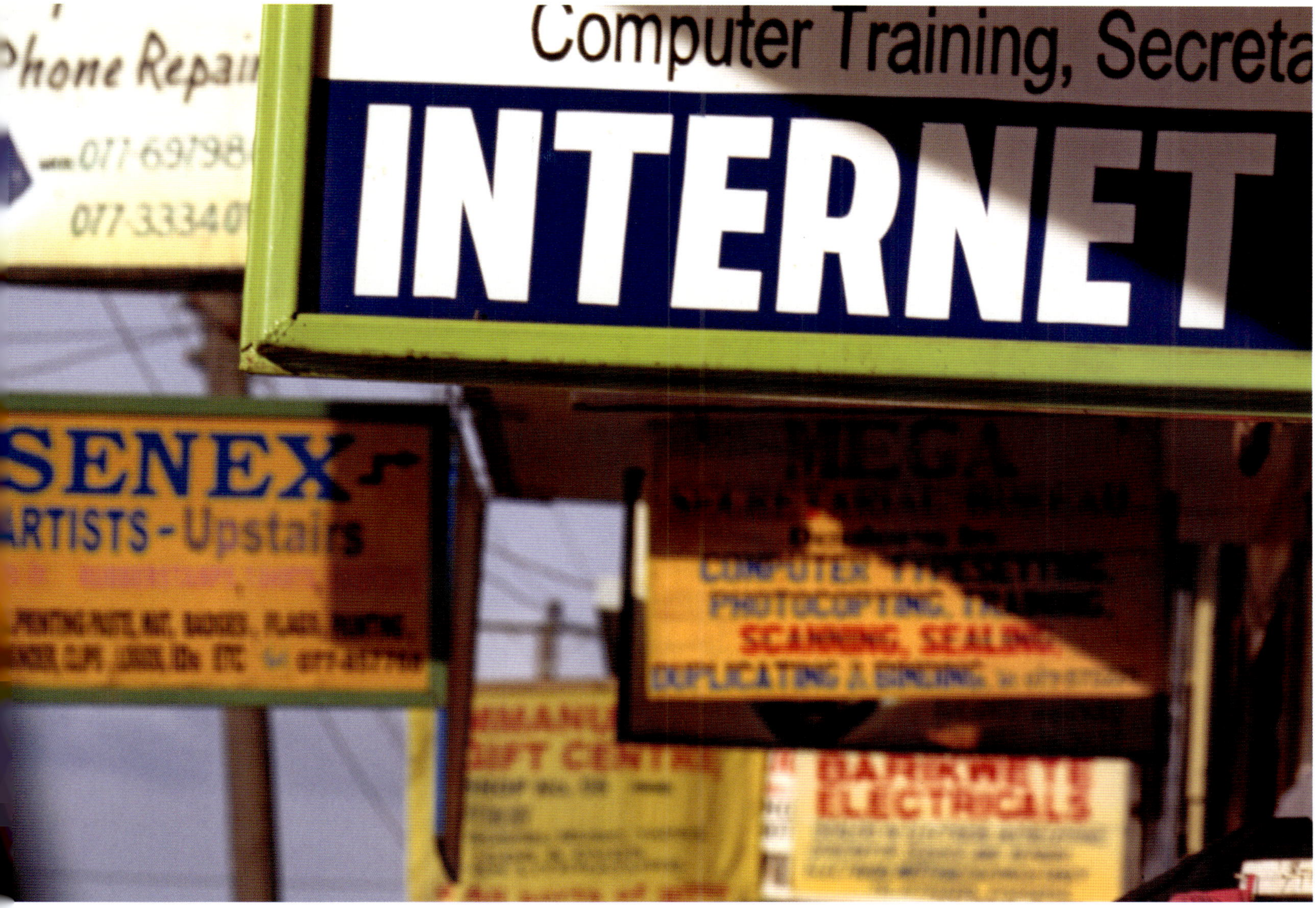

Above: Internet facilities are readily available in Kampala.

Opposite: The Kampala Sheraton is one of several international-standard hotels in the capital.

Kampala. At weekends, many Kampala residents escape the bustle of the capital and visit Entebbe, relaxing at its beach resorts and botanical gardens. The town has excellent hotel facilities and restaurants, which offer a wide range of services, depending on one's pocket and preference.

Entebbe is the site of Uganda's only international airport, which leaped from obscurity in June 1976 when an Air France flight from Israel was forcibly landed there by Palestinian hijackers. In response, Israeli paratroopers stormed the airport on 4 July 1976, freeing the hostages and exposing Amin's complicity in the hijack. A new airport was constructed at Entebbe in the early 1990s, but the disused building where the hostages were held can be visited with permission from airport staff. A few miles off the Airport Road is the Kigungu Landing Site where the first Catholic missionaries, Reverend Father Simon Lourdel and Brother Amans of the Society of White Fathers, came ashore on 17 February 1879. A small brick-walled church was erected on this site and still stands next to a memorial plaque.

The township of Entebbe itself is only a short distance up the main road from the airport towards Kampala and features a couple of international-class hotels and the lakeshore Entebbe Botanical Gardens, which was established in 1898. The gardens were originally a natural forest, used as a research ground for the introduction of various exotic fruits and ornamental plants to Uganda. Indigenous trees that were already there when the gardens were started are still in place today, as are many of the

Below: The Kasubi Tombs house the remains of four former Buganda kings.

Following pages: Bahai Temple near Kampala.

introduced exotic trees and plants. In addition to the obvious flora, there is abundant wildlife in the gardens, particularly black-and-white colobus monkeys and squirrels. Birdlife, too, is prolific and includes some species especially noted in the Lake Victoria region – such as the yellow-throated leaflove and slender-billed weaver – as well as the more common fish eagle and palmnut vulture. Forest birds include the great blue turaco and black-and-white casqued hornbill.

Close by, the Entebbe Wildlife Education Centre (UWEC) originally started as an animal orphanage in the 1920s but gradually grew to be a showplace for many animal species, including buffalo, zebra, chimpanzees, monkeys, lion, various antelopes, crocodiles, and hyenas. Birdlife at the zoo includes crowned cranes, various weavers, and captive shoebills, pelicans, parrots, and ostriches. There used to be chimpanzees here too, but in 1998 they were relocated to the forested 50 hectare Ngamba Island, which was set aside by UWEC as a sanctuary for orphaned chimpanzees. One of the most popular attractions in the vicinity of Kampala, Ngamba lies in Lake Victoria some 23 kilometres (13 miles) southeast of Entebbe, and can be visited by motorboat as a day or overnight trip, offering the opportunity to see the orphaned chimps feed and interact on a semi-natural habitat.

Another popular excursion, only an hour's drive from Entebbe, Mabamba Swamp on the northern verge of Lake Victoria is one of the most reliable sites in Uganda – make that anywhere in Africa – for sightings of the charismatic shoebill. The local fishermen who supplement their income by poling visitors around Mabamba in their dugouts are adept at finding this eagerly sought bird, with a success rate of around 90%. And even if you don't walk away with the jackpot, a heady list of consolation prizes includes pygmy goose, lesser jacana, blue-breasted bee-eater and two highly localised papyrus specialists in the form of Caruthers' cistocola and white-winged warbler.

With their contrasting atmospheres of modern urban bustle and time-warped equatorial languor, Kampala and Entebbe make for a fascinating introduction to Uganda. Entebbe, as the site of the country's only international airport, is an obvious place for natural history enthusiasts to start a tour of the country, spending a relaxed day exploring its pretty beaches, jungle-like botanical garden and popular animal orphanage. Kampala, on the other hand, is the pulsating heart of Uganda's cultural and intellectual life, not to mention its nightclub and restaurant scene, and is an ideal starting point for those seeking a funky taste of contemporary urban Africa.

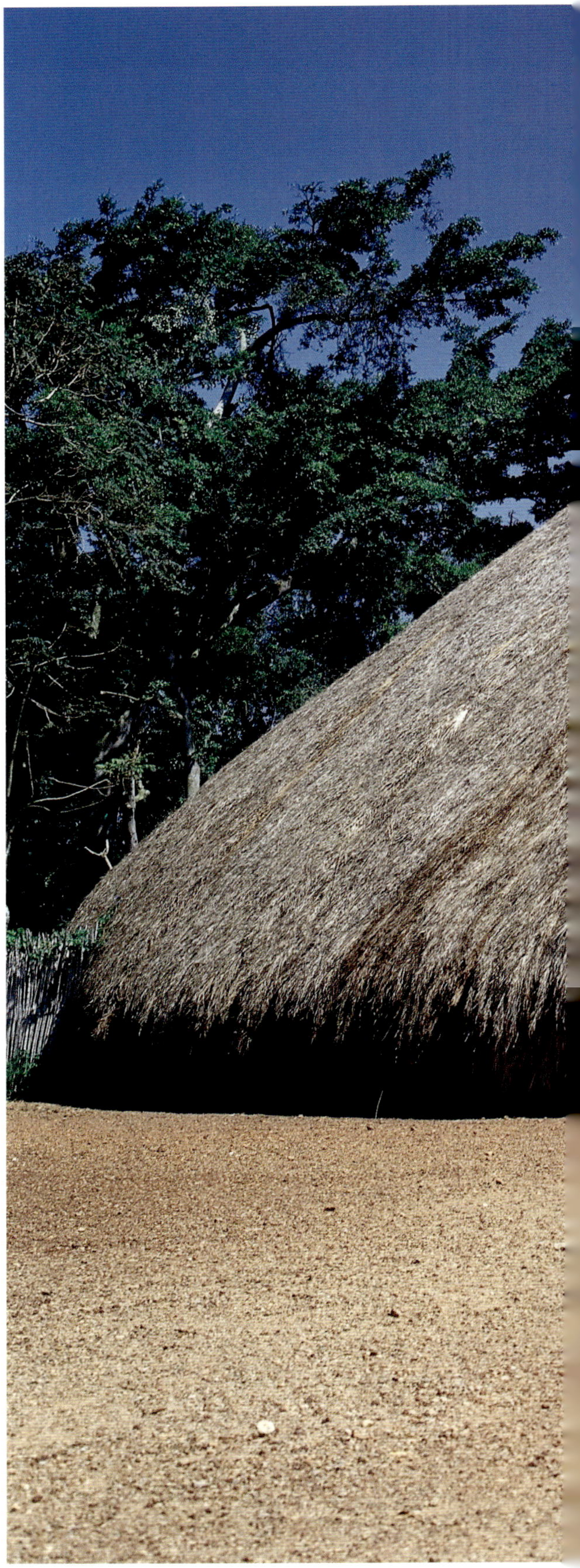

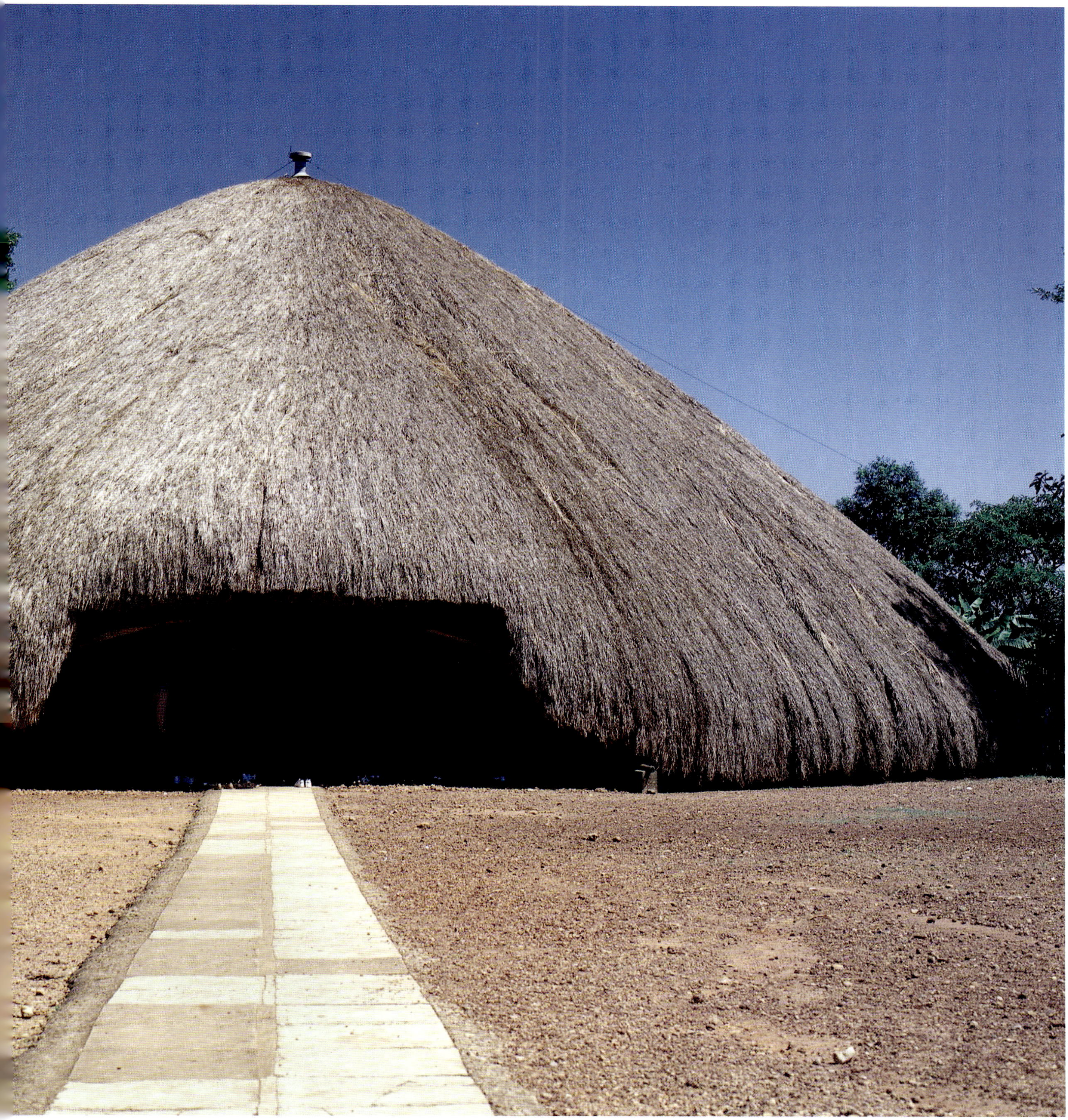

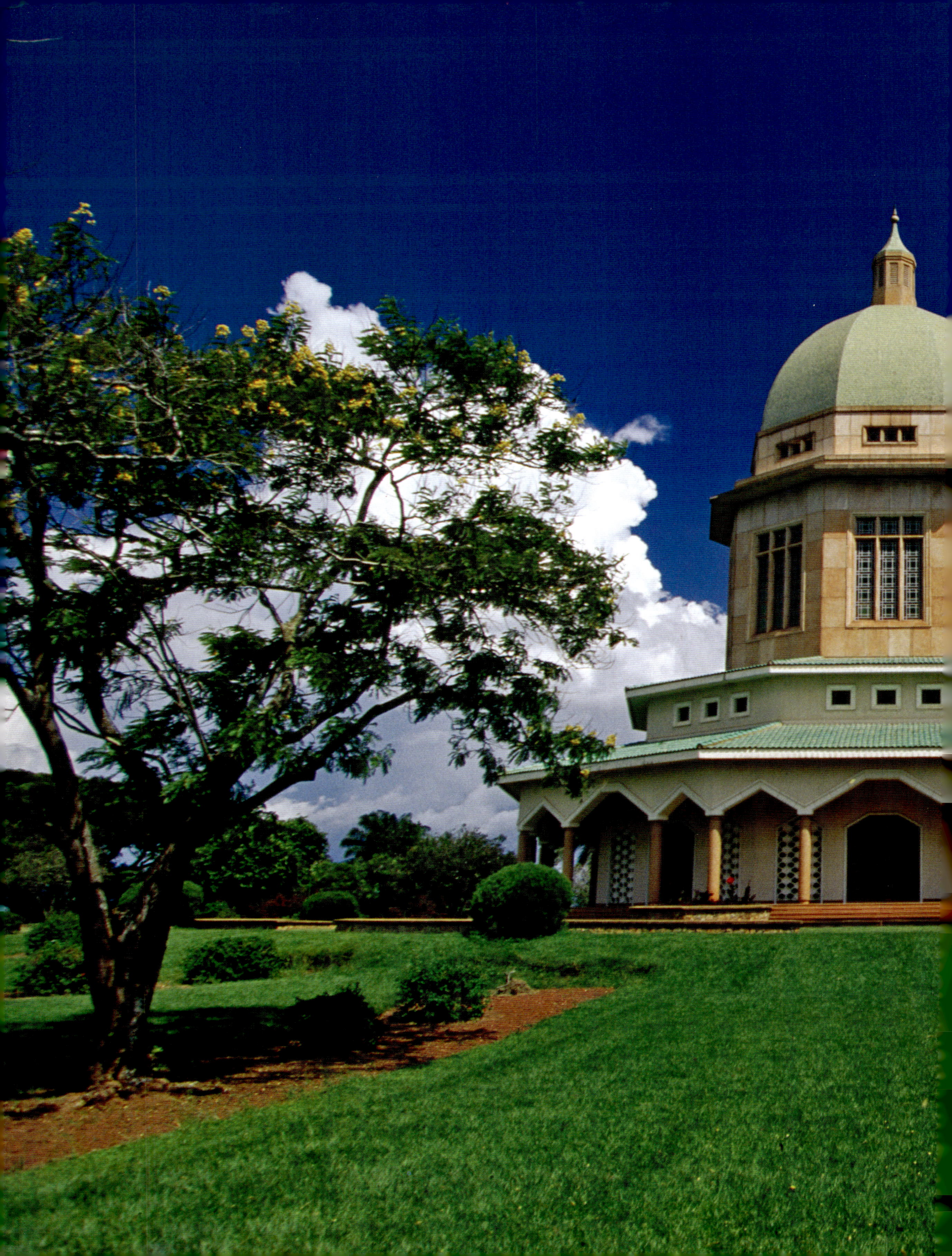

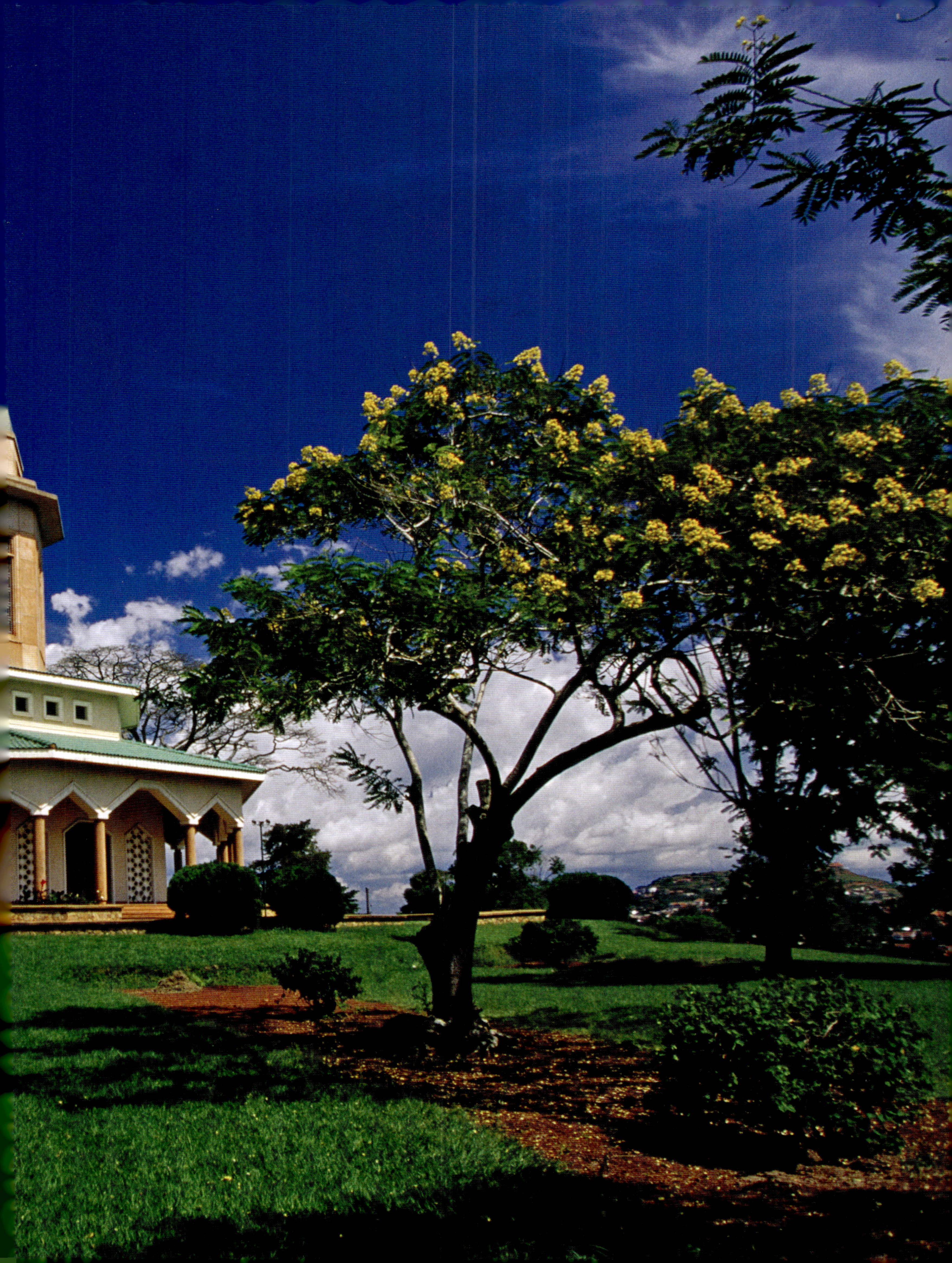

3. South-west: Gorilla Country

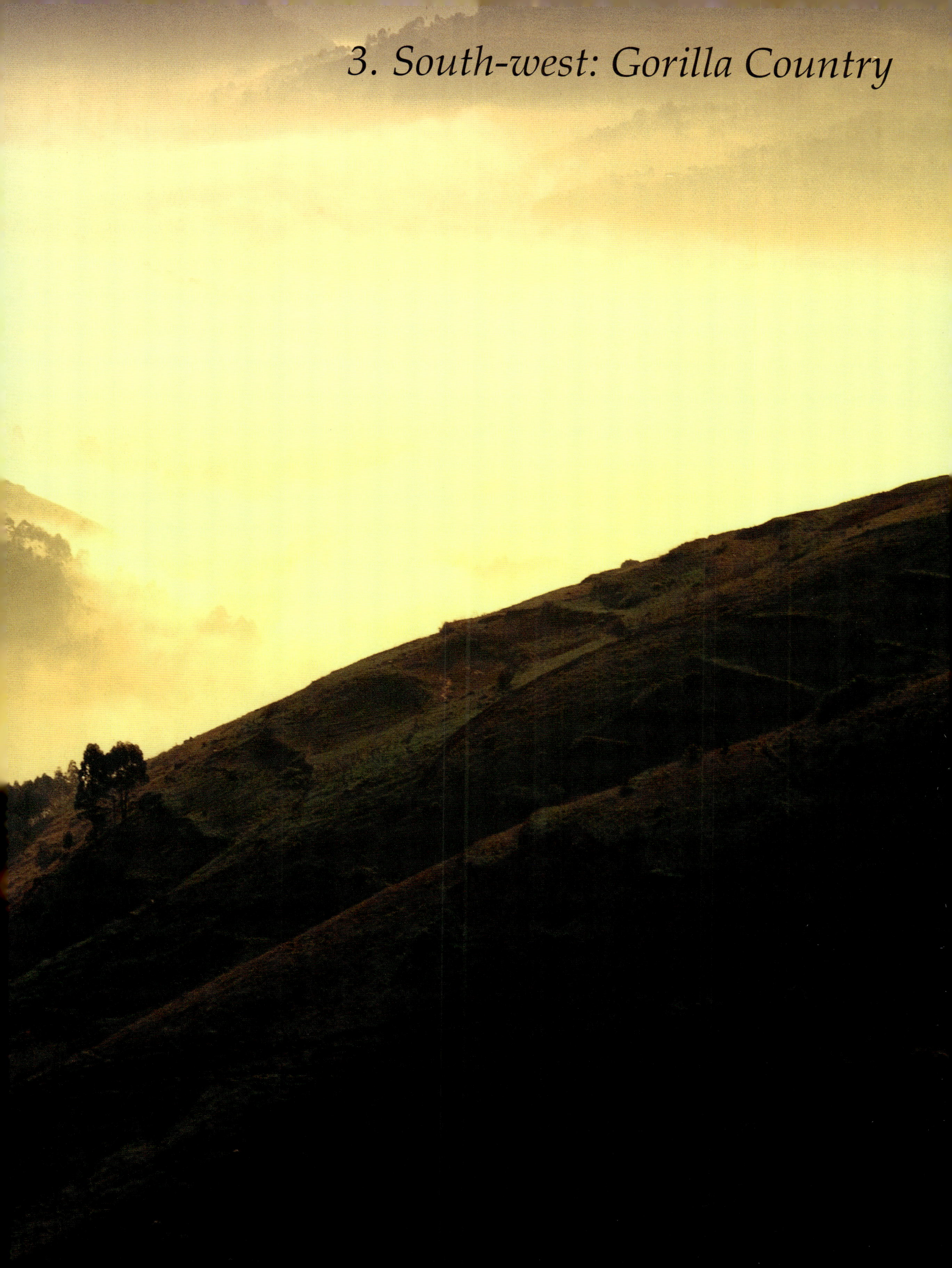

Previous pages: Hills around Kabale.

Right: Part of the Virunga Range, protected in Mgahinga National Park.

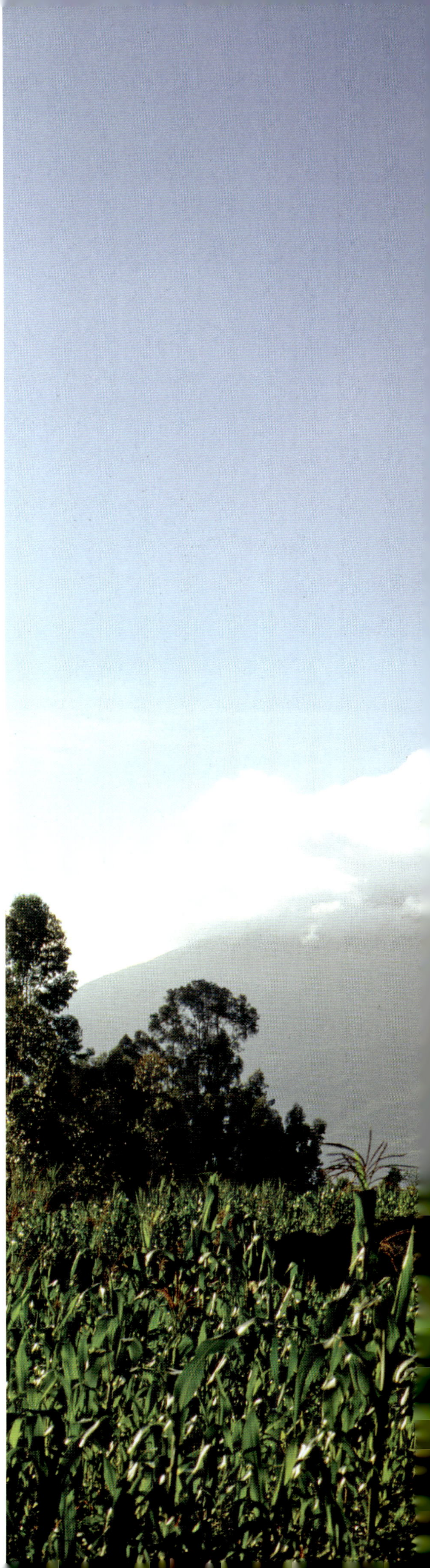

The far southwest of Uganda, all steep verdant slopes swathed in lush montane forest and terraced cultivation, is regarded by many aficionados as the loveliest part of the country. Scenically, it is most impressive for the brooding Virunga Range, a string of seven freestanding volcanic mountains that includes Mount Sabinyo, whose 3,634-metre (11,180 ft) peak forms the tripartite border with Rwanda and the DRC. It was on the rocky slopes of Sabinyo, in October 1902, that a German expedition led by Captain von Beringe, to the mutual astonishment of both man and beast, observed "a herd of big, black monkeys which tried to climb the crest of the volcano" and opened fire, causing two of the mysterious primates to tumble into a deep ravine.

"After five hours of strenuous work," von Beringe would later recall, "we succeeded in retrieving one of these animals using a rope. It was a big, human-like male monkey, one and a half metres in height, and weighing more than 200 pounds. His chest had no hair, and his hands and feet were of enormous size. Unfortunately, I was unable to determine its type; because of its size, it could not very well be a chimpanzee or a gorilla, and in any case the presence of gorillas had not been established in the area around the lakes."

As it happens, the specimen preserved by von Beringe would establish just that, when Professor Paul Matschie of the Berlin Zoological Museum recognised it as a previously undocumented type of gorilla, which he named *Gorilla beringe* in 1903. The taxonomic status of von Beringe's 'big, black monkey' has been subject to several subsequent revisions, and it remains open to debate, but most laymen know it simply as the mountain gorilla – the world's most charismatic primate. Sadly, it is also one of our most critically endangered primate taxa, with an estimated global population of around 750 divided evenly between the cross-border Virungas, whose Ugandan component is protected in the Mgahinga Gorilla National Park, and Bwindi Impenetrable National Park, which lies entirely within Uganda.

Tracking Uganda's mountain gorillas remains a singularly life-enhancing and unusually demanding wildlife-viewing experience. Setting out in the cool of the early morning, the fortunate few – just a few groups of six tourists daily – huff and puff along the steep mountain slopes, passing though lush montane forest and tall bamboo thickets to reach the place where the gorillas were observed the previous day. From here, expert trackers follow the gorilla's spoor through tangled undergrowth to their present location, a process that might take anything from ten minutes to several hours. The anticipation is heightened by the physicality of the trek, met by that imposing first sighting of a full-grown silverback (three times greater in bulk than an average human male) and often exceeded by

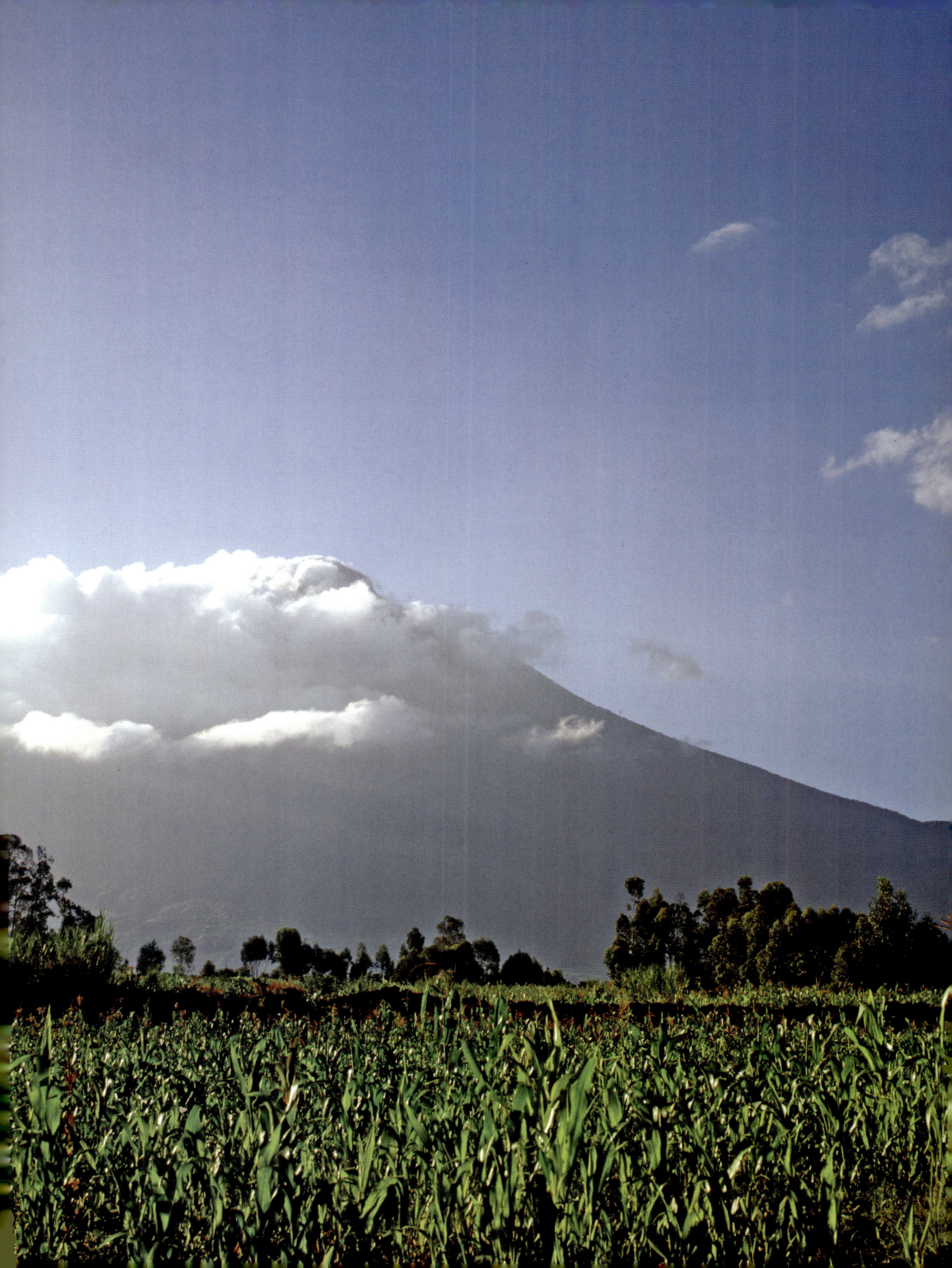

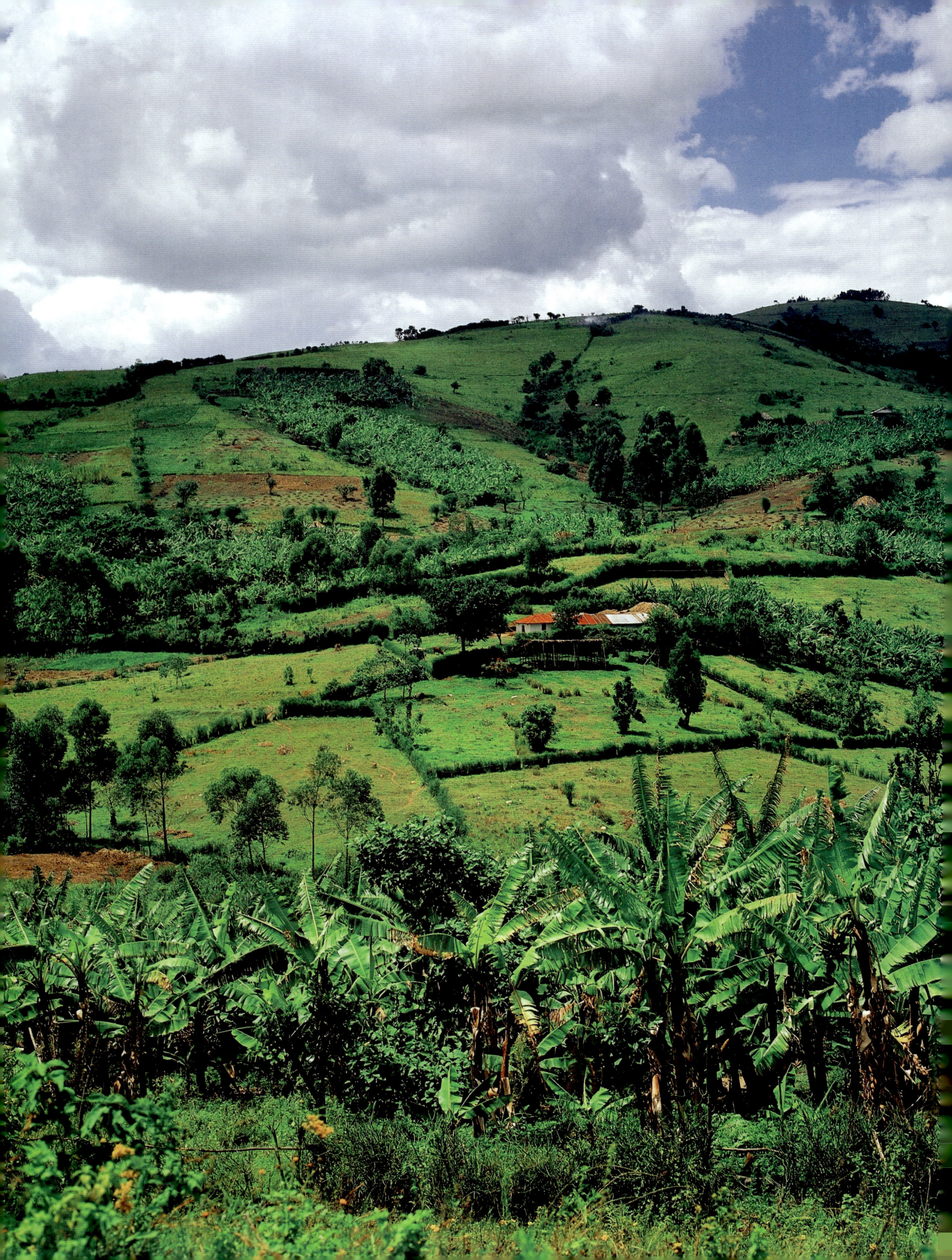

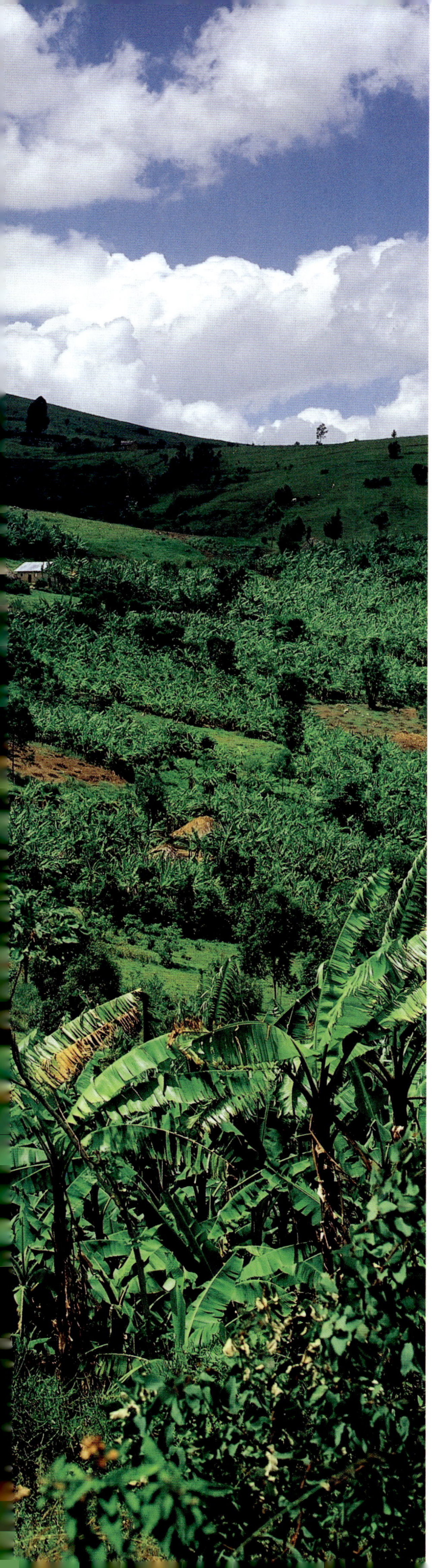

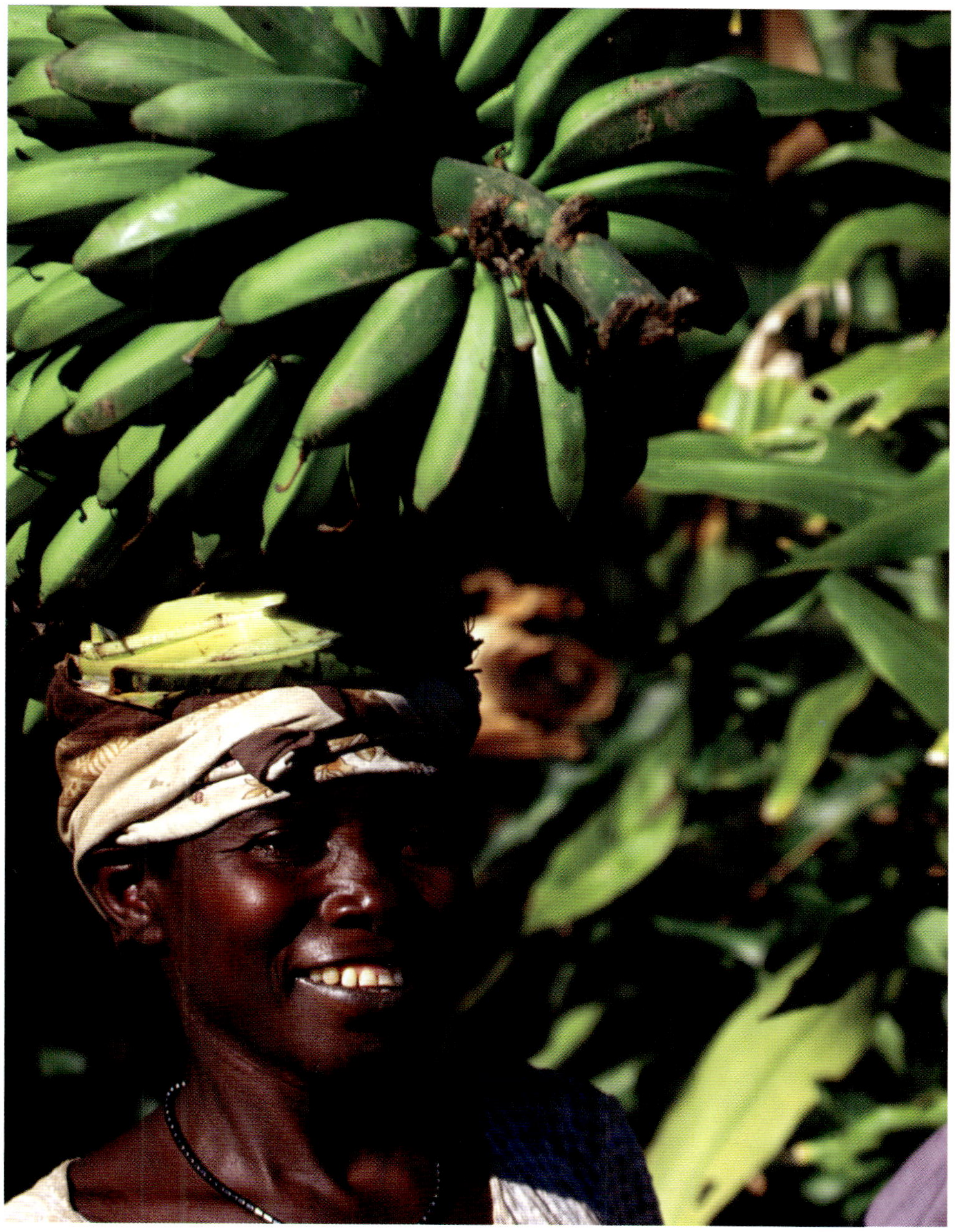

Left and above: Bananas are the staple diet of many Ugandans. Four broad categories of banana are recognised in Uganda, based on how they are eaten – matoke are boiled (rather like potatoes), gonja are roasted, mbide are distilled for banana beer, and menvu are the more familiar sweet bananas that are eaten raw.

a powerful sense of kinship experienced by most visitors. As Dian Fossey, the first person to habituate mountain gorillas to human company, once wrote: "On perceiving the softness, tranquility and trust conveyed by her eyes, I was overwhelmed by the extraordinary depth of our rapport".

Viewing the gorillas is certainly the highpoint of any visit to the southwest, for which reason many visitors rush directly from Kampala to Bwindi or Mgahinga. but for those with time to spare there is plenty to see along the way. The region boasts a number of beautiful lakes and waterfalls, particularly Lake Nabugabo, Mburo and Bunyonyi. The latter is in Kabale District, which, together with neighbouring Rukungiri and Kisoro Districts, is known as the Switzerland of Africa, largely because of the cooler climate and beautiful mountain scenery found there.

On the drive towards Masaka, the first major town coming from Kampala, huge banana plantations cover the hills and valleys as far as the eye can see, and heaps and heaps of bananas are sold by the roadside, awaiting transport to outlying districts. Not surprisingly, the staple food here and throughout the southwest is a steamed banana dish called 'matoke', and every homestead is surrounded by a cluster of the unmistakable broad-leaved banana trees. This type of banana is cooked when green. Commonly, after peeling the fruit, the banana itself is wrapped in a banana leaf and boiled in water. Meat or groundnut sauce may be added and boiled together with the bananas in the same pot. After about half an hour the matoke is ready to eat – using the fingers, while one is seated on colourful mats. To a typical Ugandan man, a meal is not a meal unless matoke is served; it's as important to him as bread is to a European. Other fruits are offered for sale on the roadside, such as mango and pineapple, which, after being purchased, can be sliced and eaten straight away – a great on-the-road healthy snack.

Of interest is the ecotourism centre in the Mpanga Forest Reserve, a 450-hectare (1,110-acre) medium-altitude rainforest, typical of that which once covered much of this region. The reserve was demarcated in the 1950s, essentially for research purposes. There is an extensive network of paths within its borders, from which visitors can view the few species of wildlife – mainly monkeys, such as the red-tailed and the vervet – and the prolific birdlife that make this forest their home. Among the more prominent of the almost 200 bird species recorded are blue-breasted kingfisher, black-and-white casqued hornbill, African pied hornbill, African grey parrot and great blue turaco. Butterflies are abundant and beautiful.

Two important Kiganda shrines lie within walking distance of the forest. Nakibinge Shrine, dedicated to a 16th century king, is housed in a small thatched building in the style of the Kasubi Tombs. The Kibuuka Shrine near Mpigi is dedicated to a war spirit from the Ssese Islands.

Opposite: Matoke is a national dish, eaten in most parts of the country, from bananas grown mostly in Buganda and western Uganda.

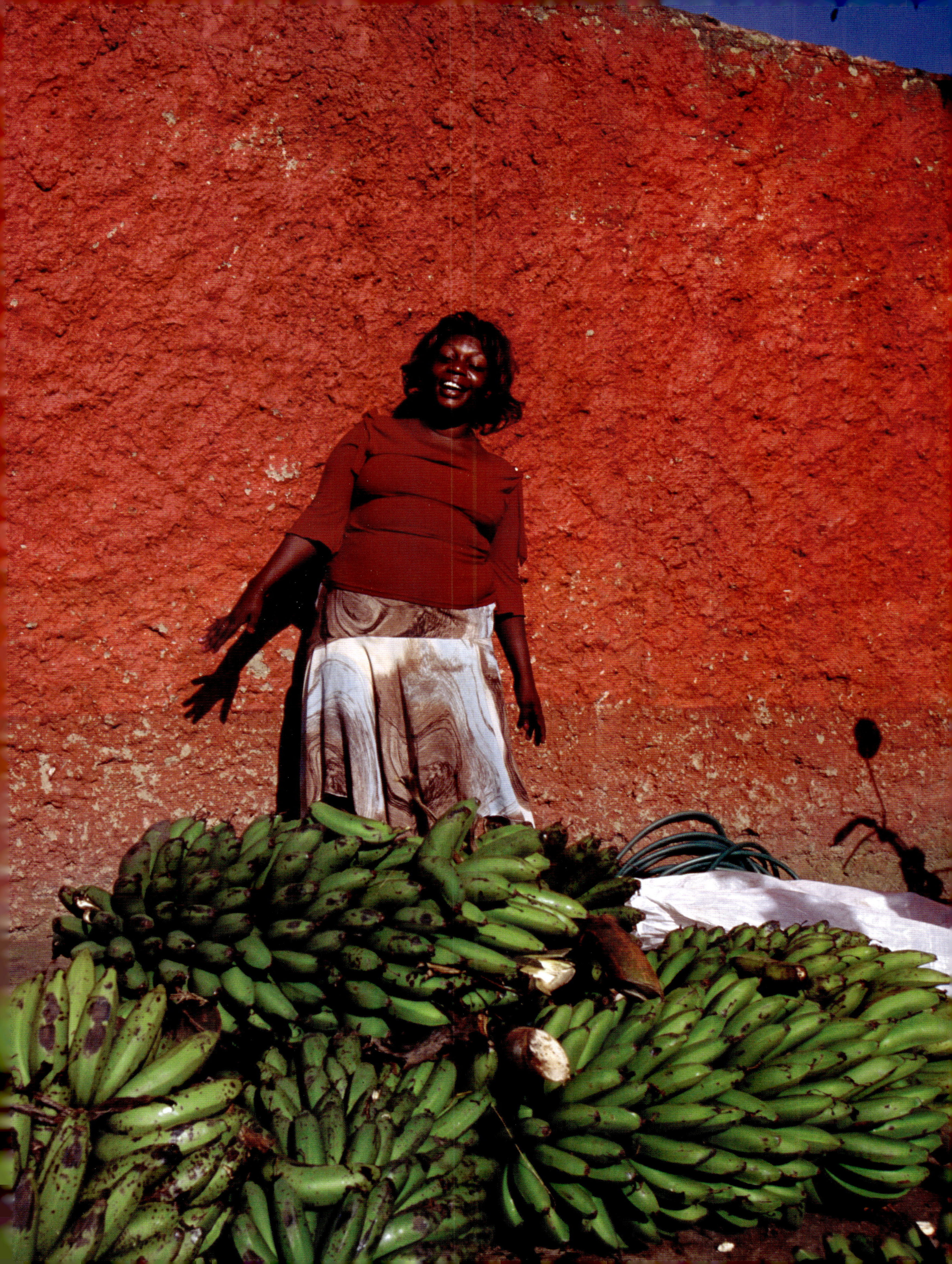

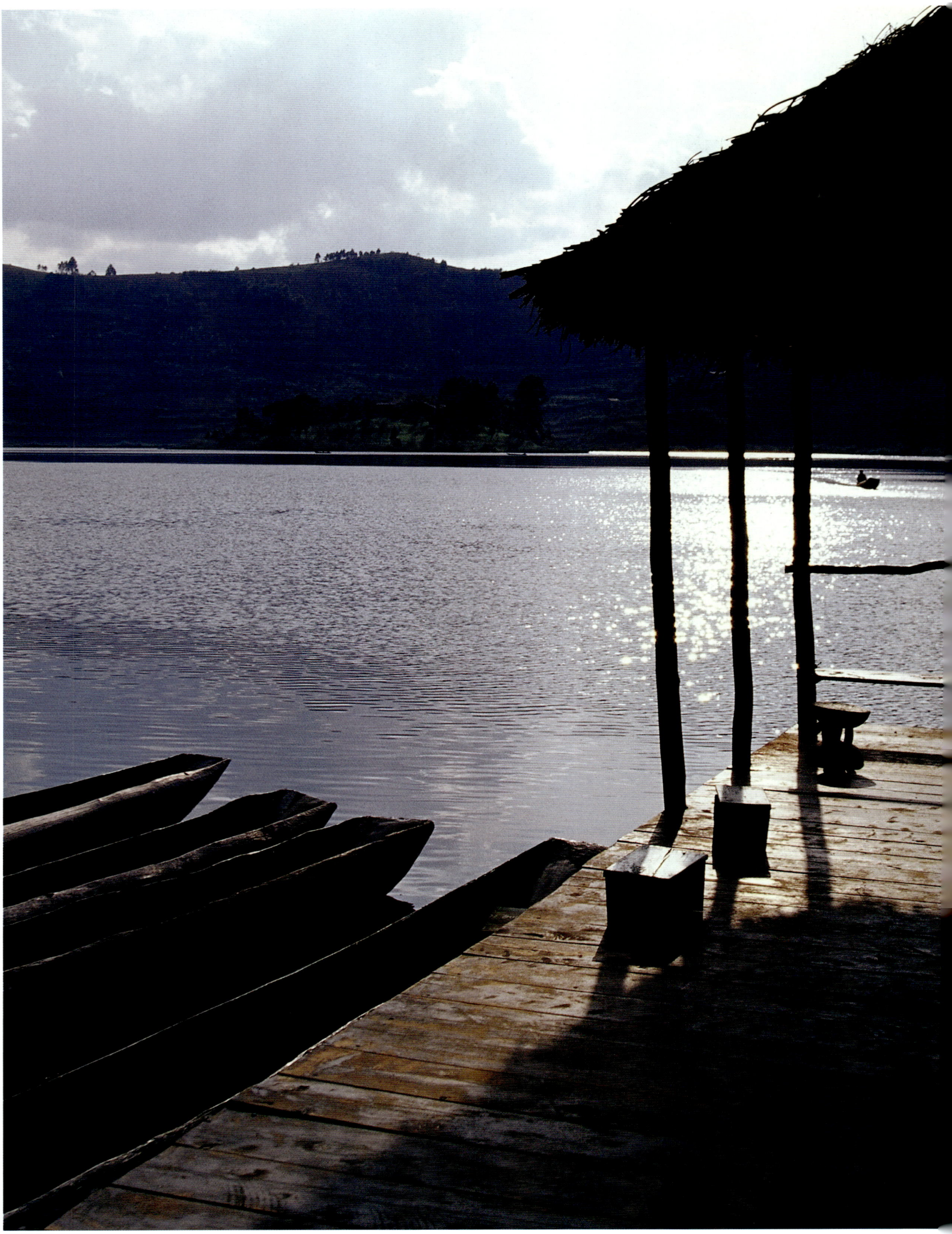

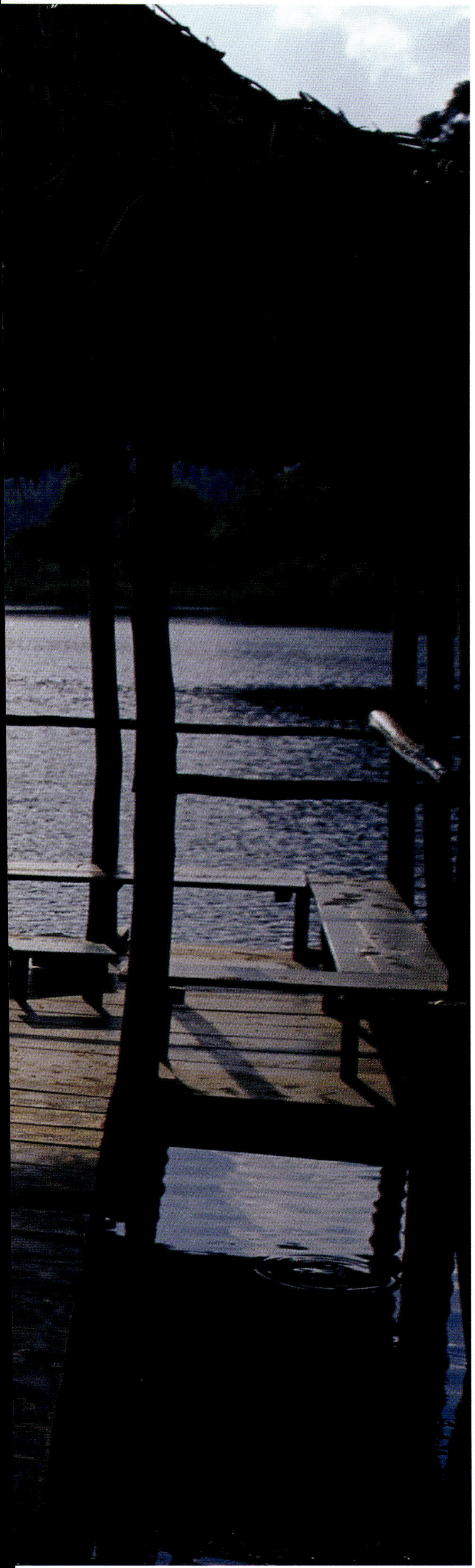

Left and following pages: Verdant hills surround Lake Bunyonyi in the Kabale area.

Nearby is Mpambire village, the home of the Royal Drum Makers. All along the roadsides in this area visitors can observe traditional drums being crafted using methods passed down through the generations. Drums have been used in Africa since time immemorial for communicating and calling people to festive occasions, and Ugandan drums are particularly well crafted. Today, drums are used extensively in traditional music and dance, and make excellent souvenirs.

Along the Masaka-Bukakata road is Lake Nabugabo, a wonderful place to spend a day or two. The area around the lake can be explored and offers sightings of some small animals and the glorious birdlife in the area – in particular the broad-billed roller, Ross's turaco, and a myriad of sunbirds, weavers, and hornbills. The lake is separated from Lake Victoria by a thin, forested sand bar.

The way to the deep south-west passes close to Lake Victoria and the offshore Ssese Islands. Truly a slice of unspoilt Africa, the 84 islands, east of Masaka, are a refuge of peace and friendliness, offering relaxing days admiring the views, watching birds, or going boating in traditional canoes. Seldom visited by travellers, Ssese shows an interesting and very different side to Uganda. They are inhabited by the Basese people – a distinct ethnic group with their own language, culture, and folklore. Primarily fishermen, the Basese also farm coffee, sweet potato, cassava, yams, and bananas. This is a place to relax, unwind, enjoy the beautiful views, and explore.

The islands are lush and well watered, with an average rainfall of more than 2,000 millimetres (80 inches) a year. The main islands of Buggala, Bufumira, Bukasa, Bubeke, and Kkome are hilly and forested (in areas where they are not cultivated) with a large variety of trees. On Buggala, in addition to the delightful views, a walk through the forests will probably bring to light a number of monkeys, some antelope, brilliant butterflies, and an overwhelming selection of water and forest birds. In particular, expect to see hornbills, barbets, turacos, weavers, and paradise flycatchers.

Heading inland from Lake Victoria, the modern village of Ntusi lies on the site of what is thought to be the most ancient large settlement in Uganda. Strong evidence suggests that the people who once lived there gave rise to the legendary and mysterious Batembuzi gods, who play a central role in Ugandan folklore. Oral history places the Batembuzi empire at between AD 1100 and 1350, and evidence in the Ntusi region confirms that a highly centralized society existed there as early as the 11th century. The ancient town is thought to have been the largest settlement in sub-Saharan Africa when it reached its pinnacle in the 12th and 13th centuries. It is believed to have been the capital of an empire stretching all the way to Lake Albert in the north. Evidence of iron smelting and ivory and wood carving has been found there by archaeologists.

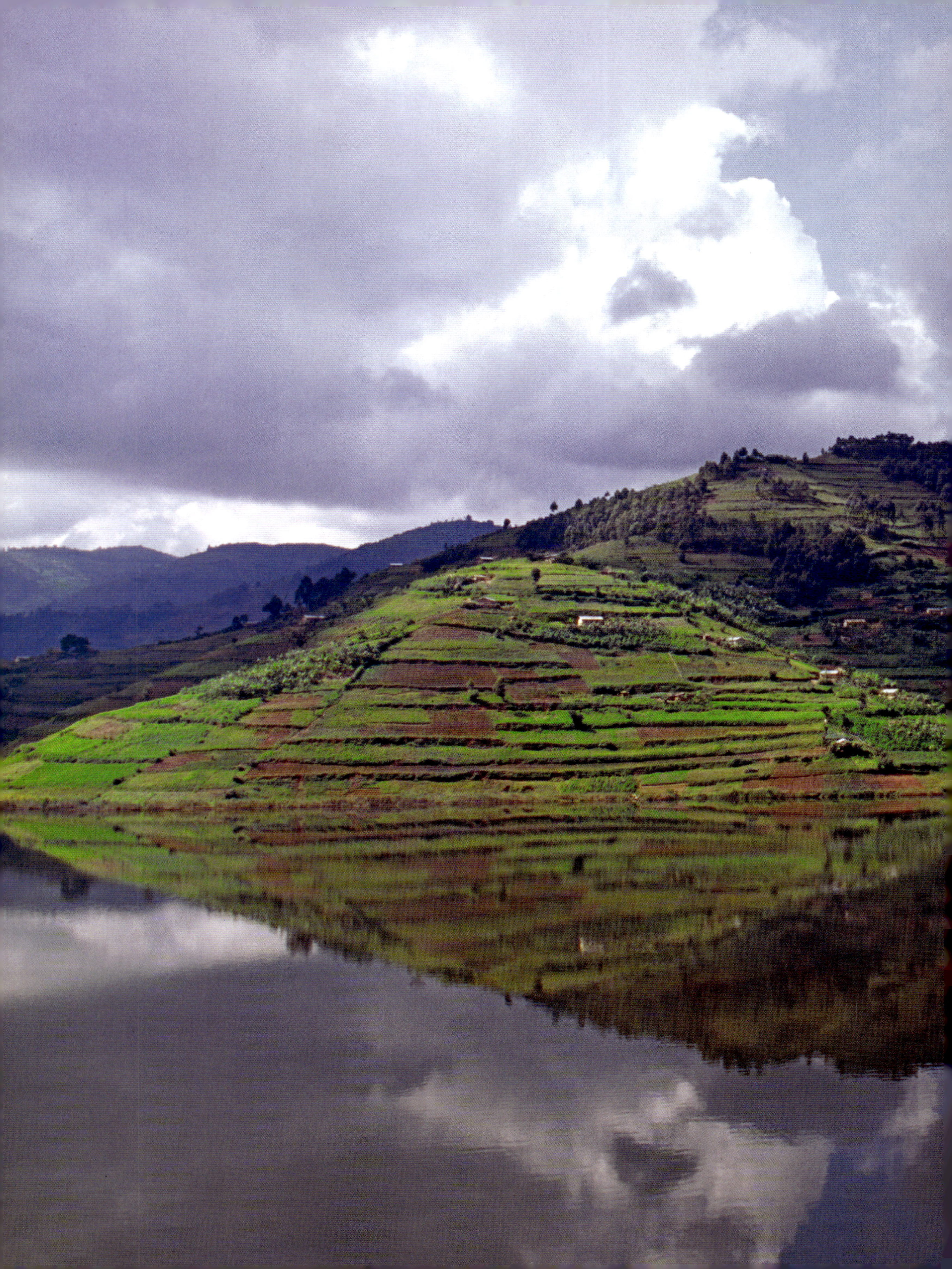

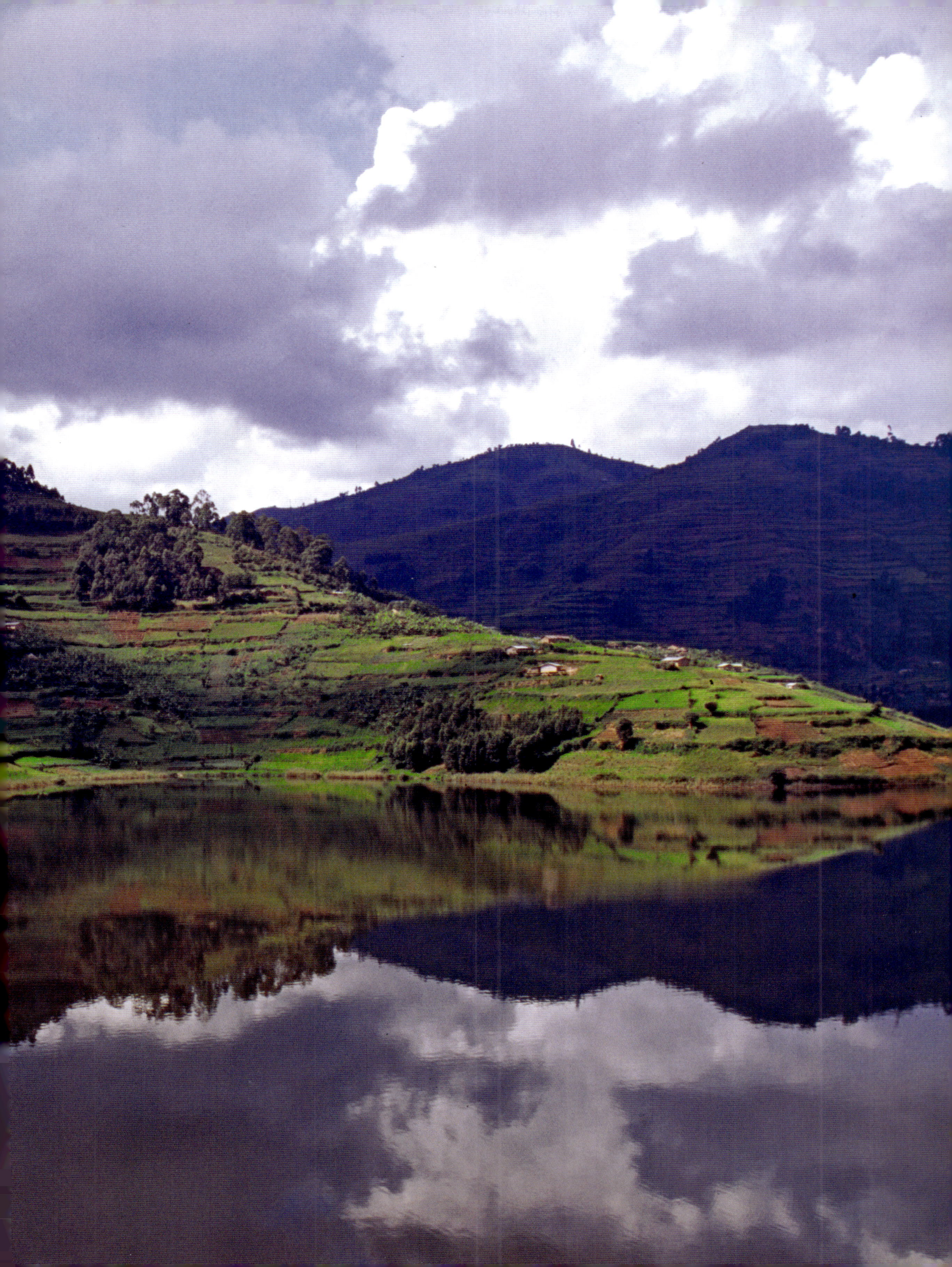

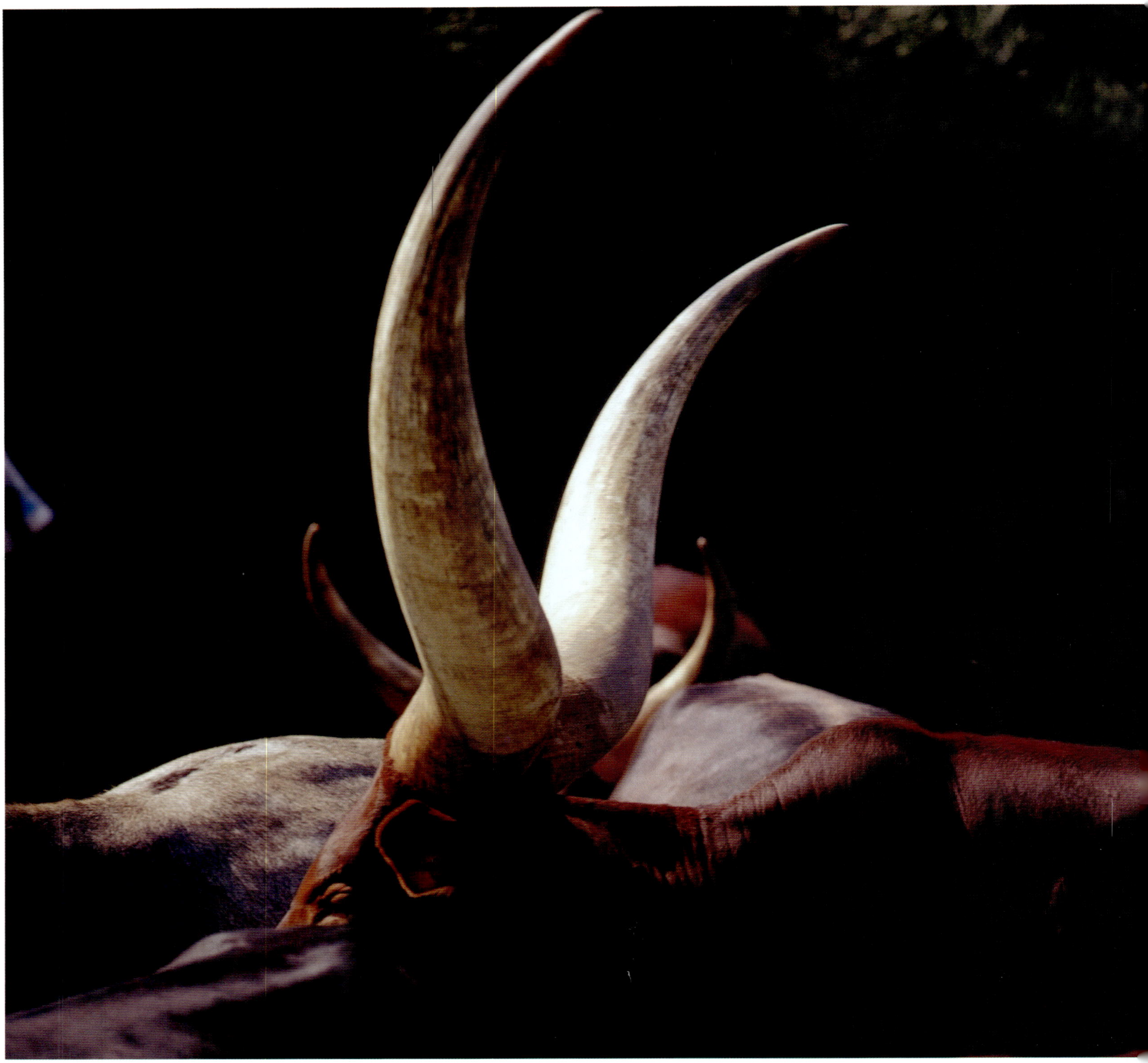

Above: The remarkable long-horned Ankole cattle.

The word ntusi means 'mound': the prominent features of Ntusi are two huge mounds, known by the local people as the 'male' and 'female' mounds. They are basically 300-year-old waste dumps containing piles of bones, pottery fragments and other refuse material. There are also several non-natural depressions around the village, the largest of which is thought to have once been a dam linked to an extensive irrigation system. The mounds and depressions are all located within a one-square-kilometre radius around the Ntusi District Headquarters and can be visited on foot from the village.

There are two other archaeological sites of interest in the area. Bigo Bya Mugenyi is the largest and most important of the several earthworks built by the Bacwezi and related kingdoms. It is thought that Bigo was a fort built to protect the southern extreme of the Bacwezi kingdom. There are two concentric sets of earthworks: an outer ditch and an inner royal enclosure built on a small hill. Local people believe the earthworks have supernatural powers and they are regarded with reverence. On the north bank of the Katonga River, upstream from Bigo, Masaka Hill is thought to have been the site of the last capital of the Bacwezi leader, Wamara. For centuries it has been used as a place of cult worship and pilgrimage. On top of the hill a circular grove of ancient fig trees is thought to have ritual significance.

Back on the main road to the southwest, Lake Mburo is one of Uganda's most low-profile but beautiful national parks. Gazetted in 1982, this 260-square-kilometre (100-square-mile) park encompasses not only Lake Mburo but also four other smaller lakes, and its accessibility from Kampala (a two-hour drive) makes it a favourite weekend getaway for the capital's residents. Mainly savannah with scattered acacia trees, the park features rolling hills, open grass valleys, thickets, woodlands, and rich wetlands. It is home to a wide variety of wildlife and birdlife; it also has a strong community extension component, trying to work closely with the local people to conserve the wildlife and other natural resources both inside and outside the park. The people in this area are traditional Bahima pastoralists, known for their famous long-horned Ankole cattle, and visitors may occasionally see the remarkable combination of cattle and wildlife grazing together.

The east side of the park features undulating, low hills broken by rocky outcrops, while in the west a series of rugged hills overlook flat-bottomed, open valleys. These grassy valleys offer the best game-viewing opportunities, with impala being the most unusual species there in Ugandan terms, as it occurs nowhere else in the country. Herds of buffalo, zebra, and the shy but magnificent eland can also be found, particularly by the waterholes during the drier seasons. Oribi and topi, seen in pairs and small groups, are abundant and easily approached. The acacia and olive woodland harbours shy bush duikers, as well as waterbuck, vervet monkeys, and baboons. The elusive klipspringer and rock hyrax can be found on the granite outcrops in the west of the park and in the rocky hills in the east.

The five lakes in the park – and several others that lie just outside the southern park boundary – are home to crocodiles and to hippos which can be seen grazing out of the water on cool mornings. The surrounding papyrus swamps hide the beautiful sitatunga, which has narrow, elongated hooves that allow it to move easily over marshy, unstable ground. Predators are seldom seen in the park. Lions were hunted out in the 1970s, but jackal, spotted hyena, and leopard still remain. Bird enthusiasts will delight in the wide variety of water and dry-land species, including the rare shoebill, southern ground hornbill and saddle-billed

Right: Terraced hillsides in Uganda's far south-west.

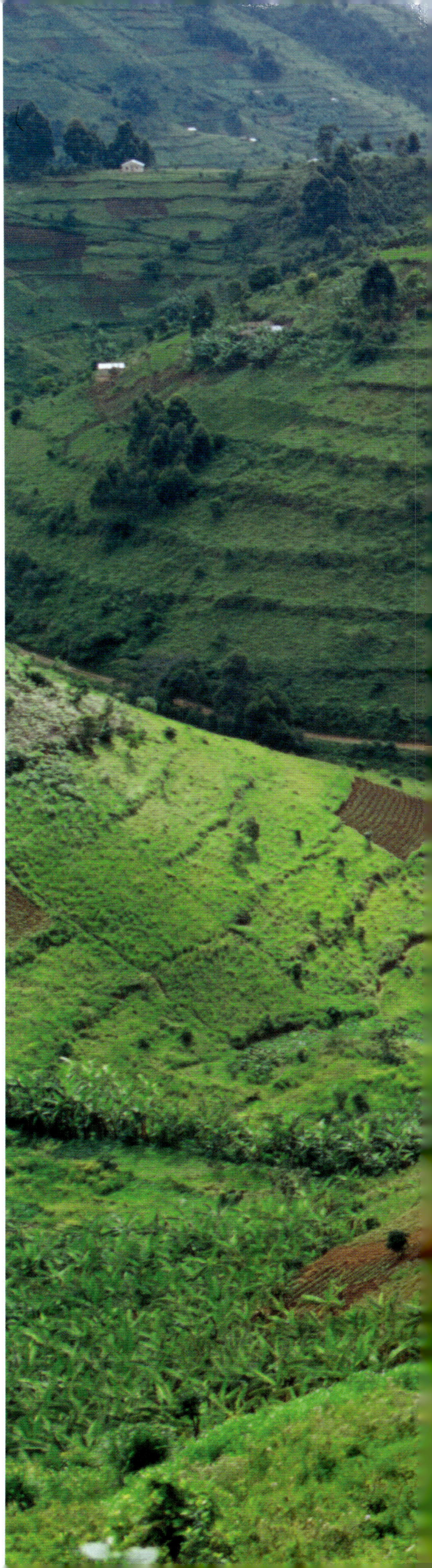

stork. The forested areas of the park are home to the beautiful Narina trogon and Ross's turaco, while the lake margin is an excellent site for the elusive African finfoot.

One of Uganda's largest, fastest growing and most overtly modern-looking towns, Mbarara is sometimes used as an overnight stop en route to the Rwenzoris or southwest, though the vastly improved state of the road make this a choice rather than the necessity it was in the past. The town has an interesting history as the capital of the Ankole kingdom, which came into being after Bacwezi folded circa AD 1500. The dynasty of the first Ankole king (omugabe), Ruhinda, maintained a strong link to Bacwezi rituals and traditions. But Ankole didn't become a driving political force until after early 18th century when the 11th omugabe, Ntare IV Kiitabanyoro (meaning 'killer of the Banyoro'), defeated the Banyoro. Over the next 100 years the Ankole kingdom grew to the point where it stretched for more than 100 kilometres (60 miles) east of Lake Albert to the Katonga River in the north and Kagera in the south. But in the late 1800s it started to crumble as a result of disease, drought, and the resurgence of Bunyoro under Kabalega. The derelict site of the old Ankole capital, Kamukazi, is just north of Mbarara, and the drum house is still standing – but the royal drum, a symbol of Ankole national unity, is long gone. Nearby and equally neglected is the Nkokonjeru Tomb, burial place of the last two Ankole kings: Kahaya II and Gasyonga II.

The gateway to the southwest and unofficial capital of the Kigezi region is the town of Kabale, which lies in a beautiful, mountainous area with steep-sided hills, neatly terraced cultivation, and many small lakes. At 2,000 metres (6,560 feet), Uganda's highest town is attractive and has a friendly mood. It is situated in an area criss-crossed by numerous tracks and paths – making it a haven for hikers. One of the most attractive places to visit is Lake Bunyonyi. Large and irregularly shaped, the lake features a number of islands and is surrounded by heavily cultivated hillsides. Other trips from Kabale include Bushara Island, the Kicumba Swamp and hot springs, and the Kisizi Falls – a 15-metre (50-foot) waterfall on the Kyabamba River near Kisizi village.

At the extreme southwest tip of Uganda, on the borders with the Democratic Republic of the Congo and Rwanda, lies Uganda's smallest national park. Covering 33.7 square kilometres (13 square miles), the Mgahinga Gorilla National Park was established in 1991 with the primary aim of providing sanctuary for the mountain gorilla, and gorilla tracking remains the most popular activity here, though it is dependent on the seasonal movements of the habituated troops. The park is an integral part of the Virunga Conservation Area and is contiguous with Parc National des Volcans in Rwanda and Parc National des Virungas in the DRC.

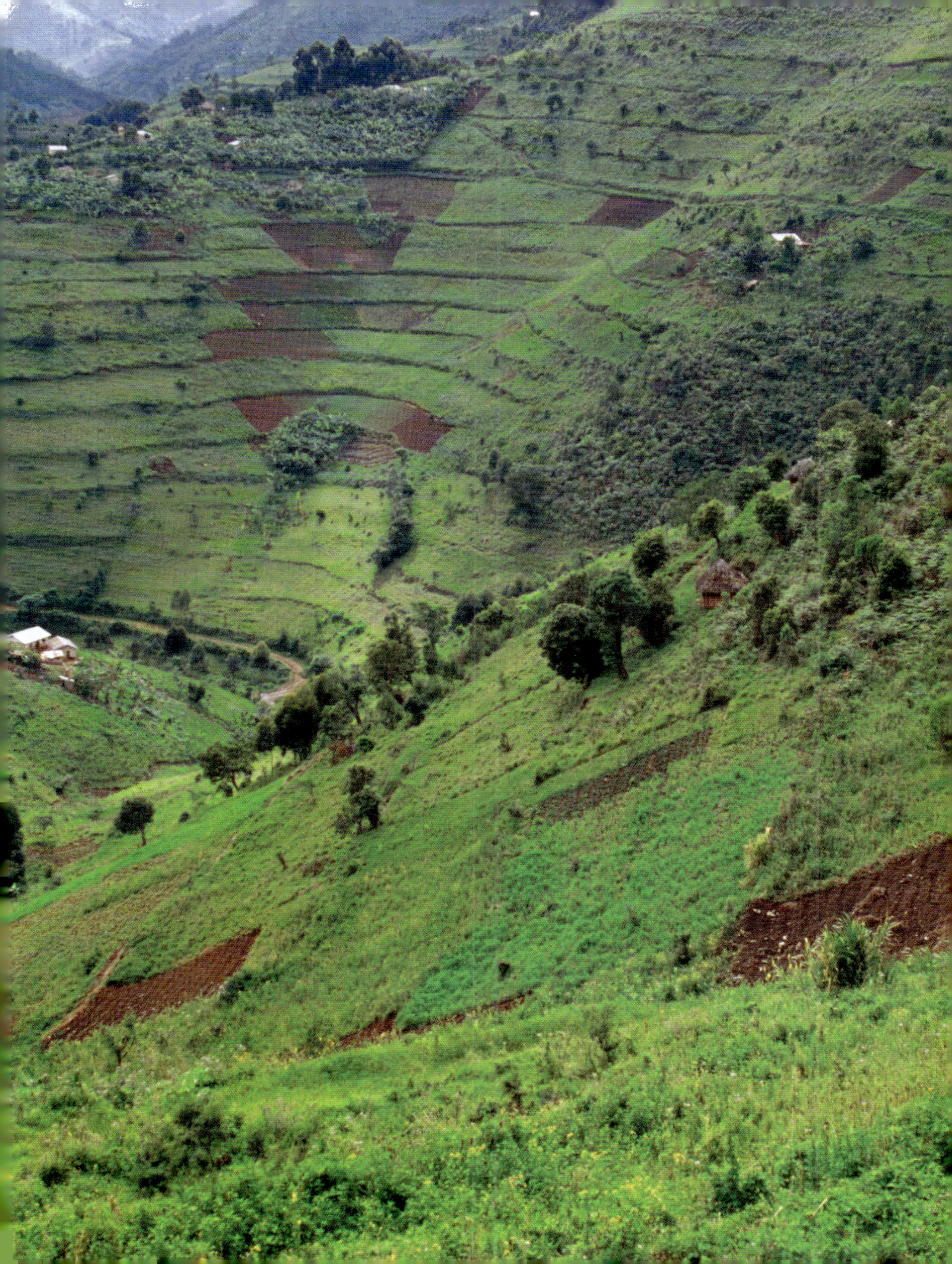

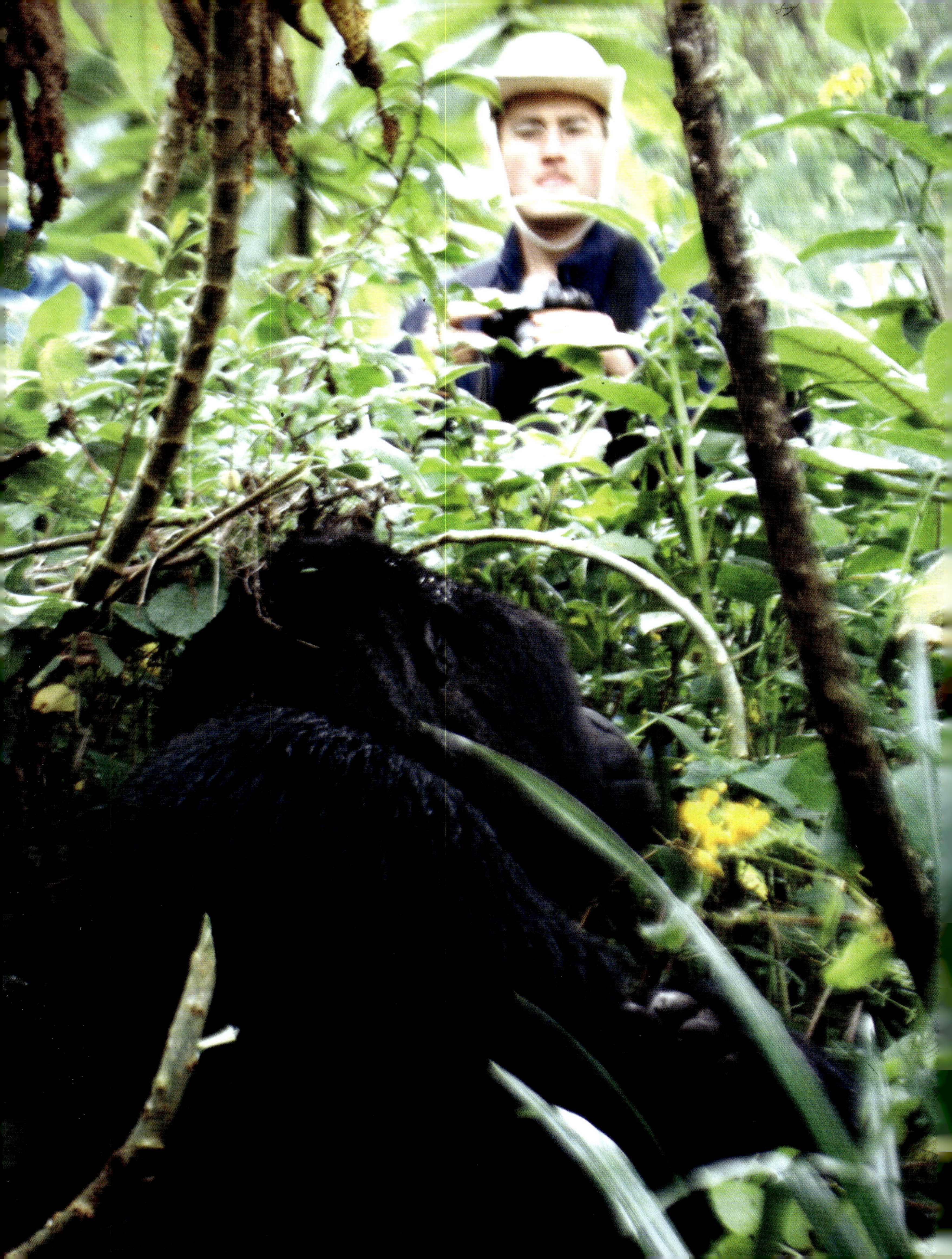

Opposite: Watching gorilla in Bwindi Impenetrable National Park

Below: Entrance to the Gorilla sanctuary.

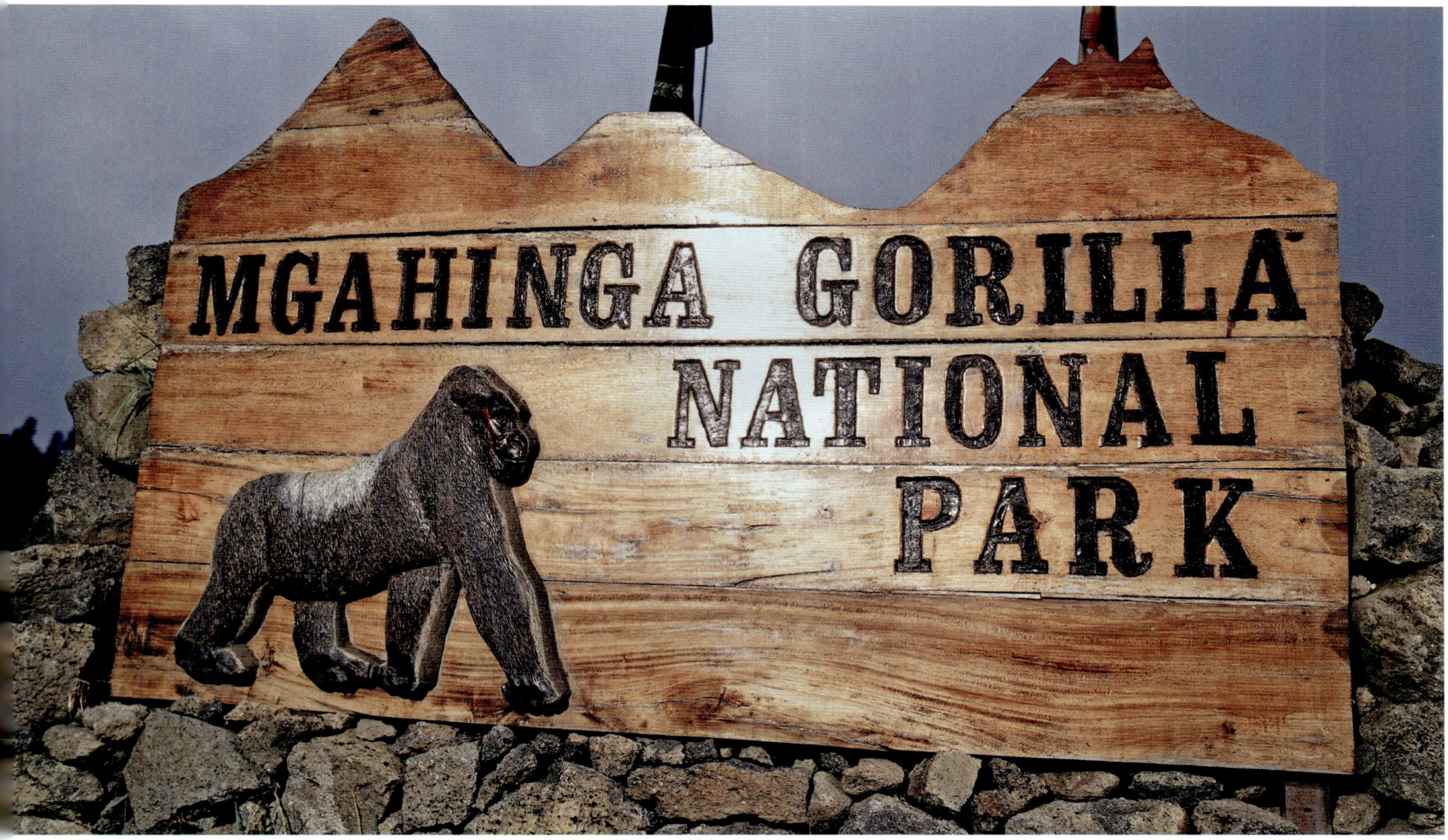

Here, in this tiny corner of the globe, one-half of the world's remaining mountain gorillas make their home.

Three extinct volcanic mountains lie within the park: Mount Muhabura, at 4,127 metres (13,540 feet), Mount Gahinga at 3,475 metres (11,400 feet), and the 3,645-metre (11,958-foot) Mount Sabinyo, whose peak lies at the intersection of the borders of Uganda, Rwanda and the DRC. Mgahinga is dominated by Afro-montane tropical rainforest, and the vegetation is typical of this terrain, with a montane forest belt, a bamboo zone, an ericaceous belt, and an alpine zone. The forest is always wet, even more so during the rains (April-May and October-November) and it contains three large swamps too. A number of exciting hikes showcase the park's dramatic views, lush vegetation, and interesting wildlife. These include challenging climbs of Muhabura and Gahinga, whose summits afford great views of Uganda, Rwanda, and the DRC. During the late Iron Age, humans sheltered at Garama Cave, which is rumoured to cut through to Rwanda.

Mgahinga supports several uniquely adapted plant and animal species. Mammals recorded – besides the endangered mountain gorilla

– include the rare golden monkey (whose extant range is also limited to the Virungas), buffalo, elephant, black-fronted duiker, bushbuck, leopard, giant forest hog, side-striped jackal, Egyptian mongoose, serval cat, golden cat, and spotted hyena. More than 185 species of birds have been recorded in the area as well, including 12 regional endemics. These include the handsome francolin, the Rwenzoris turaco and the stripe-breasted tit.

Situated within one of the most densely populated areas in rural Africa, Mgahinga is surrounded by the terraced fields of the Batwa and Bafumbira people. Now agriculturists, the Batwa lived in the forest as hunters and gatherers more than 20,000 years ago. Both ethnic groups grow crops such as potatoes, beans, and millet, and rear livestock that includes cattle, goats, sheep, and chickens. The region's main town is Kisoro, which lies on the Congolese border and forms a good base for tracking gorillas when they are in Mgahinga National Park (they often cross into Rwanda).

North of Mgahinga, on the Congolese border adjacent to the Parc National des Virungas, lies Bwindi Impenetrable National Park, where visitors who obtain tracking permits are almost certain to see one of its three habituated mountain gorilla groups. Like Mgahinga, Bwindi is one of the country's newer national parks, gazetted in 1991, and it covers 331 square kilometres (128 square miles), making it the third largest forested park in Uganda. Situated on the edge of the western Rift Valley on the highest block of the Rukiga Highlands, it is one of the largest natural forests in East Africa, and an altitudinal range of 1,160-2,607 metres (3,805 -8,553 feet) means it contains both montane and lowland forest vegetation. This ancient rainforest is one of the few in Africa to have flourished throughout the last Ice Age, and species diversity is exceptionally high, including a large number of plants and animals endemic to the region. It has a very dense, thick undergrowth – hence the name 'impenetrable' – that ensures tracking gorillas is strenuous work.

An interesting feature of Bwindi is Mubwindi Swamp, which covers an area of about two square kilometres (nearly one square mile). The park also has an extensive stand of bamboo: a rare and beautiful habitat. Bwindi's 120-plus species of mammals make it one of the richest ecosystems in Africa. There are more than 163 species of tree in Bwindi – ten of which occur nowhere else in Uganda and 16 of which show a very limited distribution elsewhere in the country. Some 346 bird species are found there, of which 184 are typical forest species, and seven are on the endangered list. In addition, Bwindi is home to more than 14 species of snakes, 27 species of frogs and toad, six chameleons, and 14 lizards, skinks and geckos. There's also an incredible variety of butterflies in the park: more than 202 species have been identified so far.

Primates are particularly abundant and include the mountain gorilla,

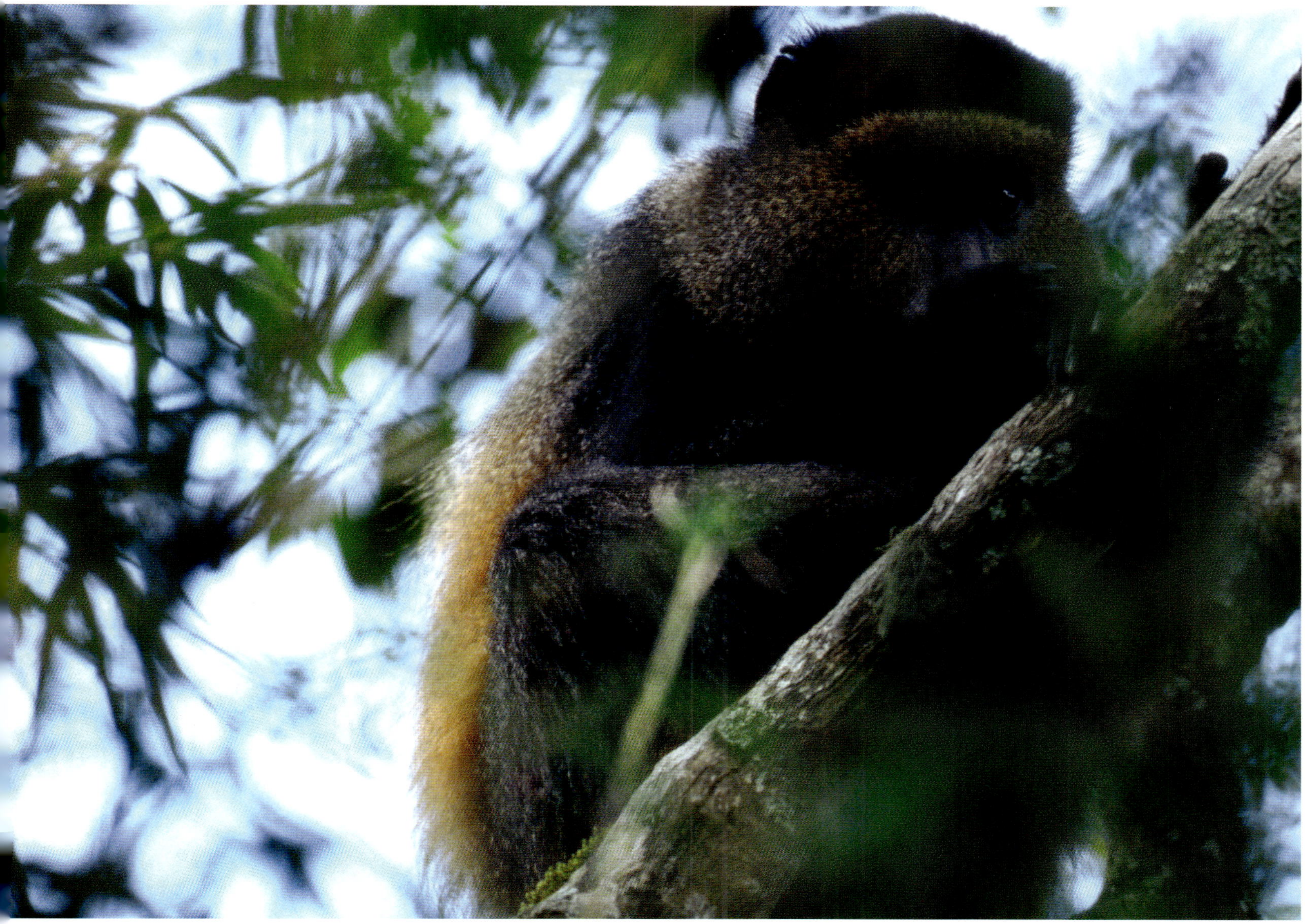

Above: Mgahinga Golden Monkey.

Following pages: The dramatic 'Mountains of the moon'.

chimpanzee, blue monkey, red-tailed monkey, L'Hoest's monkey, black-and-white colobus, baboon, potto, Demidoff's galago and needle-clawed galago. Elephants are also found in the south-east of the park around the bamboo zone and the Mubwindi Swamp. Other mammals present include the bushpig, giant forest hog, black-fronted duiker, clawless otter, golden cat, side-striped jackal, civet, genet, and many species of bats and rodents.

Buhoma, the main gorillas tracking site, is an ideal place from which to watch other primates and birds. Many monkeys can be seen along the roads, around the periphery of the park, and at the forest edge. Chimpanzees, although difficult to see, inhabit the forest adjacent to the camp and are frequently heard. This is also the richest site for birds in the park, with some 190 species on record. Of particular interest here are the Kivu ground thrush, white-bellied robin chat, red-throated alethe, collared apalis, short-tailed warbler, yellow-eyed black flycatcher, Rwenzoris batis, blue-headed sunbird, strange weaver, and Shelley's crimson-wing. It is also possible to stroll on the country roads outside the park to meet the Bakiga and the Bafumbira agriculturists who work the surrounding land.

Having enjoyed the magnificent south-west and the gentle giants that inhabit it, visitors have the choice of returning directly to Kampala or, if they have time, continuing their journey north to the famous Queen Elizabeth National Park, the dramatic Mountains of the Moon, and the spectacular Murchison Falls.

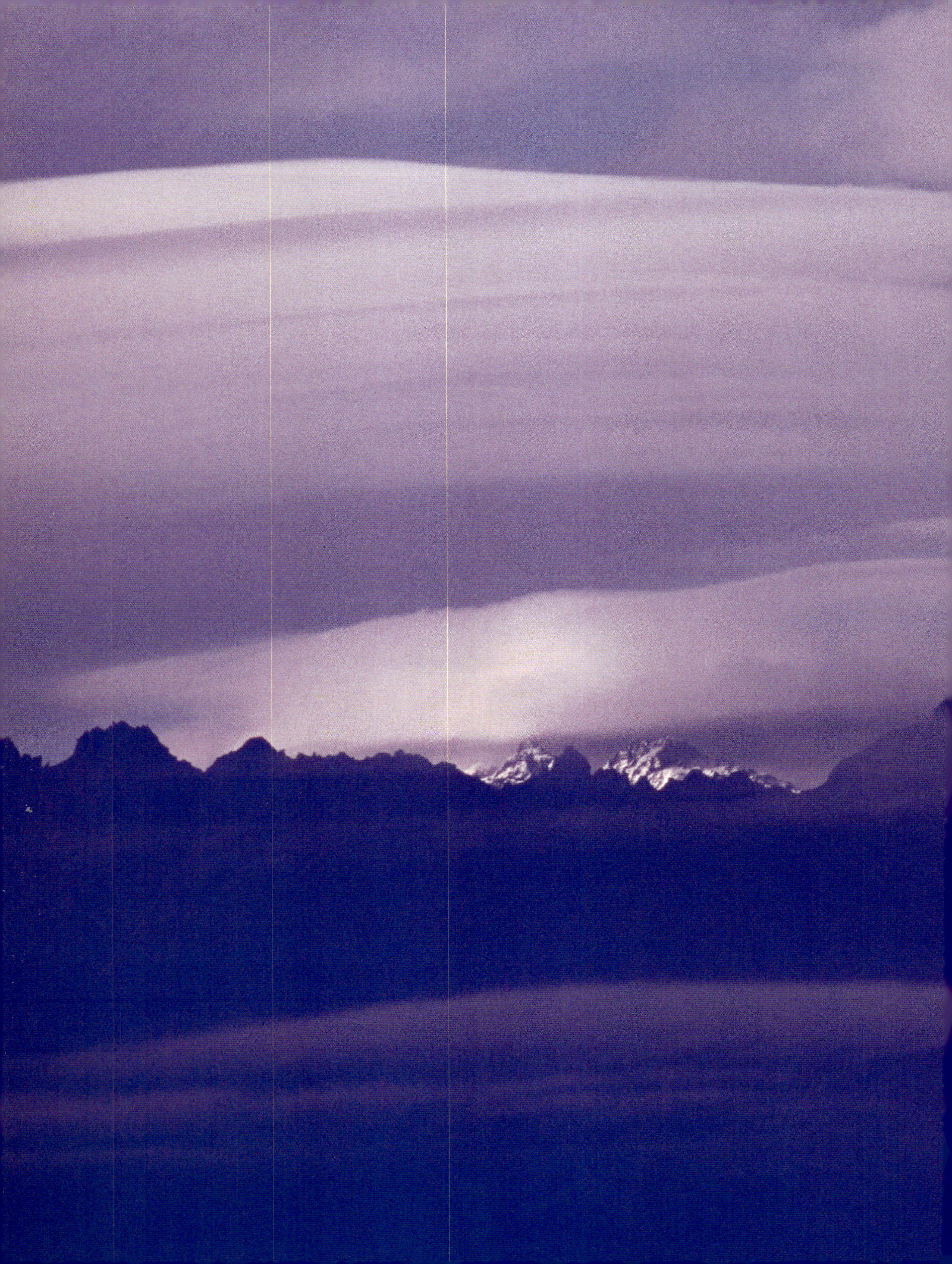

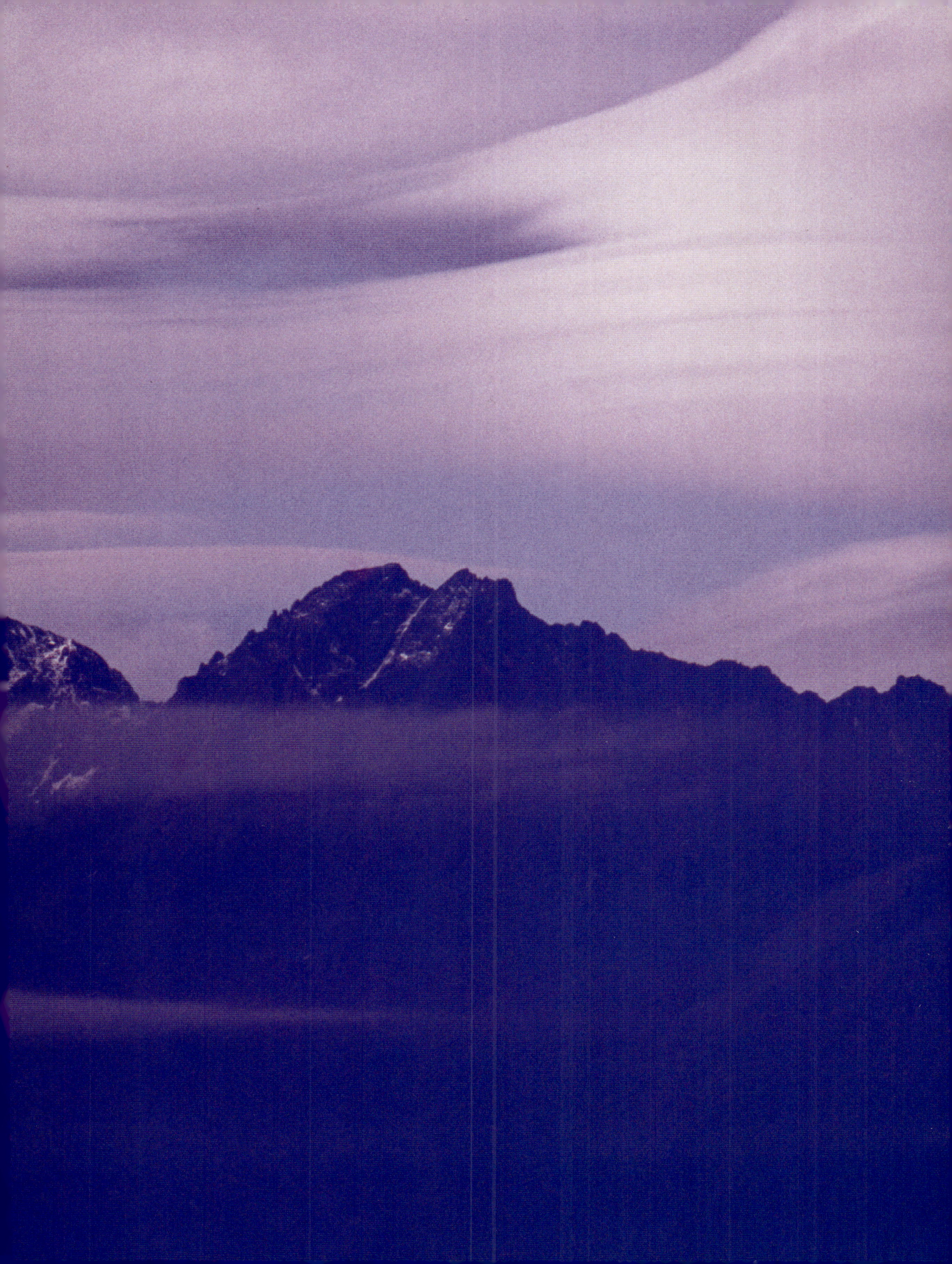

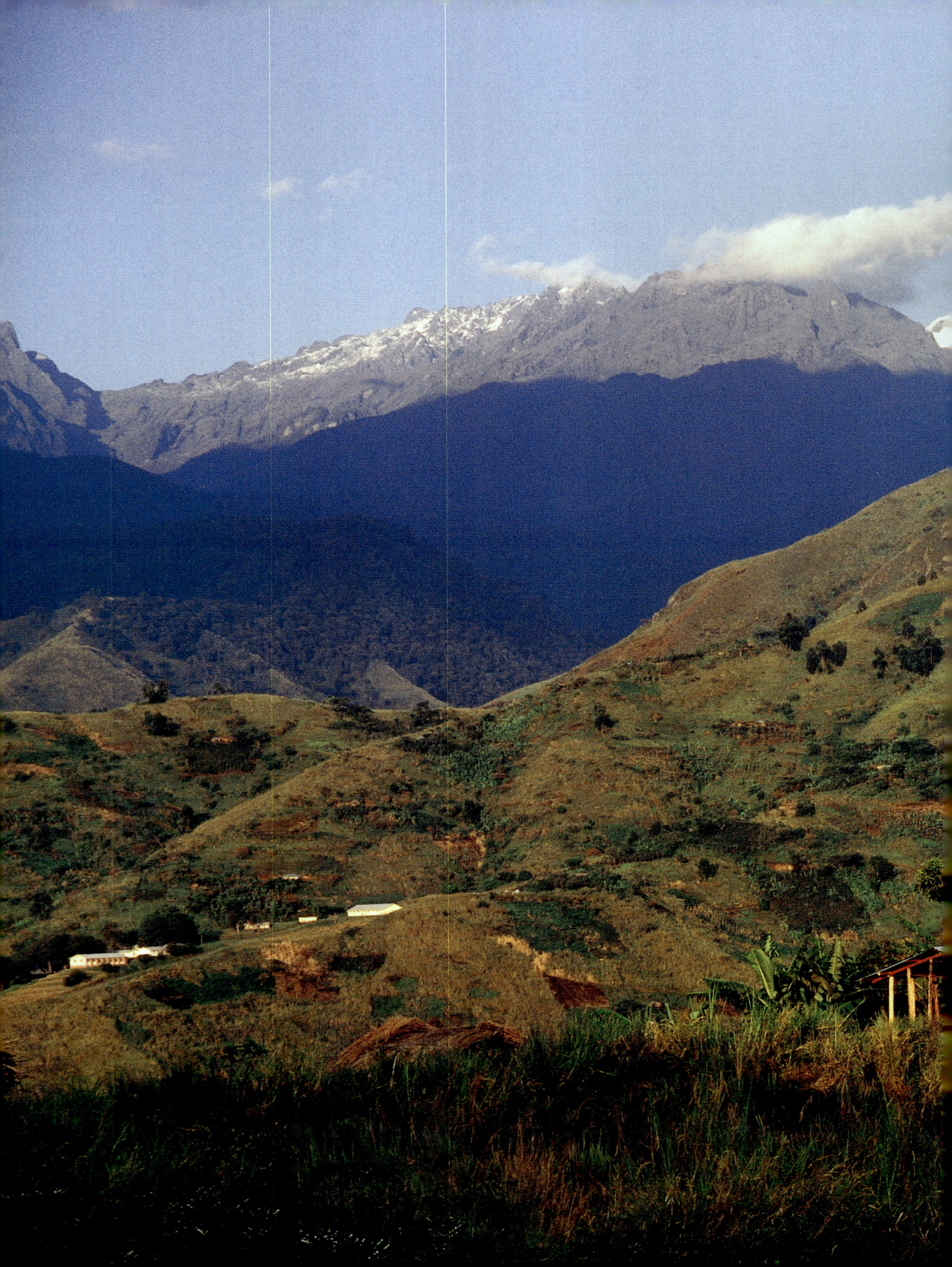

4. Queen Elizabeth National Park and the Rwenzoris

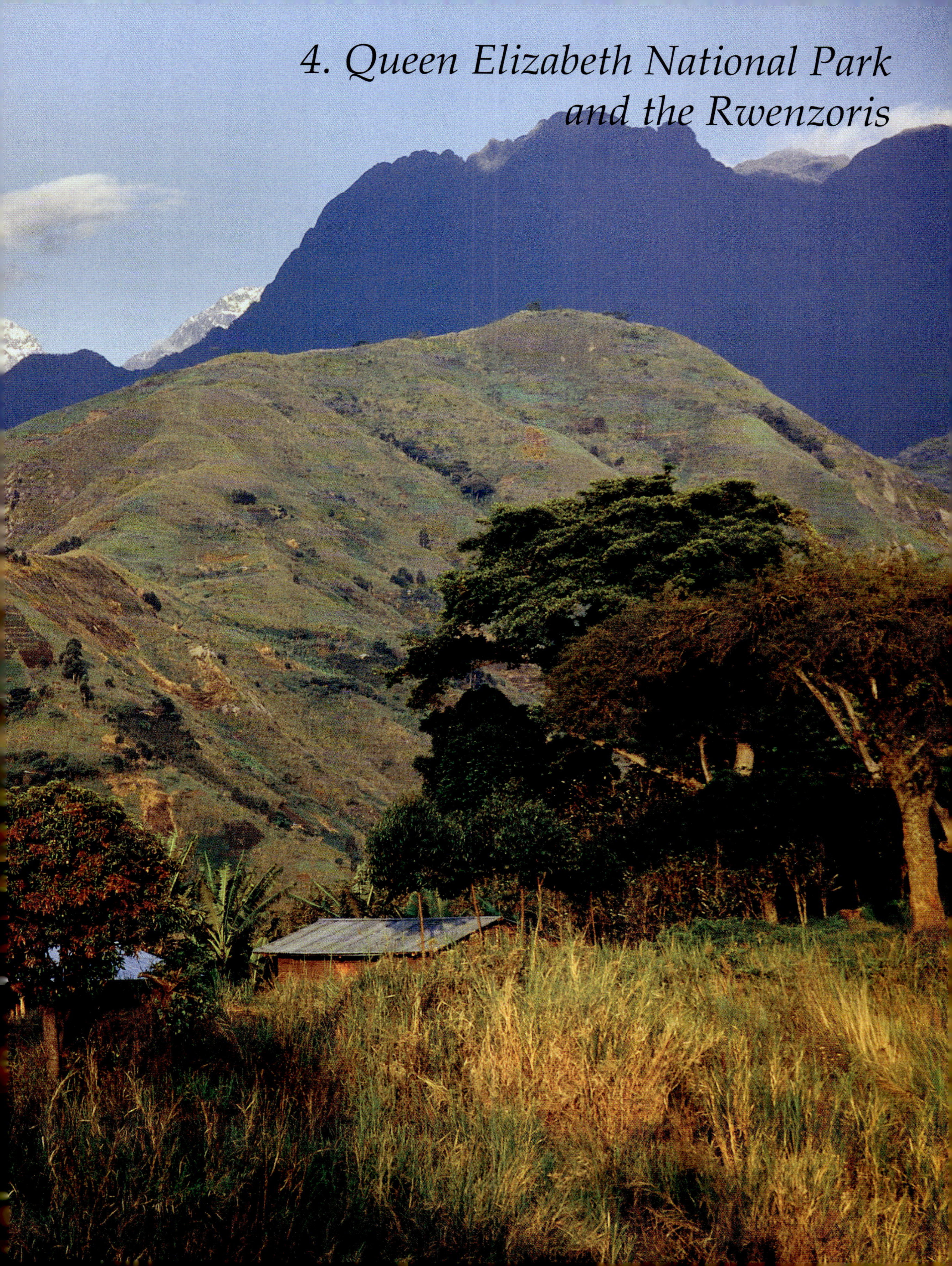

Previous pages: The Rwenzori Mountains from the foothills above Kasese.

Right: Snow-capped Rwenzoris peaks provide a tough test for climbers.

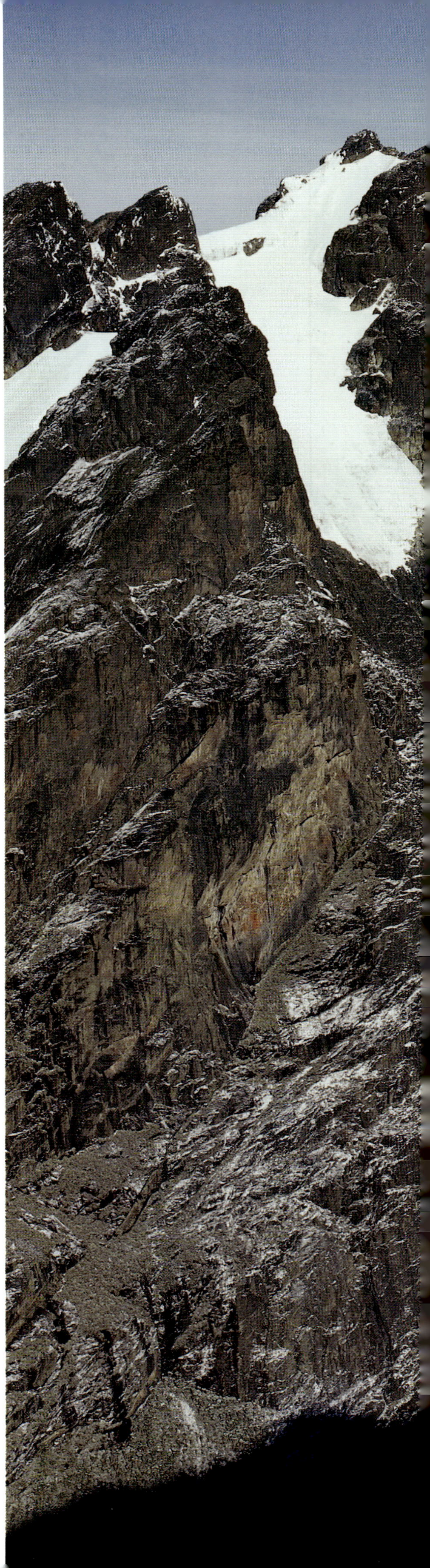

Running along the Congolese border north of Bwindi, the spectacular Rwenzoris rise from a 120-kilometre (75 miles) long and 48-kilometre (30 miles) wide base to an elevation of 5,109 metres, exceeded elsewhere in Africa only by the free-standing Mount Kenya and Kilimanjaro. It is the largest mountain range on the continent and yet its existence went unnoticed by European geographers until as recently as 1889, partly because so few outsiders reached this remote corner of Africa during the 19th century, but also because its elusive glacial peaks are habitually shrouded behind a thick veil of mist and cloud

History books accredit the discovery of the Rwenzoris to the American explorer Henry Morton Stanley. More accurately, however, it was Arthur Jephson and Thomas Parke, members of Stanley's cross-continental expedition to rescue the Emin Pasha, who first set eyes upon the magnificent snow-covered equatorial peaks. Their account was greeted with scepticism back home, but Stanley lost no time in claiming the immense massif as his own, or in identifying it as the legendary *Lunae Montes* – Mountains of the Moon – referred to as the Source of the Nile in Ptolemy's 2nd century *Geography*.

Ptolemy based his Geography on information gleaned at the Indian Ocean coast, so his snow-capped *Lunae Montes* might well have had their origin in third-hand reports of Mount Kilimanjaro or Kenya, with the relationship to the Nile being pure supposition. Nevertheless, the lunar association with the Rwenzoris has proved to be enduring, and it is apposite in more ways than one. Certainly, the Rwenzoris are the largest mountain to form part of the Nile drainage system. What's more, its upper moorland, described by Eric Shipton as "a world of fantasy where nothing is real but only a wild and lovely flight of imagination", does possess a disarmingly otherworldly quality – indeed, its barren cover of multihued heath, studded with outrageous stands of giant lobelia and groundsel, might easily pass as the set of a science fiction film.

When the cloud lifts, revealing the lunar glacial peaks and deep tarns at their base, the Rwenzoris is also perhaps the most scenically imposing and ethereal of all East African montane landscapes. It is certainly the region's most challenging target for dedicated hikers, especially during the rainy season, when the boggy trails are best avoided. As for the peaks, they went unexplored by Europeans until Luigi di Savoia's legendary expedition in 1906, and remain accessible only to experienced and equipped technical climbers. Still, for those who are up to the challenge, it is a singularly magnificent environment of glistening snow caps, massive ice-rime sculptures, awe-inspiring vegetation and unique fauna, all overhung by a eerily shrouded quality evoking Rider Haggard's 'Land of Mist'.

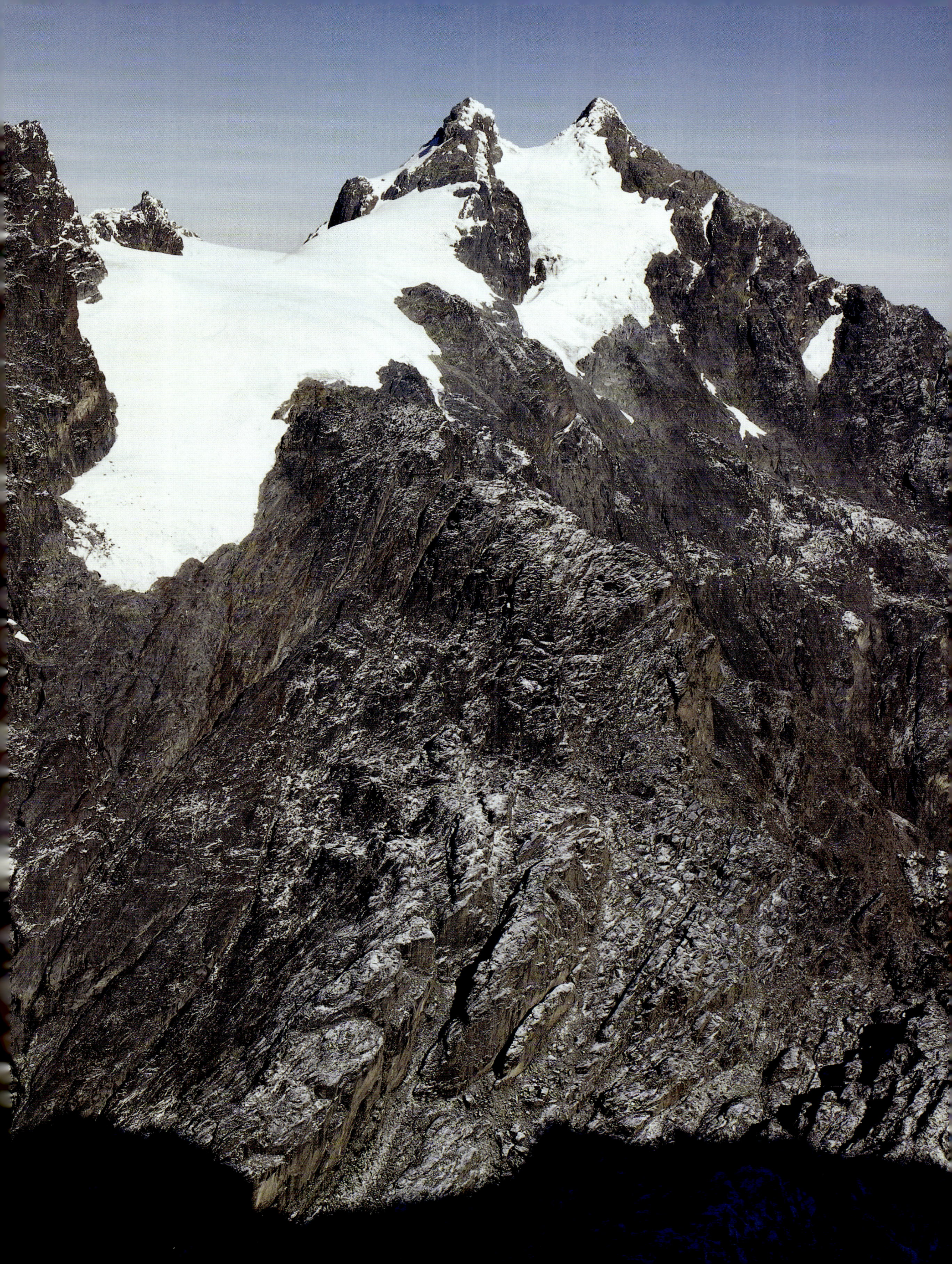

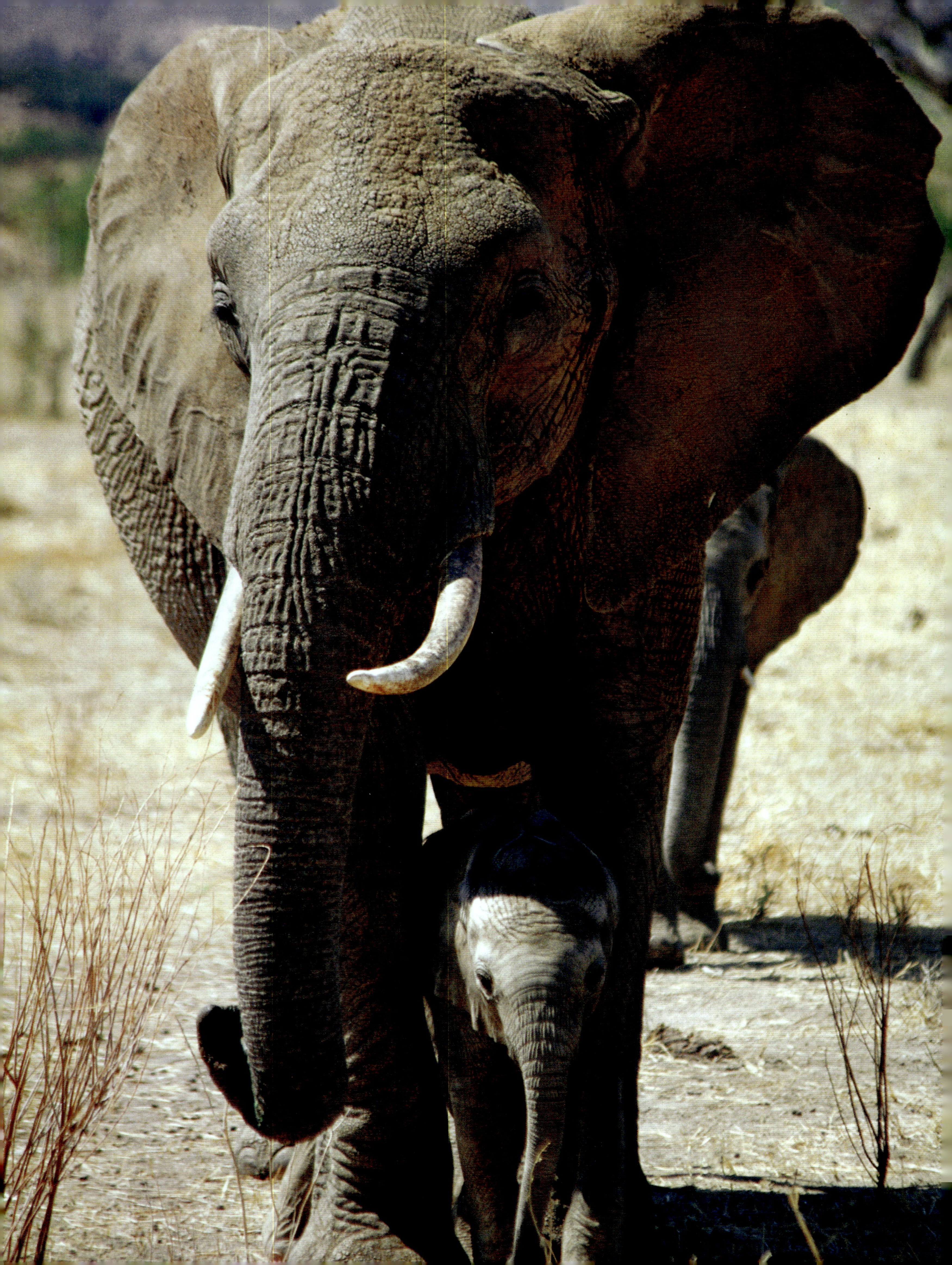

Opposite: Mother and baby. Elephants maintain a strong family structure.

Below: Dusty safari trail in Queen Elizabeth National Park.

Following pages: Elephants, their numbers depleted by heavy poaching, are now making a comeback in Uganda.

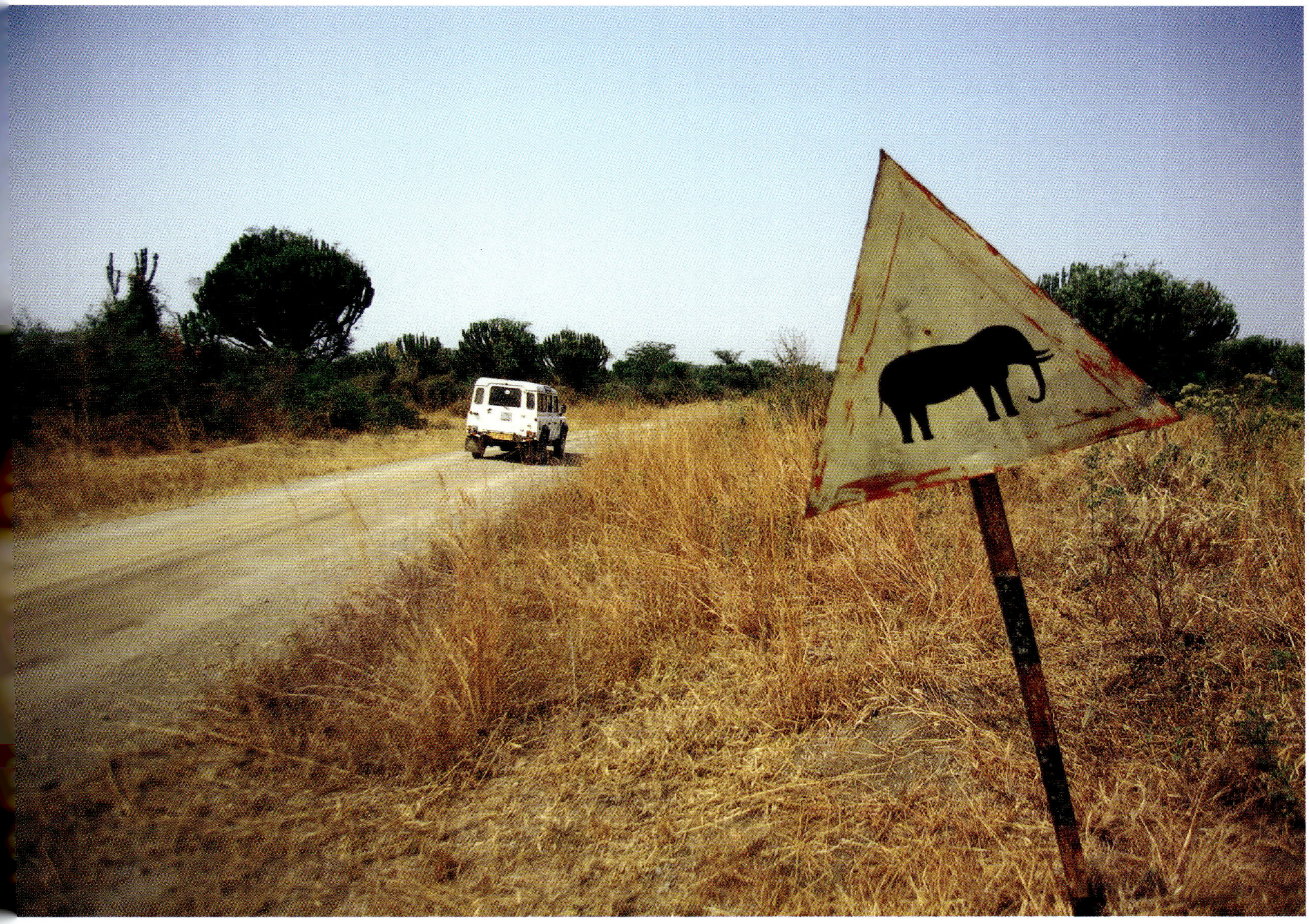

Uniquely among East Africa's largest mountains, the Rwenzoris are not volcanic in origin, but were forced up from the Albertine Rift floor at around the same time that this immense valley was created. Over time, the eroding forces of rivers and glaciers have carved out – and are still carving out – the wonderful, sculptured land mass seen today. At the centre of the range are six snow-covered peaks. The highest peak Margherita to rises 5,109 metres (16,762 feet) above sea level. Other high peaks include Alexandria (5,083 metres/16,676 feet), Speke (4,890 metres/16,043 feet), Emin (4,791 metres/15,718 feet), Gessi (4,715 metres/15,469 feet) and Luigi di Savoia (4,627 metres/15,180 feet). All terrain above the 2,200m contour was gazetted as a 996 square-kilometre forest reserve in 1941, upgraded to national park status in 1989, and inscribed as a UNESCO World Heritage Site in 1994.

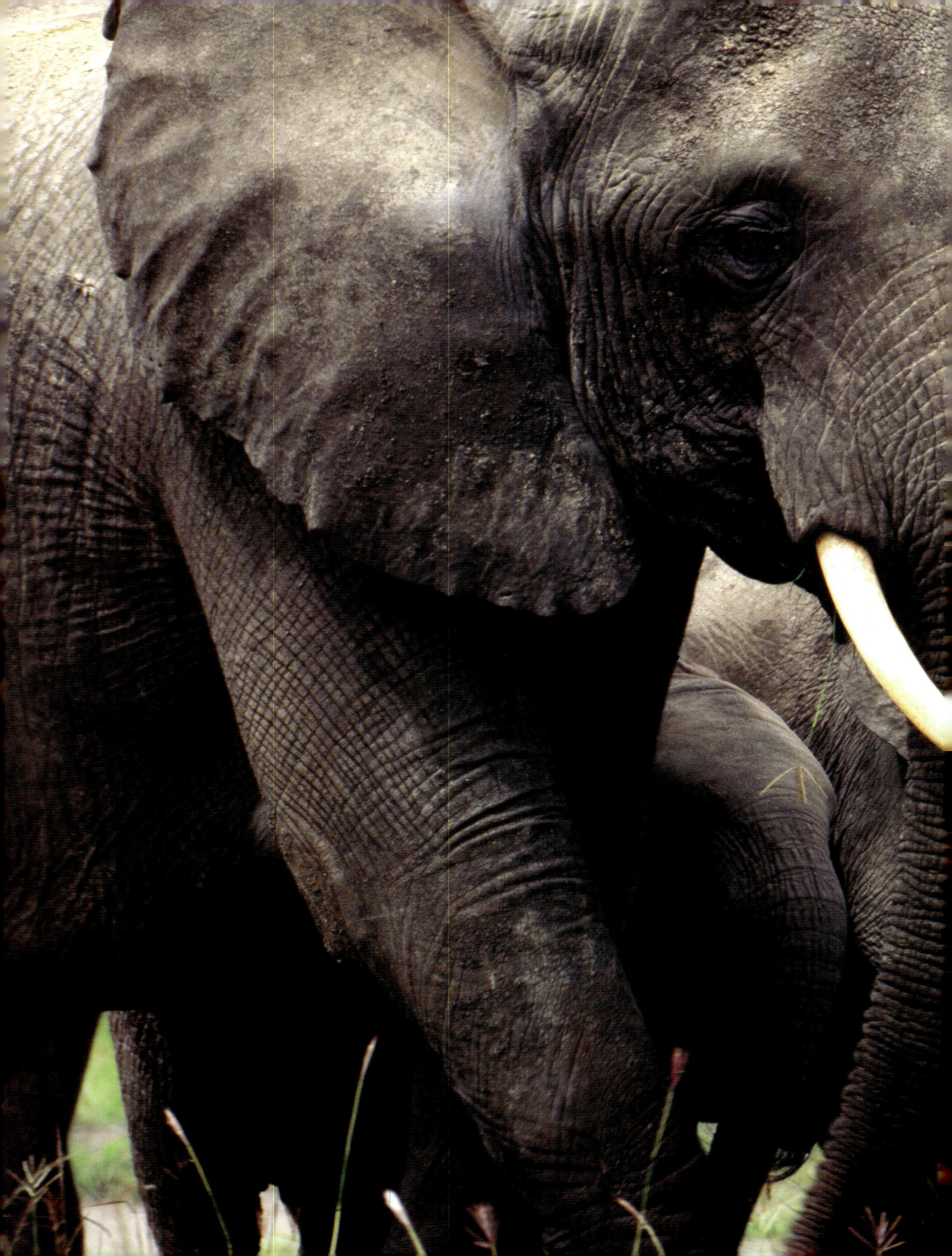

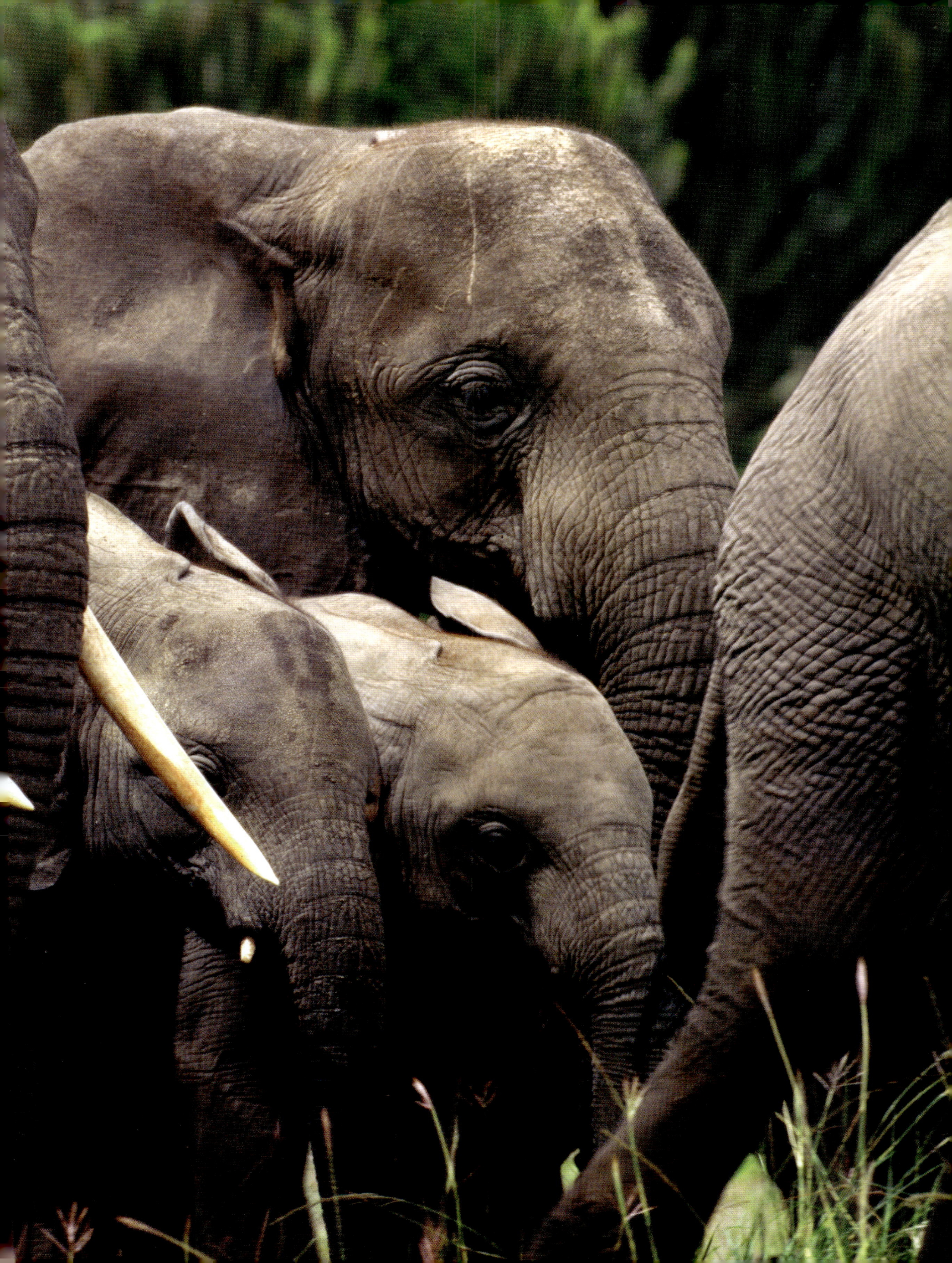

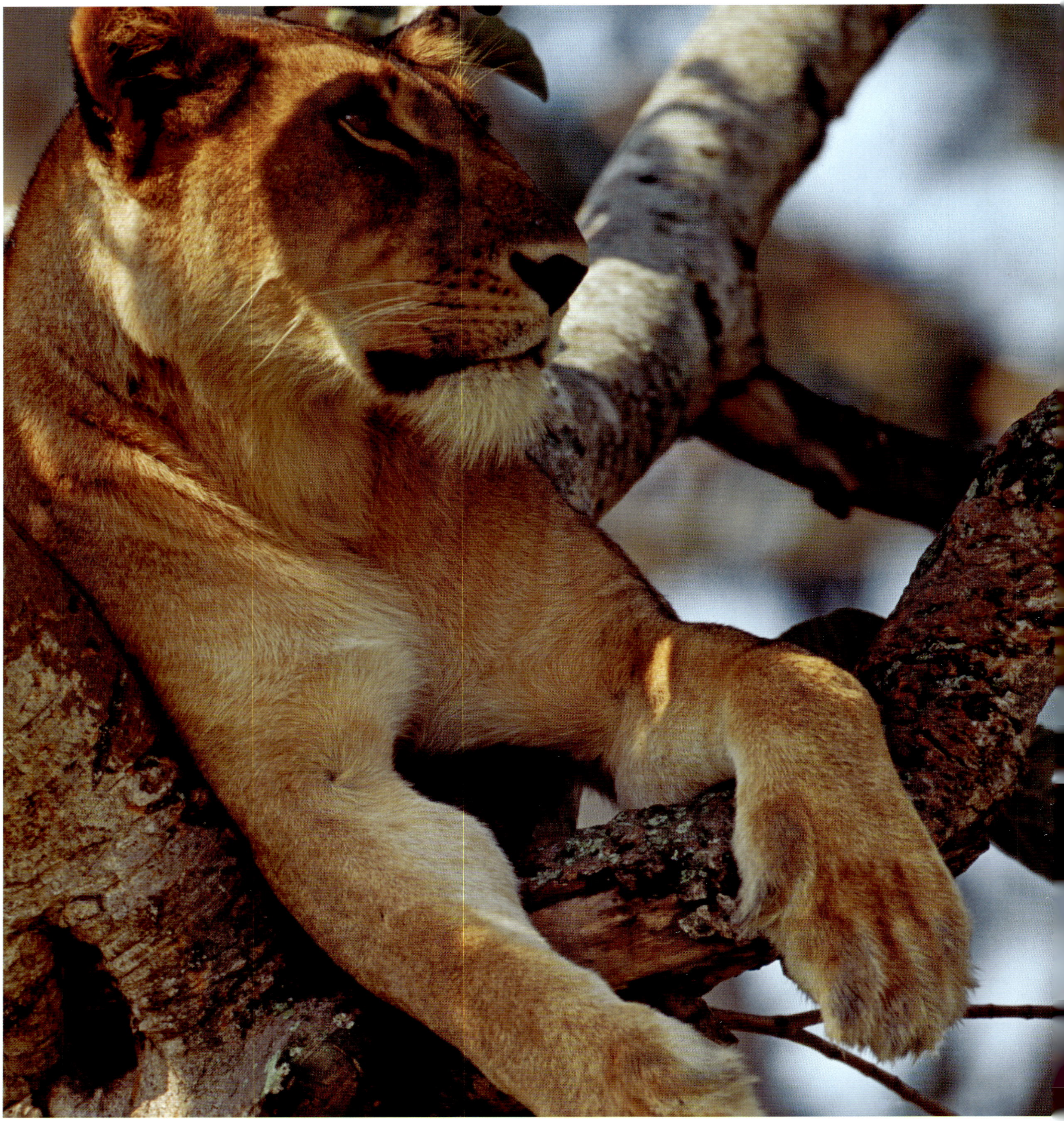

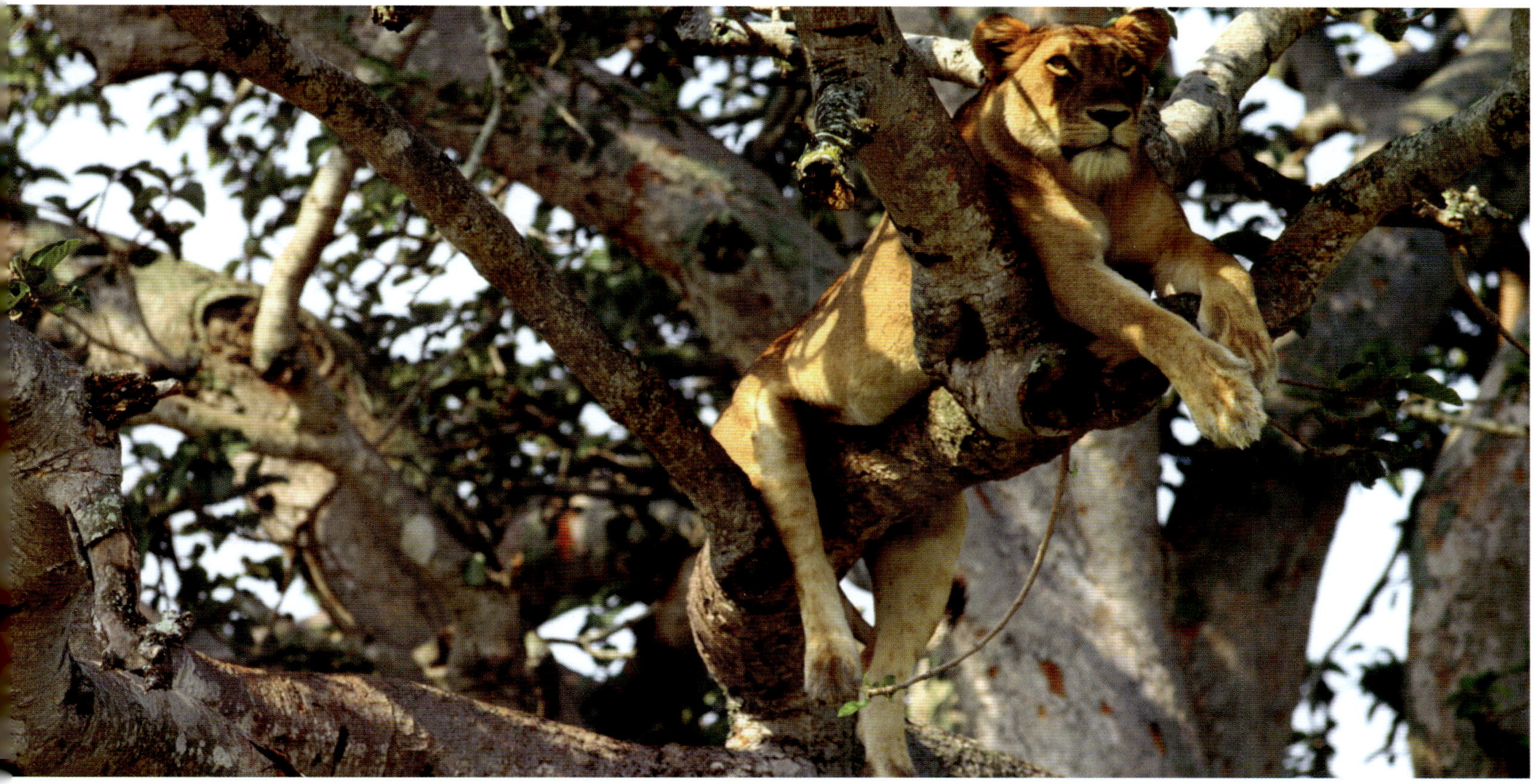

)pposite, above and right: Queen Elizabeth National Park
; a good place to see lions. Remarkably, some even climb
rees here!

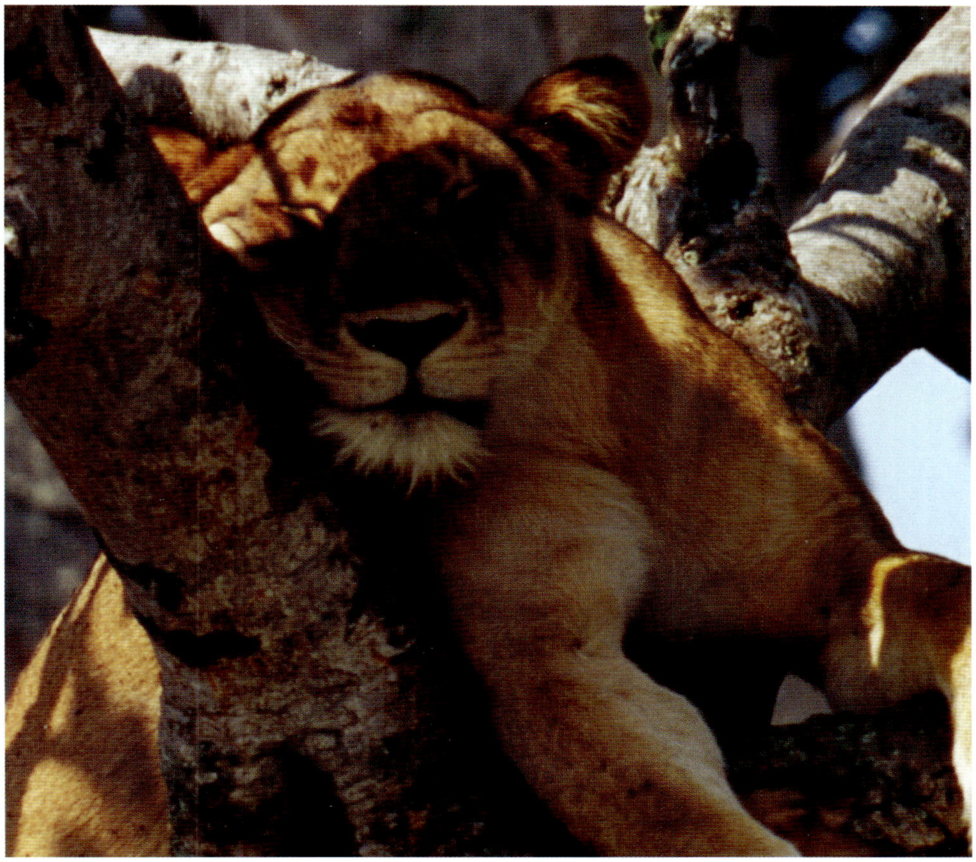

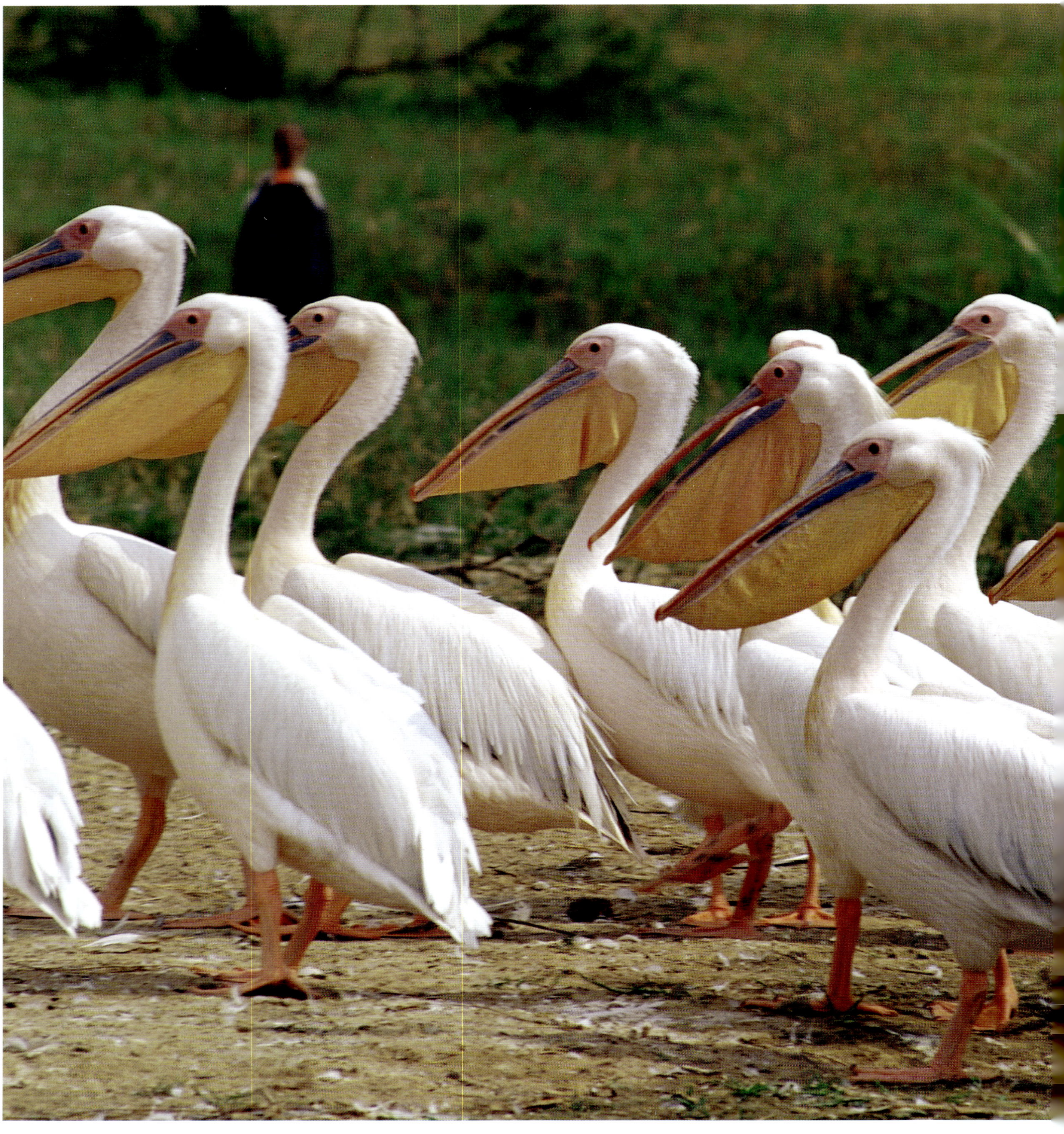

Below: Pelicans by the Kazinga Channel in Queen Elizabeth National Park.

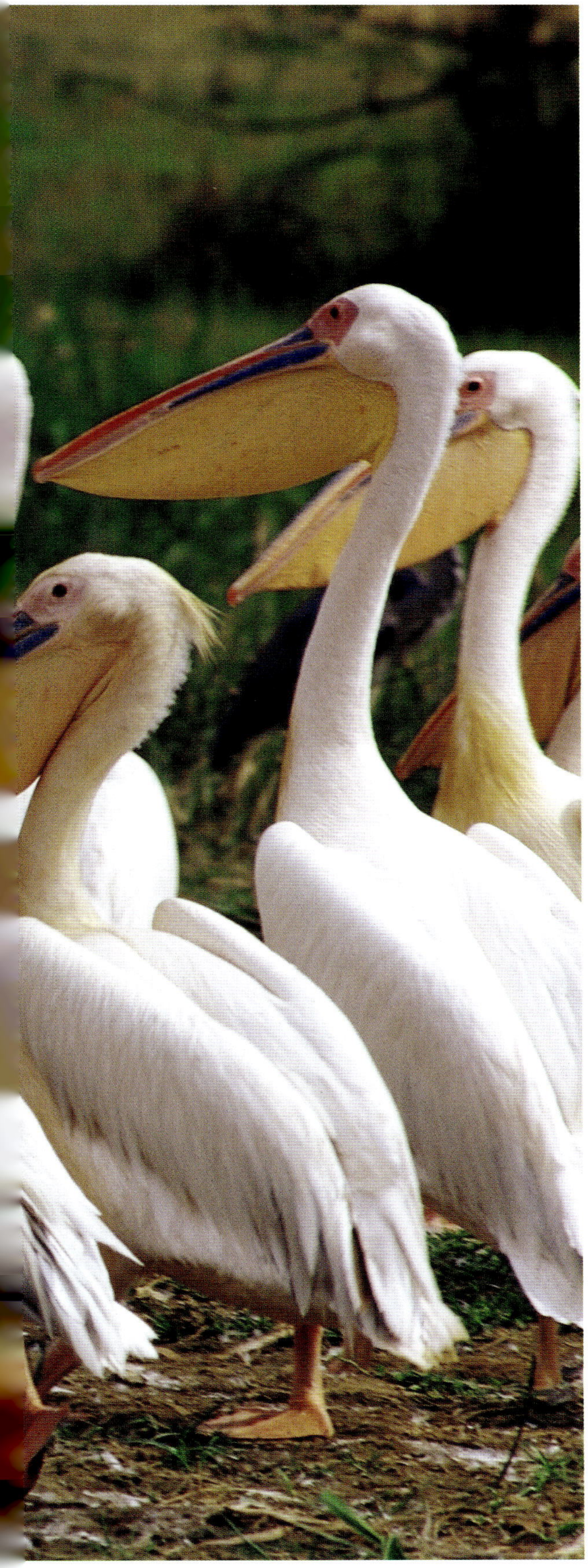

More people visit the Rwenzoris to explore and view the fascinating vegetation than to climb the peaks and glaciers. Because of the strange evolutionary pattern, common plants grow to absurd proportions. Lobelias weigh in at 60 kilos (130 lbs), while groundsel plants tower above you and heather shoots up to some 10 metres (33 feet) tall. Equally splendid are the smaller flowers, such as blackberry, cuckoo flower, and the everlastings. Primates and other mammals in the park include chimpanzee, Rwenzoris black-and-white colobus, blue monkey, elephant, bushbuck, red duiker, yellow-backed duiker, giant forest hog, tree hyrax (with its nocturnal shrieking call), serval and leopard. Forest birds include the Rwenzoris turaco, handsome francolin, olive pigeon, and white-necked raven. Above the forest zone one can see the alpine swift and the scarlet-tufted malachite sunbird, both of which are restricted to high-altitude habitats in East Africa. The weird-looking three-horned chameleon plays a powerful role in local superstitions.

The people on the lower slopes of the Rwenzori Mountains are the Bakonjo. Strong and energetic, they are well suited to life in the mountains which are an integral part of their traditional beliefs. Many local men work for the as guides and porters for tourists in the southern and western areas of the park. Some 500,000 Ugandans living below the park boundary are dependent on the Rwenzoris watershed for year-round agricultural production. Major crops include coffee, beans, maize, yams, Irish potatoes, bananas, passion fruit, and wheat.

If size counted for everything, Queen Elizabeth National Park (QENP) would scarcely feature among Africa's greatest wildlife sanctuaries. Indeed, extending across some 2,000 square kilometres (770 square miles) of the Albertine Rift floor, this relatively modestly proportioned park would fit almost 25 times into Tanzania's Selous Game Reserve. And yet measured by practically any biodiversity index, QENP is every bit as monarchic as the name it acquired after a 1954 visit by the British royal family. Its bird checklist of 612 species, for instance, comfortably exceeds that of any other protected area in Africa, if not anywhere in the world. And a tally of 95 mammal species, including 10 primates and 20 predators, would be exceptional for a reserve ten times its size.

These impressive statistics reflect an equally remarkable ecological diversity. If any one conservation area could be said to represent East Africa in microcosm, it is surely QENP. Squeezed into a relatively compact 1,978 sq km, this paragon of biodiversity protects a quite extraordinary variety of habitats, ranging from the lush rainforest of Maramagambo and euphorbia-studded grassland of Kasenyi to the vast freshwater expanses of Lake Edward and George, the steep-sided scrub-lined Kazinga Channel, the dense papyrus swamps of the country's only Ramsar wetland site,

Below: Monitor lizard grows up to two metres long.

Following pages: Mountains of the Moon are usually shrounded in rain and mist.

pretty tree-lined rivers, as well as a scattering of 70 volcanically formed craters, many of which are inundated by saline or freshwater lakes. As if that weren't enough, look skyward from the 913m lake hinterland, at least on a clear day, and you'll see the snow-capped Rwenzoris peaks looming tall on the northwestern skyline.

The park has its origins early in the 20th century, after many people fled the area when a wave of sleeping sickness plagued the country. Between 1925 and 1947, these abandoned areas became two wildlife reserves: Lake George and Lake Edward. In 1952, the reserves were merged into Kazinga National Park. Two years later, when Queen Elizabeth of Britain visited the park, it was renamed in her honour. During the Idi Amin regime, the park was renamed Rwenzoris National Park, but it regained its original name in 1991, when the Rwenzori Mountains National Park was gazetted. The park has been designated as a Biosphere Reserve for Humanity under the auspices of UNESCO.

The obvious starting point for exploring QENP is the bulbous Mweya Peninsula, which is flanked by Lake Edward to the northwest and the Kazinga Channel to the southeast, and connects to the mainland by a narrow rock isthmus perhaps twice as wide as the road that traverses it. Here, the shady clifftop patio of the park's oldest and largest safari lodge offers a grandstand seat over one of the most tremendous views in Africa, with large herds of buffalo and elephant regularly to be seen drinking on the channel's opposite shore, dwarfed by the magnificent Rwenzoris peaks. The peninsula is also home to plentiful hippo, warthog and waterbuck, while a habituated troop of banded mongooses is often seen scampering around the lodge gardens, and the rich birdlife includes the dazzling black-headed gonolek, red-throated sunbird and slender-billed weaver.

There's plenty more wildlife to be seen on the two-hour launch trip along the Kazinga Channel that leaves from a jetty below the lodge. Buffalo, hippo, waterbuck and kob can be taken for granted, while elephant are a near certainty from late morning to mid-afternoon, and lion and leopard emerge at dusk. Monitor lizards are unusually prolific here too, and waterbirds are everywhere, ranging from perky wagtails to the spectacular pelicans that roost near the channel mouth. The game-viewing tracks that run through the dense woodland overlooking the channel's north bank harbours similar wildlife, and is probably the only location anywhere in Africa where the hirsute giant forest hog is regularly encountered in daylight.

The other important game-viewing circuit north of the channel is the Kasenyi Plains, a short-grass savannah studded with tall euphorbia clusters and acacia thickets. The near-endemic Uganda kob congregates

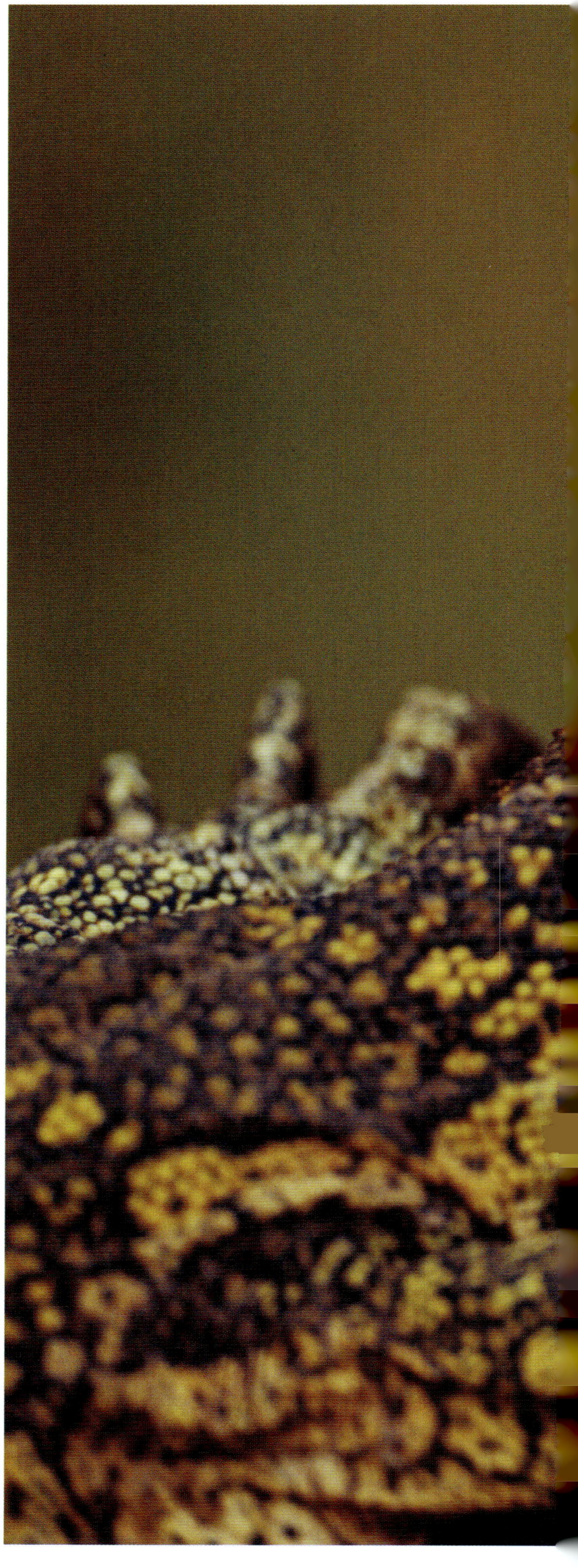

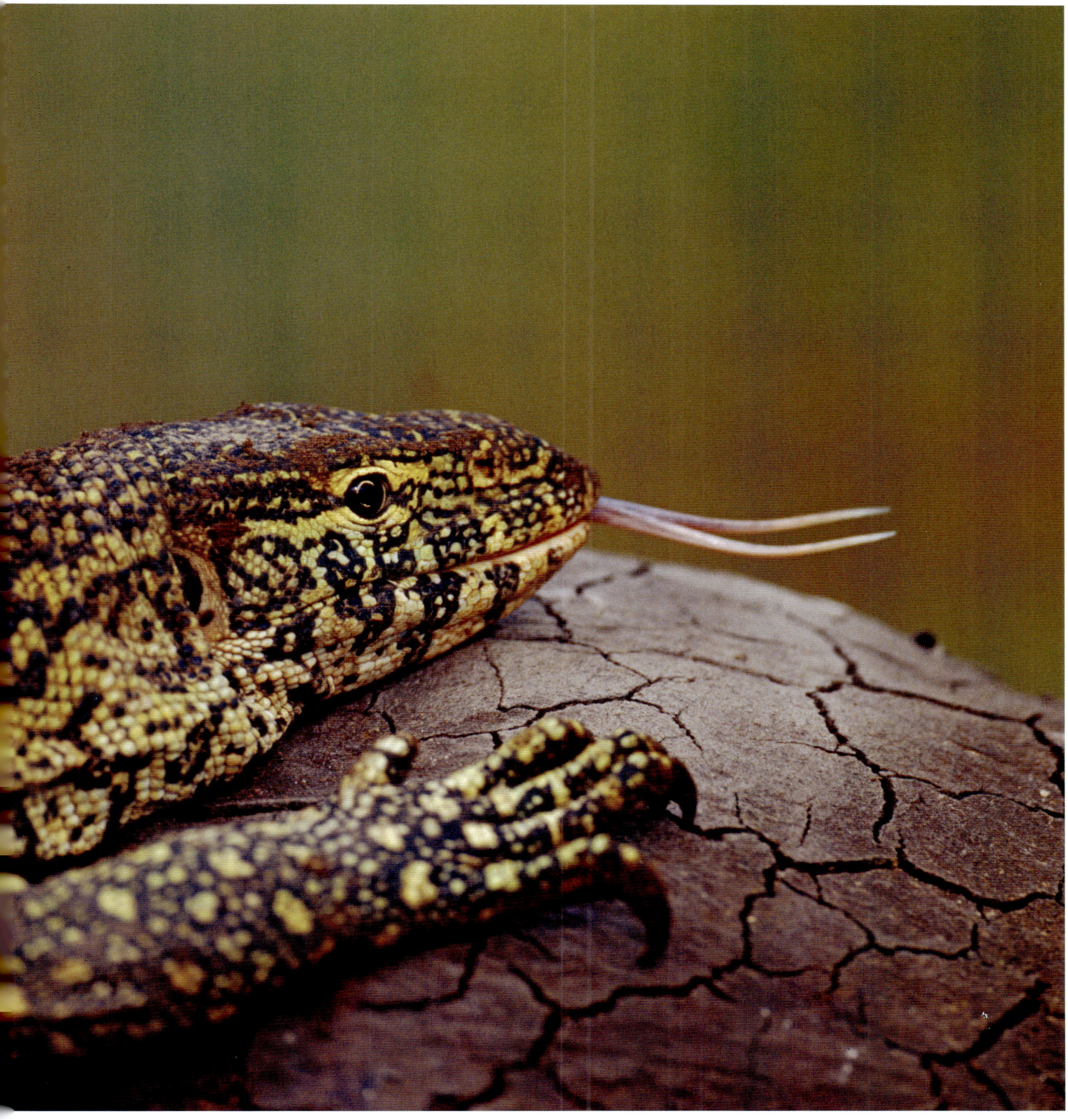

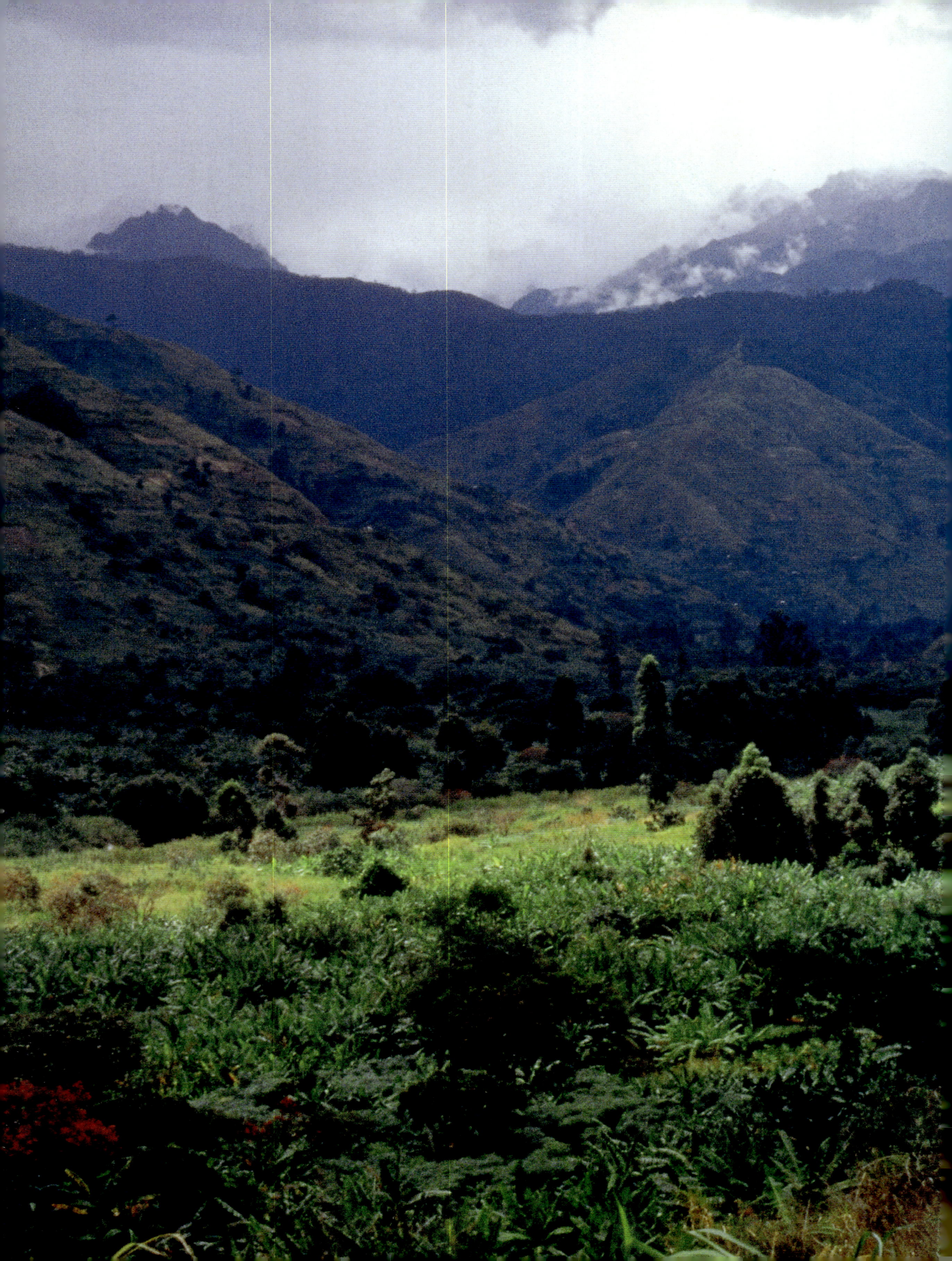

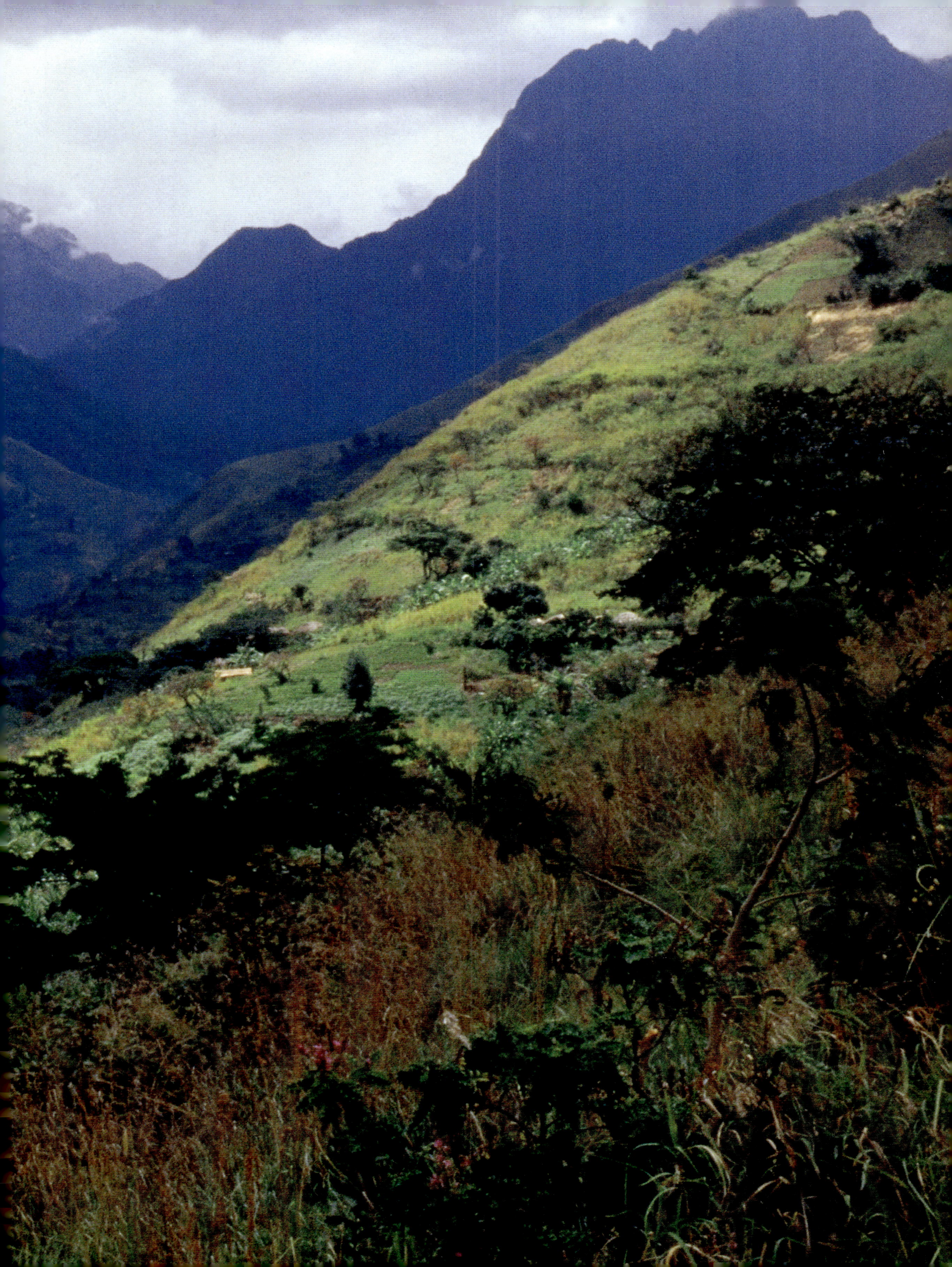

Right: A typical scene in western Uganda, with an evening shower approaching a small banana plantation.

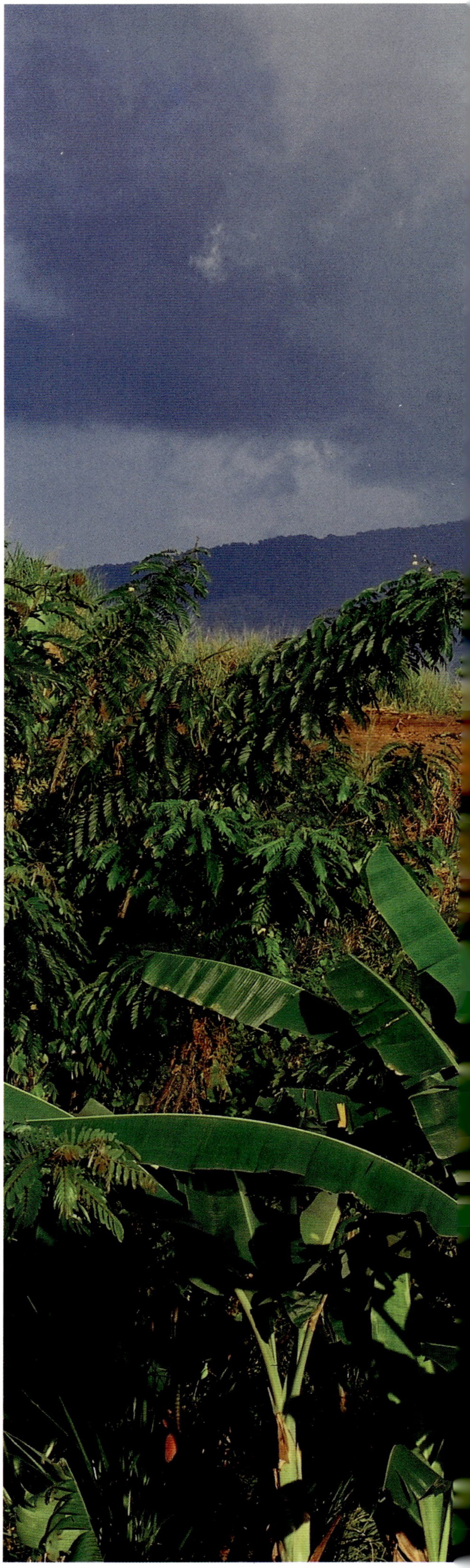

here in its thousands, along with buffalo and bushbuck, providing rich pickings to several lion prides, whose presence is often revealed by the kob's wheezy alarm call. Grassland birds such as crowned crane are common here too, but a more intriguing birding possibility is Ramsar-listed Kikorongo Swamp, an avian hotspot that extends from Lake George to the smaller Lake Kikorongo and harbours such localised species as shoebill, papyrus gonolek and papyrus canary. If it's scenery you're after, Crater Drive forms a rough and circuitous alternative to the main road between Kasenyi to Mweya, and spectacular views over a succession of craters formed by the volcanic upheaval that characterised this currently stable part of the Rift Valley for much of the last half-million years. Back at Mweya, the salt-rich Katwe Crater Lake was fiercely contested by the area's rival kingdoms in pre-colonial times, and is still mined for salt today, this despite the compellingly bleak appearance that led E J Wayland, an early European visitor, to describe it as a "stifling and malodorous… fiend-made meeting place for the Devil and his friends".

An altogether more sumptuous crater lake called Nyamasingiri, 10 kilometres south of Katwe as the crow flies, but considerably longer along the solitary bridge that crosses the Kazinga Channel to link the north and south of the park, is the tourist centrepiece of the lush Maramagambo Forest. Comprised of five interlocking flooded craters, this lovely lake is the site of the exclusive Jacana Lodge, whose fine in-house wildlife viewing includes black-and-white colobus, red-tailed monkey, L'Hoest's monkey and olive baboon clattering through the forest canopy between the lodge and a nearby campsite, and African finfoot and fish eagle on the lake. Chimpanzees are regularly heard at Maramagambo, but to see these charismatic apes you must visit the nearby Chambura Gorge, a spectacular deep chasm whose 16 kilometres length supports around 40 individuals.

The most remote and compelling sector of QENP is Ishasha, a mesmerising vista of rolling grassland and jungle-like forest patches bounded by Lake Edward and the Ishasha River, and bypassed by a rough dirt road connecting Bwindi to Mweya. This untrammelled wilderness is best known for the extraordinary behaviour of its tree-climbing lions, which currently number about 40 individuals split across three prides. True, there are other parts of East Africa where lions climb trees upon occasion, most famously Lake Manyara in northern Tanzania, but Ishasha is unique in that this behaviour is so deeply ingrained as to occur practically on a daily basis – and it has done at least since 1952, when Douglas Willocks wrote of "lions that climbed fig trees and lay in them all day keeping a sleepy eye on the antelope herds". Quite why they do this is a matter for conjecture – possibly it's purely opportunistic since Ishasha

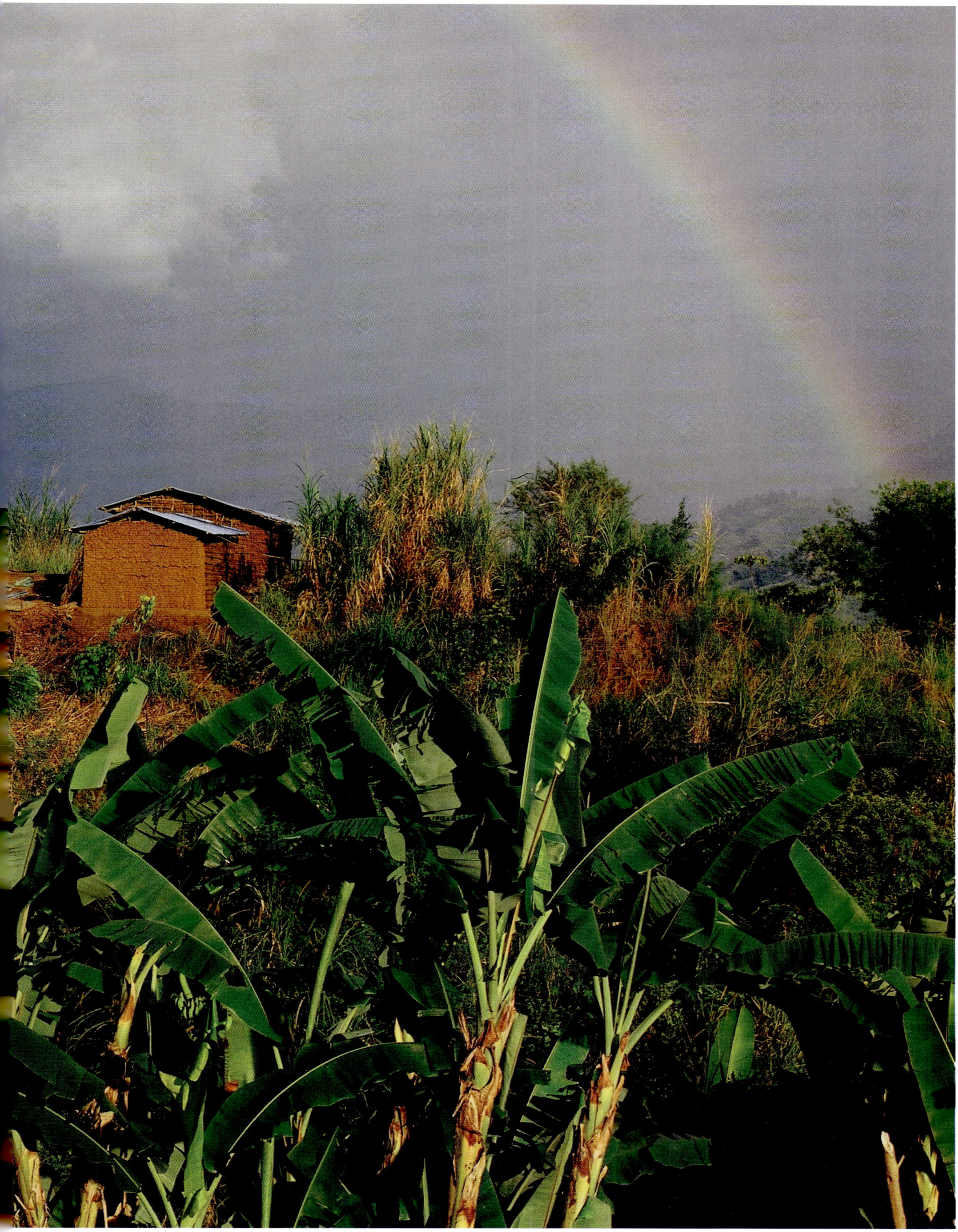

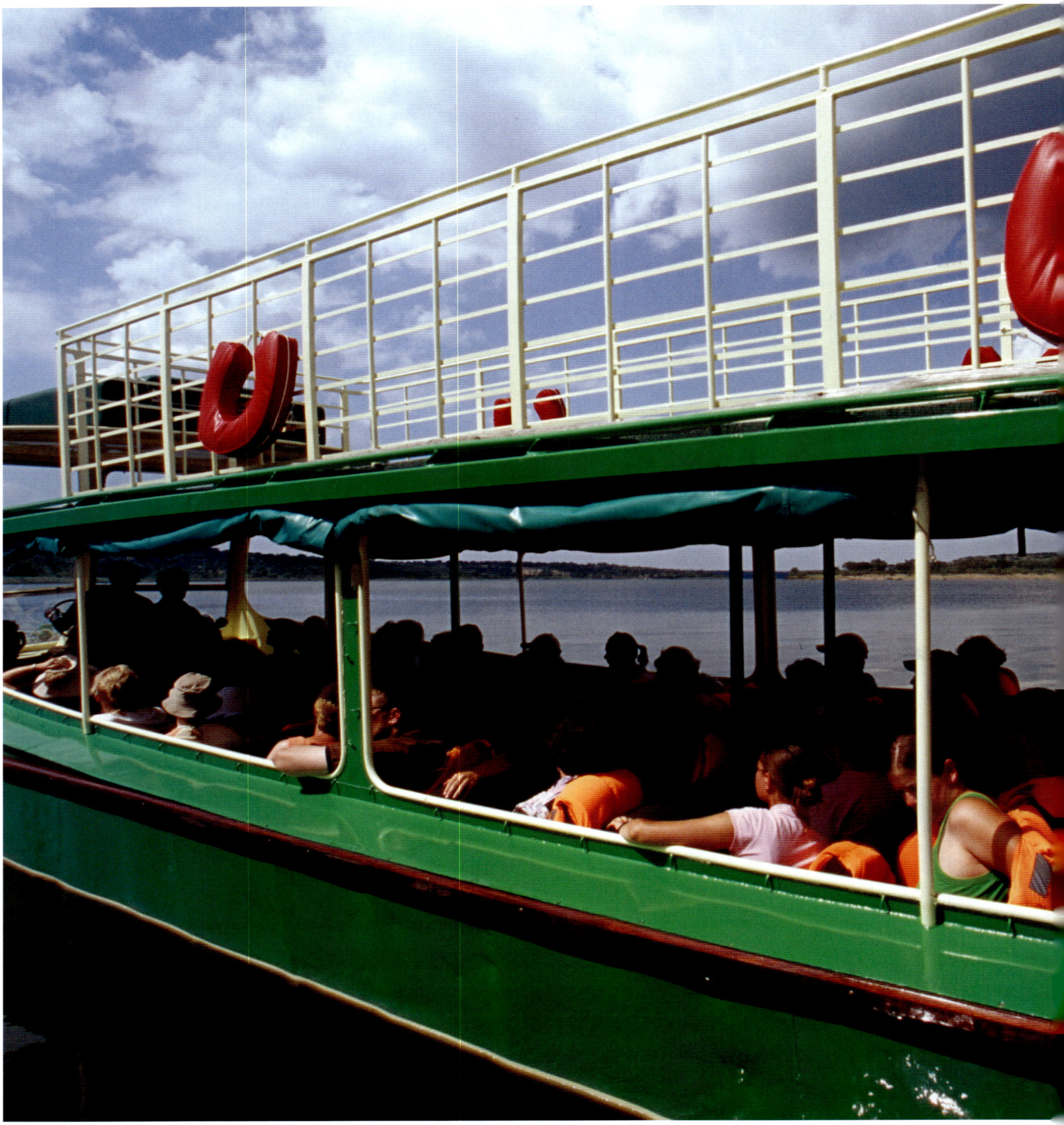

Below: Visitors enjoying the Kazinga Channel boat trip.

Following pages: Sunset over the grand expanse of the mythical Rwenzori Mountains

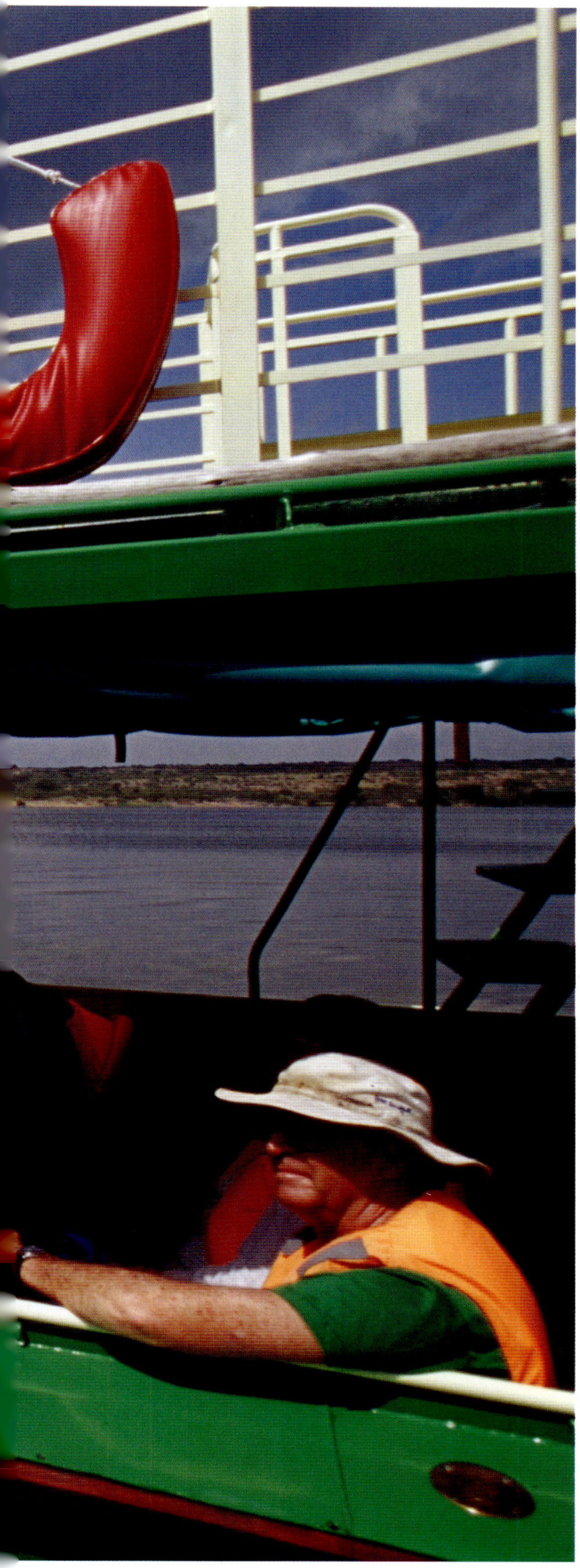

boasts a high concentration of sycamore figs with heavy low limbs suited to L-plate clamberers – but there's no doubt that the sight of a lion pride slumbering high in the canopy is extraordinarily satisfying to veteran safarigoers.

Ishasha's wildlife doesn't stop there. Large herds of buffalo are commonplace, and often contain striking ochre coloured individuals as a result of interbreeding with the red forest race of the neighbouring Congo. Elephant and kob are common too, and the area harbours an isolated population of topi. Hippos and crocs cluster in the Ishasha River, whose banks are home to bushbuck, acrobatic black-and-white colobus, and several of the choicer items on QENP's avian checklist, including black bee-eater, Ross's turaco, double-toothed barbet, black-necked weaver, red-headed bluebill and Cassin's grey flycatcher. Another draw for birders is the marshy Lake Edward Flats, a good site for the enigmatic shoebill, and other waterbirds such as dwarf bittern, painted snipe, blue-headed coucal and spotted crake.

The present-day health of QENP is all the more remarkable when one considers the crippling level of poaching it experienced during and immediately after the Amin era. Between 1971 and 1980, the elephant population tumbled from 4,000 to 150 survivors, buffalo from 18,000 to fewer than 8,000, and lion were hunted close to extinction. Today, by contrast, an estimated 2,500 elephant and 10,000 buffalo roam the park, along with 35,000 Uganda kob, and the lion population stands at around 250, population densities that compare favourably with, say, the Kruger Park. But to view QENP merely as another 'big game destination' feels monumentally reductive. With a scenic impact matched by few wildlife reserves and a combined diversity of plains and forest creatures second to none, this astonishing and infinitely rewarding tract of soil and water is arguably the closest thing in existence to a one-stop microcosm of non-arid East African habitats.

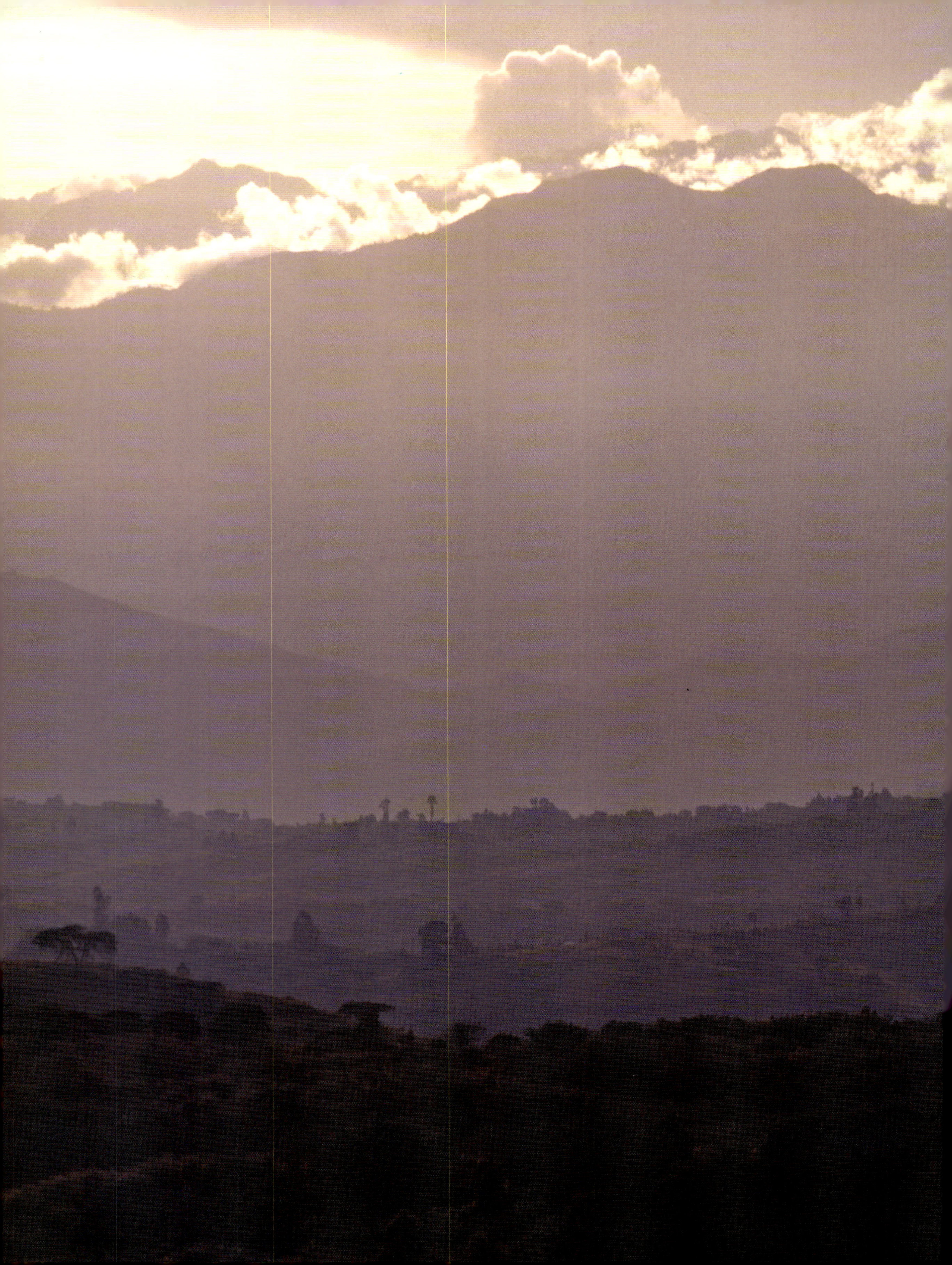

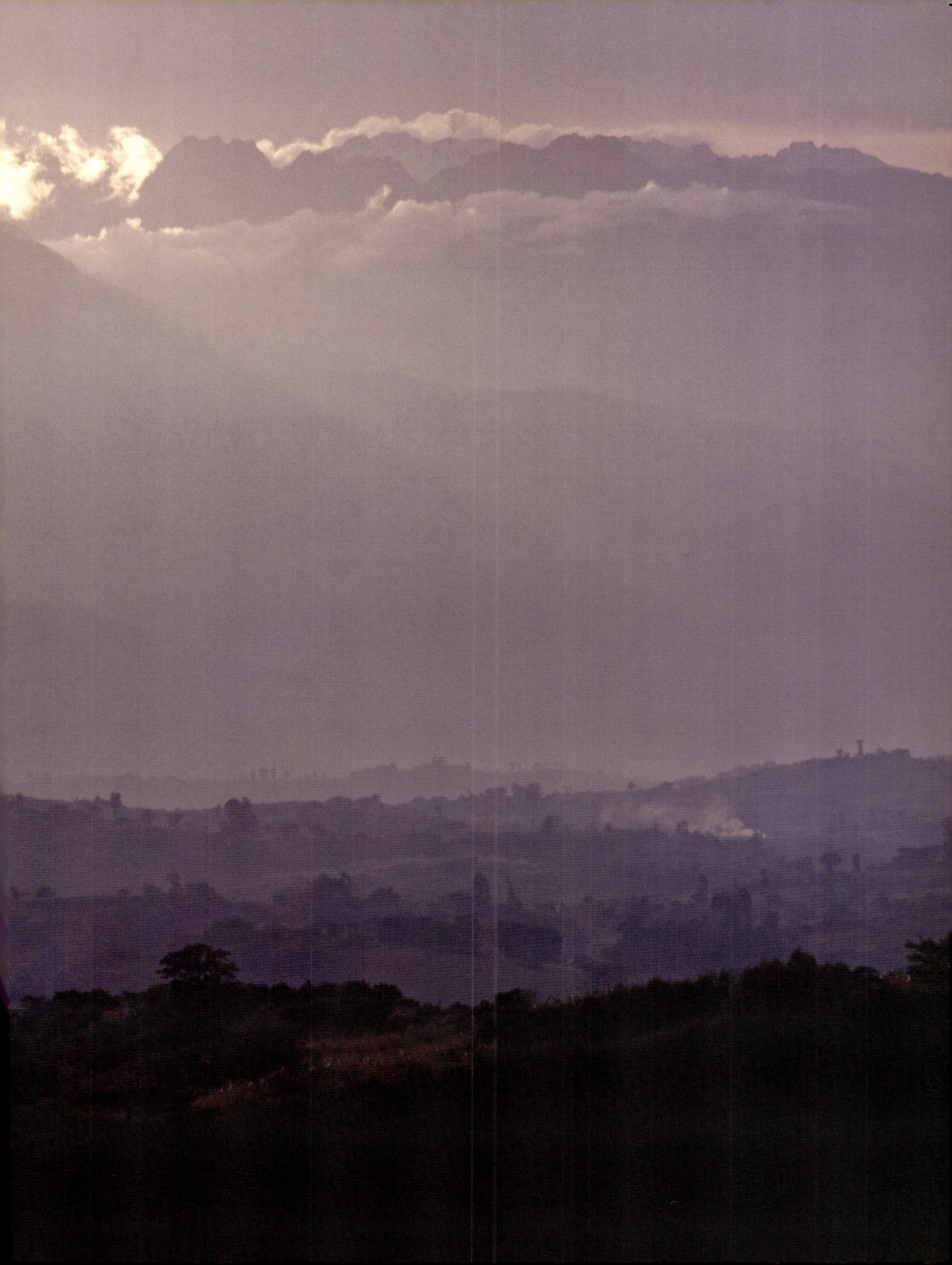

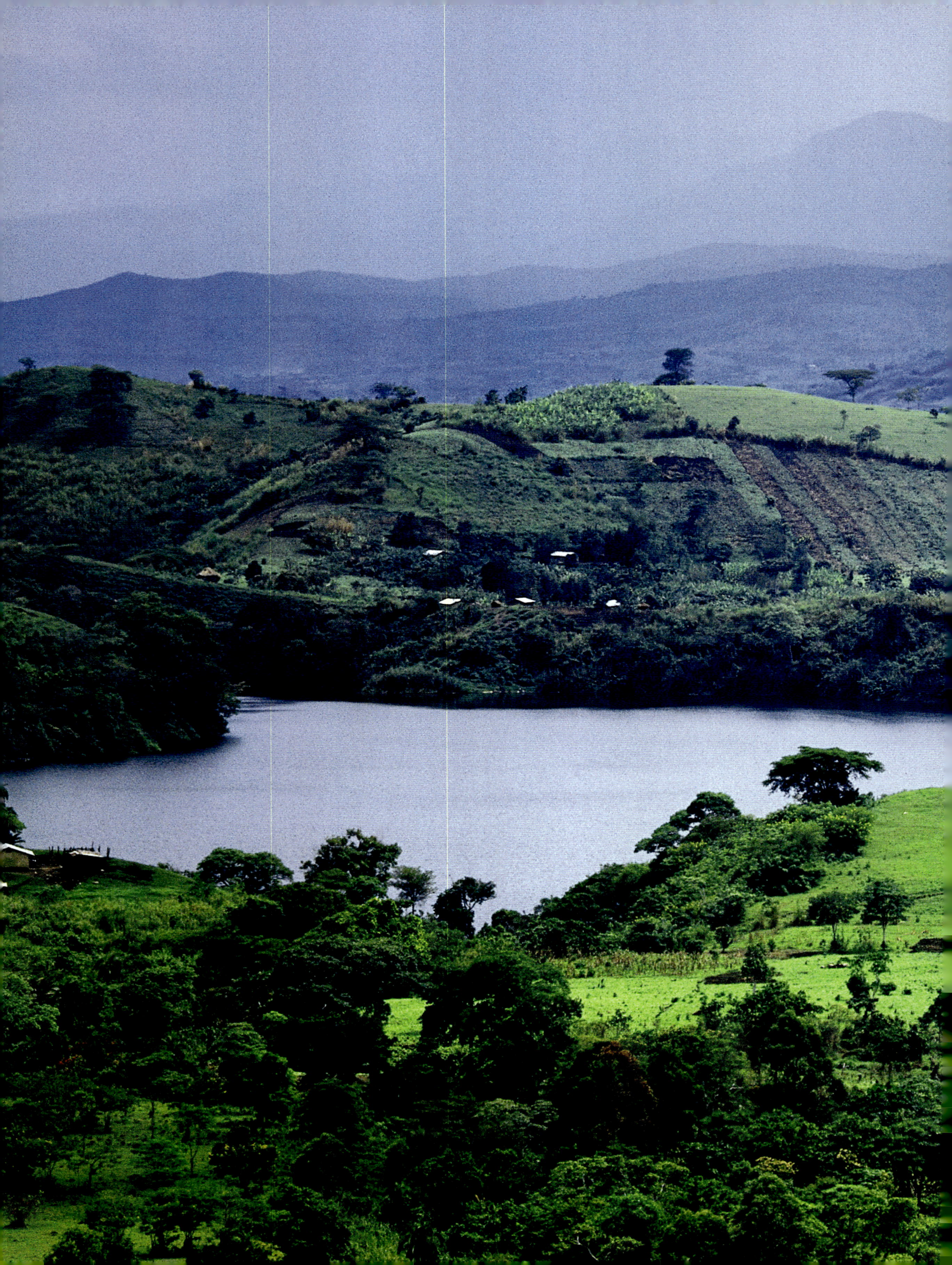

5. *Fort Portal and the Forests of Toro*

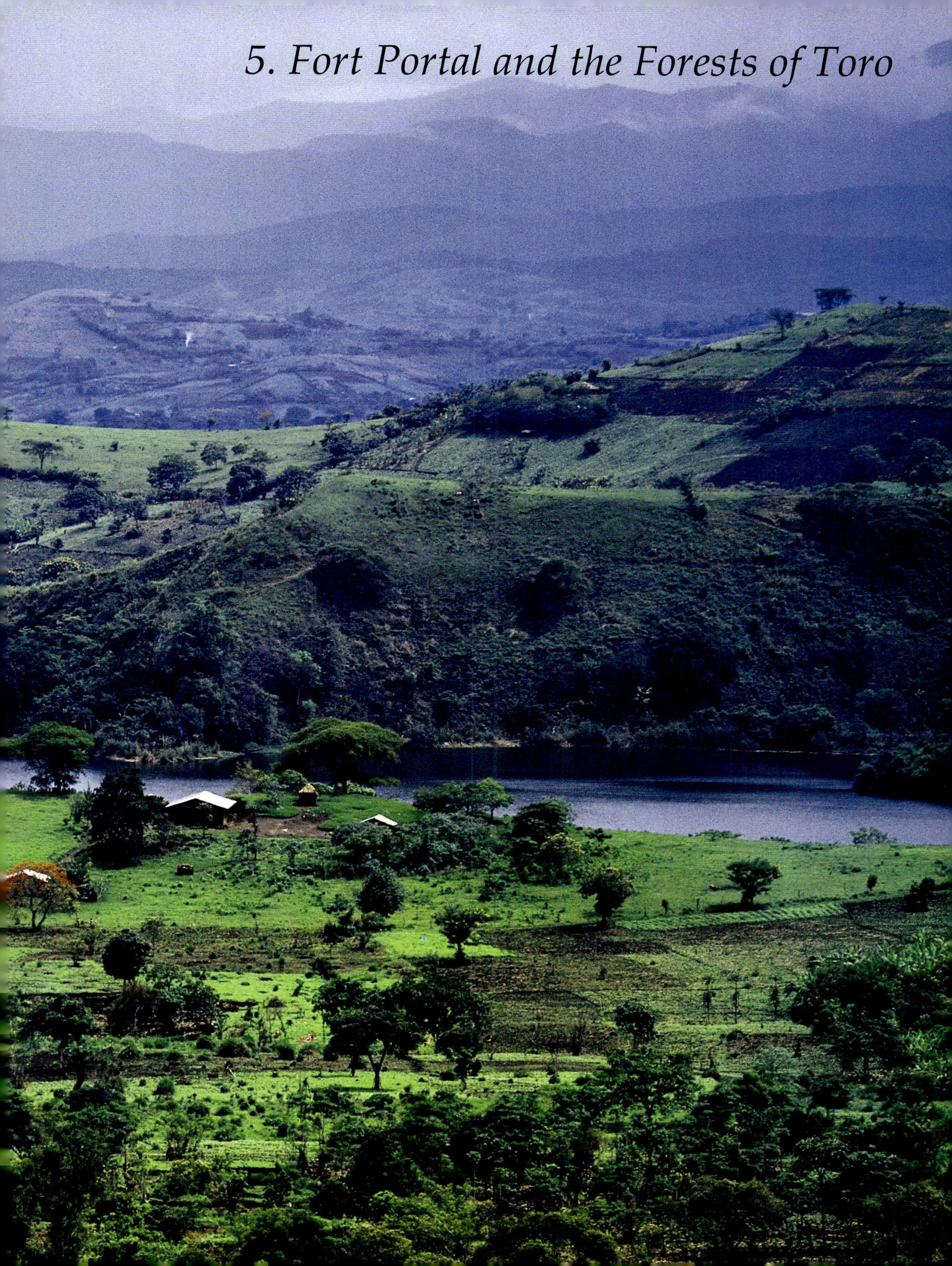

Set on the moist, verdant northern footslopes of the Rwenzoris, Fort Portal has the unusual distinction of being named after a relatively obscure figure who never set foot anywhere in the vicinity. The personage in question is Sir Gerald Portal, British Consul-General of Zanzibar, who visited Kampala in 1893 to formalize Ugandan protectorateship and died of malaria soon afterwards. Little remains of the fort, which stood close to the present-day golf club, but the eponymous town is one of the most attractive in Uganda, surrounded by crater lakes, caves and tea estates, and well based for visits to the primate-rich Kibale Forest and scenic Semliki Valley.

Fort Portal is the capital of the Toro Kingdom, the youngest of Uganda's traditional kingdoms, founded circa 1825 by a rebel Banyoro prince called Kaboyo, but co-opted back into Bunyoro by King Kabalega 50 years later. The kingdom was restored by Britain in 1891, and Kasagama was installed as king in recognition for his role in the defeat of Kabalega. Like other Kingdoms in Uganda, Toro was abolished during the Amin era and its royal family was forced into exile. Following the restoration of the monarchy in 1995 under Museveni, the kingdom has been ruled by the world's most youthful monarch, Oyo Nyimba Kabamba Iguru Rukidi IV, only three years old at the time of his coronation. Perched on a hill above Fort Portal is the large circular palace built in the 1960s for Kasagama's son and successor, Rukidi III, who is now buried alongside his father at the Karambi Tombs, 5 kilometres out of town.

A mere 10 kilometres west of Fort Portal, following a bumpy dirt road along the precipitous northern Rwenzoris foothills, the Semliki Valley opens up in all its geographical immensity. To the immediate right are the sheer walls of the Rift Escarpment, while the aptly named Blue Mountains rise to 2,500m in the distant DRC. To the left, shrouded in clouds, rise the austere glacial peaks of the Rwenzoris. Cupped within this imposing natural amphitheatre is the green swathe of the Ituri Forest, which extends over thousands of square kilometres into the dark heart of the Congo Basin, while the Semliki River forms an intermittent weave of serpentine silver flowing along the Congolese border into the distant southern tip of Lake Albert, shimmering far below.

The Semliki Valley houses two of Uganda's most intriguing and divergent protected areas. Separated by a northern spur of the Rwenzoris foothills, Semliki Wildlife Reserve consists of open grassland rolling down to the swampy southern shore of Lake Albert, while Semuliki National Park protects the Ugandan extension of the sweltering Ituri Forest, home to a host of species found nowhere else in East Africa.

Set aside as a forest reserve before it was gazetted in 1993, the 220-square-kilometre (85-square-mile) Semuliki National Park is relatively

Previous pages: Pretty crater lake near Fort Portal.

Opposite: Statue of Sir Gerald Portal in Fort Portal town.

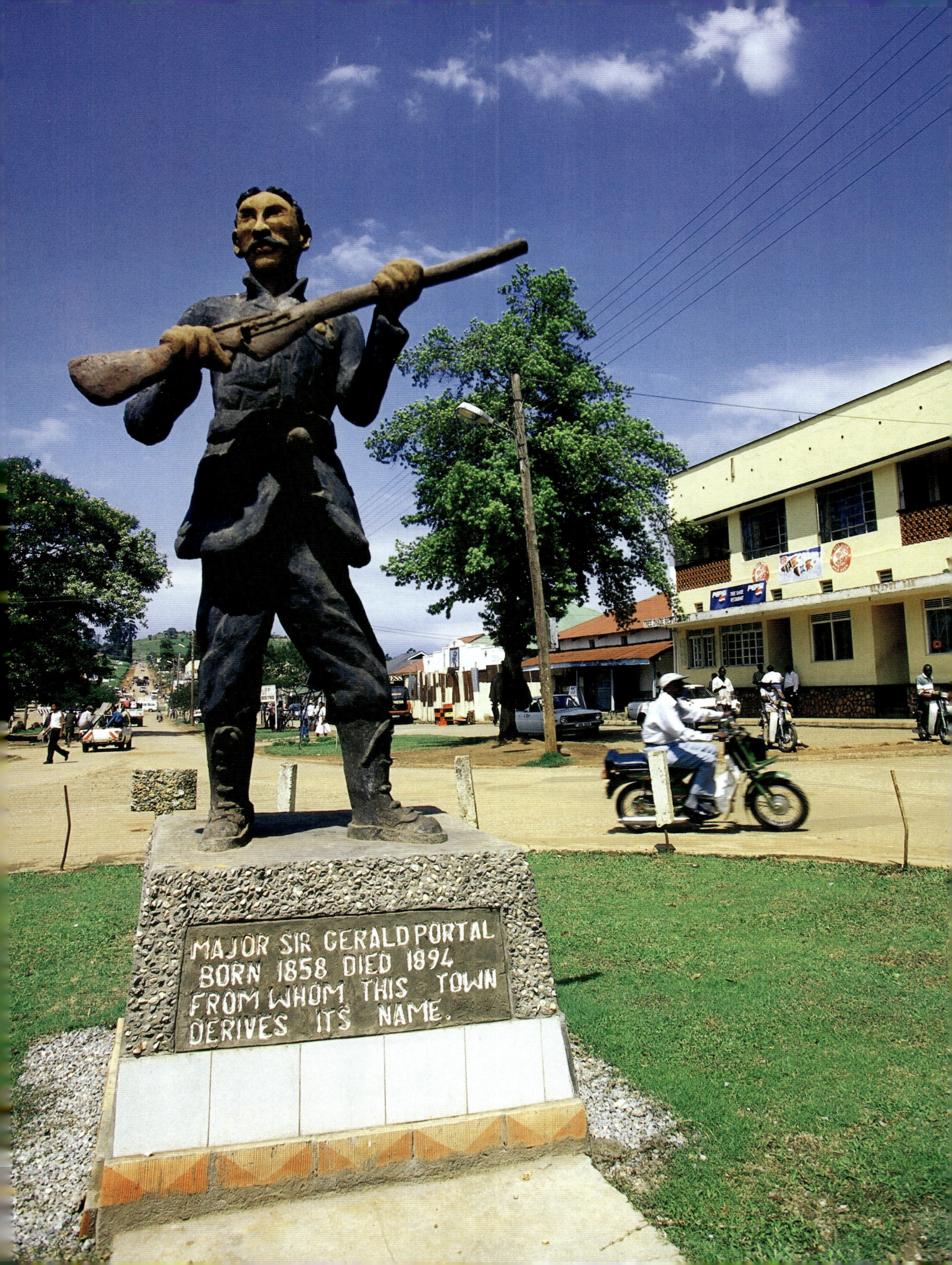
MAJOR SIR GERALD PORTAL
BORN 1858 DIED 1894
FROM WHOM THIS TOWN
DERIVES ITS NAME.

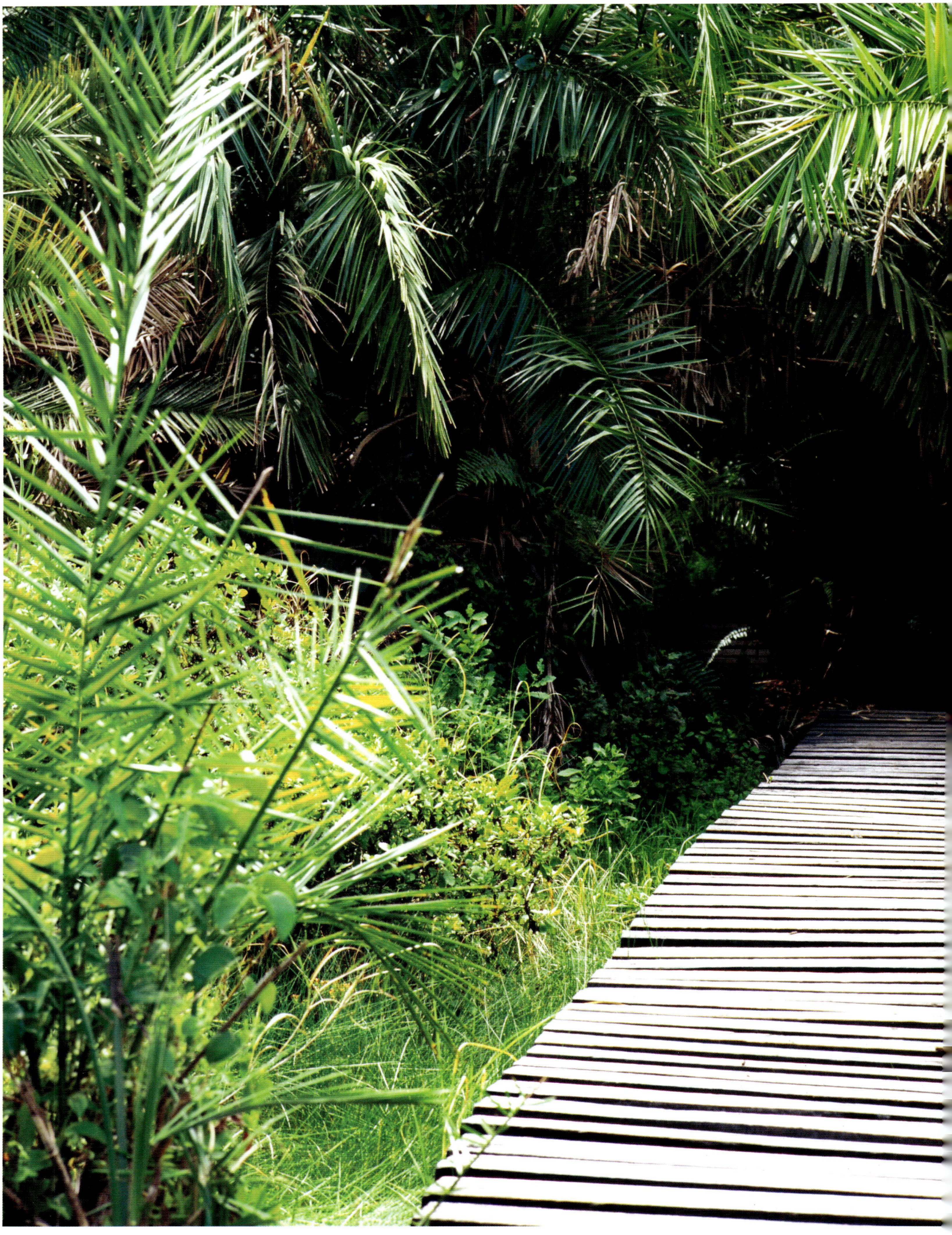

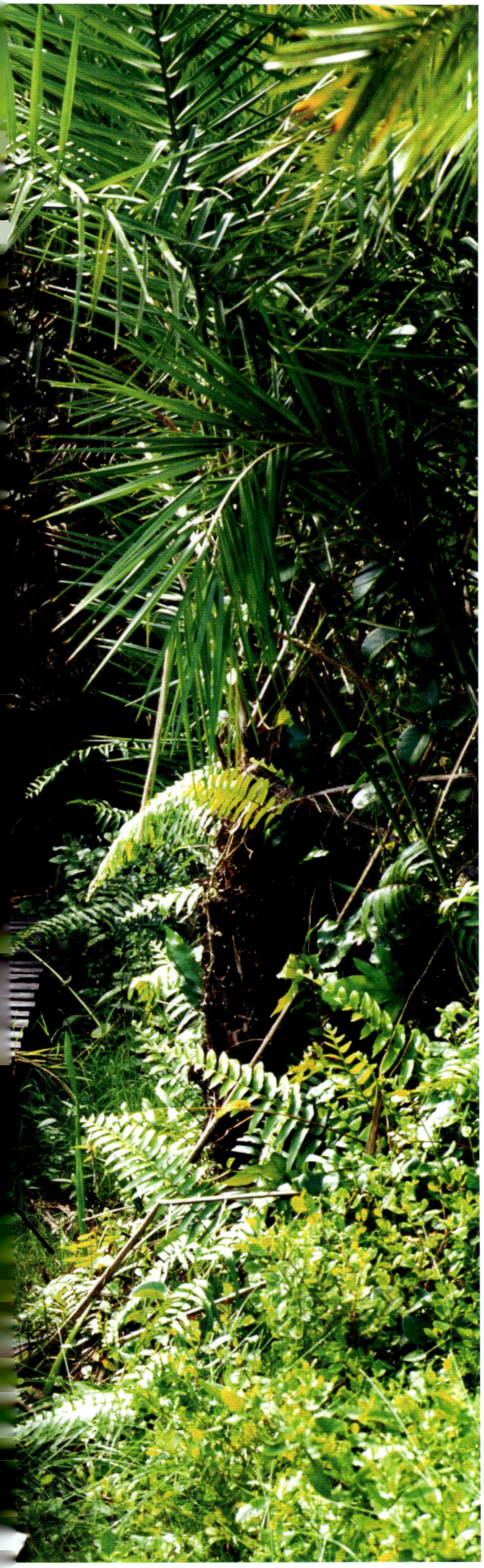

Left: Nature walk at Semuliki National Park.

Following pages: Hot springs in Semuliki National Park.

untouched by tourism, despite protecting the country's only significant stand of tropical lowland forest, which is characterized by a more diverse vegetation than other Ugandan forests, and has a moister, denser undergrowth as a result of having no real 'dry season'. The local people are the Bamba and Bakonjo ethnic groups, mainly coffee and cocoa growers. There is also a small number of Batwa Pygmies, traditional forest dwellers who were forcibly removed from the forest when it became a national park, although they continue to gather medicinal plants from within, and generally welcome visits from the rare passing tourist.

One of the specialized micro-habitats of the park is caused by the Sempaya hot springs, which erupt from the ground through a saline stalagmite-like sculpture at a scalding 106°C (223°F). It is a primeval, evocative sight, linked to the same tectonic activity that created the Rift Valley and Rwenzoris Mountains. The pungent bubbling water is rich in salt and sulphur, while the surrounding mud supports a strange lungfish-like creature fed upon by an unusually large population of shorebirds. Large mammals also frequent the hot springs, which form a natural salt lick, while the surrounding forest is good for primates, with grey-cheeked mangabey, red colobus, black-and-white colobus and red-tailed monkey all regular. Semliki is the only East African stronghold for the water chevrotain, a superficially duiker-like relic of an ancient ungulate family that shares several structural features with pigs and is regarded to be ancestral to all modern-day antelopes, deer, cows and giraffes.

Semliki is renowned among birdwatchers for its remarkable checklist of 400 species, which includes a full 35 Guinea-Congo biome endemics known from no other locality in East Africa, among them the immense black-wattled hornbill, Nkulengu rail, spot-breasted ibis, African piculet and Congo serpent-eagle. The scarcity of many of these localised specials, not to mention the density of the forest, mean that it would be deliriously optimistic to expect a short visit to the national park visit to yield anything like a full contingent. Still, no birdwatcher could fail to arrive without heightened anticipation at the prospect of ticking a few excellent 'lifers'. The truly dedicated could set up a 3-4 day camping trip along the Kirumia Trail, which follows the eponymous river and a series of associated oxbow lakes to the banks of the Semliki, where monkeys play in the trees and elephant and buffalo occasionally come to drink.

The 555-square-kilometre (214-square-mile) Semliki Wildlife Reserve is Uganda's oldest protected area, gazetted as in 1932 as the Semliki Wildlife Reserve. Back then, its legendary abundance of wildlife included tens of thousands of Uganda kob, numerous buffalo, the forest race of elephant (so common it was referred to locally as a 'Semliki rat'), and an impressive density of predators – indeed, the Kenyan hunter Brian Herne

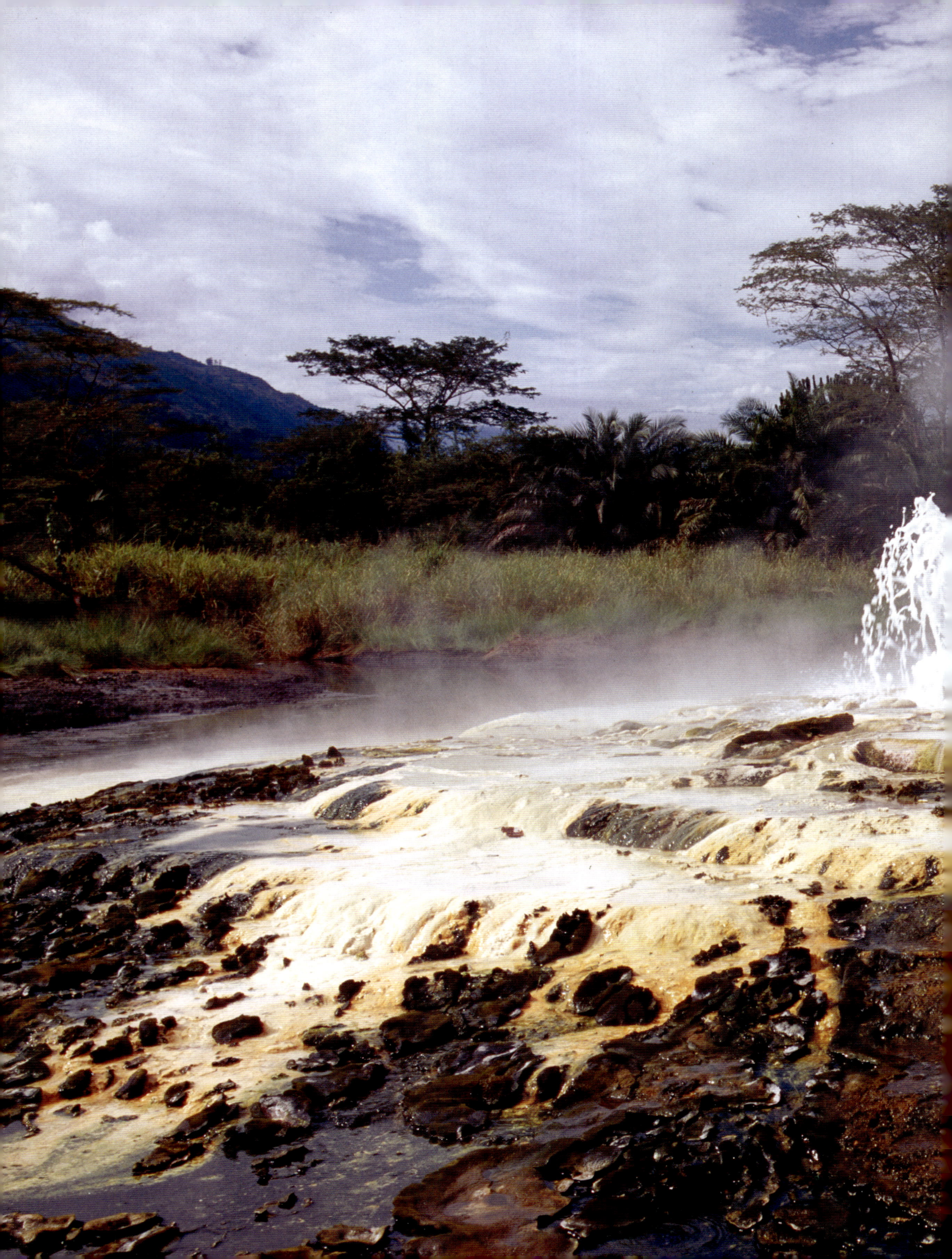

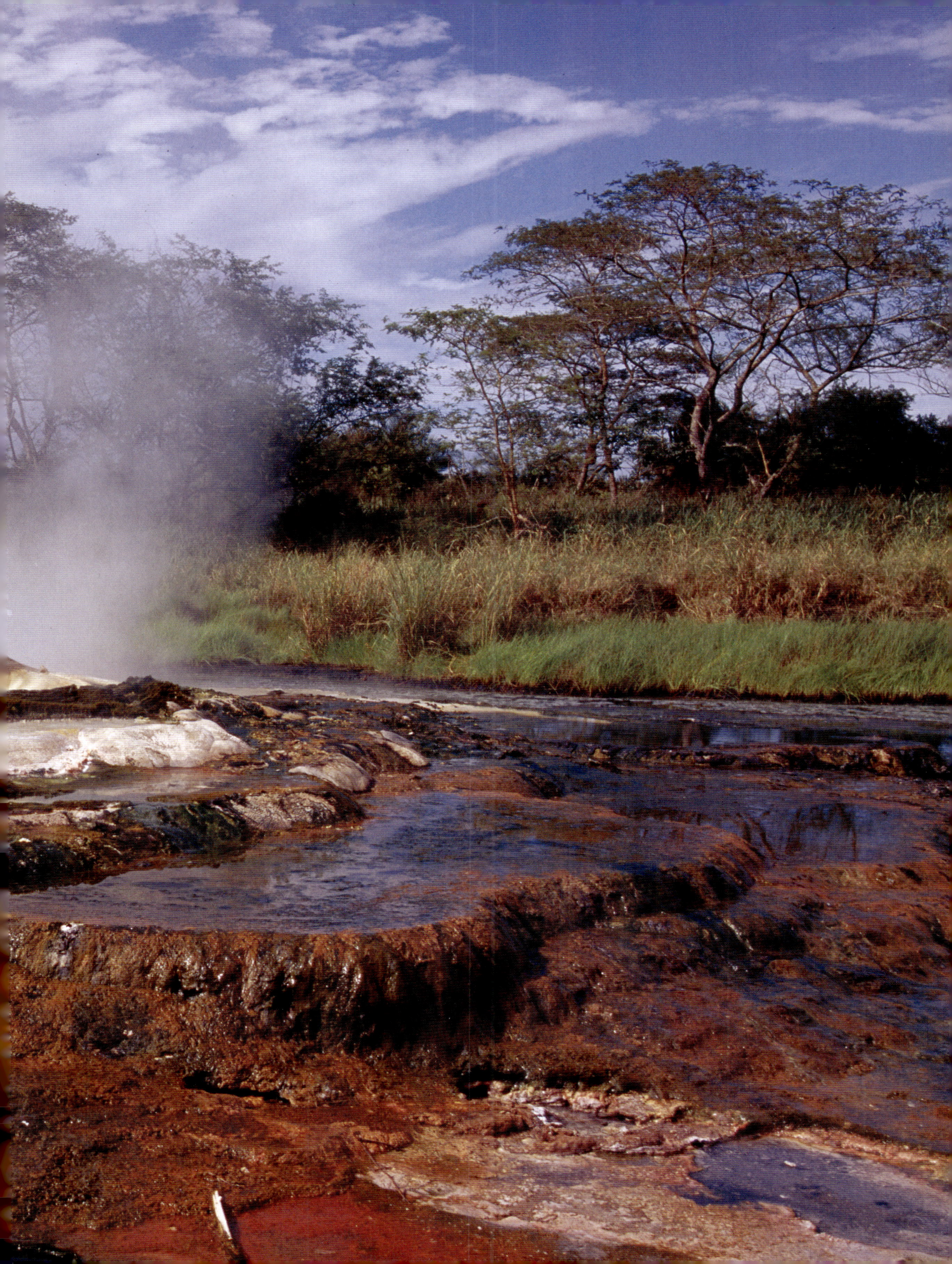

once wrote that he had "never seen so many big lions in other parts of Africa". Semliki was devastated by poaching during the years of unrest, but this trend is slowly reversing, and lion and spotted hyena have both recolonised the reserve since the turn of the millennium. The part of Lake Albert bordering the reserve is one of the top locations for shoebill and other water-associated birds, ranging from flotillas of great white pelican to breeding colonies of the dazzling red-throated bee-eater.

Contiguous with Queen Elizabeth National Park to the southwest, the 766-square-kilometre (296-square-mile) Kibale Forest National Park protects a moist medium-altitude transitional forest habitat with an extremely diverse fauna and flora, including some 335 bird, 60 mammal and 145 bird species. Probably the most accessible of the country's large forests, it was originally set aside as the Kibale Forest Corridor Game Reserve, part of a migratory route between Queen Elizabeth and Murchison Falls National Parks for elephant and other large game.

Today, Kibale Forest is best-known as Uganda's premier destination for tracking habituated chimpanzees. Unfortunately, this pursuit tends to be a little more hit-and-miss than gorilla tracking, mainly because chimps are far less sedentary creatures than gorillas, often covering dozens of kilometres daily as they search for food sources – and they can move seriously quickly through the tangled forest undergrowth. You're most likely to get lucky during the fruiting season, when the guides know which trees the chimps favour, and if you do, these delightful apes, more closely related to humans than to any other living creature, are tremendous fun to watch as they squabble and play in the canopy.

Chimps aside, Kibale Forest supports the largest variety and highest density of primates in Uganda, and has thus been the site of much behavioural research by primatologists. The tally of 13 primate species of primate includes a high density of the red colobus monkey, which is rare elsewhere in Uganda, but is easily seen in the forested environs of Kanyanchu tourist camp. Also present are black-and-white colobus, red-tailed monkey, blue monkey, L'Hoest's monkey, grey-cheeked mangabey and olive baboon. Other wildlife includes bushbuck, red duiker, blue duiker, bush pig, civet, buffalo and giant forest hog which are present, but rarely seen. In addition, Kibale harbours Uganda's largest population of forest elephant, which frequent Kanyanchu for brief periods during the rainy season, but are almost never seen, though their spoor is abundant.

The ethnic groups who live near the park are the Batoro and the Bakiga, many of whom grow cash crops – such as coffee – and eucalyptus trees for timber. Many local villages are also involved in the tourist industry, one such being Bigodi, which lies outside the park boundaries just 5 kilometres from Kanyanchu. Adjacent to this tiny village, the community-owned

Opposite: Male Uganda Kob protecting its mating territory, the small circle of trampled grass surrounding him.

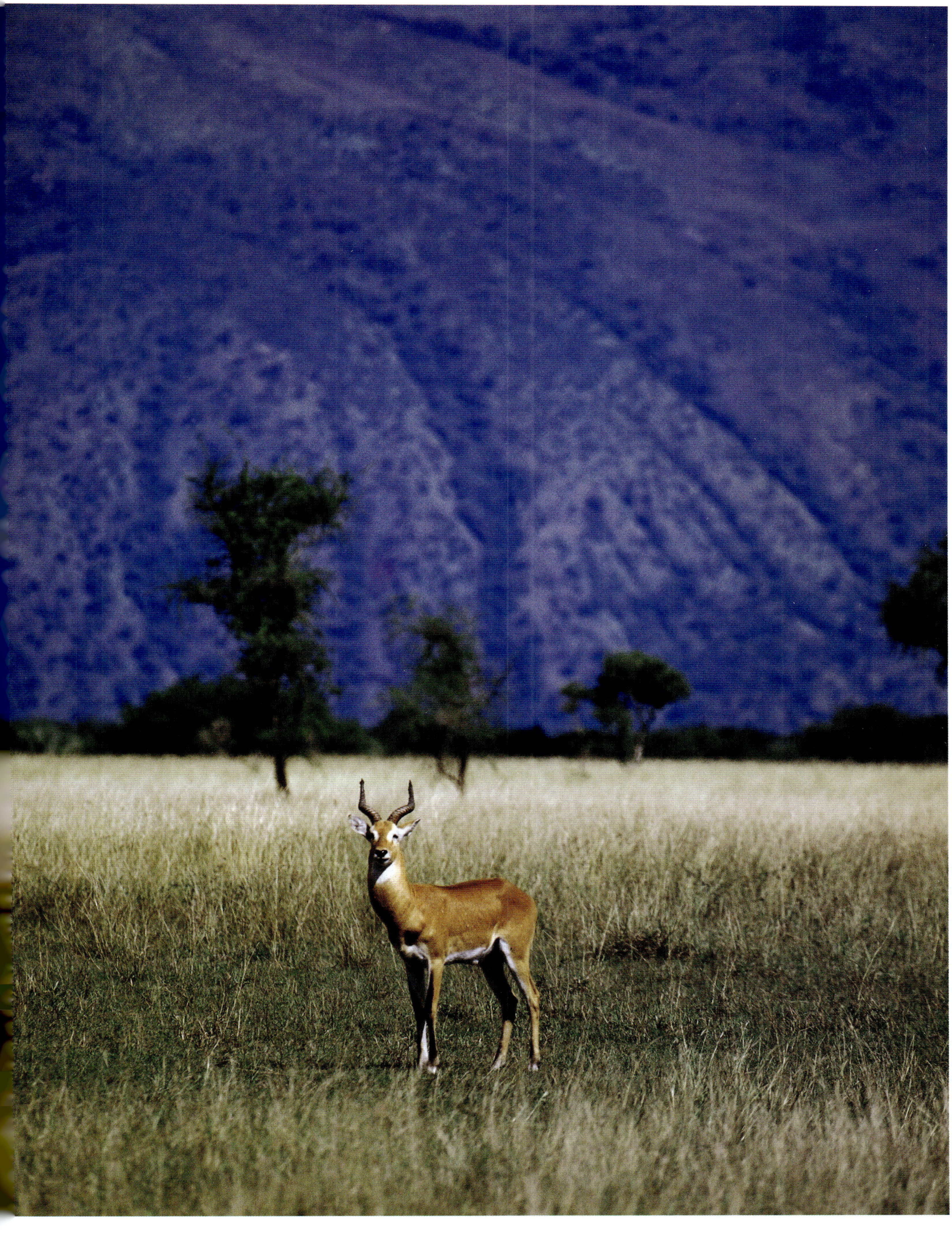

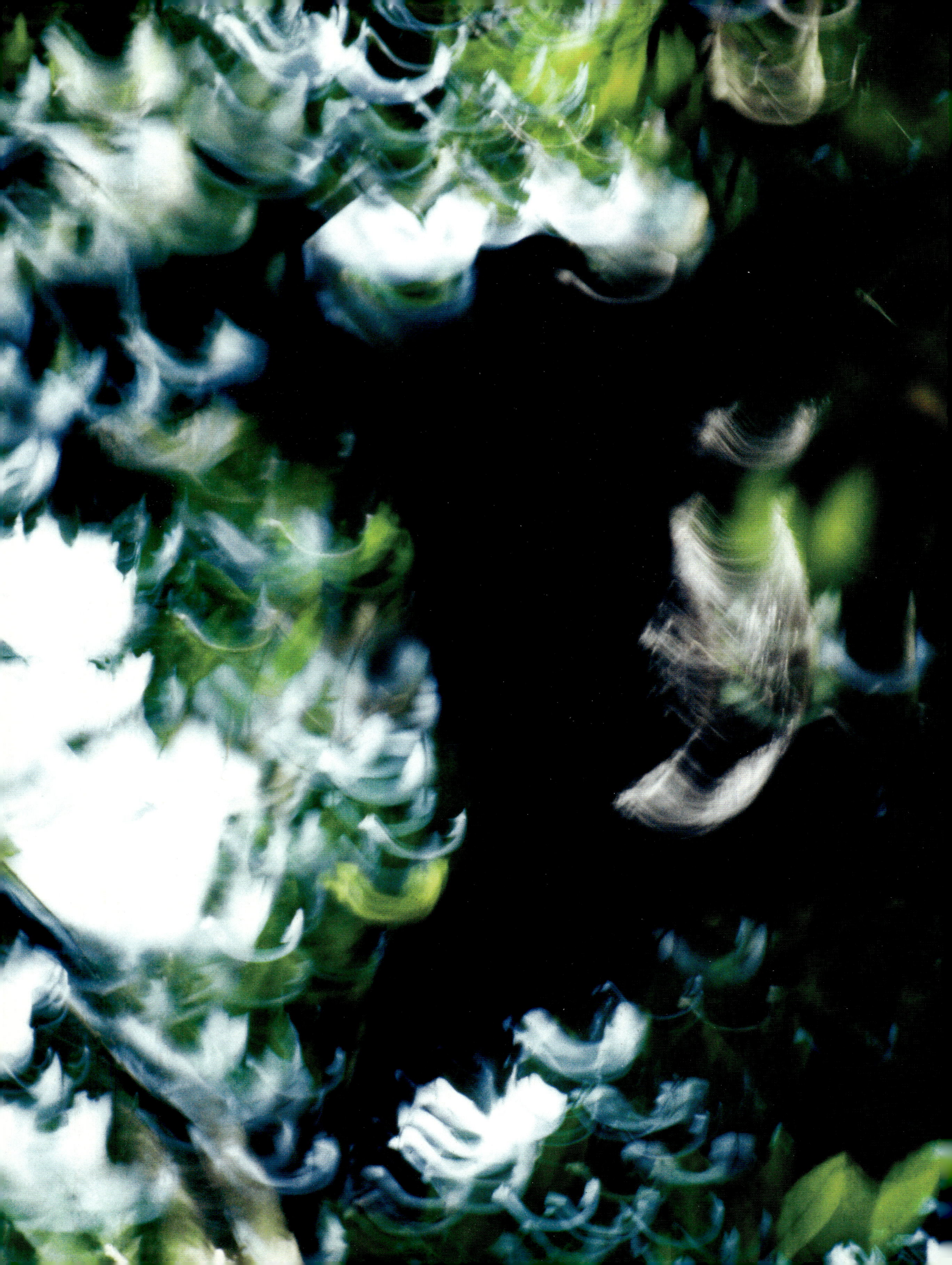

)pposite: Chimpanzee climbing in the forest ɲ Kibale Forest National Park.

'ollowing pages: Nkusi Falls on the extreme side f Lake Albert.

Bigodi Wetland Sanctuary offers a great introduction to East Africa's rainforest fauna. Clear views from the swamp edge into the gallery forest allow for good sightings of red colobus, black-and-white colobus, grey-cheeked mangabey, red-tailed and possibly L'Hoest's monkey, and the guides really know their stuff when it comes to the swamp's varied forest avifauna, which includes squawking African grey parrot, yellow-billed and double-toothed barbets, and a trio of colourful turacos. The nearby Kasenda Crater Lake Field, whose 30-odd lakes are each a different shade of blue or green, is also serviced by several excellent community projects, notably the Lake Nkuruba Nature Reserve, protecting the beautiful jungle-fringed lake for which it is named, Visitors can go boating on the lakes, the water is safe for swimming, and the birdlife is prolific. Local legend has it that the chain of lakes was created by Ndahura, the first Bacwezi king, when he retired to the area after abdicating in favour of his son, Wamara.

South of Kibale Forest, the Katonga River forms the southern boundary of the 208-square-kilometre (80 square-mile) Katonga Game Reserve, which is traversed by the river's many tributaries. Only recently developed for tourism, the reserve protects a network of forest-fringed wetlands along the Katonga River. Best explored on foot and by canoe, Katonga supports some 40 mammal and at least 150 bird species, many specific to wetland habitats. Most visible are elephant, waterbuck, reedbuck, colobus monkeys and river otter. This is one of the best places in Africa to look for the elusive sitatunga, a semi-aquatic antelope with webbed hooves that forages almost exclusively in swamps.

Those heading eastward from Fort Portal along the new 332-kilometre surfaced road to Kampala might want to break the journey at Mubende, which lies within easy striking distance of several interesting archaeological sites. These include the Munsa Earthworks, which surround three large interconnected rock shelters, and an ancient shrine reached by stone stairs in a cave in Semwama Hill. The rock shelters were thought to hold up to 100 people and are traditionally linked to Prince Kateboha of the mediaeval Bacwezi kingdom.

Excavations at Mubende Hill suggest it was occupied about 500 years ago, and oral tradition connects the site to Ndahura, founder of Bacwezi. Since this legendary kingdom collapsed, the hill has drawn a number of Bacwezi-related cults to its shrine, which is centred on the 400-year-old and 40-metre (130-foot) high Nakaima Tree. Named after Ndahura's wife, who was renowned for her mystical powers, the Nakaima Tree is believed to contain Ndahura's spirit and has been a site of worship for centuries, guarded by a hereditary line of priestesses (also called Nakaima) of the Basazima clan. The last Nakaima died in 1907, and her regalia is now on display in the National Museum in Kampala – as are two large pots that were unearthed near the tree, apparently once used in religious rituals.

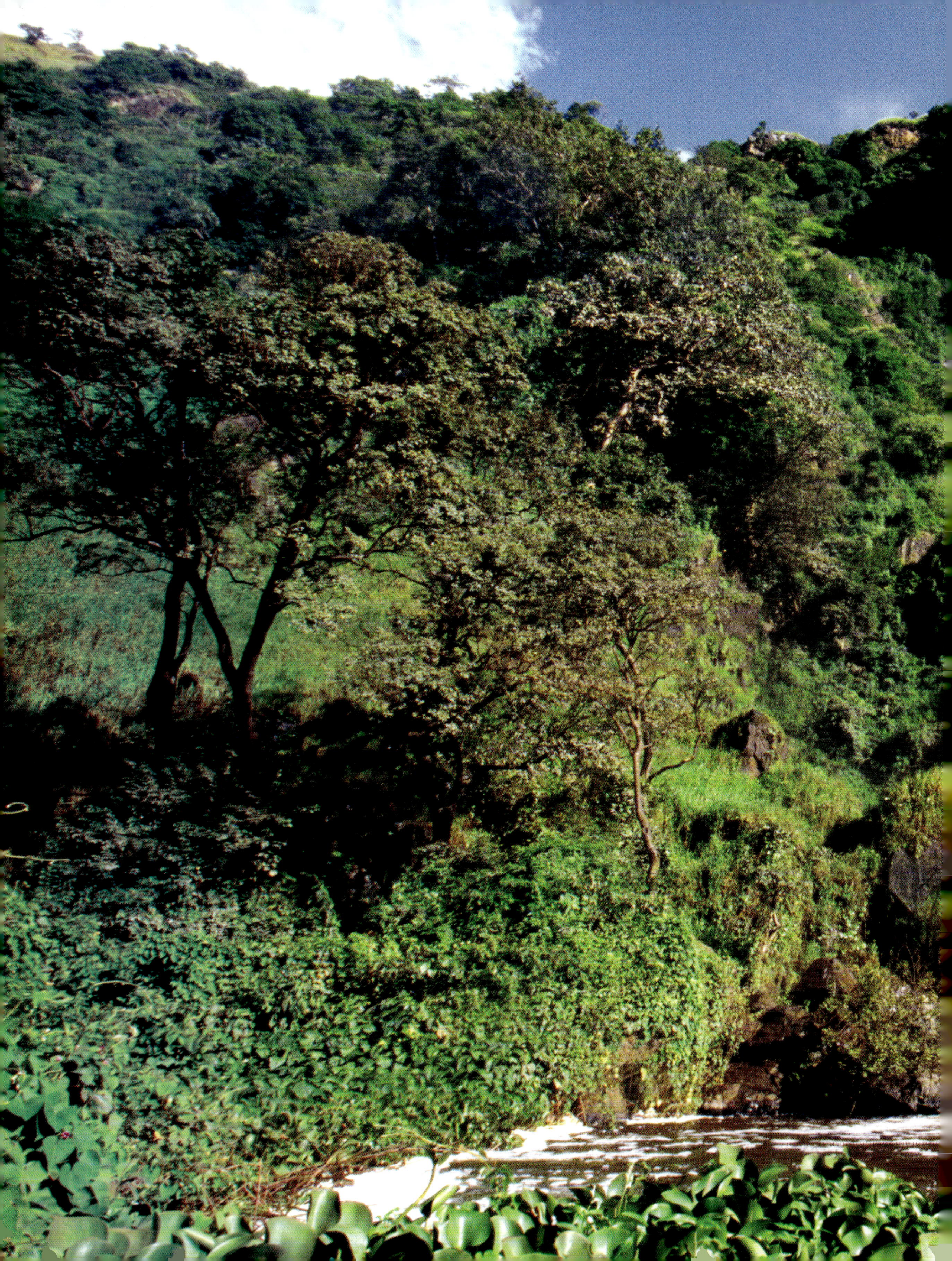

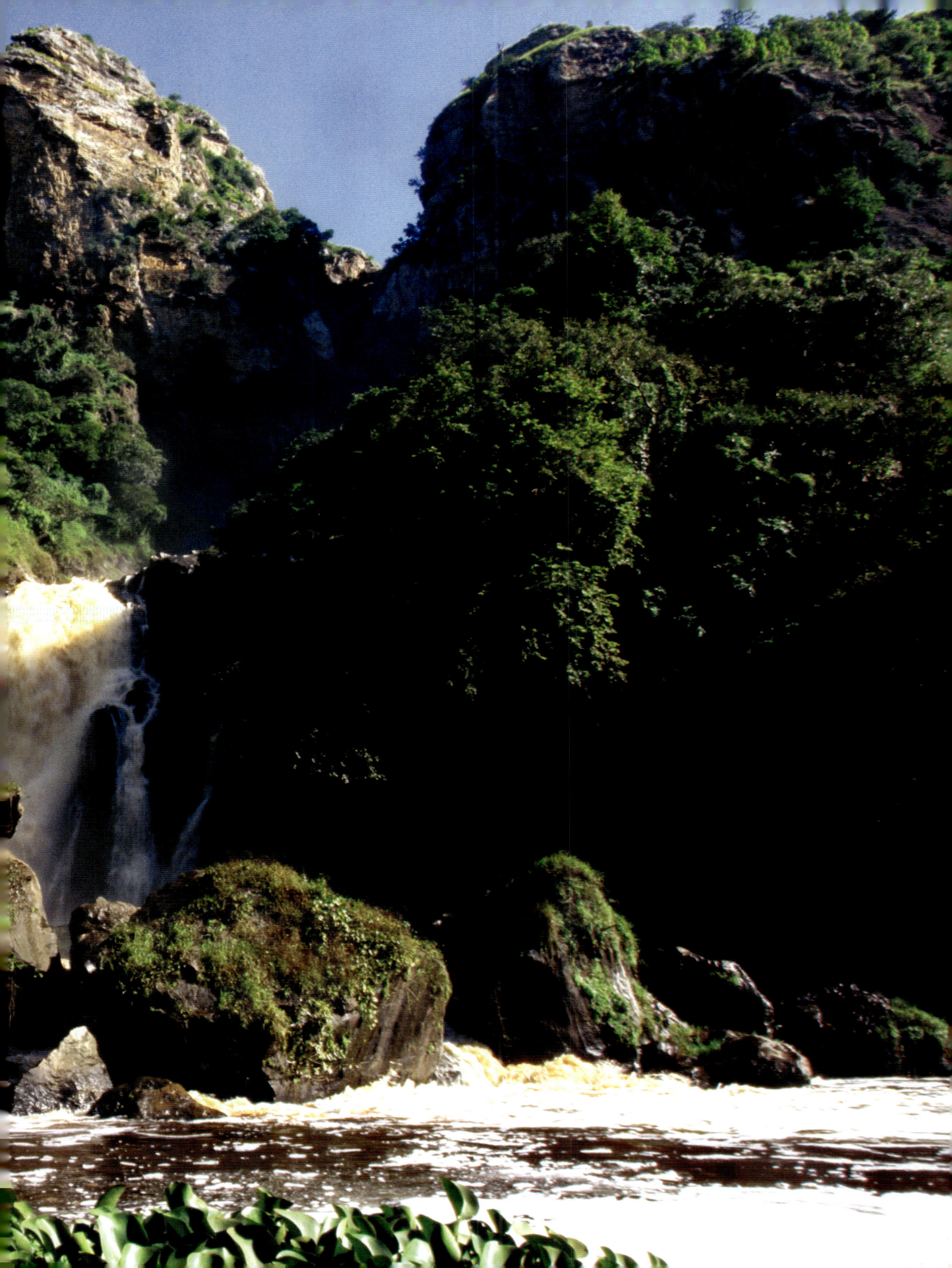

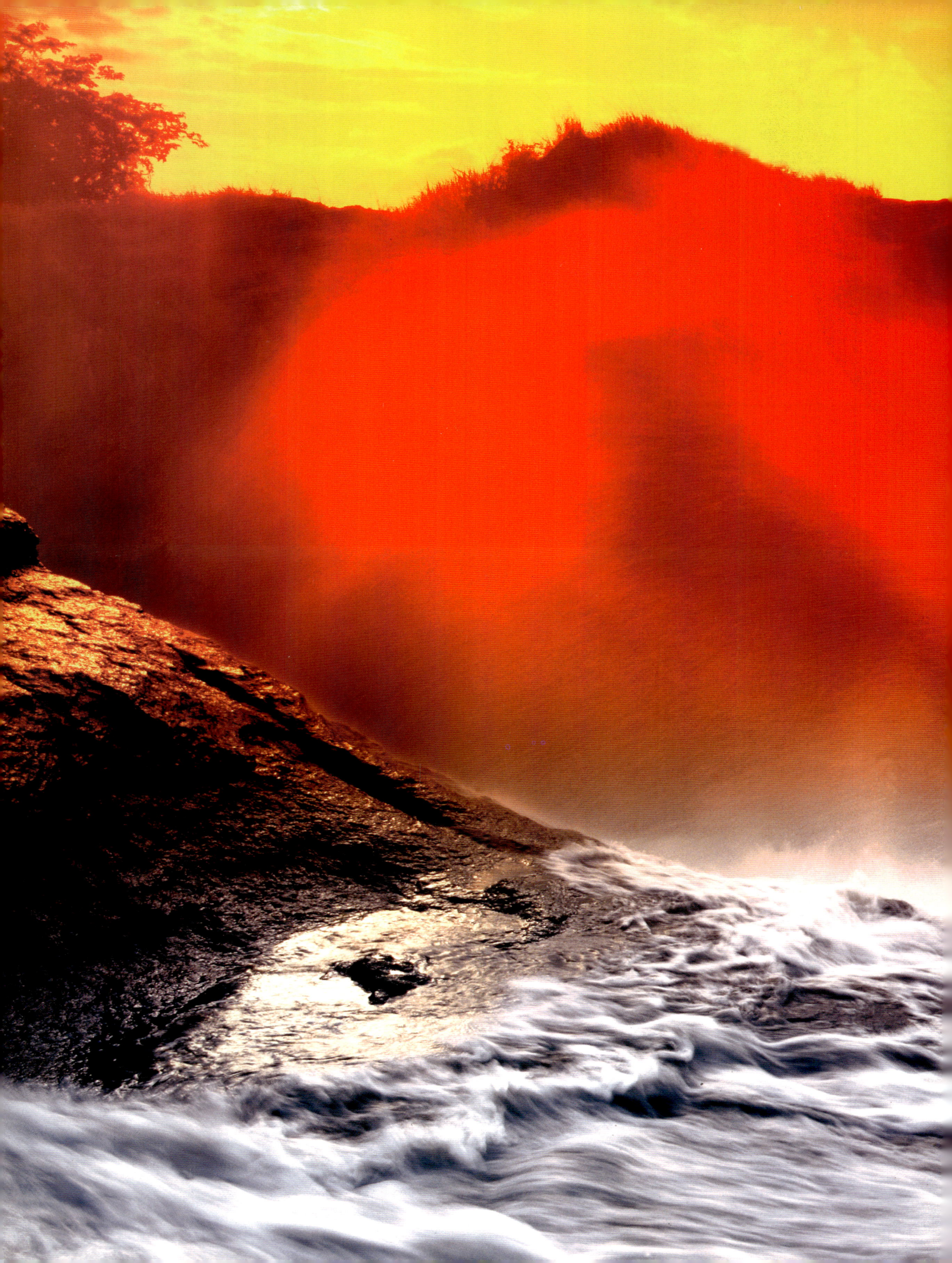

6. *Murchison Falls and the Northwest*

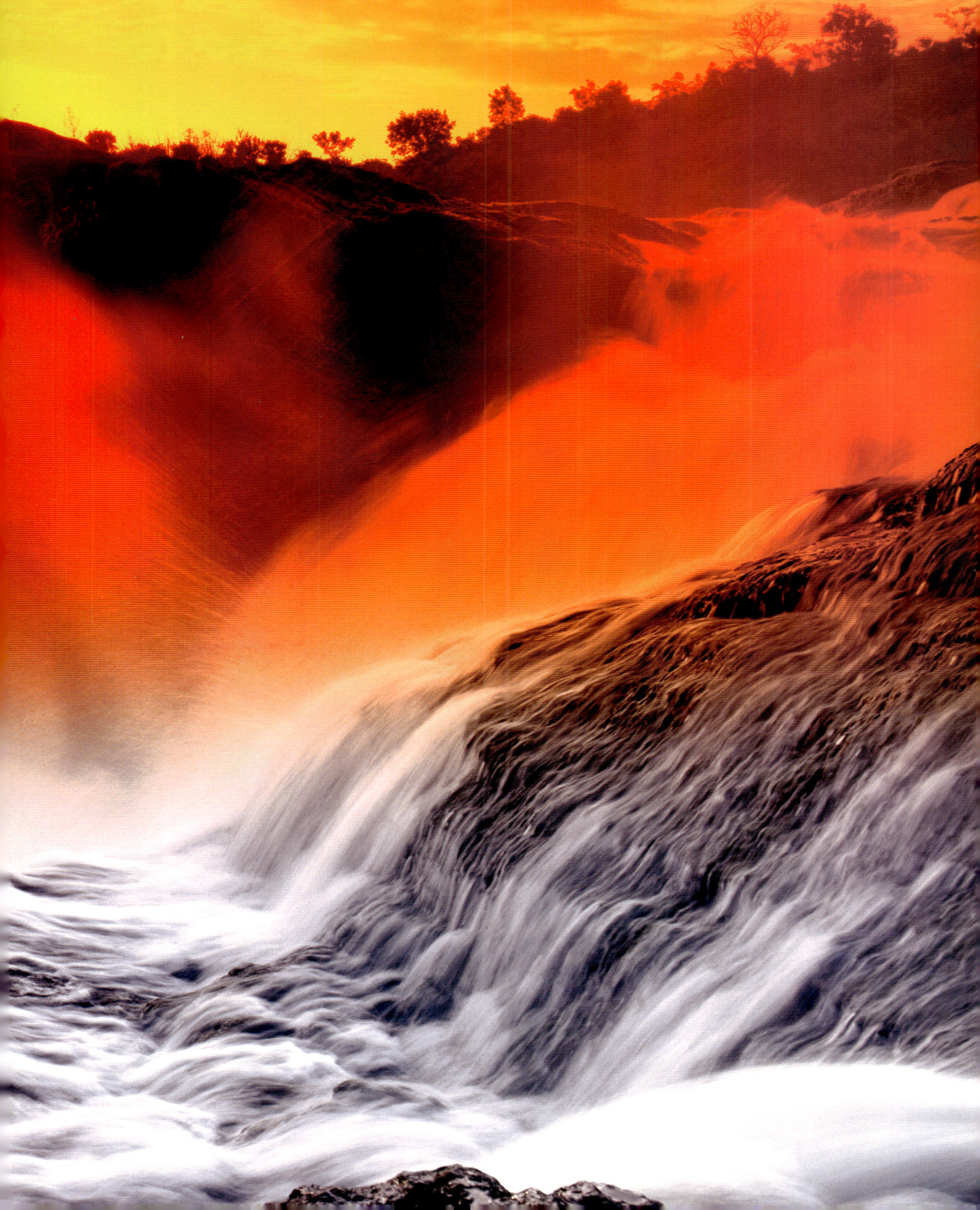

Previous pages: The thundering Murchison Falls, where the mighty Nile is funnelled through a 7-metre (23-foot) cleft in the rocks.

Below: Locals travelling down the Nile River by boat. In the foreground the sign for the station started by Charles Gordon and Emin Pasha in the 1800s.

Sir Samuel Baker, the first European to explore the lower reaches of the world's longest river, described the waterfall he named in honour of Sir Roderick Murchison (president of the Royal Geographical Society) as 'the most important object through the entire course of the While Nile'. True, there's not much in the way of competition for this accolade, but Murchison Falls is undeniably one of the most spectacular cascades in Africa. Here, the world's longest river, following its hitherto wide and sluggish course between Lakes Kyoga and Albert, is funnelled through a seven-metre (23-foot) gap in the rift escarpment, exploding out of the other side in a brutally energetic plume of cacophonous white foam.

Overhung by a permanent mist-cloud and subtly hued rainbow, this thunderous 43 metre (141 ft) waterfall forms the centrepiece of Uganda's largest conservation area, Murchison Falls National Park. Situated to the northwest of Kampala, this spectacular 3,840-square-kilometre (1,483-square-mile) park protects some of Africa's wildest and most pristine scenery, while its tangled plains, rolling palm-studded hills and sweltering forests support an abundant and diverse fauna, with some 76 mammal and 480 bird species recorded to date. But the park's dominant geographic feature is the mighty Nile, which bisects it from east to west for a distance of 115 kilometres (70 miles), its banks fringed by brooding borassus palms, lush riparian woodland dominated by leafy mahogany and fig trees, and dense beds of papyrus, before it flows into the northeastern tip of Lake Albert and then out again towards the Sudanese border.

An unforgettable highlight of any visit to Murchison Falls is the twice-daily launch trip that follows the Nile for 17 kilometres (10 miles) from the park headquarters at Paraa to the base of the waterfall. As the boat chugs along the beautiful river, gargantuan crocodiles leer menacingly from the sandbars, conferences of hippo grunt in the shallows, docile waterbuck and squint-eyed buffalo stare on in bemusement, and an occasional elephant or giraffe makes its way down to drink. The birdlife is fantastic, with dazzling red-throated bee-eaters breeding in the mud-banks, pied kingfishers hovering effortlessly above the water, fish eagles emitting their memorable piercing duet, African skimmers darting above the water surface, and a variety of herons, plovers, geese, waders and cormorants pacing the shore. For those fortunate enough to see one, however, the undoubted avian star of the park in the shoebill, a prehistoric-looking slate-grey papyrus dweller whose gigantic proportions are matched by its bizarre clog-sized bill. This feast of wildlife viewing climaxes at a rock below the falls, where the power of the roaring water is awesome.

In the 1960s, Murchison Falls harboured Africa's densest elephant population, an estimated 16,000 head at a density of four individuals per square kilometre. A 1969 aerial census counted 26,500 buffalo, 16,000

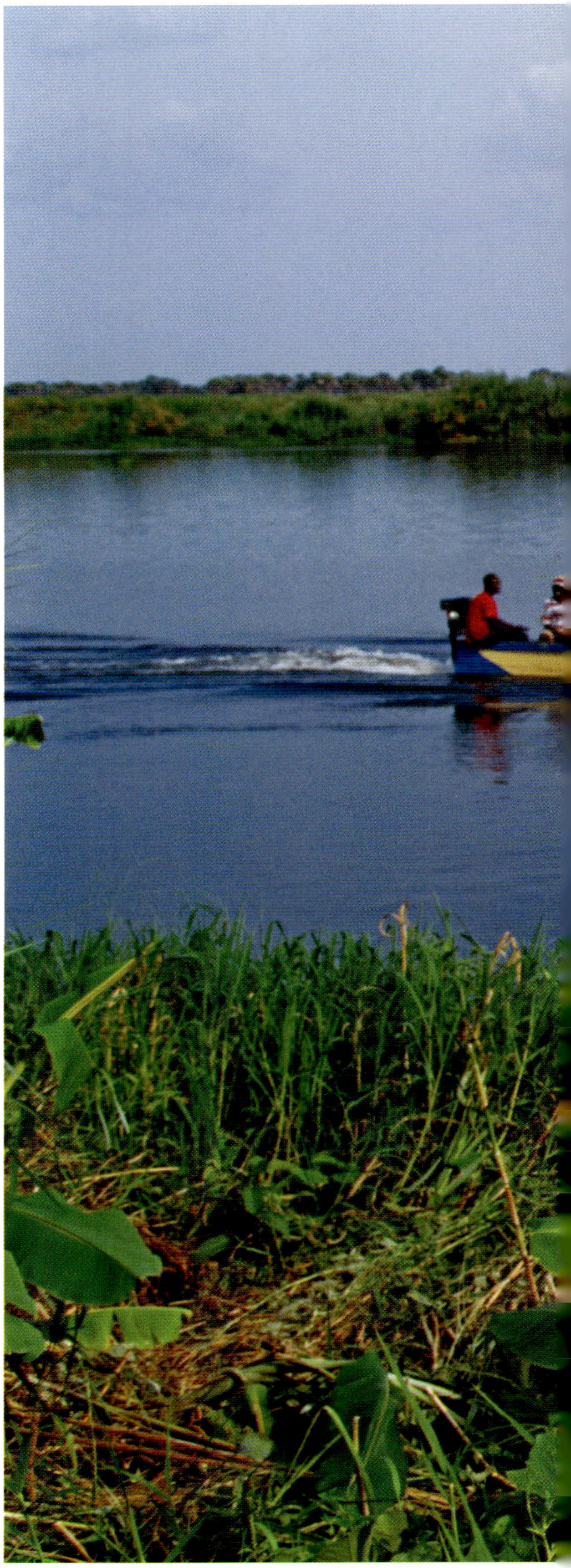

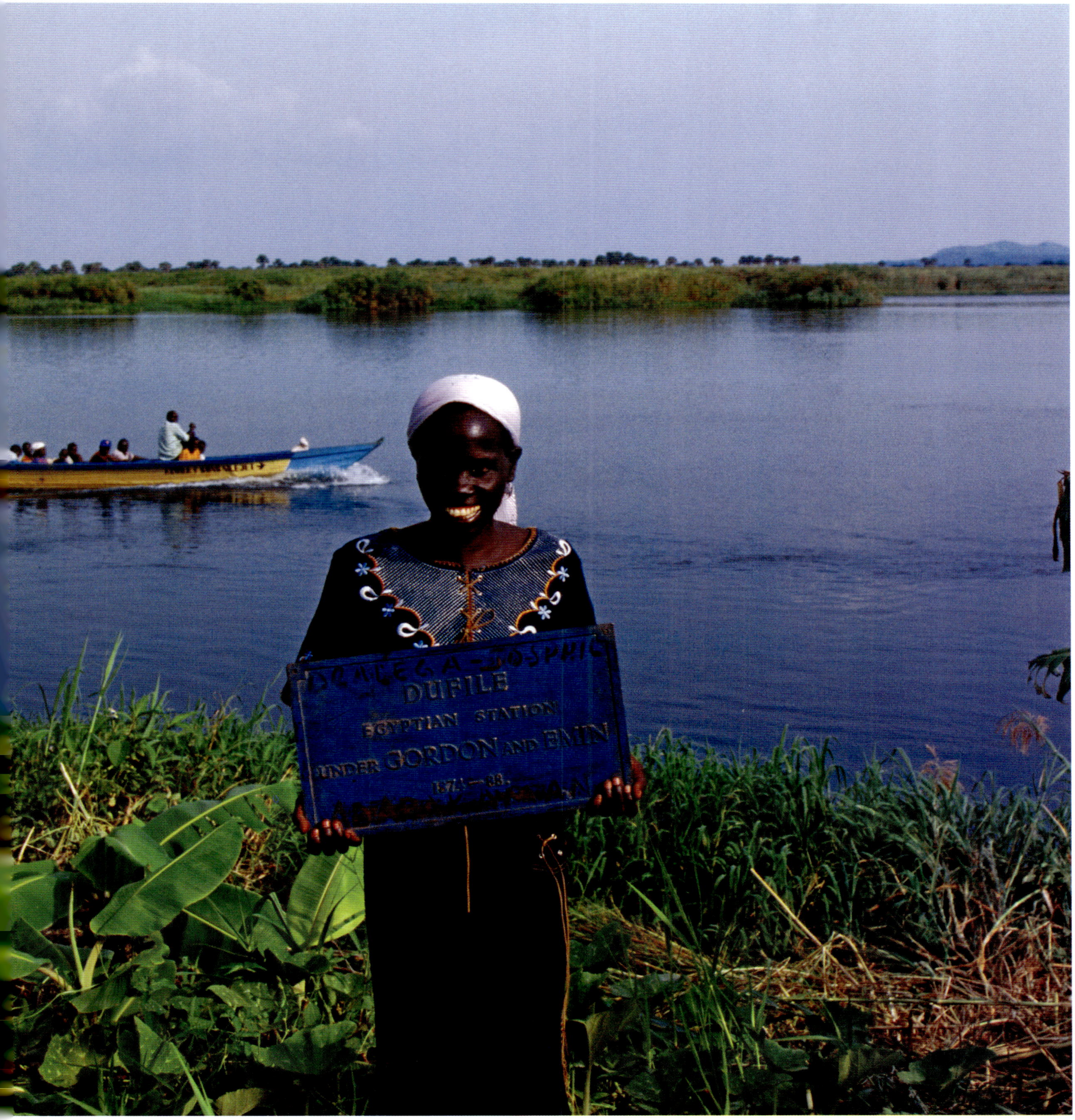
DUFILE
EGYPTIAN STATION
UNDER GORDON AND EMIN

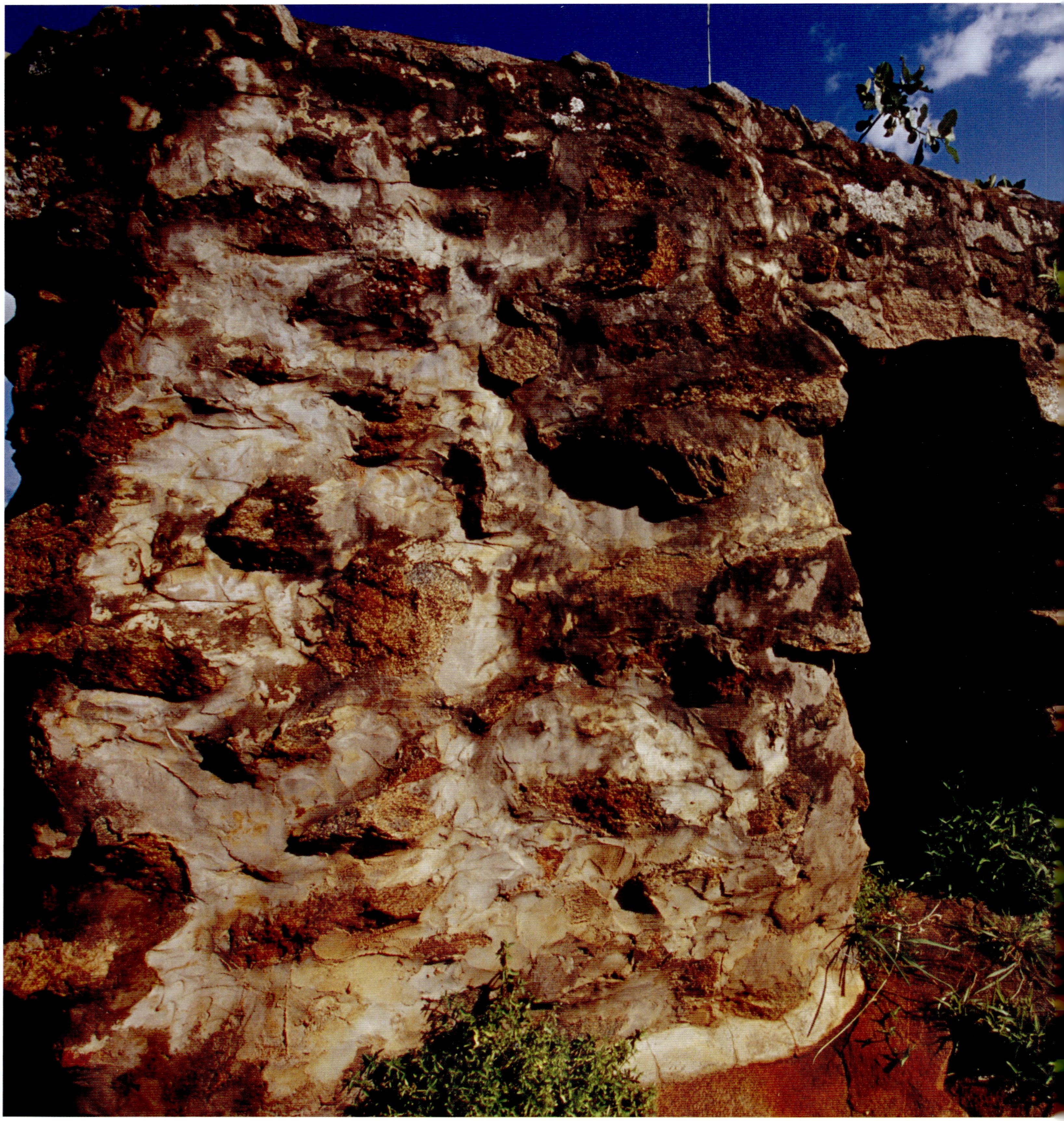

Below: Remains of the building stands with a 700-metre-long (2,300 foot) defence ditch and rampart, which enclose a stately tree filled park.

Following pages: Young man fishing in the Nile near Karuma Falls.

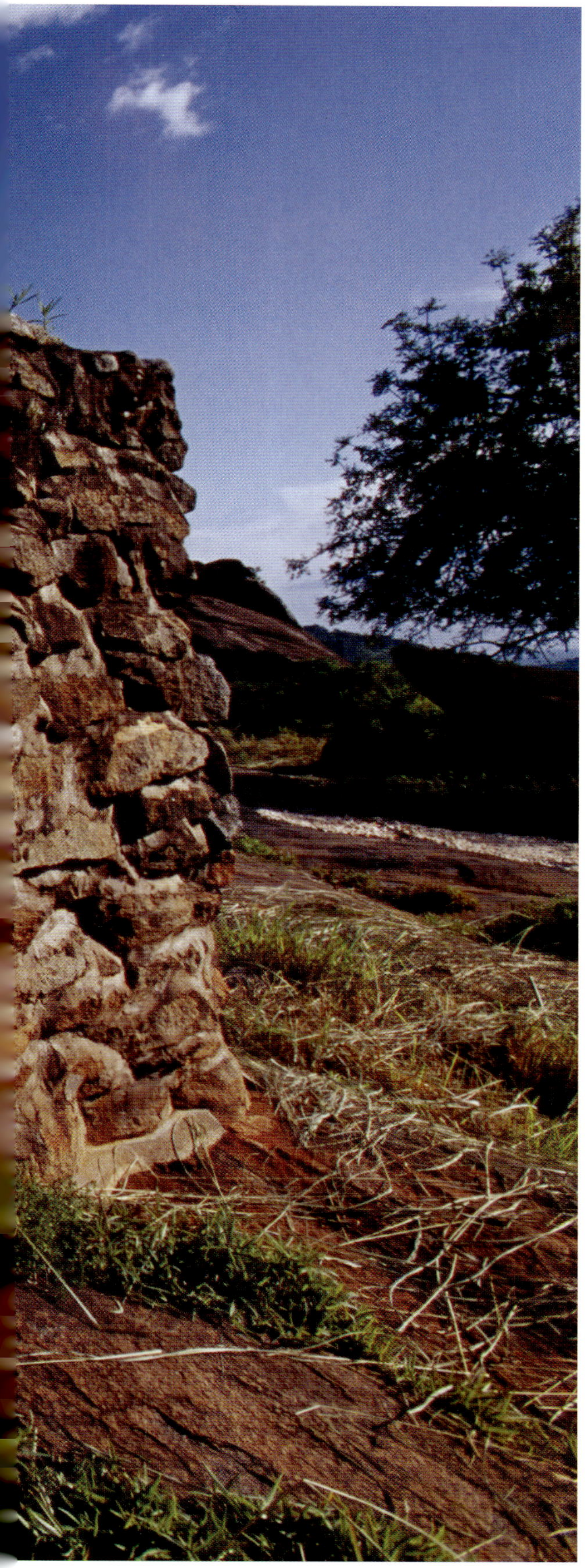

Jackson's hartebeest and 30,000 Uganda kob, and the park also harboured significant herds of black rhino, the highly endangered northern race of white rhino, and large numbers of lion. By the late 1980s, following two decades of civil war and poaching, the park contained just 250 elephant, 1,000 buffalo, 3,000 hartebeest and 6,000 kob, its rhino had been poached to oblivion, and dwindling giraffe and lion populations were headed the same way. Over the past few years, however, the great healer has worked its magic, and recent estimates place the elephant population at 1,200, while buffalo number around 10,000 and lion more than 200.

Wildlife concentrations are highest along the rough tracks of the Buligi and Wankwar circuits, which run along the north bank of the Nile Delta as it flows into Lake Albert. In the early morning, lions are often seen here, lying or walking conspicuously in the open grassland, though they tend to retreat into the shade in the heat of the day, while side-striped jackal are also quite common. Studded with tall borassus palms, the rolling grassland also supports large herds of buffalo and Uganda kob, some seriously impressive tuskers, and substantial numbers of the diminutive oribi antelope, shaggy-coated Defassa waterbuck and doleful-faced Jackson's hartebeest. The otherwise rare Rothschild's giraffe is often seen here in herds of 50-plus head, which stalk through the grassland looking for suitable browsing.

Game-viewing tracks south of the river are less rewarding, but they do offer access to a thrilling viewpoint above Murchison Falls, where the Nile can be seen gathering momentum before making that violent and deafening plunge into the Rift Valley floor. Otherwise, big game is less conspicuous here than the tsetse flies to which this beautiful park owes its existence. Tsetse flies were responsible for a serious outbreak of sleeping sickness between 1898 and 1915, and since the only effective way to combat this disease was to evacuate the region, some 13,000 square kilometres (5,000 square miles) were depopulated between 1907 and 1912. Murchison Falls National Park was gazetted forty years later, in July 1952, and although sleeping sickness has long since been eradicated, the park remains.

Most of the national park supports a cover of rolling savannah and tall grassland, though the bush becomes increasingly thick in the higher and wetter areas to the south and east. In the far southeast, this graduates into the Rabongo Forest, a closed canopy evergreen forest dominated by ironwoods, and inhabited by a varied selection of forest birds and primates, including black-and-white colobus and chimpanzee. Although Rabongo is seldom visited by tourists, a few wooden bandas are available for hire in a forest glade overlooking a pretty stream, and chimp tracking and other guided forest walks are available.

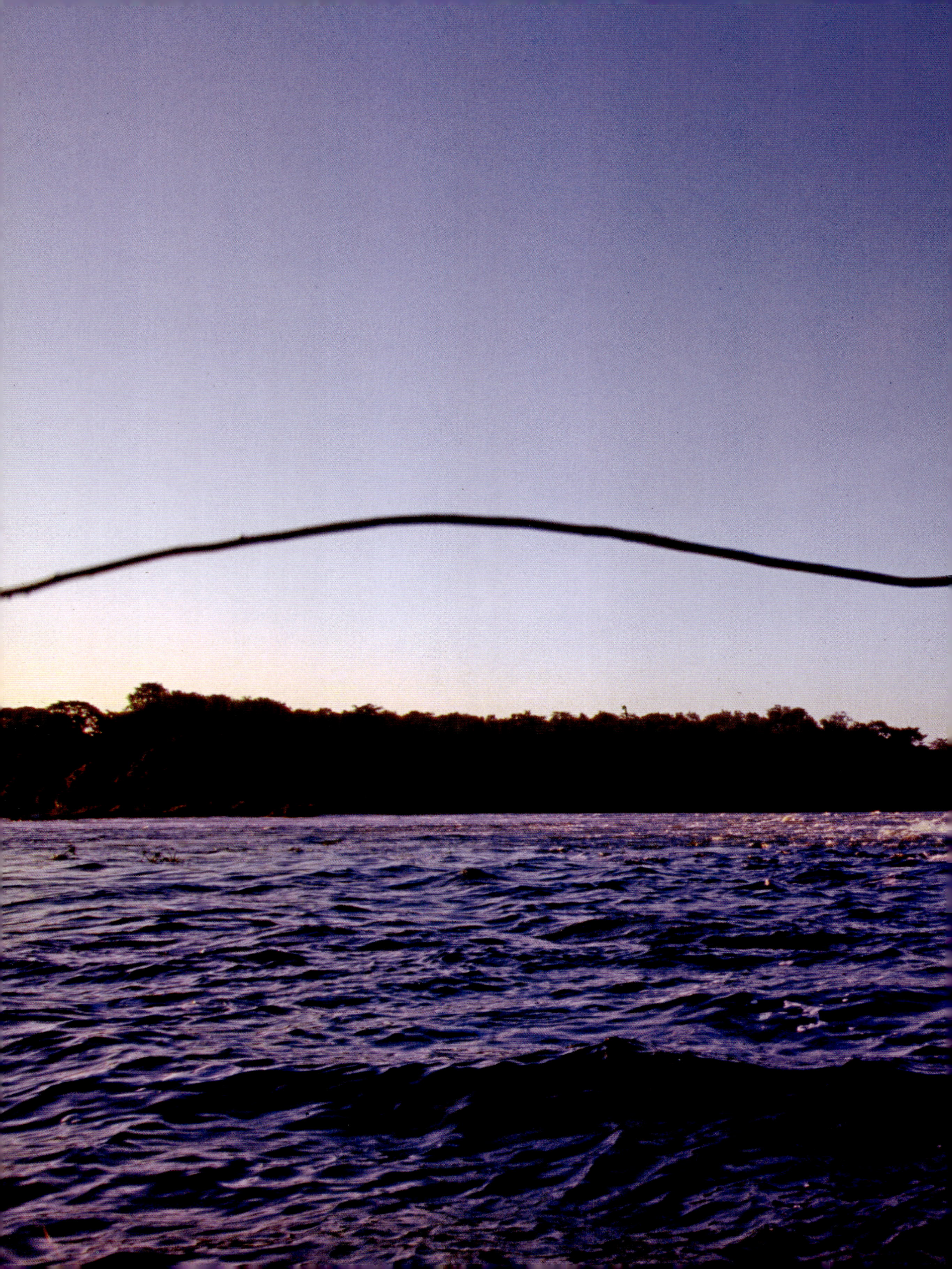

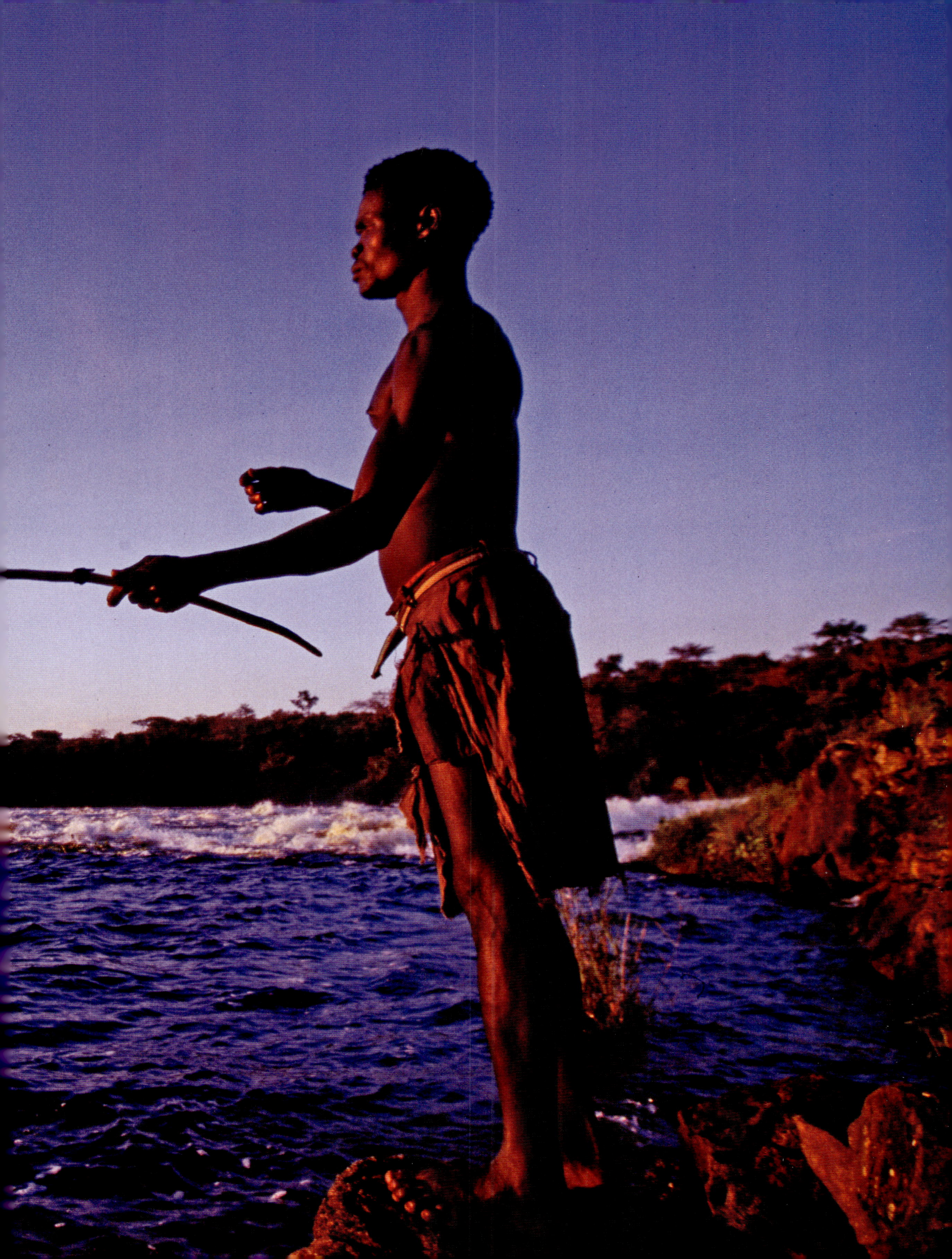

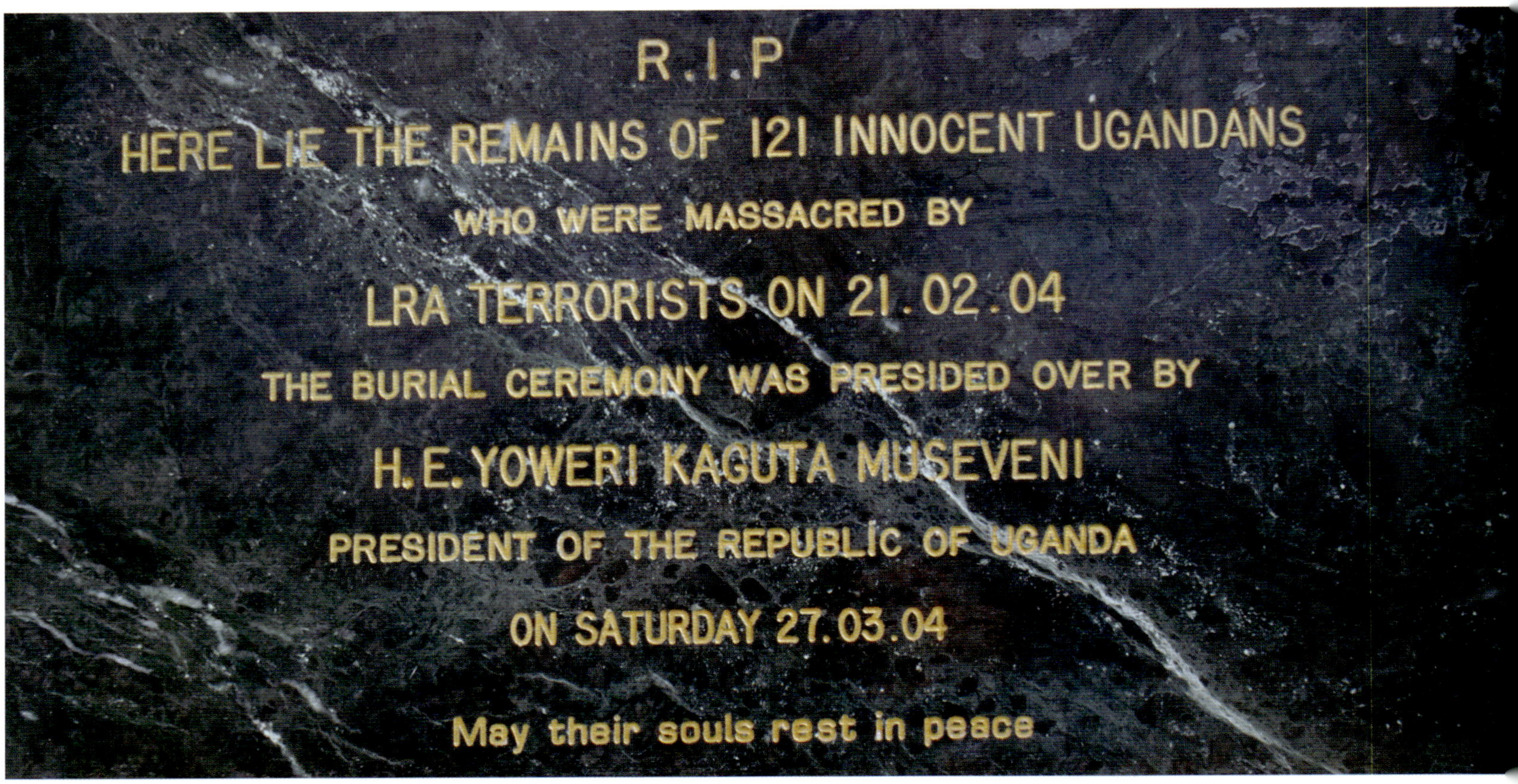

Above and opposite: Ugandan President H.E Yoweri Museveni unveiled a monument in September 2004 at Banyoni camp.

Even better for forest birds and primates is the Budongo Forest Reserve, which abuts the park's southern border, where it is bisected by the main road to Masindi and Kampala. This legendary forest supports a population of around 800 chimpanzees, and one chimp community has been habituated for tourist visits from the Kanyiyo Pabidi campsite, which lies alongside the main Masindi road. Other common primates include the red-tailed monkey, blue monkey and black-and-white colobus, while scaly-tailed flying squirrel, tree pangolin, potto, black-fronted duiker, blue duiker and giant forest squirrel are less easily seen .

But Budongo is best known perhaps for its checklist of 366 bird species, which includes a remarkable 60 west-central African specials recorded from fewer than five locales in East Africa. The best base for birders is the Busingiro tourist site, which lies about 40 kilometres west of Masindi. Indeed the so-called Royal Mile, 10 kilometres from Busingiro, is often cited as offering the finest forest birding in Uganda. With such riches on display, it is difficult to talk in terms of highlights, but even a short visit is likely to yield the likes of Cassin's hawk-eagle, white-thighed hornbill, yellow-footed flycatcher and a trio of colourful forest kingfishers (chocolate-backed, blue-breasted and African dwarf). Because the forest has been opened up by sawmills over many years, a network of forest roads and tracks makes exploring – and bird-watching – easy.

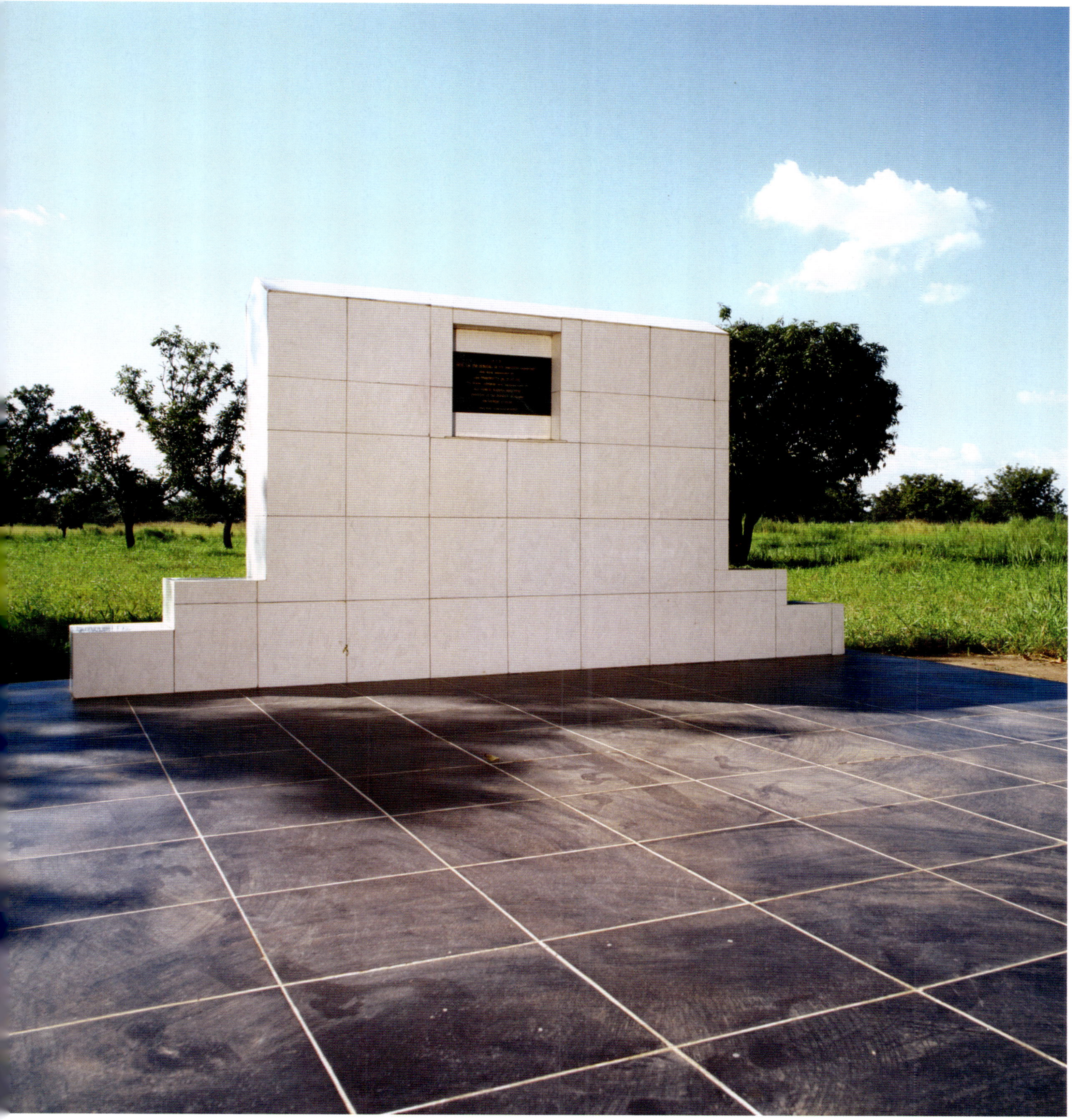

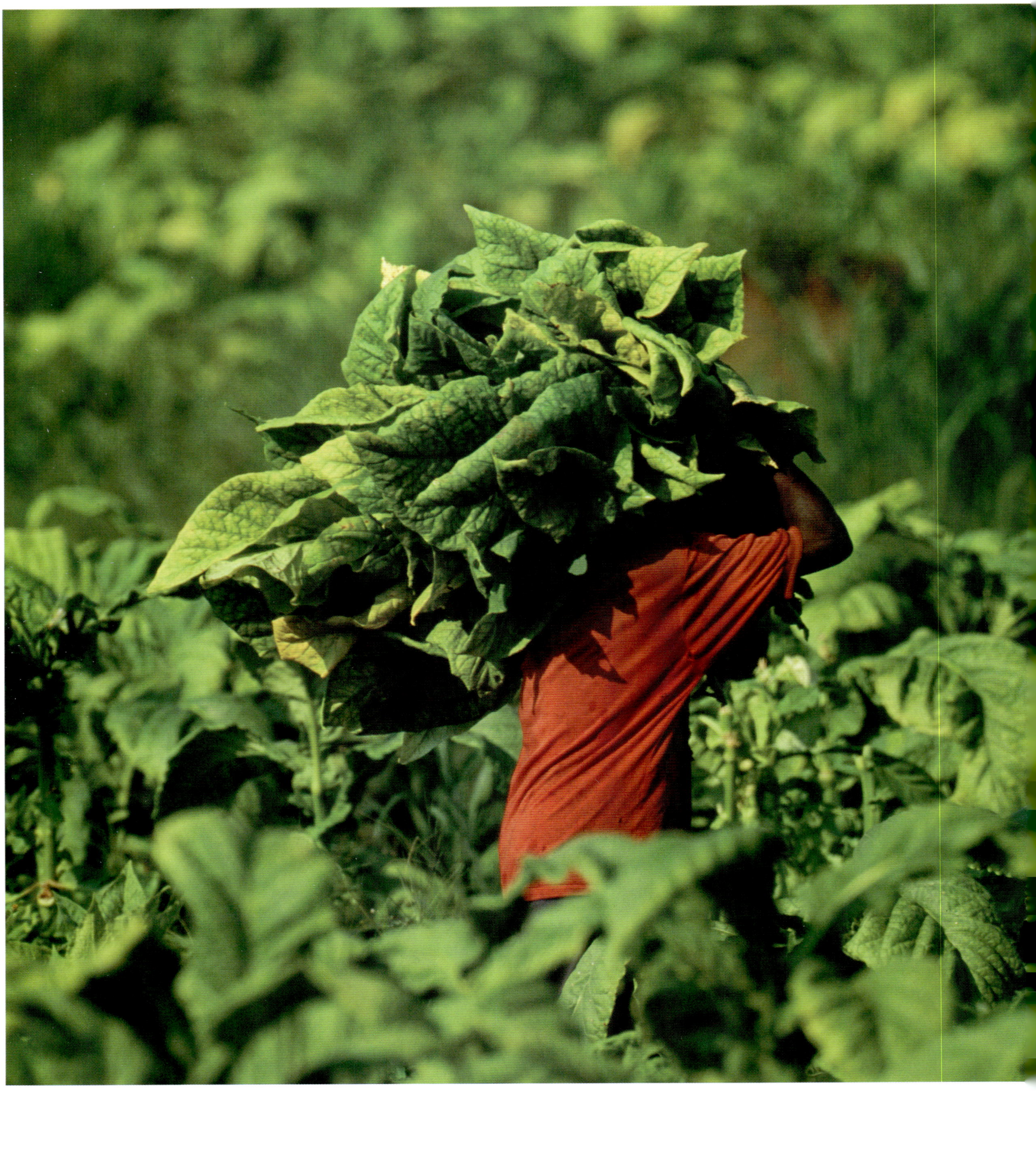

Opposite: The West Nile region, is Uganda's main tobacco-growing area.

Following pages: Mt Otzi.

Busingiro lies alongside a longer and relatively little used road that connects Masindi to Murchison Falls National Park via a spectacular descent of the Rift Valley escarpment, with views across the shimmering waters of Lake Albert to the distant DRC. The first European to see this vast 6,400-square-kilometre (2,500-square-mile) inland sea was the aforementioned Baker, who named it after Queen Victoria's consort. The lake runs along the Rift Valley floor for 160 kilometres (100 miles) – far too long for one end to be seen from the other – and is enclosed on either side by the precipitous Rift walls, which appear as hazy blue ranges from the opposite shore. It is fed by the Victoria Nile and the Semliki River, and forms the source of the Albert Nile, which runs north into Sudan to converge with the Blue Nile at Khartoum.

On the shores of Lake Albert, west of Kigorobya, are the Kibiro hot springs and salt works, where traditional salt-extraction methods are still practised. The lake, particularly the northern tip near Murchison Falls National Park, is a fishing centre, with plentiful tilapia, tiger fish, and Nile perch (known locally as mputa). The perch in particular grow to huge sizes, and many anglers have set records there, such as the 102 kilo (225 lb) specimen taken on rod and line from a boat, and some of up to 165 kilos (364 lbs) snared by net fishermen.

The main port on the Uganda shore is Butiaba, whose backwater status today belies its significance as a transport hub in the colonial era, when it was the terminus for a regular steamer service that extended the Mombasa-Malindi trade route into the Congo, and was also a key landing site for early seaplane flights between Cairo and East Africa. Butiaba is also where Humphrey Bogart and Katherine Hepburn were based during the filming of The African Queen, and where in January 1953 a plane carrying Ernest Hemingway and his wife Mary crash landed and burst into flames, an accident that led to a spate of premature obituaries for the American writer.

The Hemingways spent several days recuperating from the plane crash at the Masindi Hotel, a still functional colonial edifice that remains an important landmark in the town of Masindi, which most visitors pass through en route to Murchison Falls and the Budongo Forest Reserve. Aside from this characterful old hotel and its shady grounds, Masindi is a fairly humdrum place, though Kihande Hill just outside the town centre is now the site of the Bunyoro king's palace. En route between Masindi and Kampala lies the sprawling expanse of Lake Kyoga, a large but rather amorphous body of shallow water flowed through by the Victoria Nile before it reaches Murchison falls.

Travellers heading between Masindi and Fort Portal must pass through Hoima, which lies a few kilometres from Mparo, the capital from where

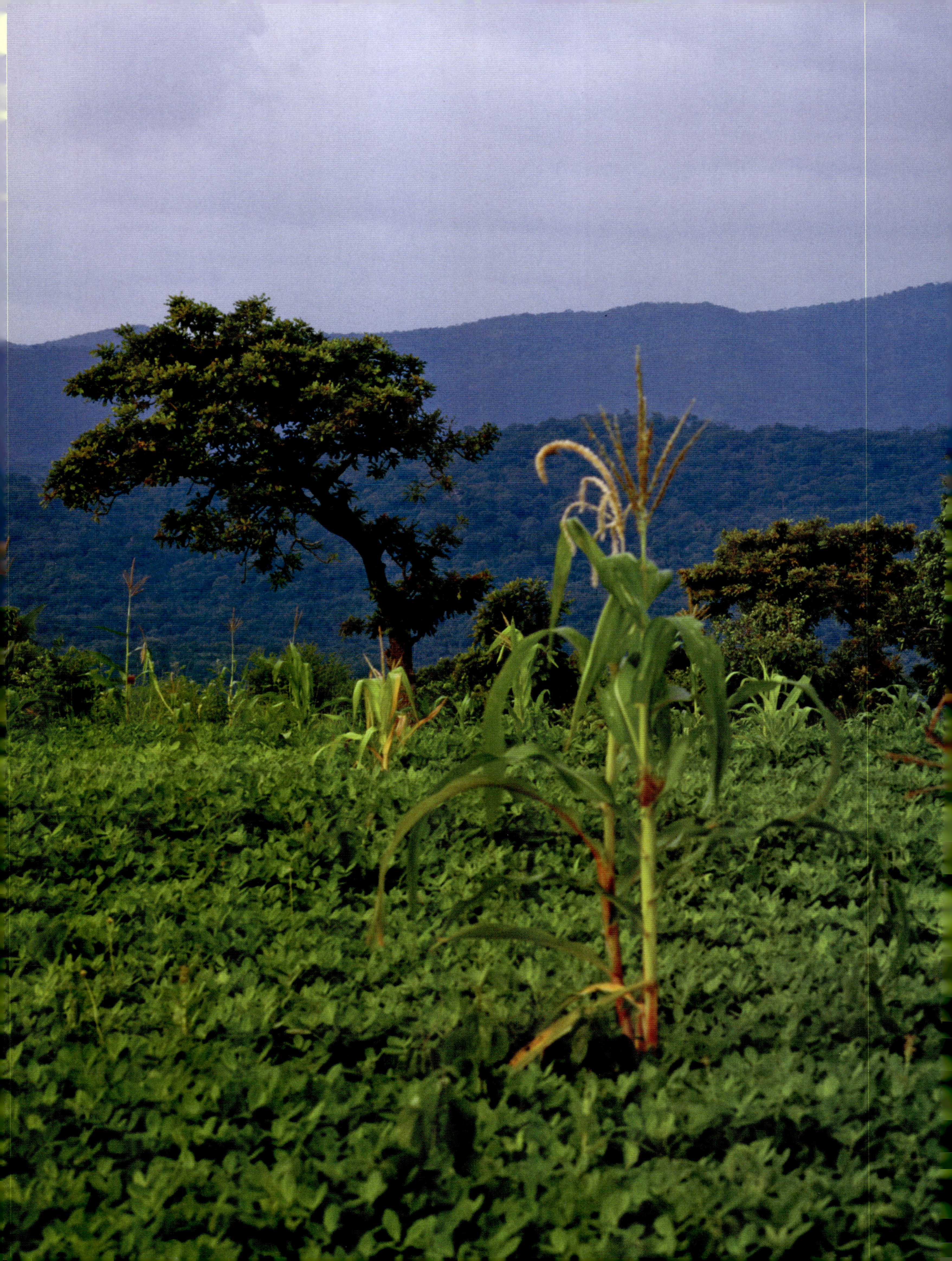

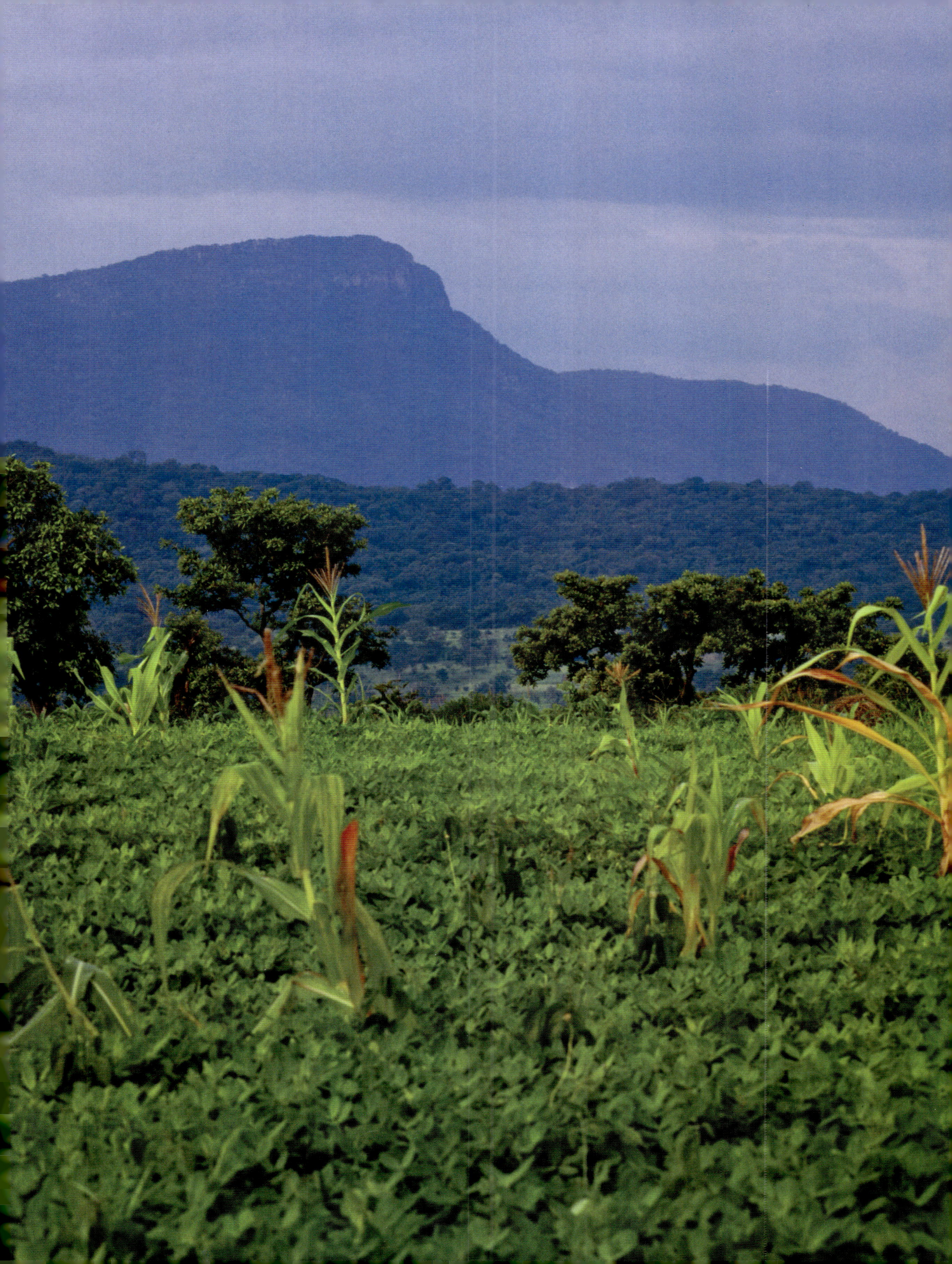

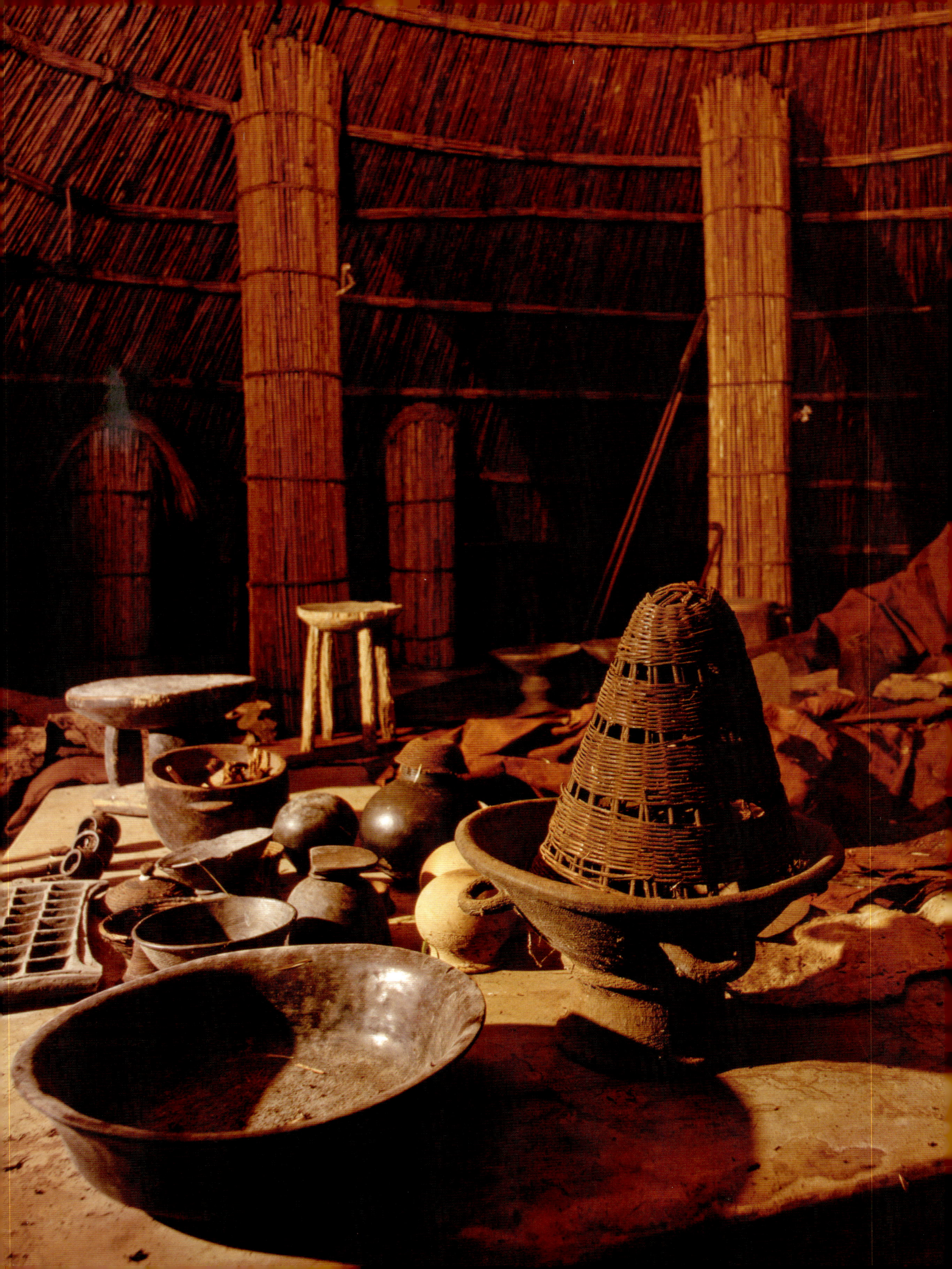

Opposite: Mparo treasures.

Below: Plaque marks the spot where Kabalega and the Emin Pasha met in 1877.

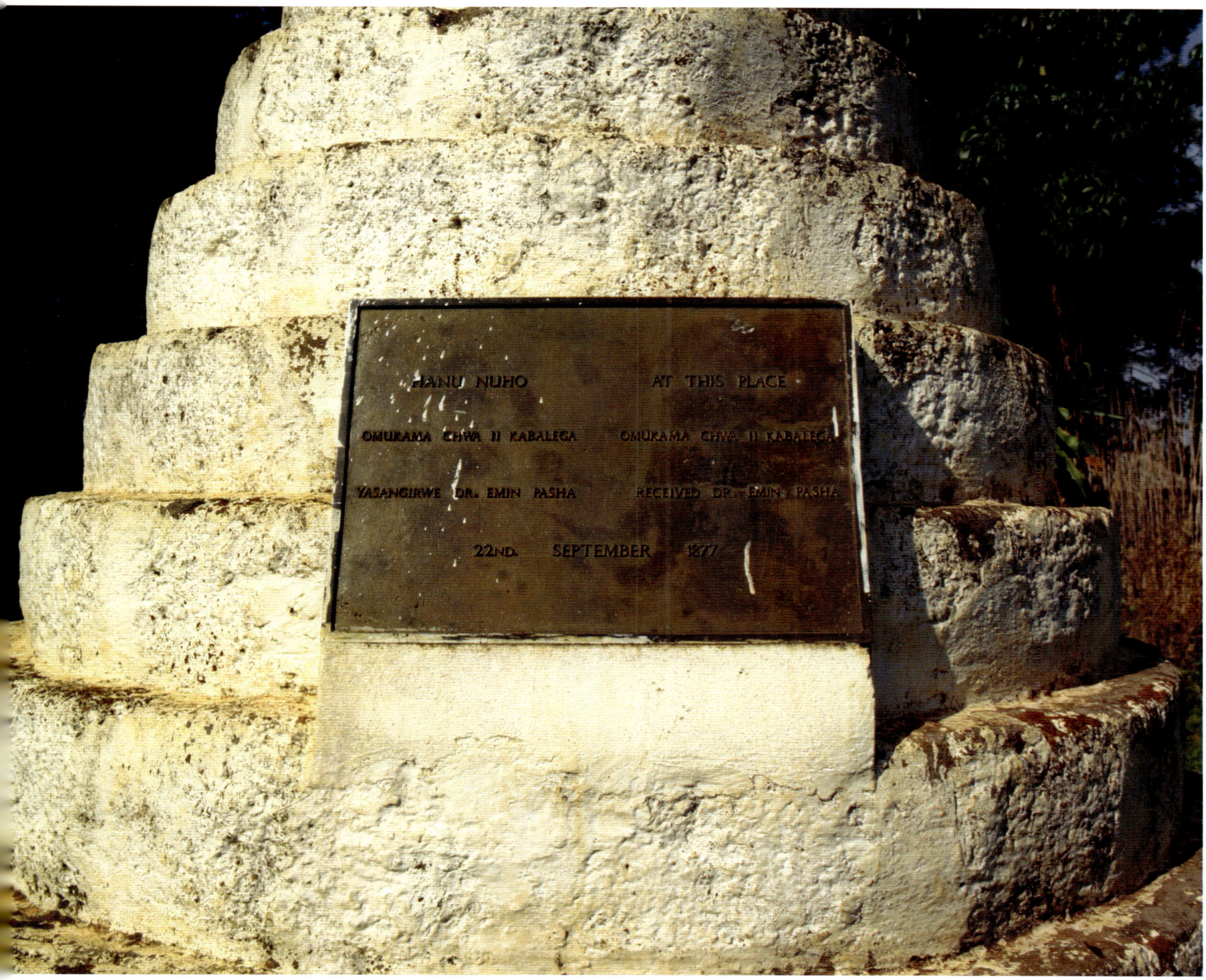

the Banyoro leader Kabalega led raids into the neighbouring Toro and Buganda kingdoms before his capture in 1894. The former capital now houses the Mparo Tombs, where Kabalega and several of his successors (including his son, Tito Winyi) are buried. The burial site is a large enclosure made of natural materials, and Kabalega's grave is housed in a domed construction similar to that of the Kasubi Tombs in Kampala, although smaller. The grave is surrounded by many of Kabalega's personal effects. Outside the main enclosure is a plaque marking the spot where Kabalega met the Emin Pasha in 1877.

Opposite: Elephants in Murchison Falls National Park are thriving again.

Below: African Buffalo provides a handy perch for the white cattle egret and a flock of piapiacs.

Following pages: Sunset over the River Nile, the most prominent feature of Murchison Falls National Park.

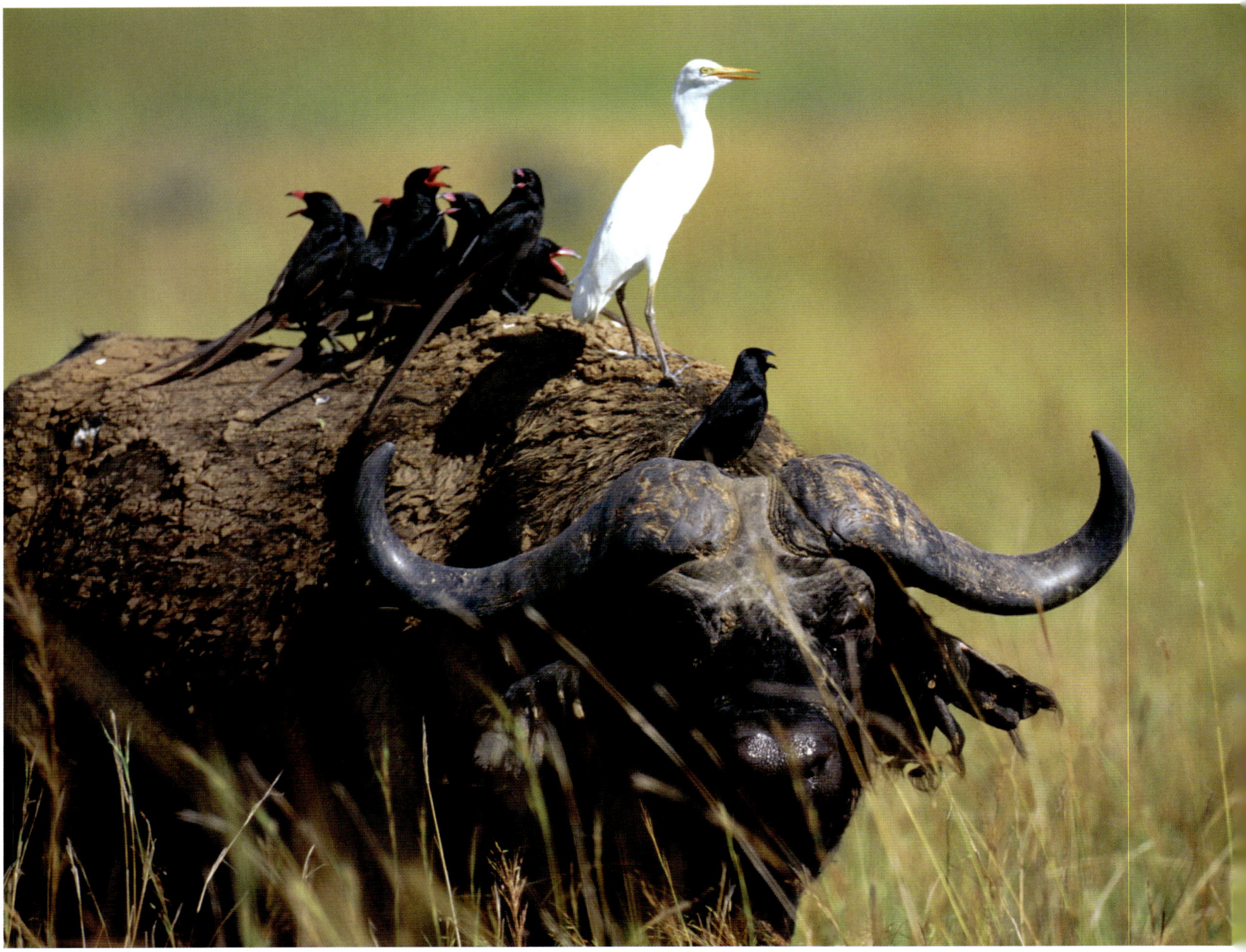

Although most of the area north of Murchison features wide plains and is sparse in population, around the towns of Gulu, Kitgum, and Lira agriculture is well developed, with many small farms growing simsim (sesame), groundnuts, millet, and cotton. Gulu is the largest Ugandan town in the north, but it sees few tourists. There is an airstrip, a police station, and several lodgings. Throughout the town visitors can see and can buy some of the handicrafts of the area, including baskets, pottery, and ironwork. South of Gulu the road leads to the Karuma gate of Murchison Falls National Park, where the Nile cascades over 23 kilometres (14 miles) of rapids in a breathtaking maelstrom that includes the Karuma Falls and Goragung Falls.

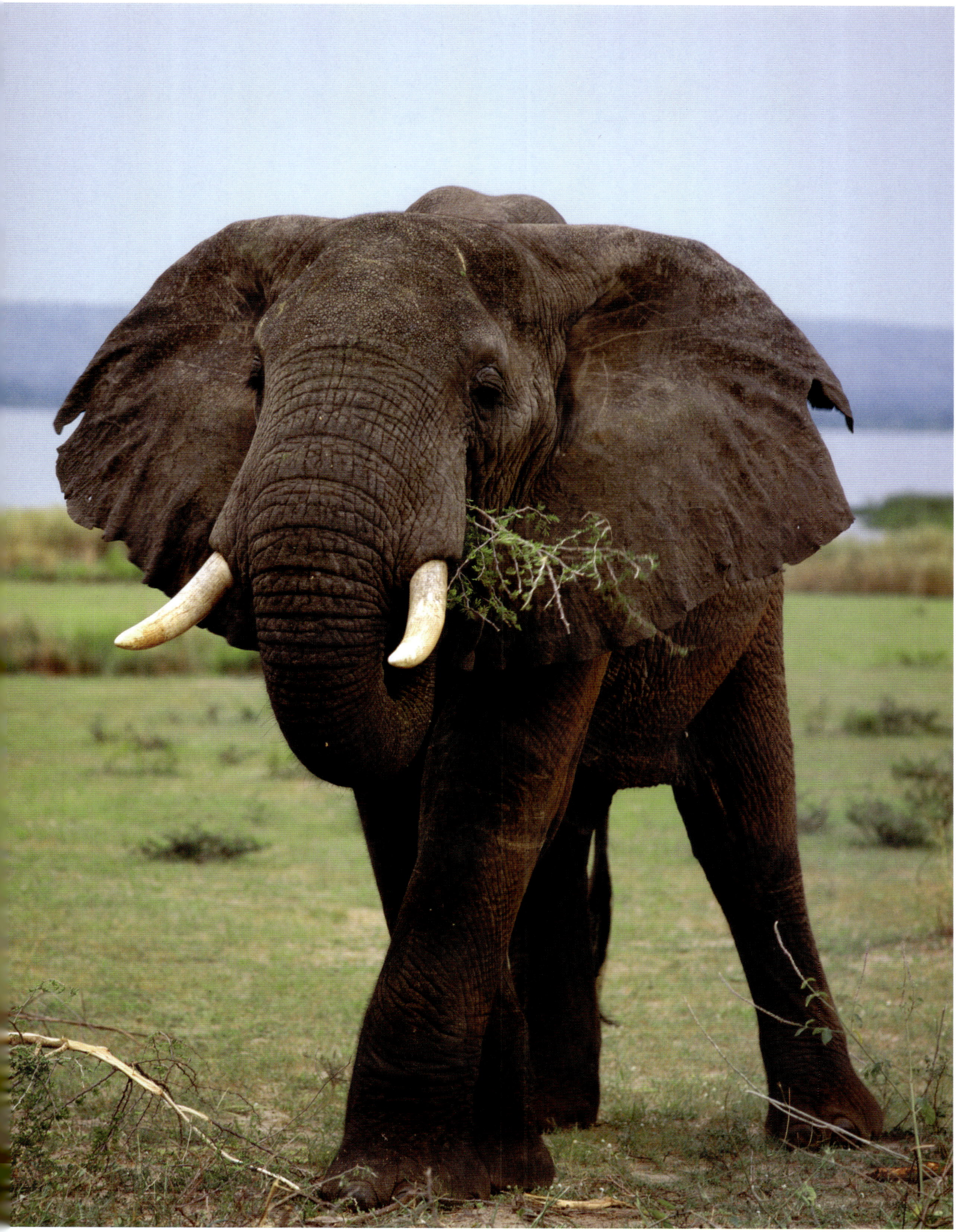

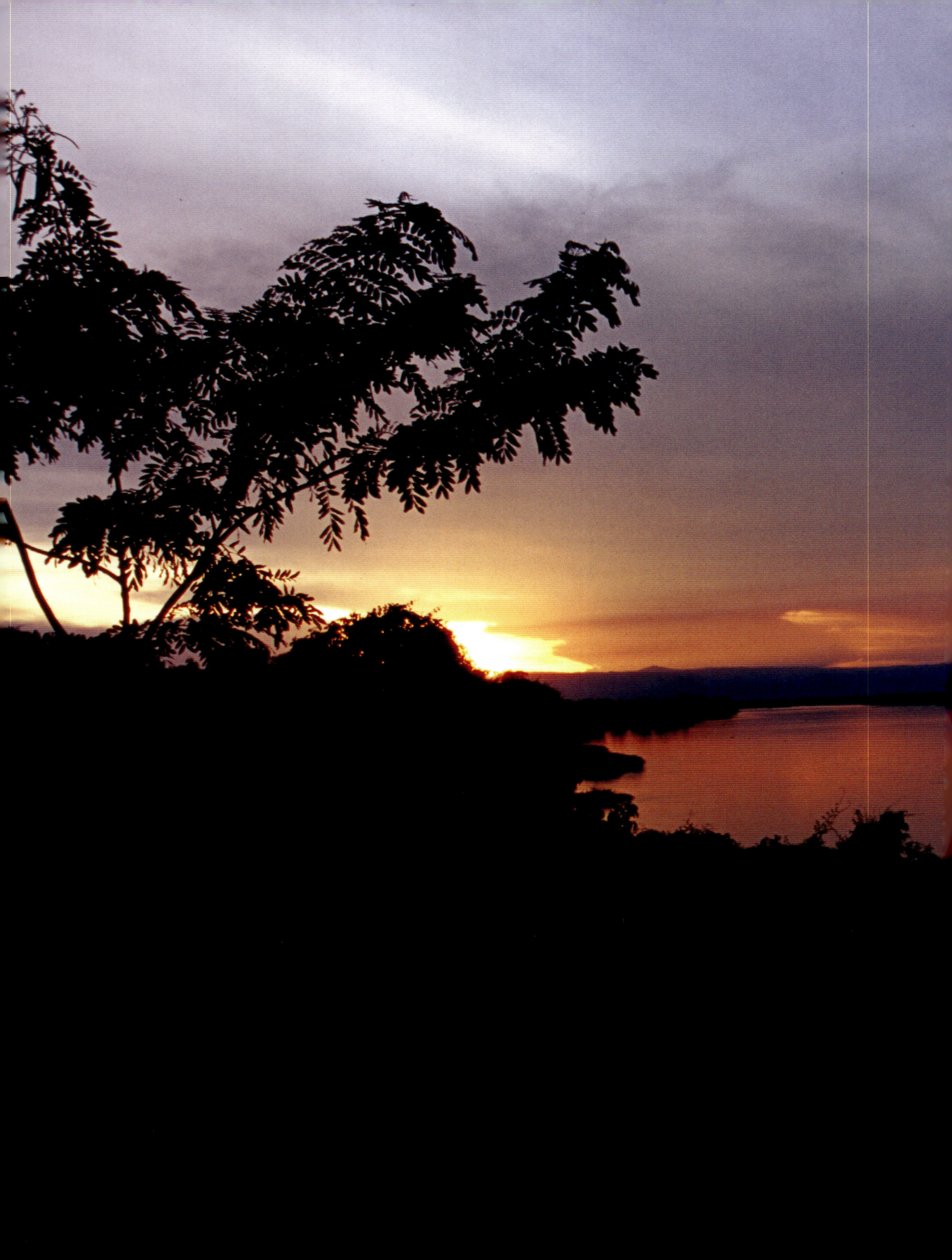

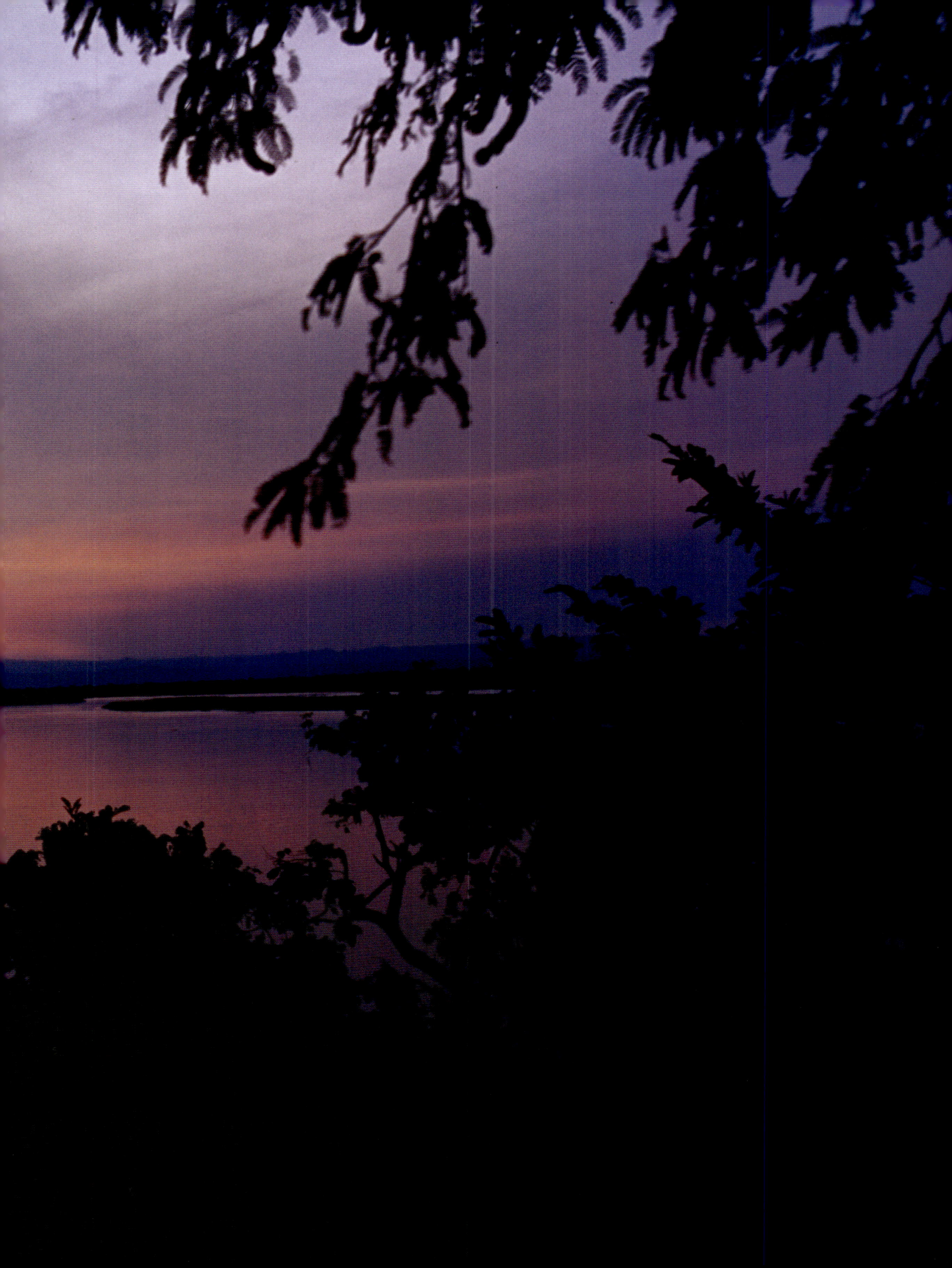

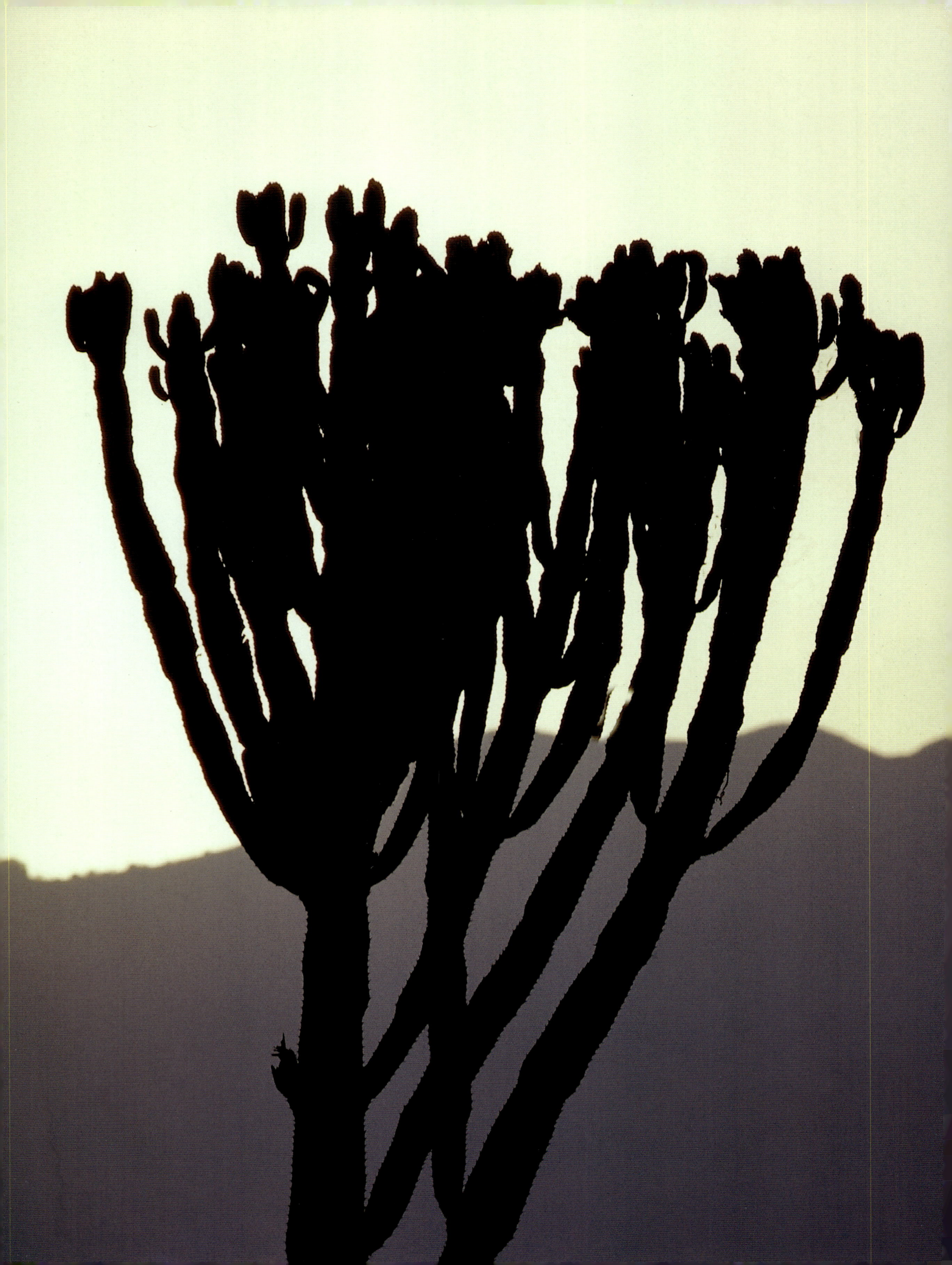

7. The East: Remote and Wild

Previous pages: Mount Moroto at dawn.

Right: Mount Elgon's summit crater, accessible to hikers as it requires no technical climbing skills.

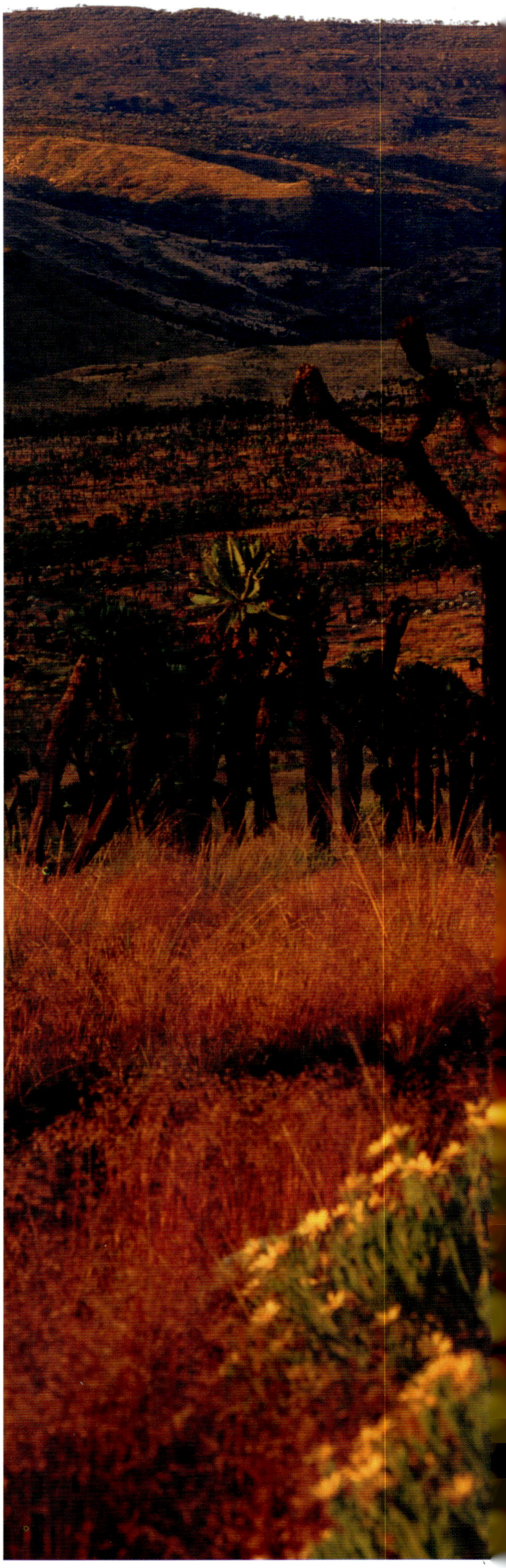

In 1892, the English soldier and explorer John Hanning Speke, following a lengthy stay at the Buganda capital of Kampala, undertook a 80 kilometres (50 mile) trek eastward along the shores of Lake Victoria to see the powerful waterfall that marked the beginning of a river known locally as Kiira, in reference to the loud roar it made as it plunged into the big gorge. Of course, locals knew nothing of where this river eventually led, or of its ages-long significance for humanity, but Speke recognized the roaring cascade as the point where the Nile started its 6,400-kilometre-long (4,000-mile) journey via Sudan and Egypt to the distant Mediterranean.

Speke described his discovery thus: 'We were well rewarded, for the "stones", as the Waganda call the falls, was by far the most interesting sight I had seen in Africa... It attracted one to it for hours – the roar of the waters, the thousands of passenger fish leaping at the falls with all their might, the Wasoga and Waganda fishermen coming out in boats and taking posts on all the rocks with rod and hook, hippopotami and crocodiles lying sleepily on the water, the ferry at work above the falls, and cattle driven down to drink and the margin of the lake, made... as interesting a picture as one could wish to see.'

The source of the White Nile – on which Sudan and Egypt have always depended for their livelihood and sheer existence – was probably the most hotly debated geographic riddle of the era of African exploration. And Speke's assertion that the Nile rose in Lake Victoria met with strong resistance in Europe, where acknowledged experts such as Sir Richard Burton and David Livingstone postulated a more southerly source near Lake Tanganyika. Only in 1874/5, when Henry Morton Stanley circumnavigated both great lakes, was Speke's hunch confirmed to be correct. By then, however, Speke had been dead for a full decade, victim of a self-inflicted gun wound – hunting accident or deliberate suicide, nobody knows for sure.

Speke had christened the site Ripon Falls, after a former president of the Royal Geographical Society. But as he noted, it was known locally as the Stones (Ejjinja, in the Luganda tongue), most probably in reference to the large sacrificial rock that can still be seen at the site. Ripon Falls is no longer, having been submerged during the construction of the hydro-electric Owen Falls Dam in 1947. But the old Luganda name of Ejjinja survives, albeit slightly corrupted, as that of the country's second largest city, Jinja, which sprawls attractively along the east bank of the river as it departs the lake.

The first informal European settlement at Jinja was founded in 1900, when the site was selected as the best place for the telegraph line between Kisumu and Kampala to cross the Nile. A year later, the colonial governor Sir Harry Johnston relocated his Busoga headquarters from Iganga –

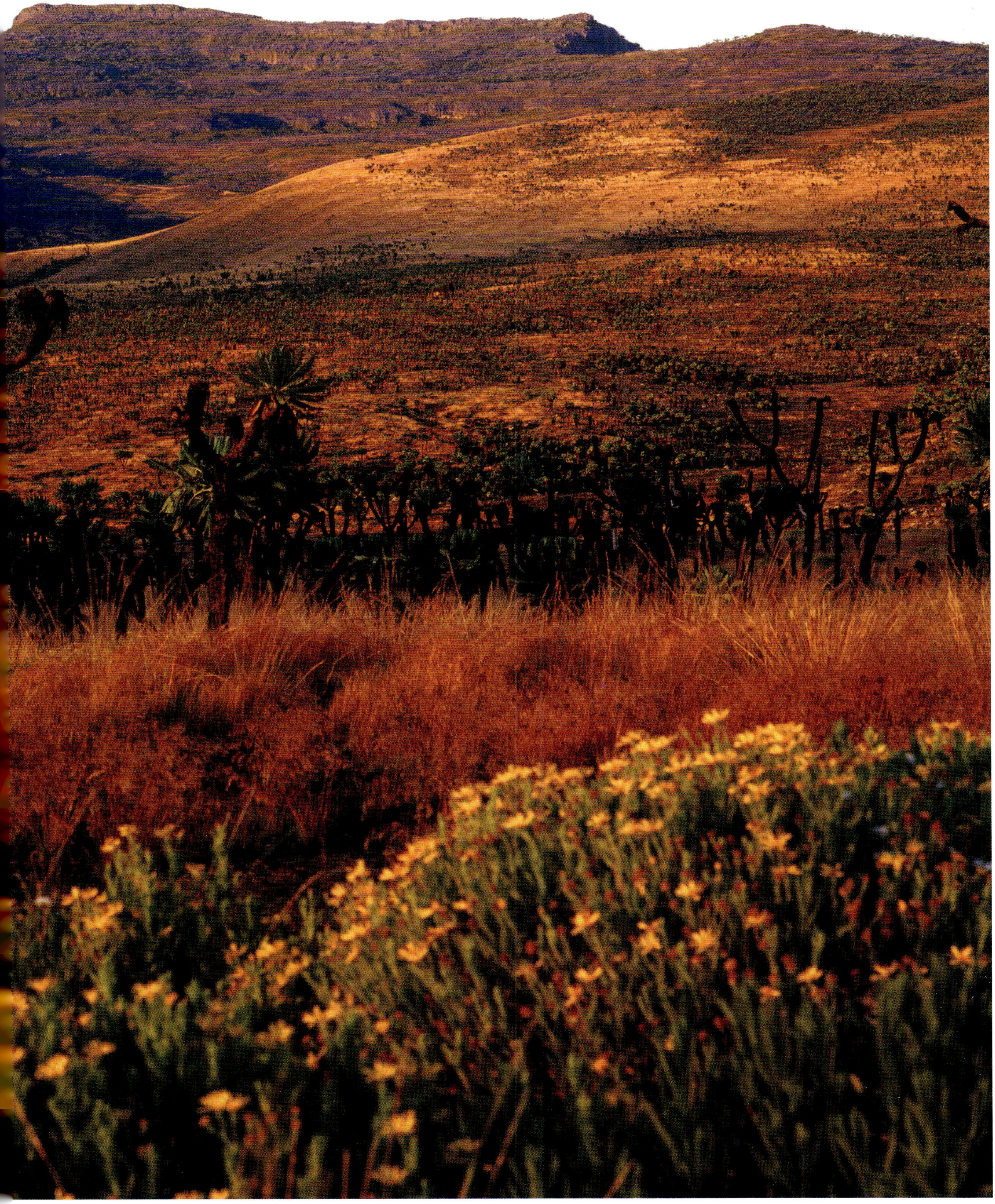

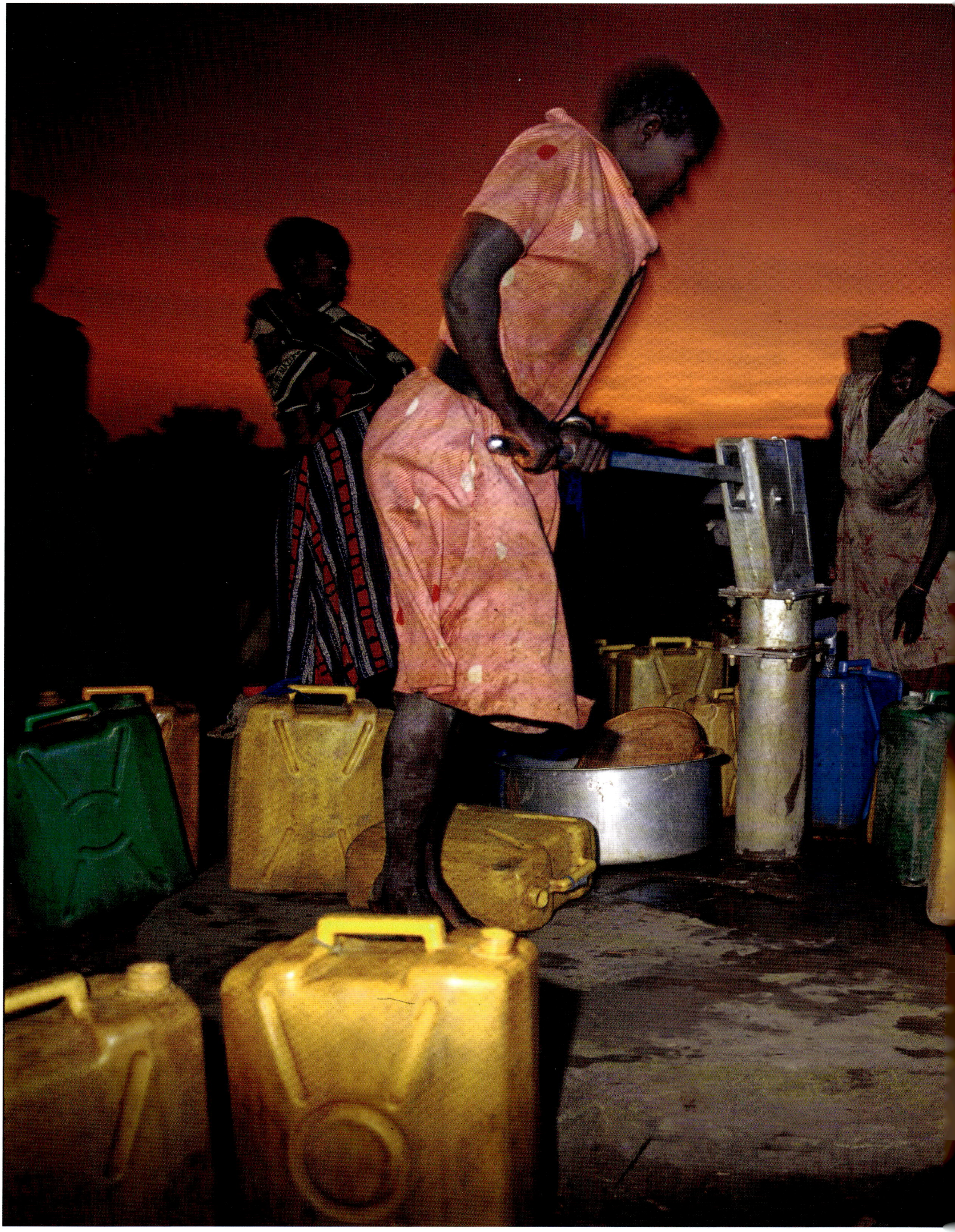

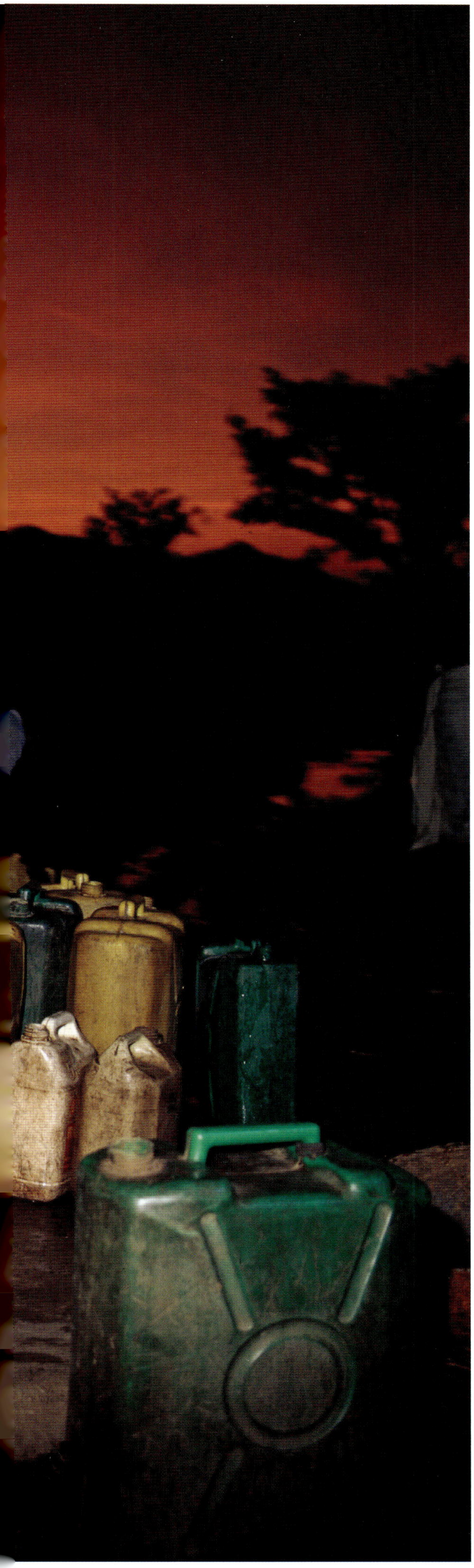

Left: Pumping water is a daily chore in remote rural areas. Piped water is a luxury outside the major towns and cities.

Following pages: Mount Loirot, a giant granite extrusion in the Labwor Hills of Eastern Uganda.

32 kilometres (20 miles) away in the east – to Jinja. The same year saw the railway line from Mombasa reach Kisumu, on the Kenyan side of the lake east of Jinja, and a steamer service was established to serve the different parts of the lake. For the first few years Jinja developed slowly as the Busoga District headquarters. The only item traded with the coast was ivory. Though cotton was introduced in Buganda in 1903 and was soon being grown in the eastern province, it was not to grow in this part of the country in quantities sufficient to stimulate trade for some years.

As early as 1908, Sir Winston Churchill recognized that: 'Jinja is destined to become a very important place in the future of central Africa . . . in years to come the shores of this splendid bay may be crowned with long rows of tropical villas and imposing offices and the gorge of the River Nile crowded with factories and warehouses.' In the years that followed, that prophecy became a reality. In 1912, the colonial administration constructed a railway connection from Jinja northward to the cotton-growing district of Namasagali, allowing for direct shipment of this important product to Kisumu.

The construction of the Owen Falls hydroelectric scheme gave Jinja a tremendous advantage in attracting industry. Opened by Princess Elizabeth of Great Britain in 1952, this tribute to modern engineering prowess harnesses the Nile's waters to generate electricity not only for Uganda, but also for Kenya, Tanzania and Rwanda. As you enter Jinja from the direction of Kampala, there is no mistaking the tall Owen Falls Dam and associated hydroelectric plant, which was further developed in 1999 and gained several additional turbine generators in 2000. Look out for brilliant rainbows in the water that gushes out of the sluices when they are open – usually for at least a couple of hours daily, depending on the amount of water in the artificial lake.

An important impetus behind the economic development of Jinja was provided by the Asian settlers who came to East Africa to work on the Uganda Railway in the late 19th century. Most famous among these entrepreneurs were Nanji Kalidas Mehta, who pioneered Uganda's sugar industry at Lugazi (40 kilometres/25 miles west of Jinja), and Muljibhai Madhvani, whose massive sugar estate at Kakira bankrolled a business empire that included the region's largest steel mill and textile factory. The town centre boasts some fine Asian architecture dating to this period of expansion, most notably Madhvani House, which was built on Main Street in 1919. Jinja's fortunes declined following Amin's expulsion of Asians in 1972, and his attempt to 'Africanise' their confiscated businesses was an abject failure, but the city has gradually started to prosper again under Museveni, who allowed the returned Asian exiles to repossess their expropriated property.

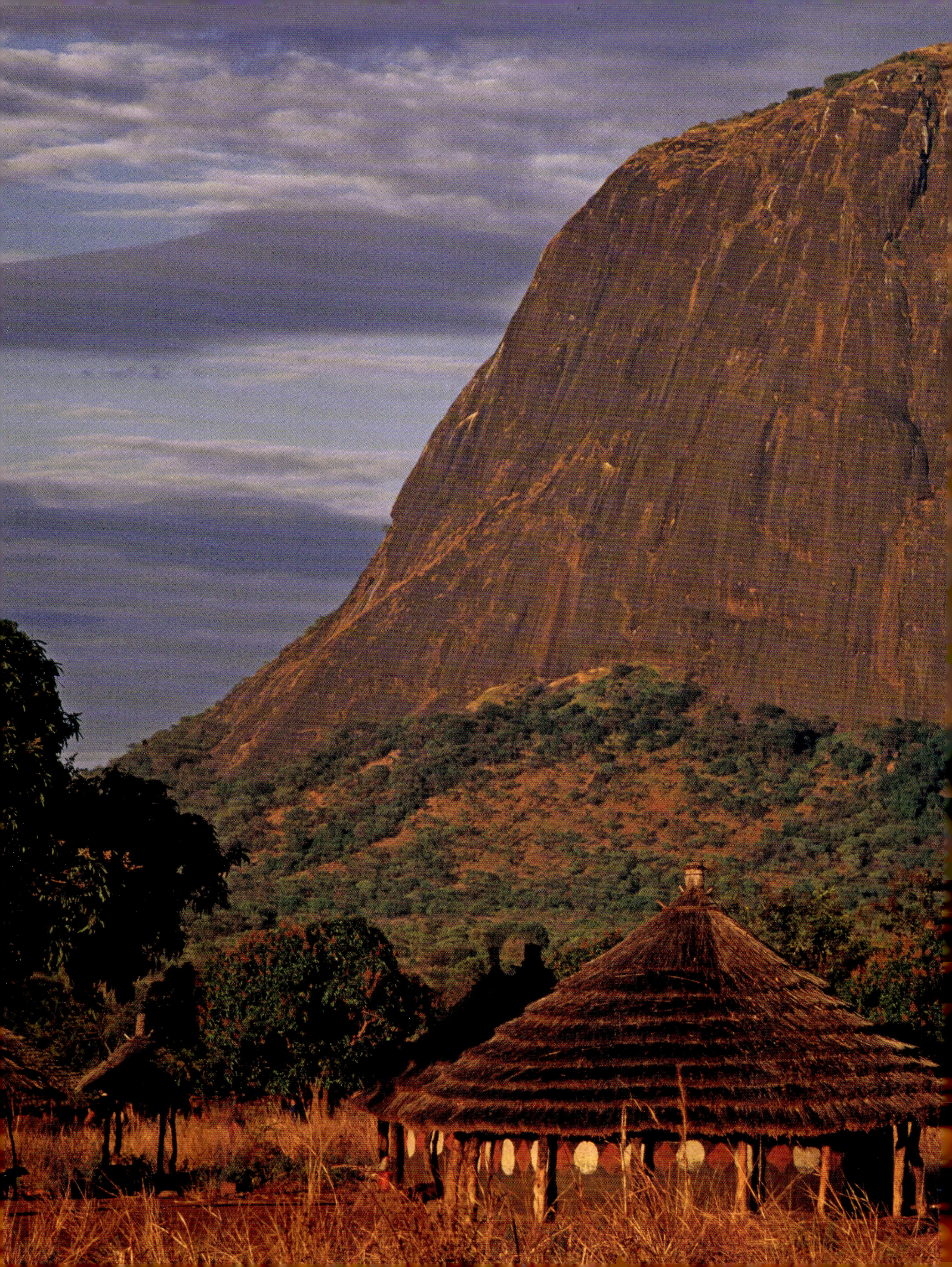

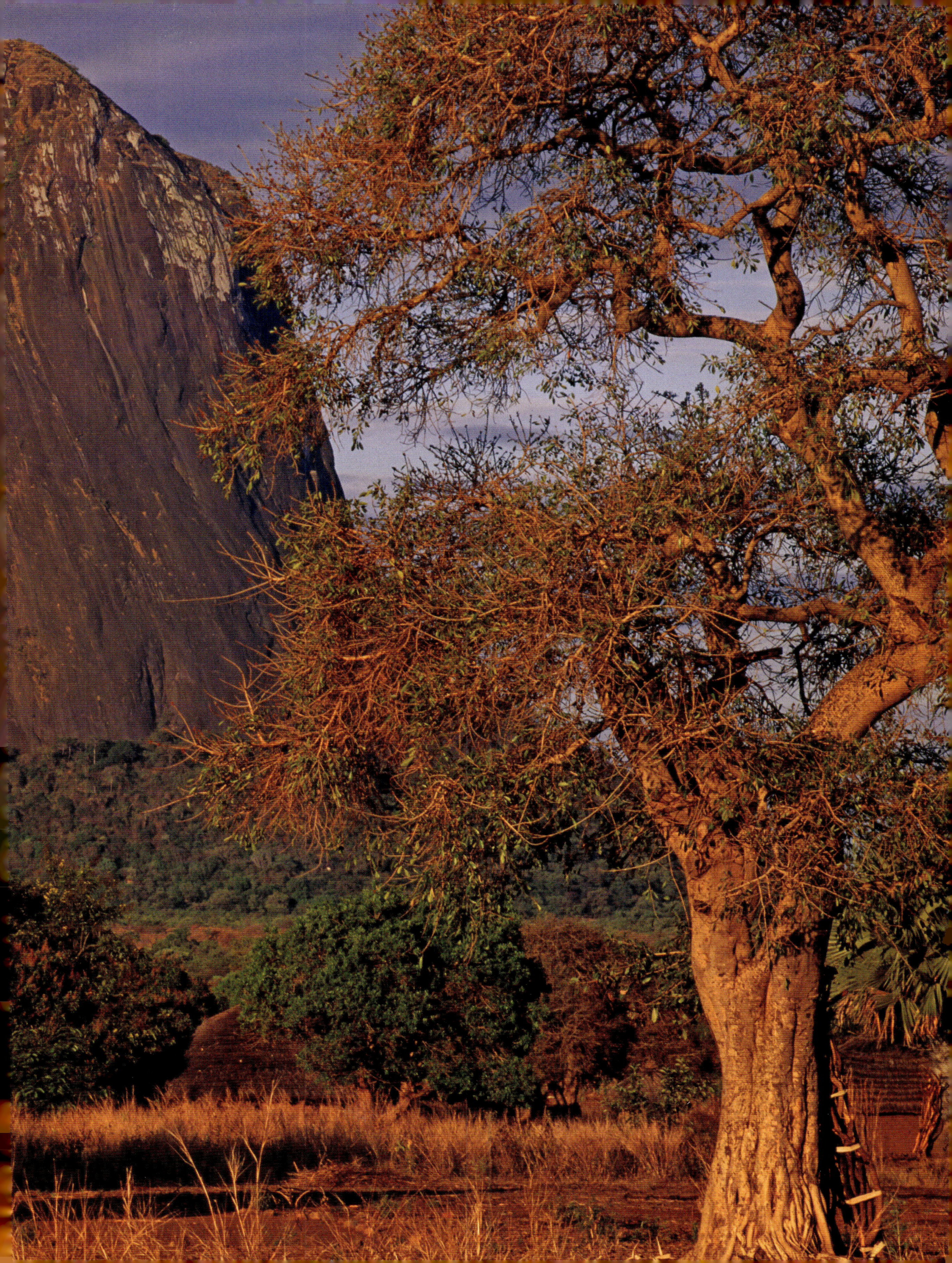

Below: White water rafting on the Nile.

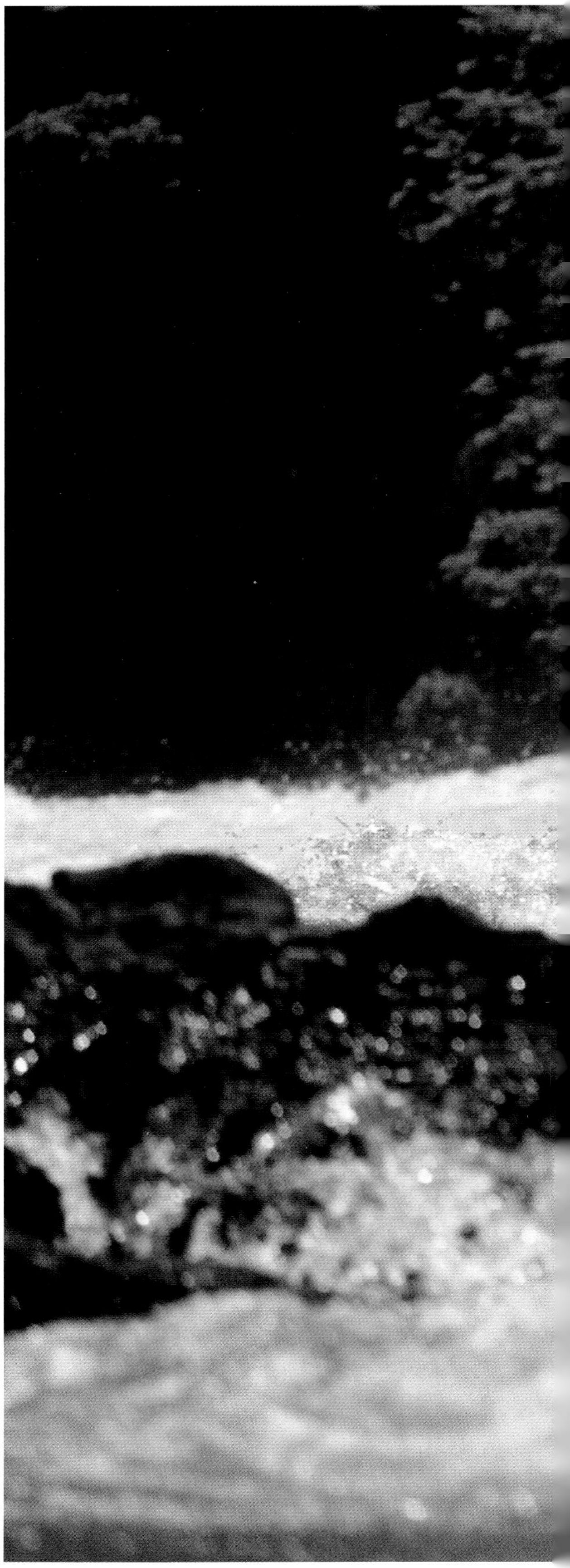

Jinja remains Uganda's second largest town and an important East African industrial centre. Together with Njeru, the township on the opposite side of the Nile, the city supports a population of around 150,000. For tourists, Jinja offers a variety of recreational activities, from sailing to golf. Its main attraction, however, is the Source of the Nile, which is now a picnic site, with a plaque marking the spot where the world's longest river departs from Lake Victoria. On the opposite bank stands an obelisk that marks the place where Speke stood and gazed in wonder at the sight before him. Other beauty spots in and around the town centre include the golf club and yachting club on the shores of Lake Victoria – both welcome visitors. So too does Nile Breweries, the countries largest beer producer, which runs free guided tours during normal office hours on Tuesdays to Fridays. After the tour, you can visit a small gift shop selling a limited selection of branded clothing and other items such as watches, key rings, pens, coasters, etc.

Jinja residents once used to hear lions roaring around nearby Bugungu Hill, and elephant and buffalo also roamed the area, while the riverbanks were thick with crocodiles and hippos. Today, you'd be lucky to see any wildlife larger than a marabou stork or monitor lizard in the immediate vicinity of Jinja, but the Mabira Forest Reserve, back on the road towards Kampala, is a good spot for monkeys and butterflies, and it ranks as one the country's most important ornithological sites, with more than 300 bird species recorded, including several rarities. Sadly, the future of this richly biodiverse forest is uncertain, with a strong possibility that at least one-third of its 300 square kilometres will be sacrificed to make way for sugarcane plantations.

Over recent years, Jinja has been usurped as a tourist centre by Bujagali Falls, a series of rapids on the forest-fringed Nile about 10 kilometres downriver of its source. Held sacred by locals, Bujagali is named after a powerful river spirit that has manifested itself in at least 30 successive human reincarnations over the centuries, each of whom has proved their claim by floating across the rapids on a magical piece of barkcloth. The last uncontested Bujagali died without nominating an heir in the 1970s, and the identity of his successor has been the subject of a heated dispute, though most villagers believe the spirit resides in a local called Ja-Ja, who crossed the rapids by barkcloth while evading military arrest during the Amin era.

Not so long ago, Bujagali was serviced by one obscure and peaceful picnic site that attracted a handful of travellers annually. Today, it is East Africa's premier adventure tourism centre, serviced by half-a-dozen hotels and backpacker lodges. The main activity here is white-water rafting and kayaking along the Nile north of Jinja, a 50 kilometres stretch

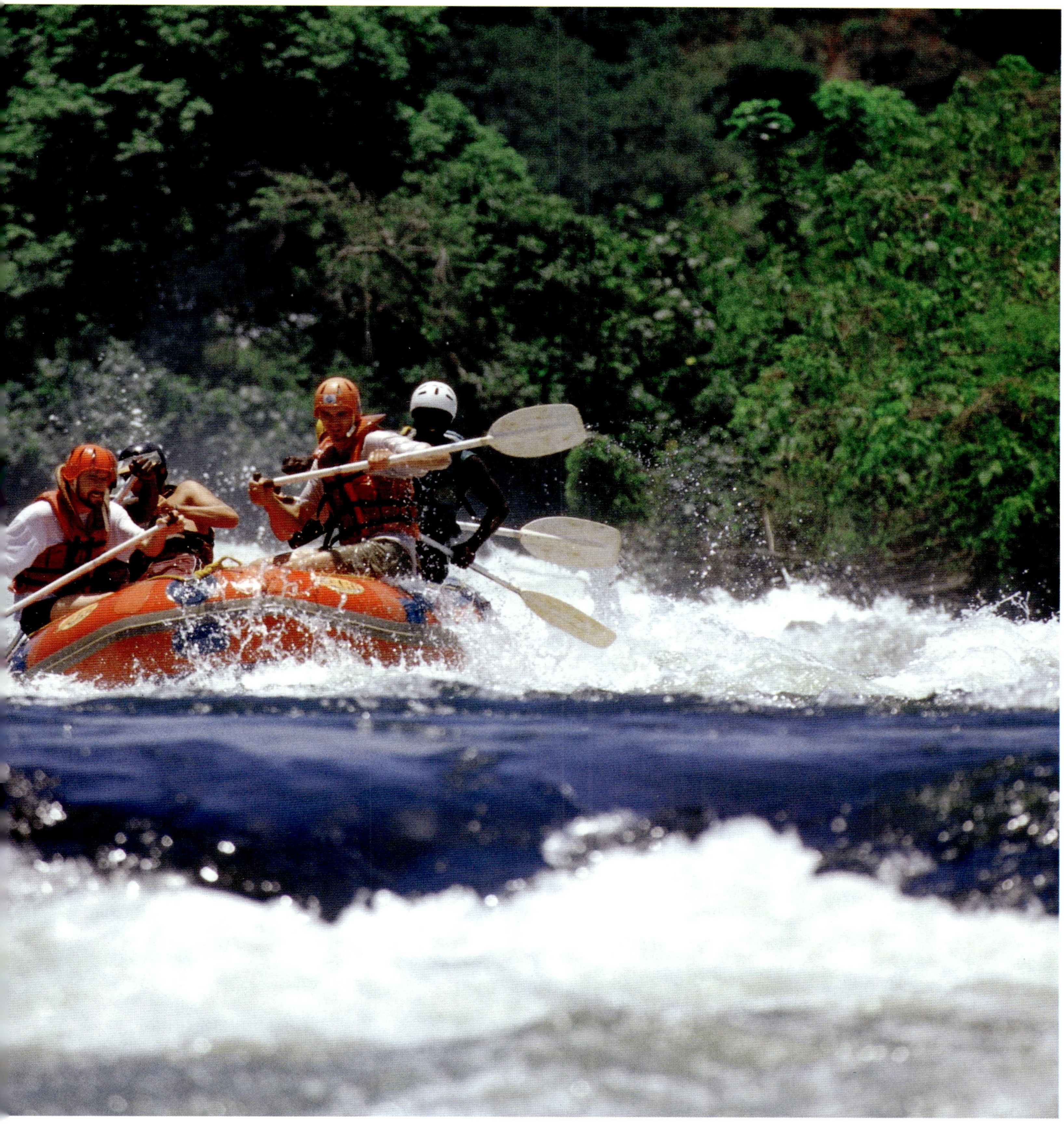

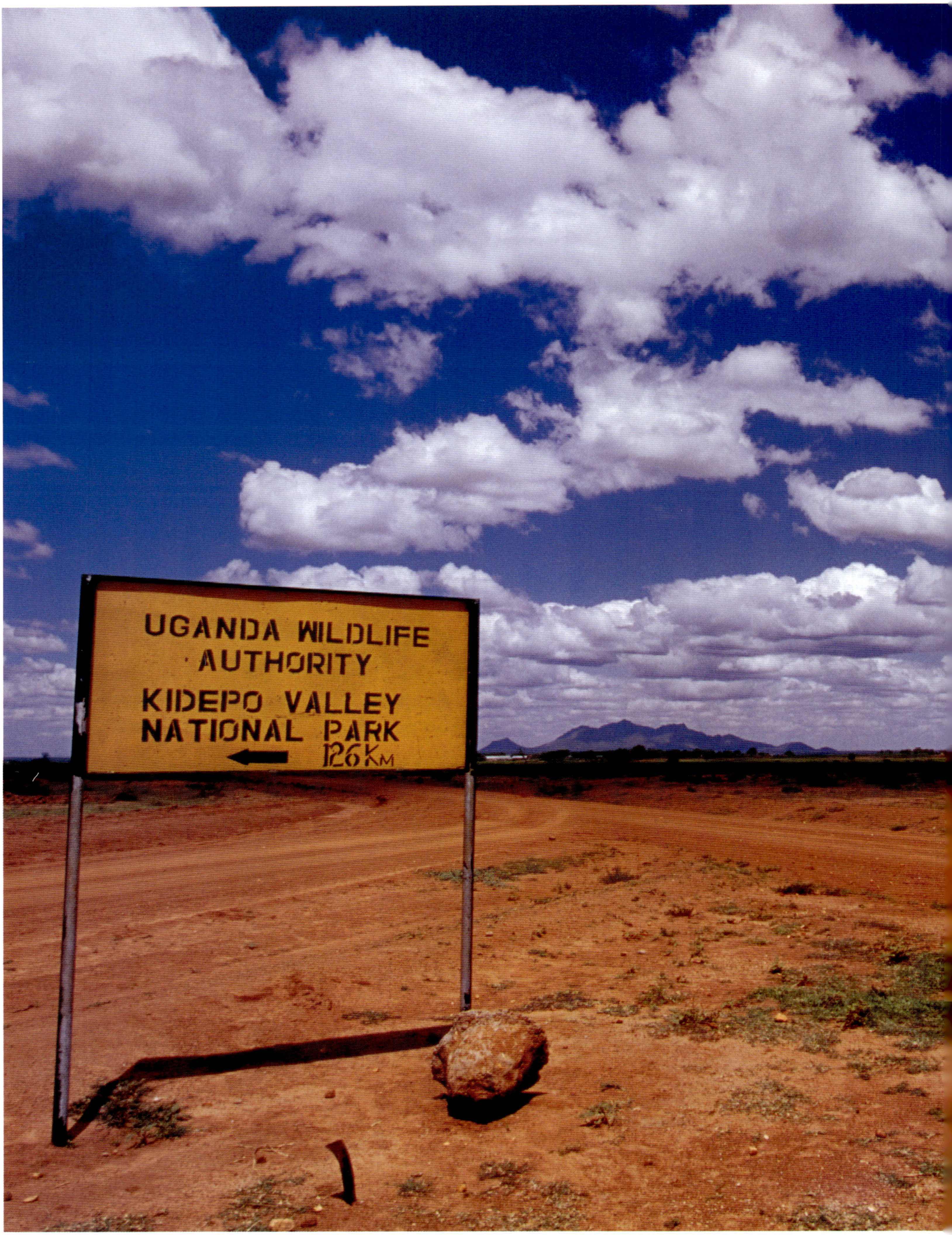
UGANDA WILDLIFE
AUTHORITY
KIDEPO VALLEY
NATIONAL PARK
126 KM

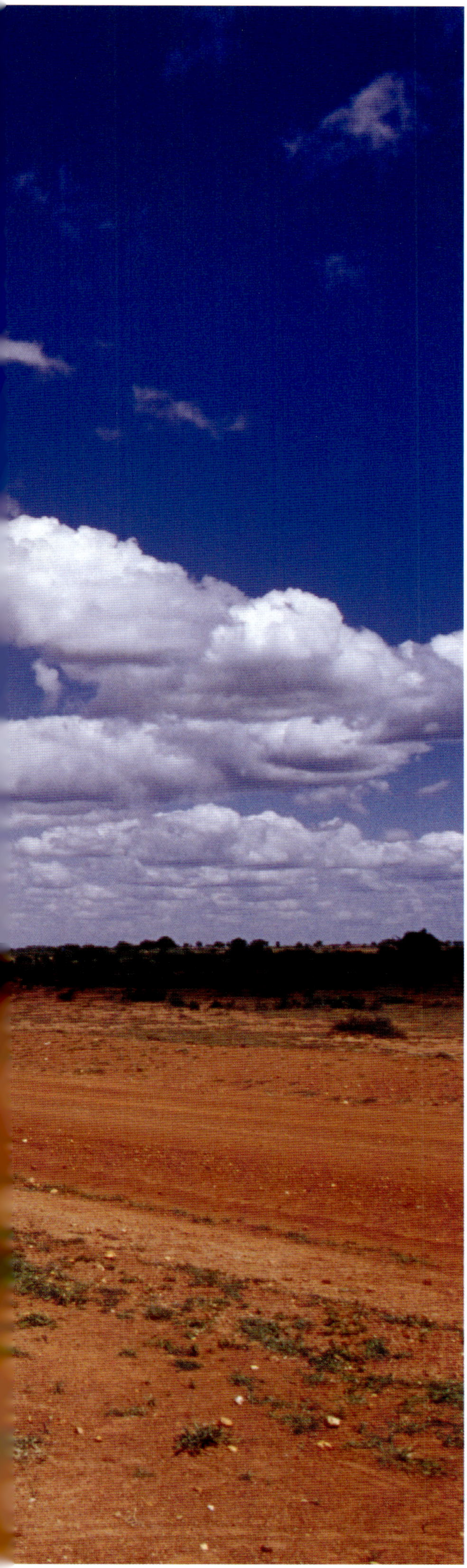

Left: Road sign to Kidepo Valley National Park, truly one of Uganda's most spectacular parks.

of river punctuated by several Grade Five rapids every bit as exhilarating as the famous Zambezi Gorge below Victoria Falls. Additional activities include bungee jumping. Horseback trips and quad-biking, but it's also a relaxed and scenic place to spend a few days enjoying the lively backpacker scene, lush riverine scenery, and thick riparian woodland rattling with birds and monkeys.

Aside from Jinja, two substantial towns in the southeast are of marginal interest to visitors. The smaller of these is Tororo, whose wide pavements, straggling flowering trees and timeworn colonial-era façades pay testament to its former prosperity. A more convincing reason to stop over here is Tororo Rock, a steep volcanic plug that protrudes several hundred metres above the town's southern skyline, and can be climbed in about one hour for panoramic views towards Mount Elgon and Lake Victoria.

Far more inherently attractive is Mbale, Uganda's third-largest town, nestled at altitude of around 1,200m in below Nkokonjeru, a 2,347m spur of the Mount Elgon massif whose rocky face is run down by several waterfalls. Mbale was founded by the controversial Muganda administrator and soldier Semei Kakungulu, who subjugated much of eastern Uganda as an agent of the British Crown before his overzealous methods caused the administration to retire him to a piece of land below Nkokonjeru in 1902. A natural centre for trade, the town supported around 3,000 African, Greek, Arab, Indian and Swahili traders by 1904, and was made the regional capital a year later. Few travellers pass through Mbale, but it's a pleasant lively town, less obviously scarred by the events of 1971-86 than most in Uganda, and its leafy suburbs make for a pleasant afternoon stroll.

Situated on the outskirts of Mbale, Nabugoye Hill is the spiritual home to the Abayudaya community of Ugandan Jews founded by Kakungulu in 1920. Kakungulu's original version of Judaism was a confused hotchpotch of customs that, for instance, placed as much emphasis on the Christian baptism of children as on the severing of their foreskins! The community subsequently moved closer to the Jewish mainstream and it thrived until 1971, when Idi Amin closed 32 synagogues, banned Judaism, and ordered its followers to convert to Christianity or Islam. Today, the Abayudaya community amounts to roughly 500 individuals, who have yet to gain the acceptance of other Jews, but who welcome sympathetic visitors, and are notable for their distinctive music, which sets Jewish prayer texts to African melodies and rhythms.

The most important landmark in the Mbale area is Mount Elgon, or Masaba as it is known to locals. Elgon is an extinct volcano that formed about 24 million years ago and had its last major eruption some 10 million years ago, though its violent origin is still evident in the hot

Opposite and below: Kidepo Valley National Park offers a great diversity of wildlife: 80 species, more than in any other Ugandan Park.

Following pages: The town of Soroti, 19 kilometres (12 miles) east of one arm of Lake Kyoga.

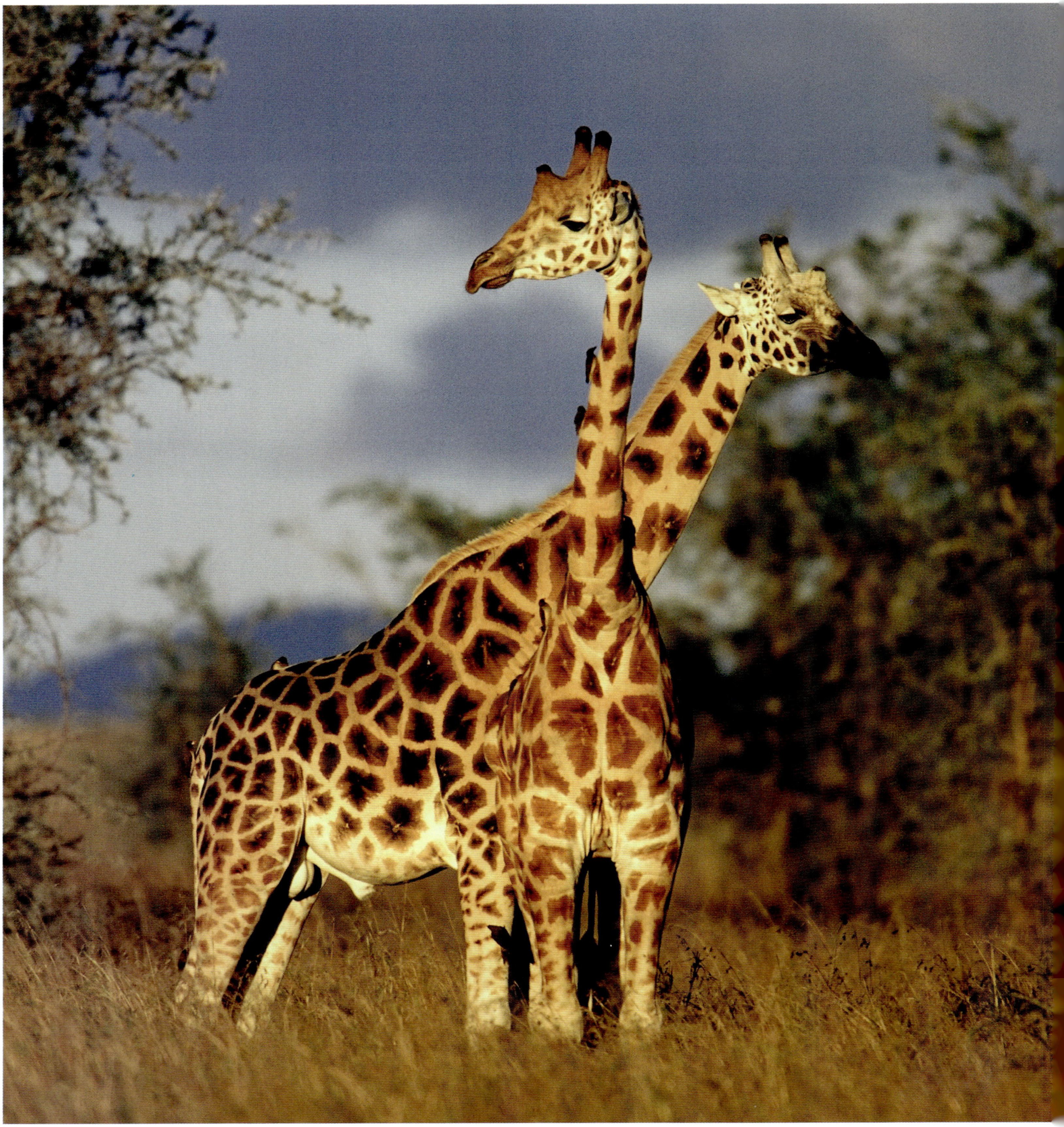

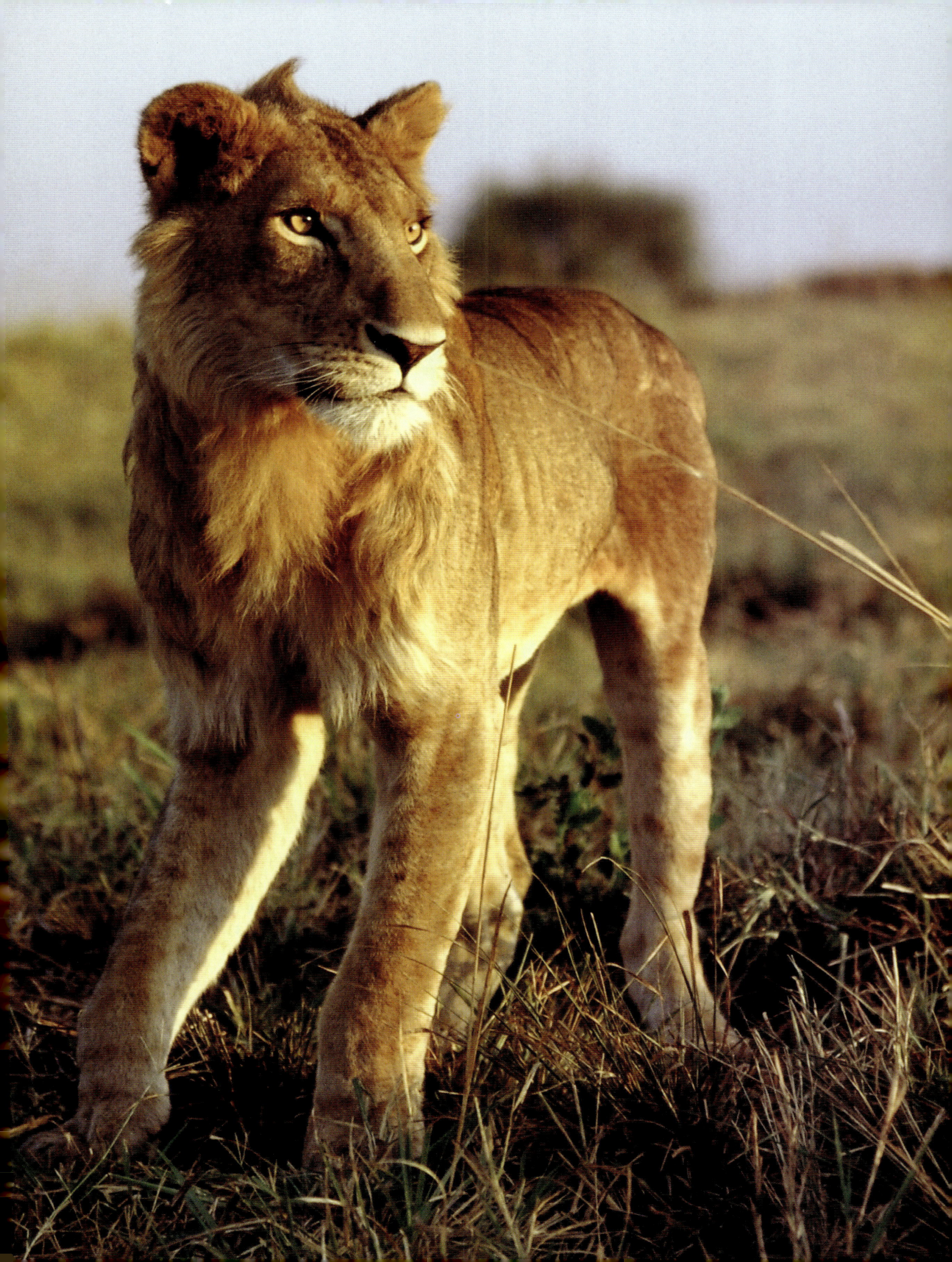

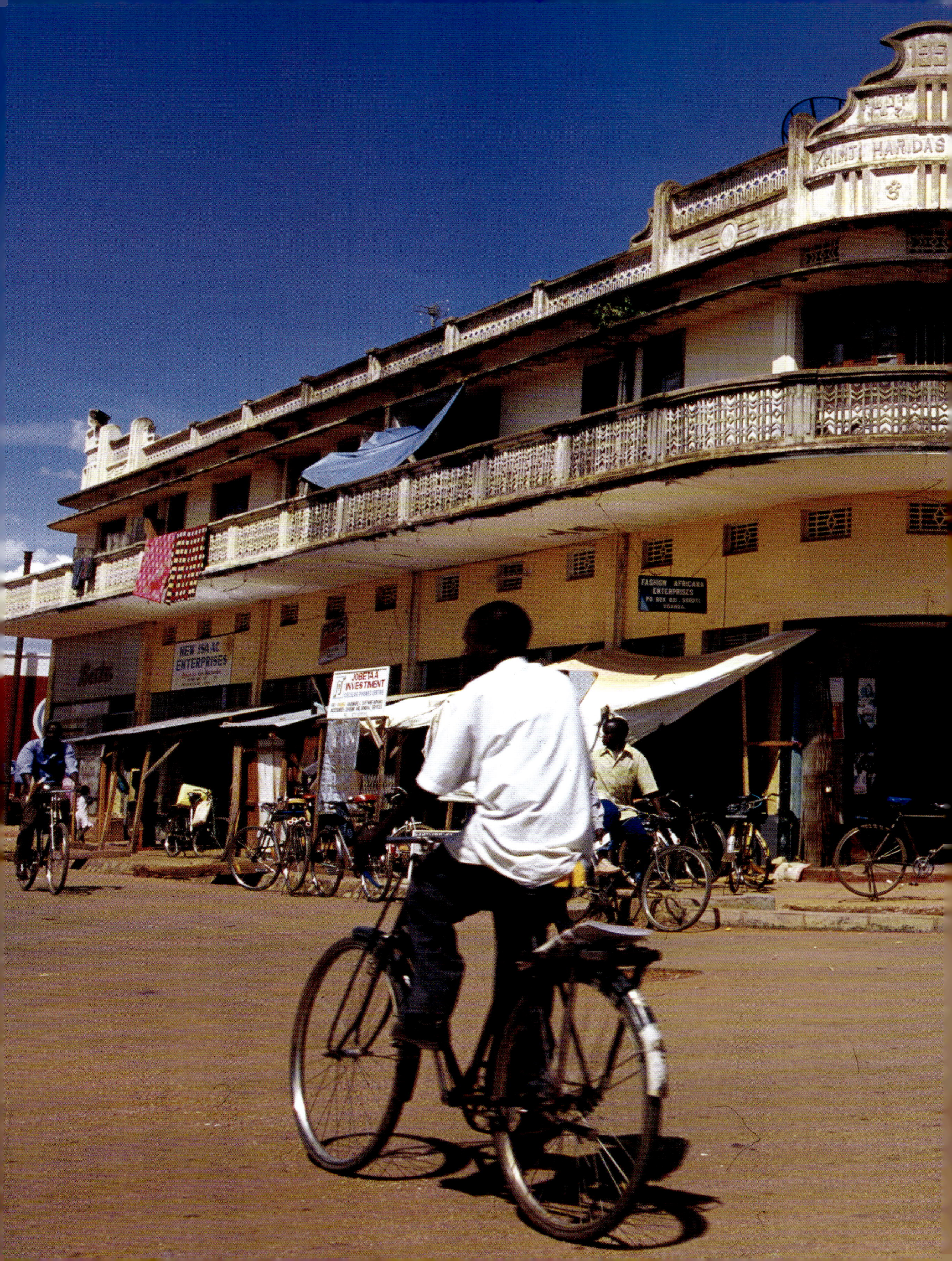
KHIMJI HARIDAS
NEW ISAAC ENTERPRISES
JOBETAA INVESTMENT
CELLULAR PHONES CENTRE
FASHION AFRICANA ENTERPRISES

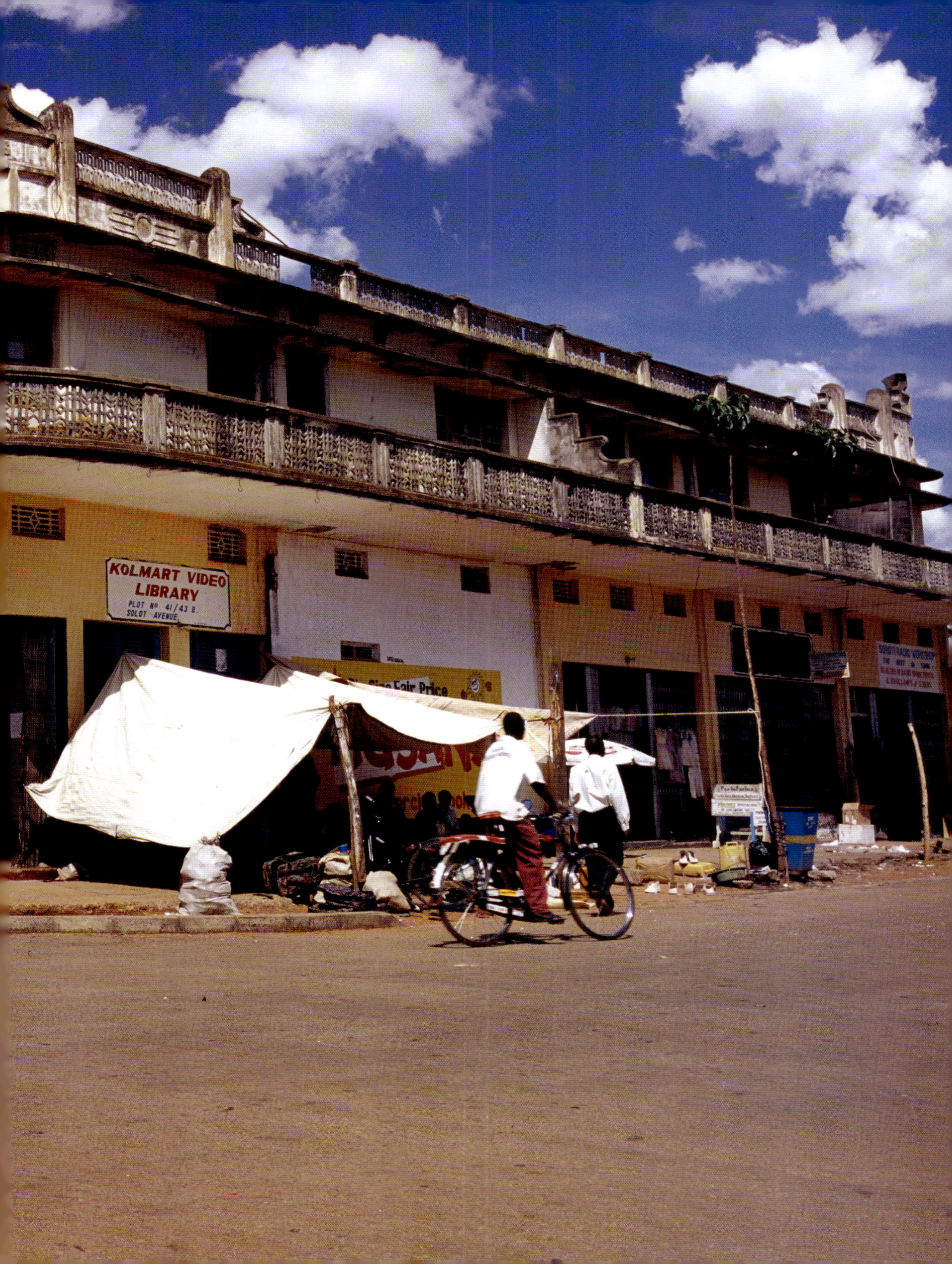
KOLMART VIDEO LIBRARY
PLOT No 41/43 B.
SOLOT AVENUE

Opposite: Spectacular Sipi waterfall on Mount Elgon.

Below: Trekking on Mount Elgon.

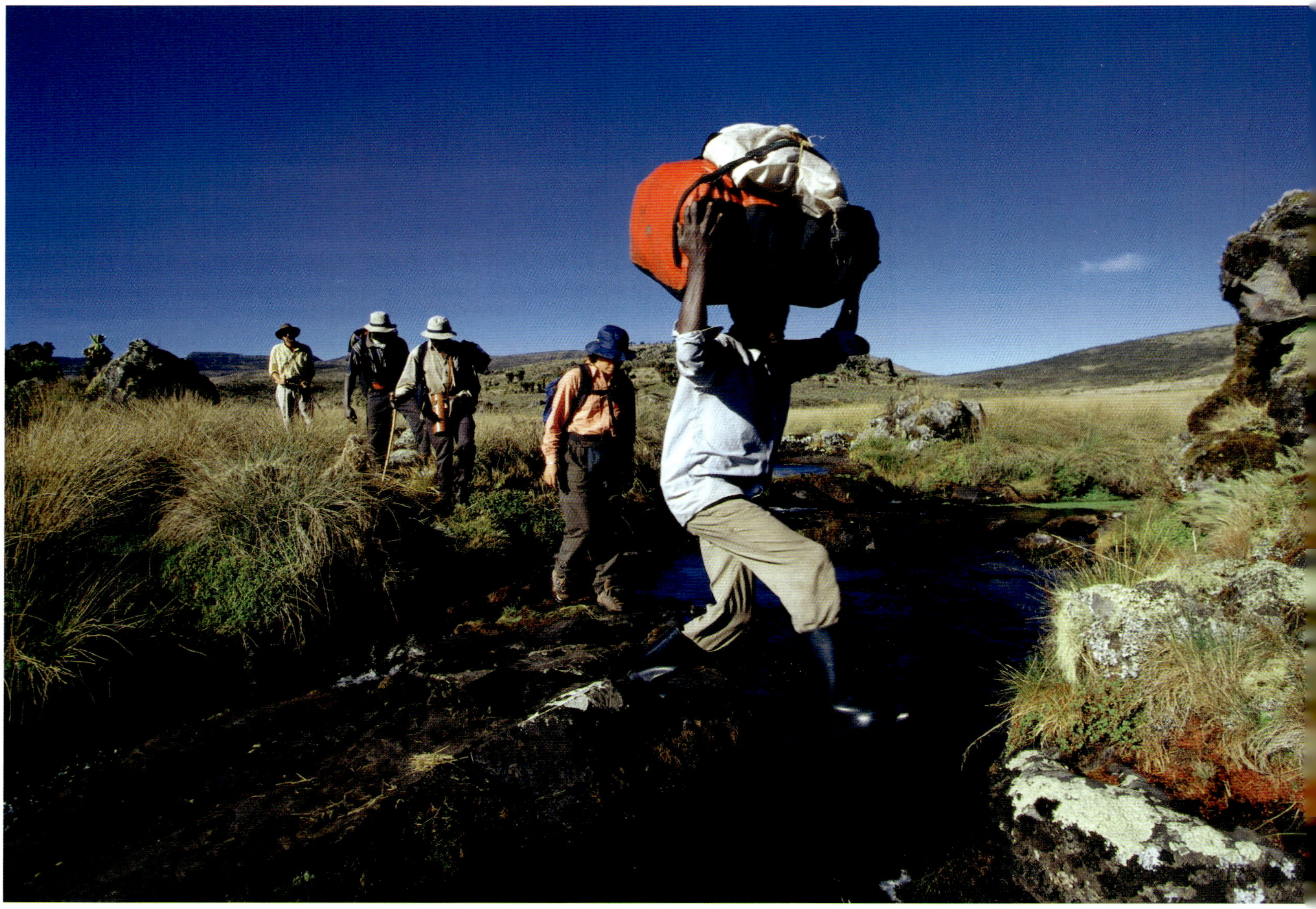

springs that bubble out of the caldera floor. Its highest peak Wagagai reaches an elevation of 4,321 metres (14,176 feet) above sea level, making it one of the ten tallest mountains in Africa, but its immense base – the largest of any standalone volcano in the world, with a diameter of 50 kilometres (30 miles) – suggests it must once have been far taller than Kilimanjaro is today.

Besides volcanic forces, many other geological events have shaped Mount Elgon. The many crater lakes in the mountain's caldera were gouged by glaciers, which extended from the summits down to about 3,500 metres (11,500 feet) during the Pleistocene era. The same glaciers gouged a deep gash out of the eastern wall, creating what is now the Suam Gorge. Rock falls and landslides, in addition to the growth of astounding vegetation, have enhanced the fascinating, tumbled landscape.

Years of land-use practices and a growing population have had

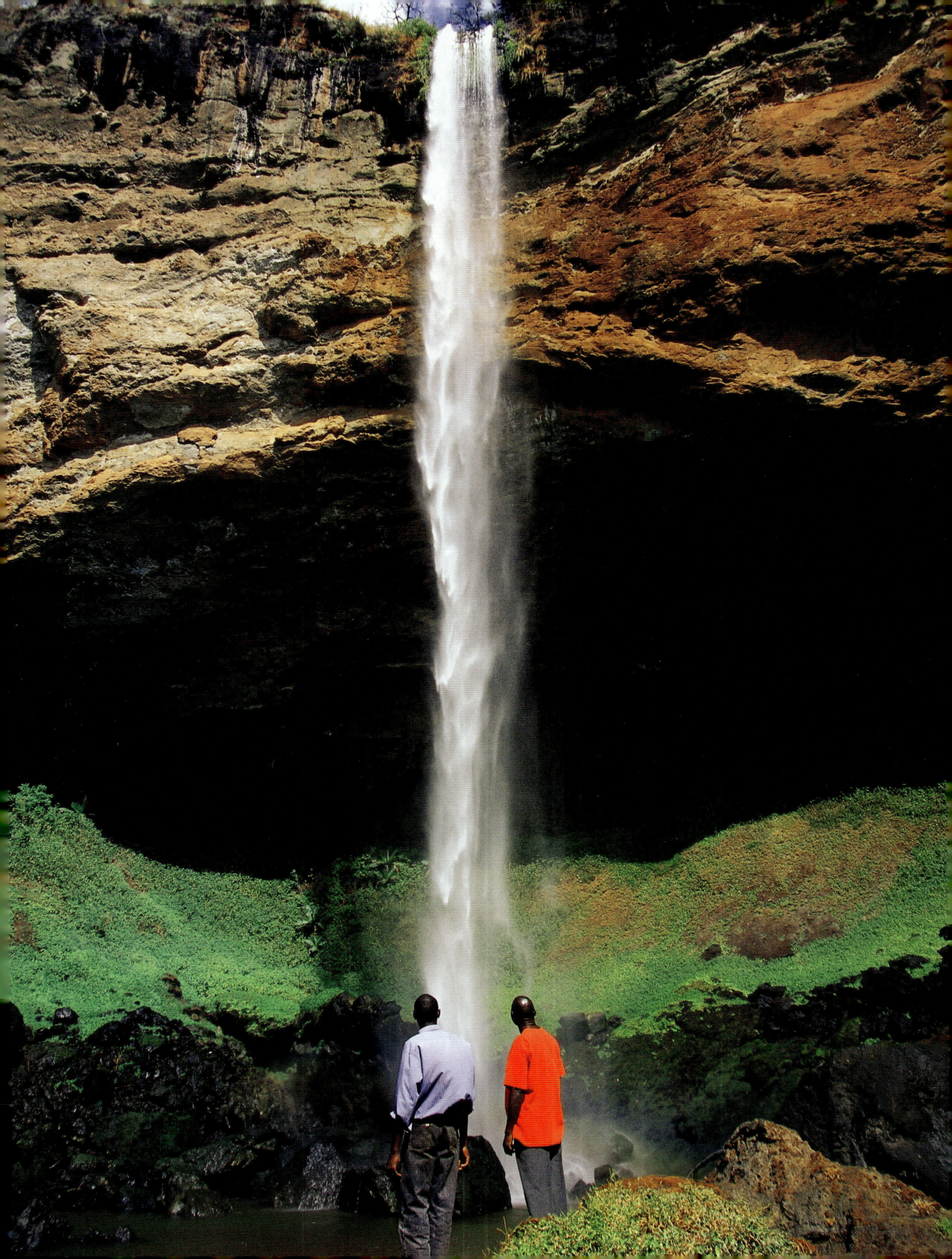

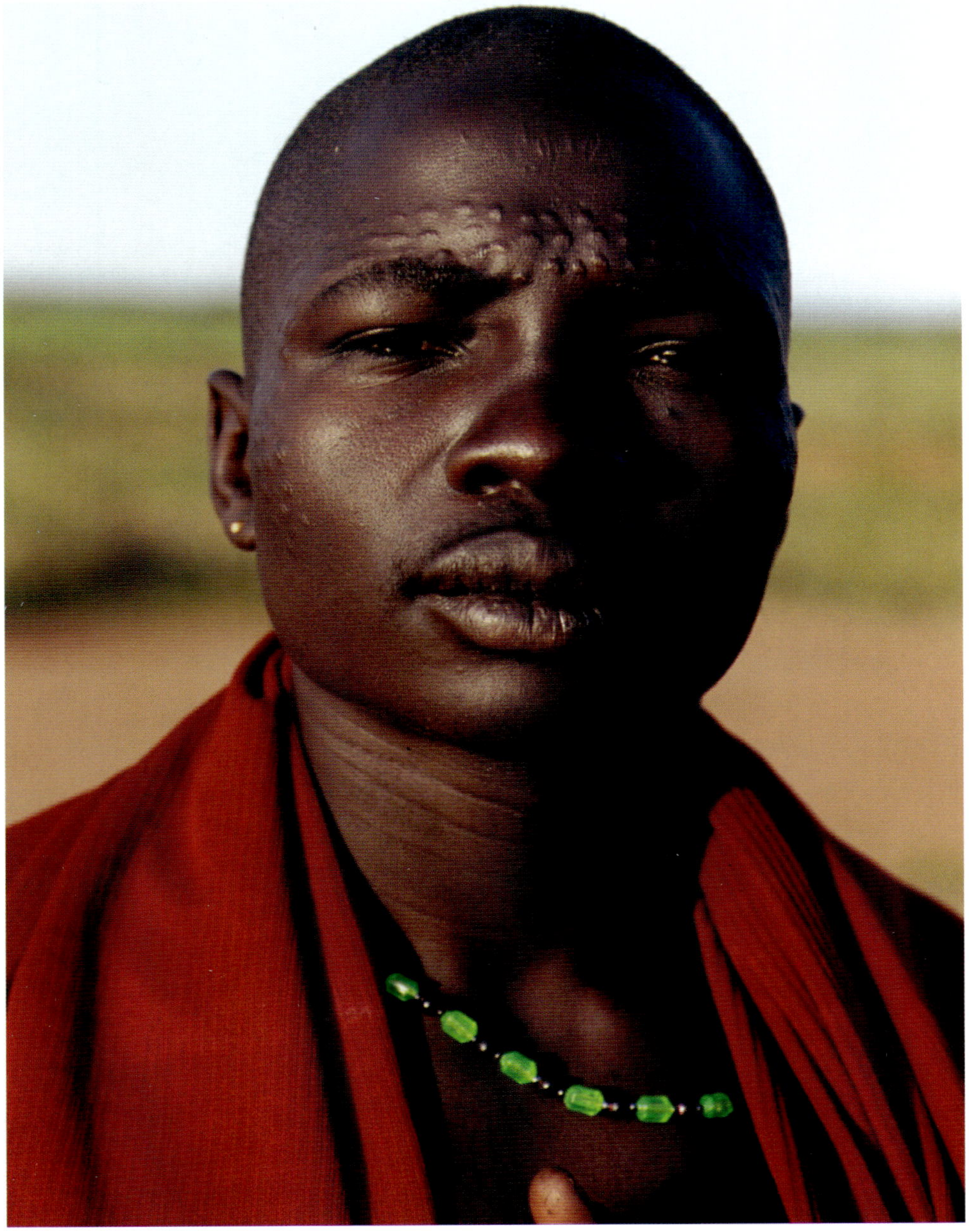

Left and opposite: The Karamoja man and girl.

Following pages: Village in the remote foothills south of Kidepo Valley National Park.

their effect on the area, which is one of the reasons why the 1,145-square-kilometre (442-square-mile) Mount Elgon National Park was gazetted in October 1993. The park is primarily concerned with conserving and restoring the original forest that once covered the slopes, enabling the mountain to continue its essential role as a major watershed. However, the park also supports a fair variety of wildlife, though much of it is shy. Mammals include olive baboon, blue monkey, black-and-white colobus, buffalo, bushbuck, black-fronted duiker, tree hyrax, bushpig, leopard and spotted hyena, while elephants, once confined to the Kenyan side of the border, are also returning. Birds, of course, are prolific, with a checklist topping 300 that includes Ross's turaco, casqued hornbill,

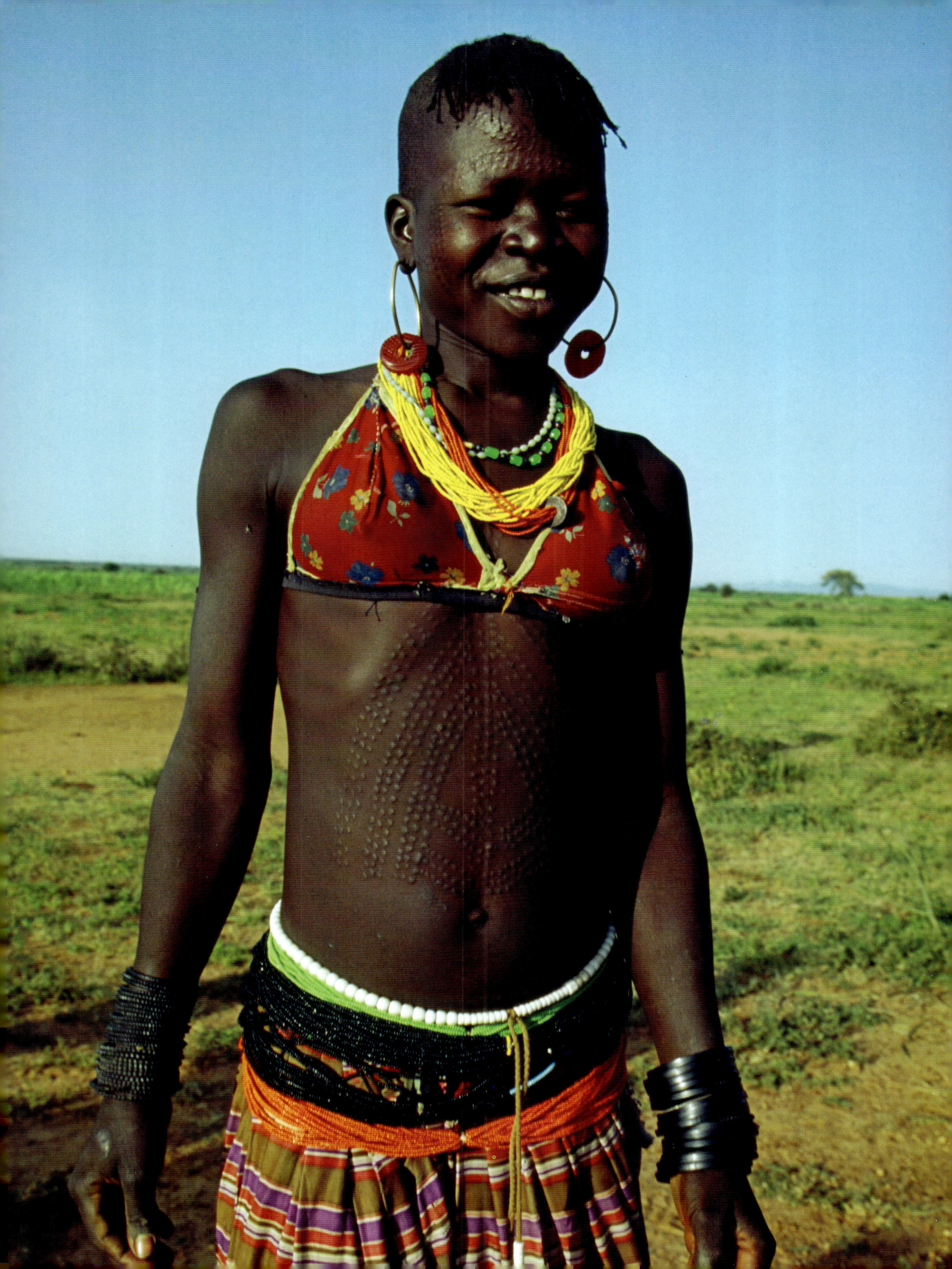

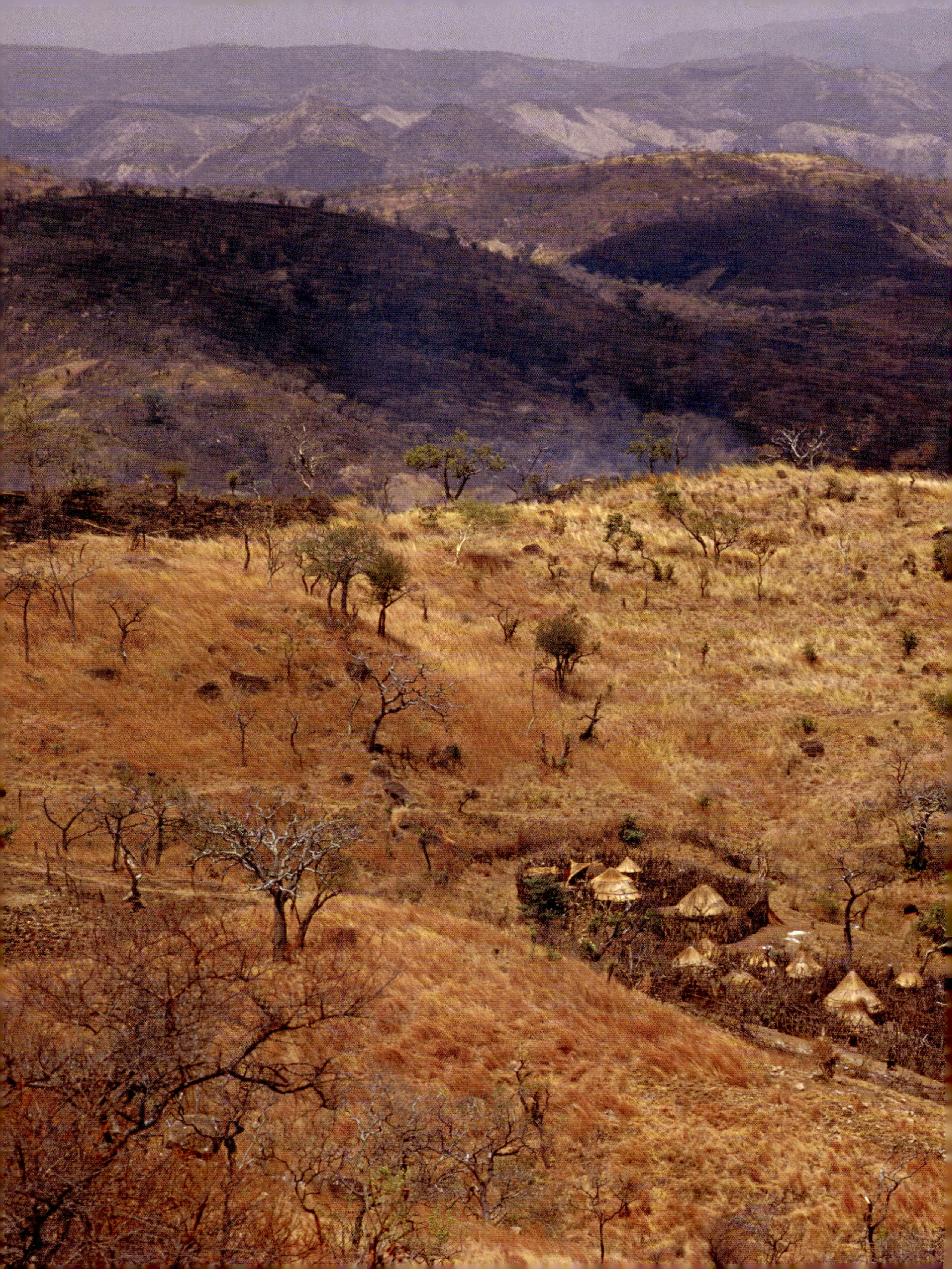

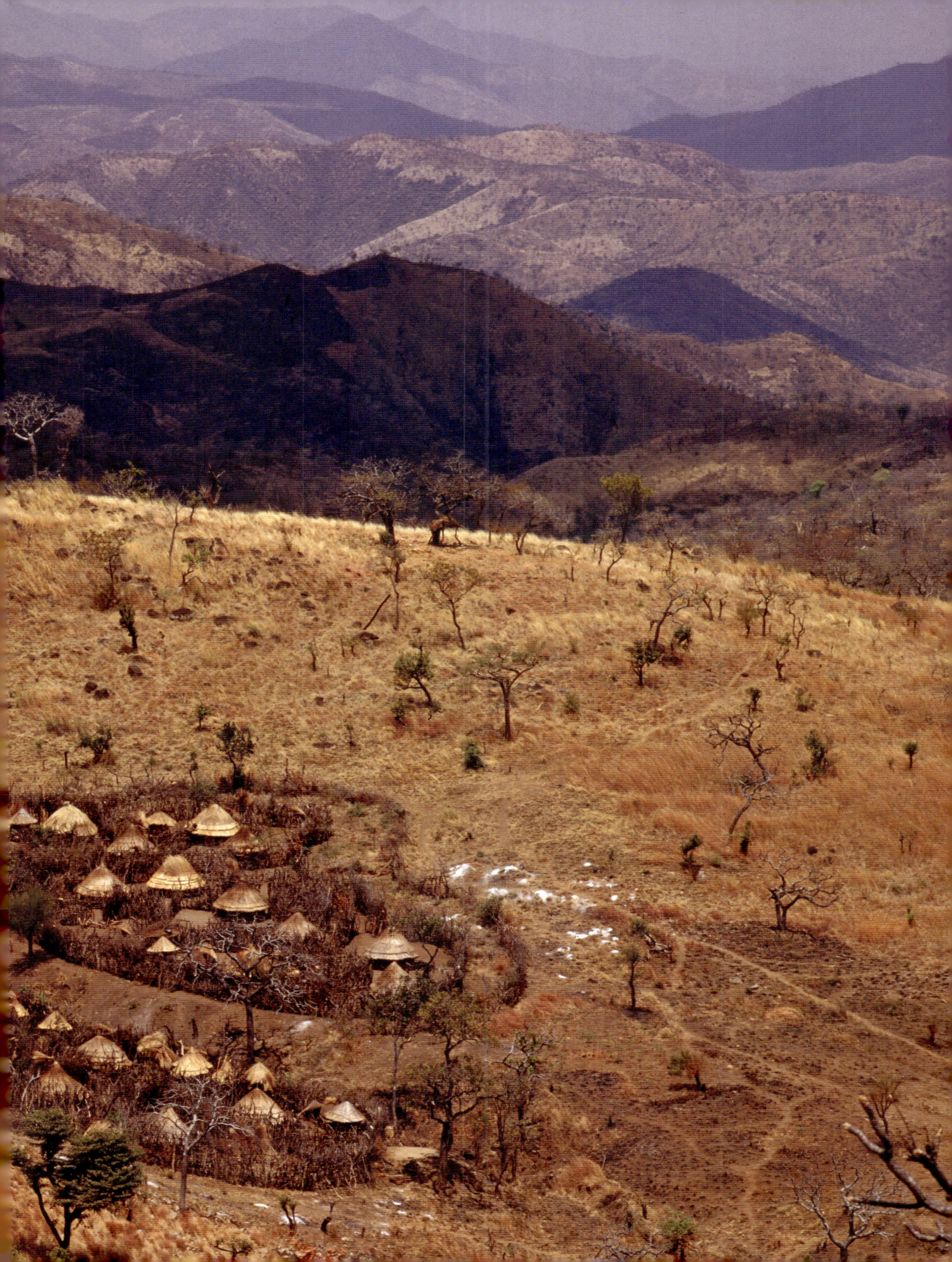

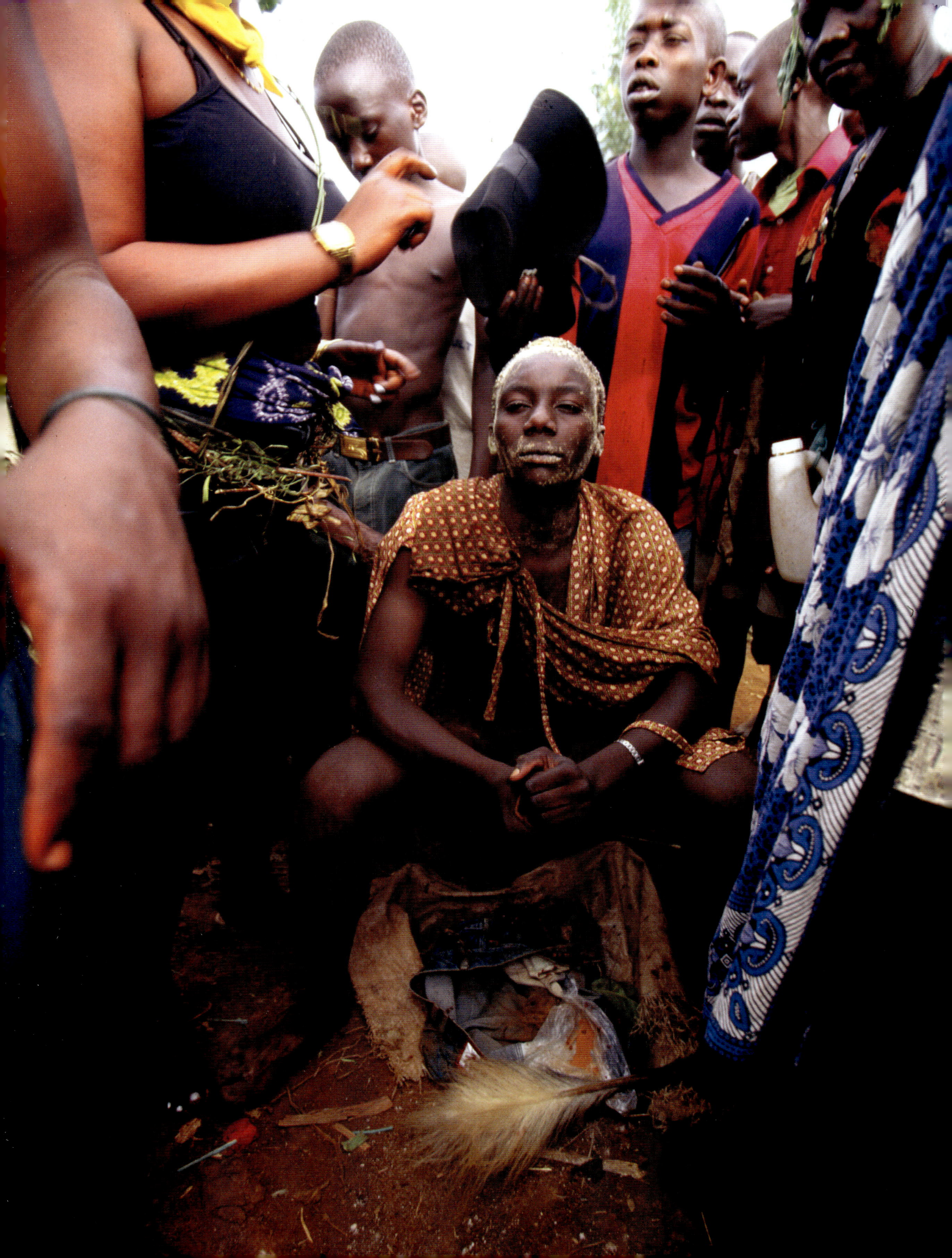

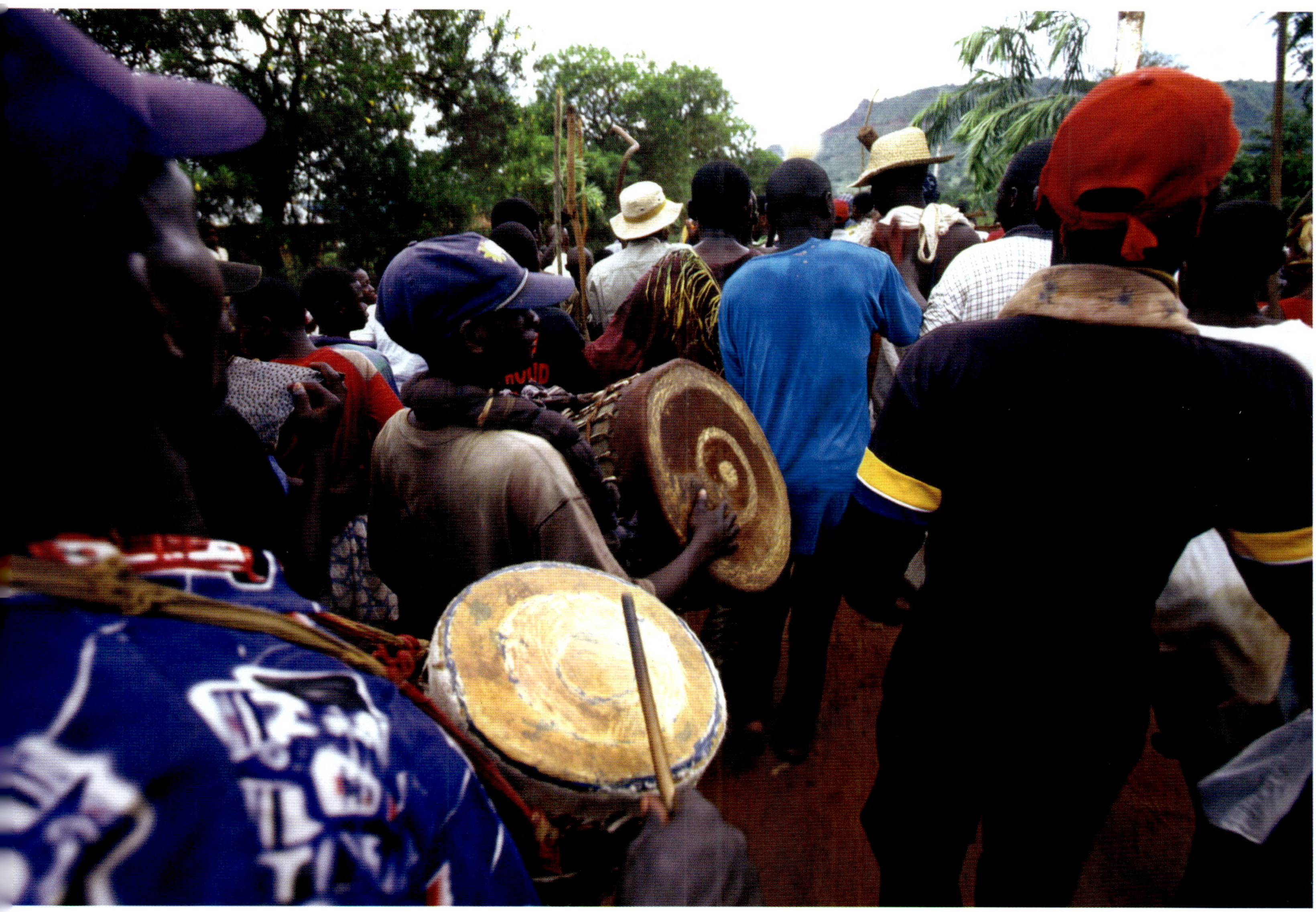

bove and opposite: Bugisu circumcision ceremony, round the town of Mbale.

crowned eagle, lammergeyer and many less conspicuous species not recorded elsewhere in Uganda. Other attractions include ancient cave paintings close to the trailhead at Budadiri, and spectacular caves and hot springs within the crater.

With its waterfalls, caves, hot springs, mountain vegetation and fascinating caldera, Mount Elgon is an exciting place to explore. It is ideal for climbers seeking a less strenuous alternative to the Rwenzoris Mountains, as scaling Elgon requires no technical climbing skills, and all major summits are accessible to hikers. The beautifully wooded slopes, smaller scale, and milder climate make Mount Elgon a wonderful wilderness experience that is often overlooked by tourists. The services of the local guides, porters, and park rangers are highly recommended, but optional. There are two main trails in the park, Sasa and the Piswa, and a recommended potion is to ascend Mount Elgon via the

Right: The IK (Teuso) dance.

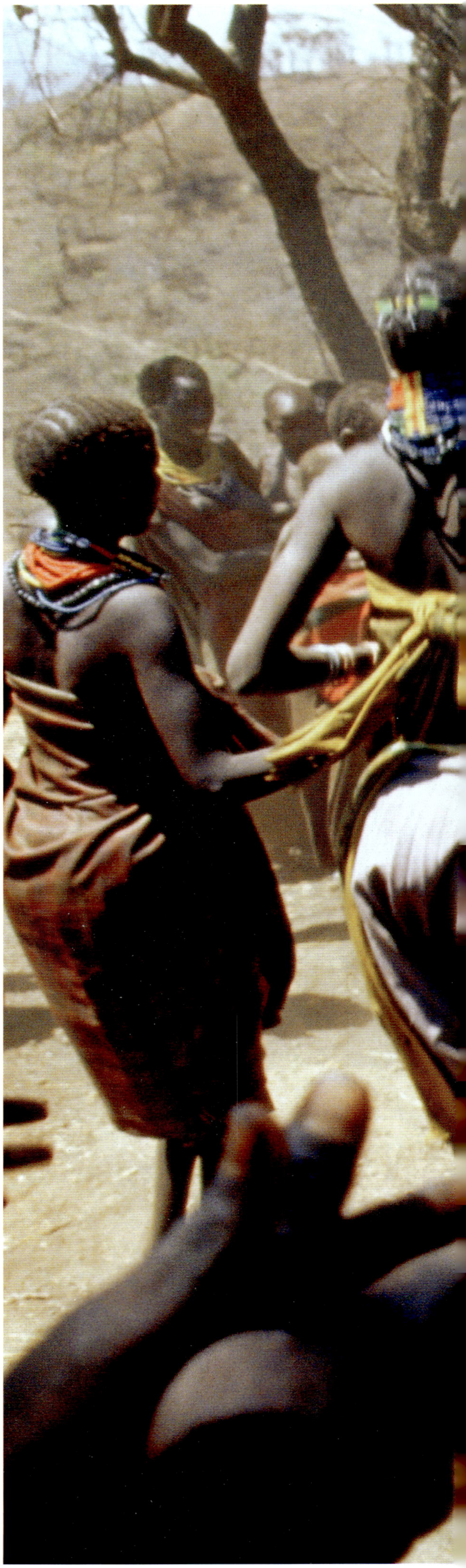

Sasa trail and descend via the Piswa trail, allowing six days for the trek. This will include an ascent of the highest peak, Wagagai, a visit to the caldera, and climb to Jackson's Point, the second highest peak.

The hike will take trekkers through the mountain's four altitudinal vegetation belts. In descending order, these are the Afro-alpine zone, the sub-alpine or heath zone, the bamboo zone, and the montane forest. The largest number of plant and animal species exist in the montane forest, but the high elevation areas have much to offer as well. The vegetation there has adapted to the extreme weather conditions in bizarre ways, as seen in the giant groundsel, giant lobelia, and giant heather which are common in the area. Two types of giant groundsel are also endemic to the area. Bamboo forests grow in the southern and western parts of the park, with shoots growing up to 15 metres (50 feet) tall. There are also many beautiful wild flowers in the park.

The area around the park is largely occupied by the Bagisu people, one of the few ethnic groups in Uganda that still practises traditional circumcision. The area is particularly worth visiting between August and December of even numbered years, when the renowned – and conspicuous – Bagisu circumcision ceremonies take place. Mainly agriculturists, the Bagisu grow crops that include coffee, matoke (bananas), millet, potatoes, beans and peas. Their terraced coffee plantations can be seen throughout the area. The Bagisu also rear some cattle, sheep, and goats, and use the donkey as a beast of burden.

A popular goal outside the park is the Sipi Falls, which lies about 60 kilometres (35 miles) from Mbale by road. The Sipi River rises on the upper slopes of Mount Elgon before cascading down the foothills over 7 kilometres to form a series of four pretty waterfalls culminating in a 99m drop at an altitude of 1,775m outside the small trading centre of Sipi. The resorts here make an agreeable base for gentle day walks in the hills, and offer spectacular views over the Kyoga Basin and glimpses of the Elgon peaks. The most popular walking trail, only 20 minutes in each direction, leads from behind the post office in Sipi trading centre to the base of the main waterfall, where a small entrance fee is levied. More ambitiously, a day hike leads from the main waterfall to the three smaller falls upstream, one of which has a tempting swimming pool at its base.

Between Sipi and Kapchorwa, a fork to the right leads to the Mount Elgon Exploration Centre, an excellent base for those who wish to explore the lower slopes of the mountain on day hikes. The centre lies at the centre of a network of trails through grassy meadows and montane forest studded with waterfalls. Monkeys are plentiful, and birdwatchers can hope to see a good selection of highland birds, several of which are eastern species at the most westerly extreme of their range.

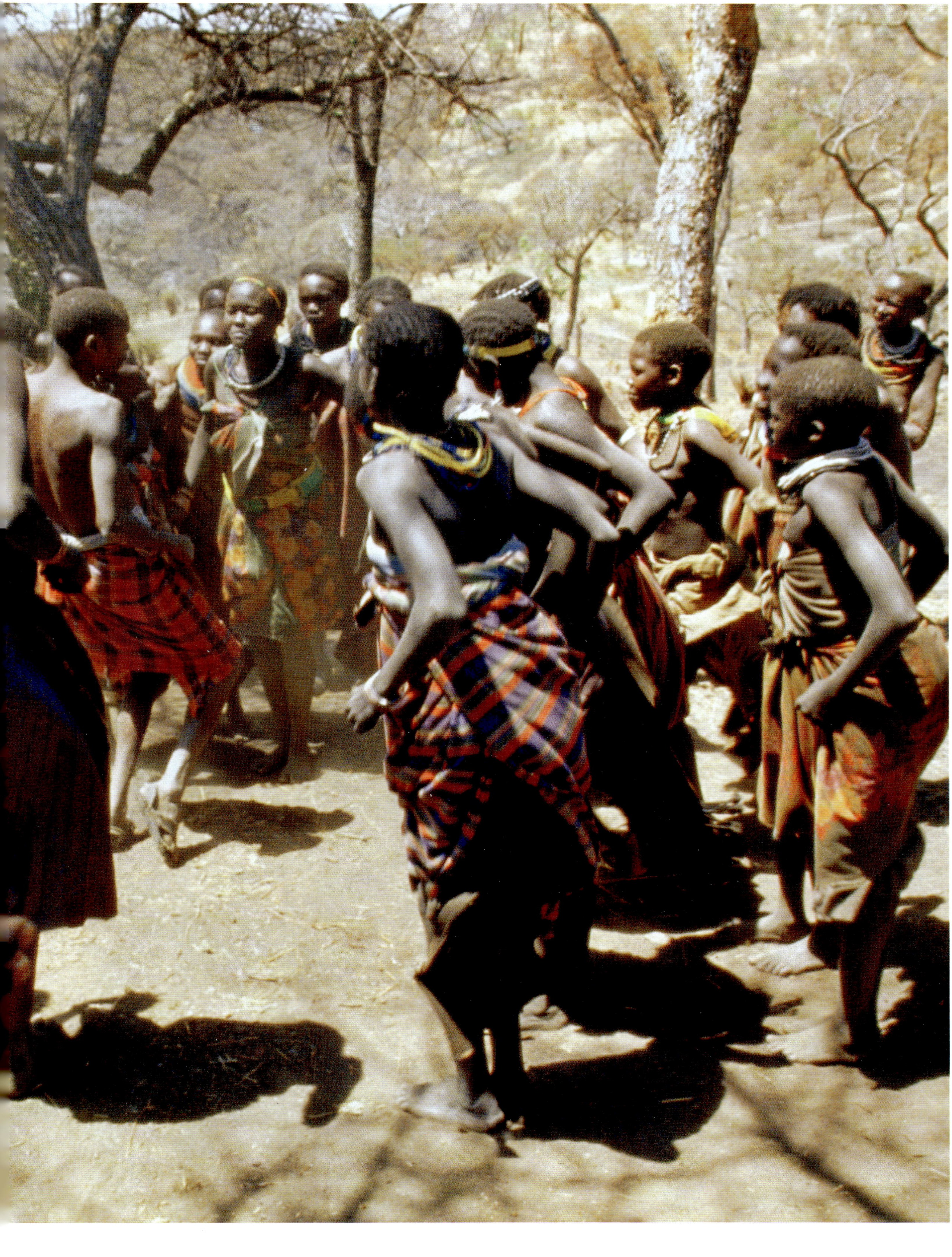

Opposite: Karamoja celebrations.

Below: IK (Teuso) girl.

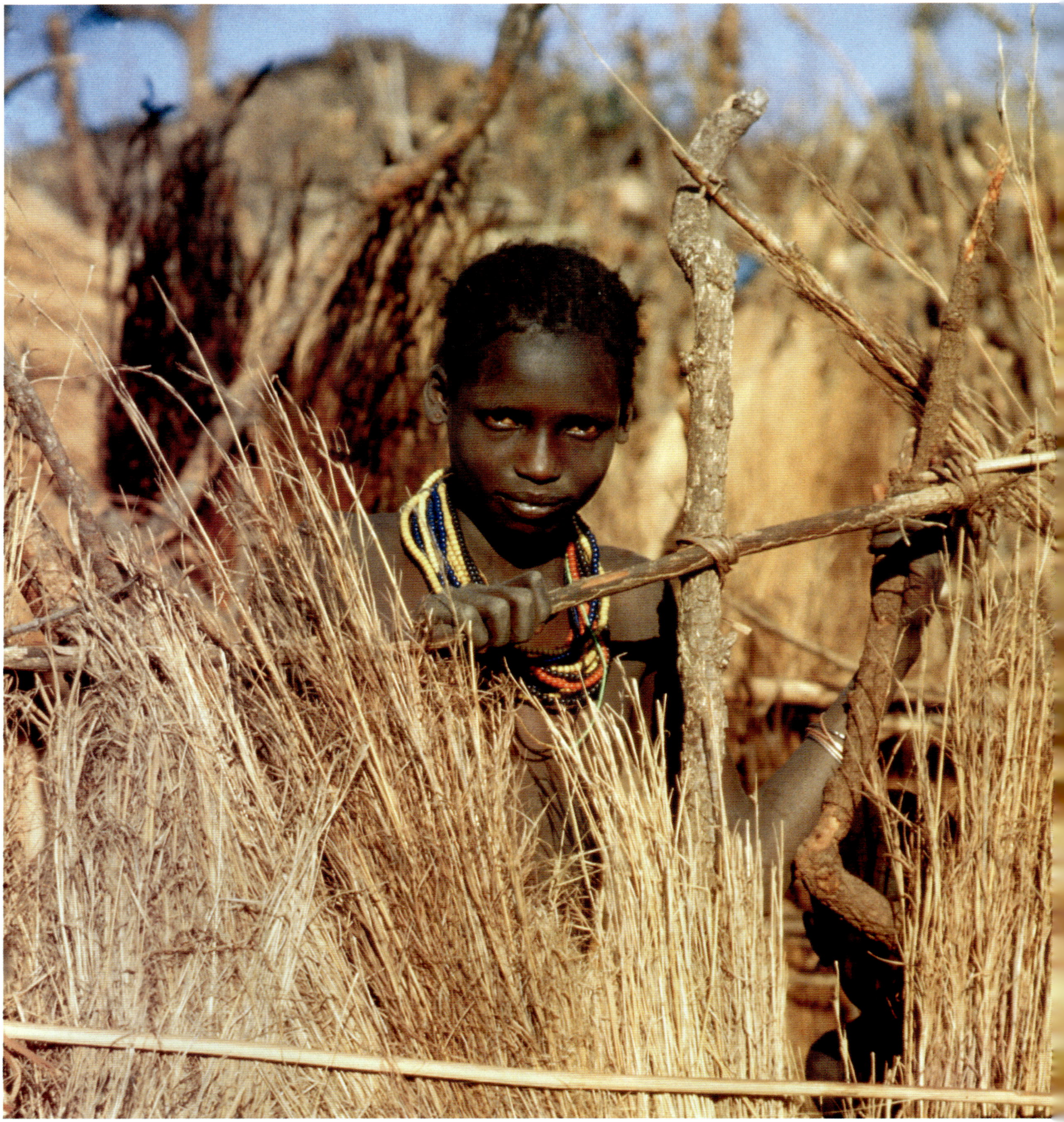

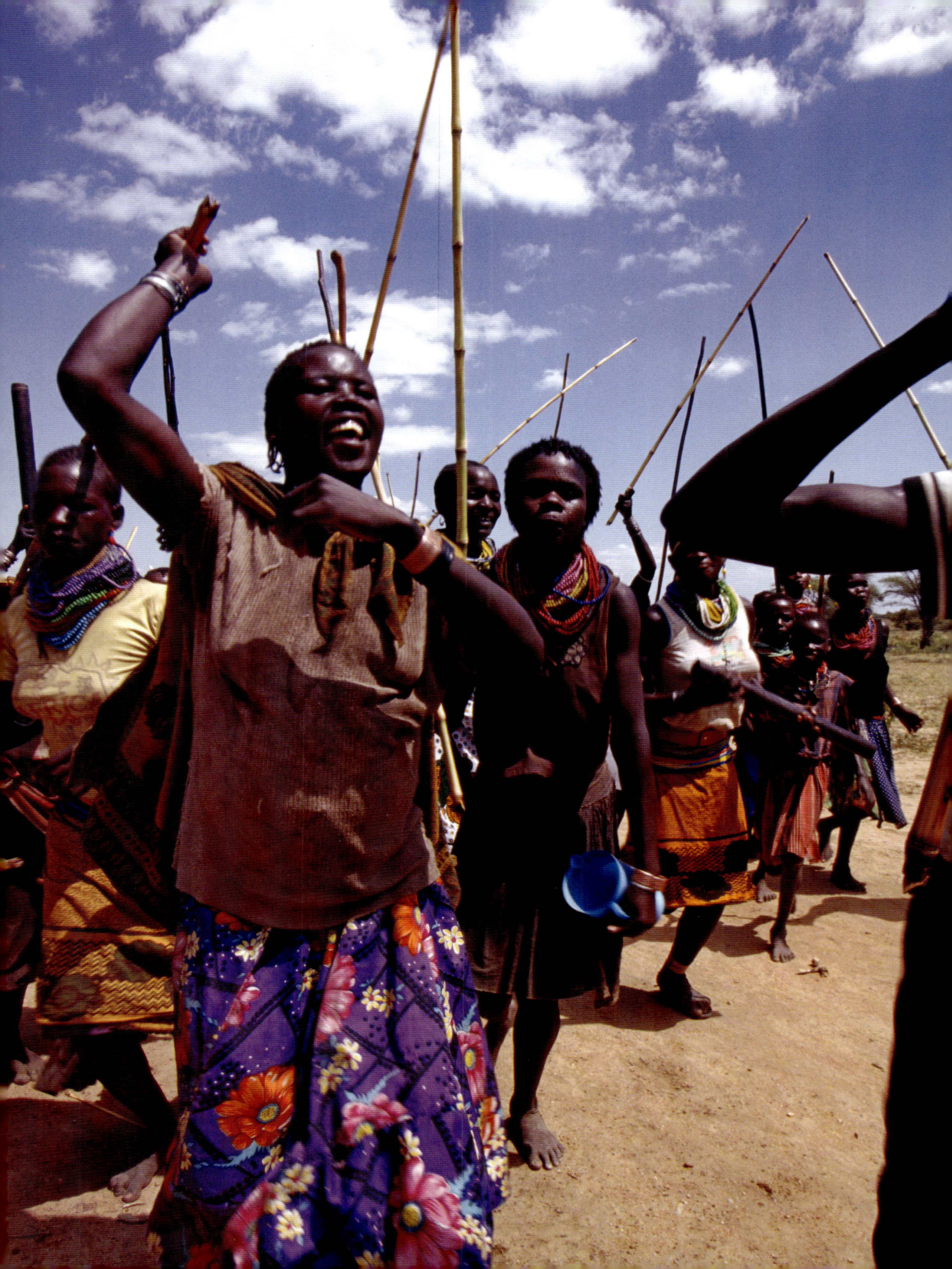

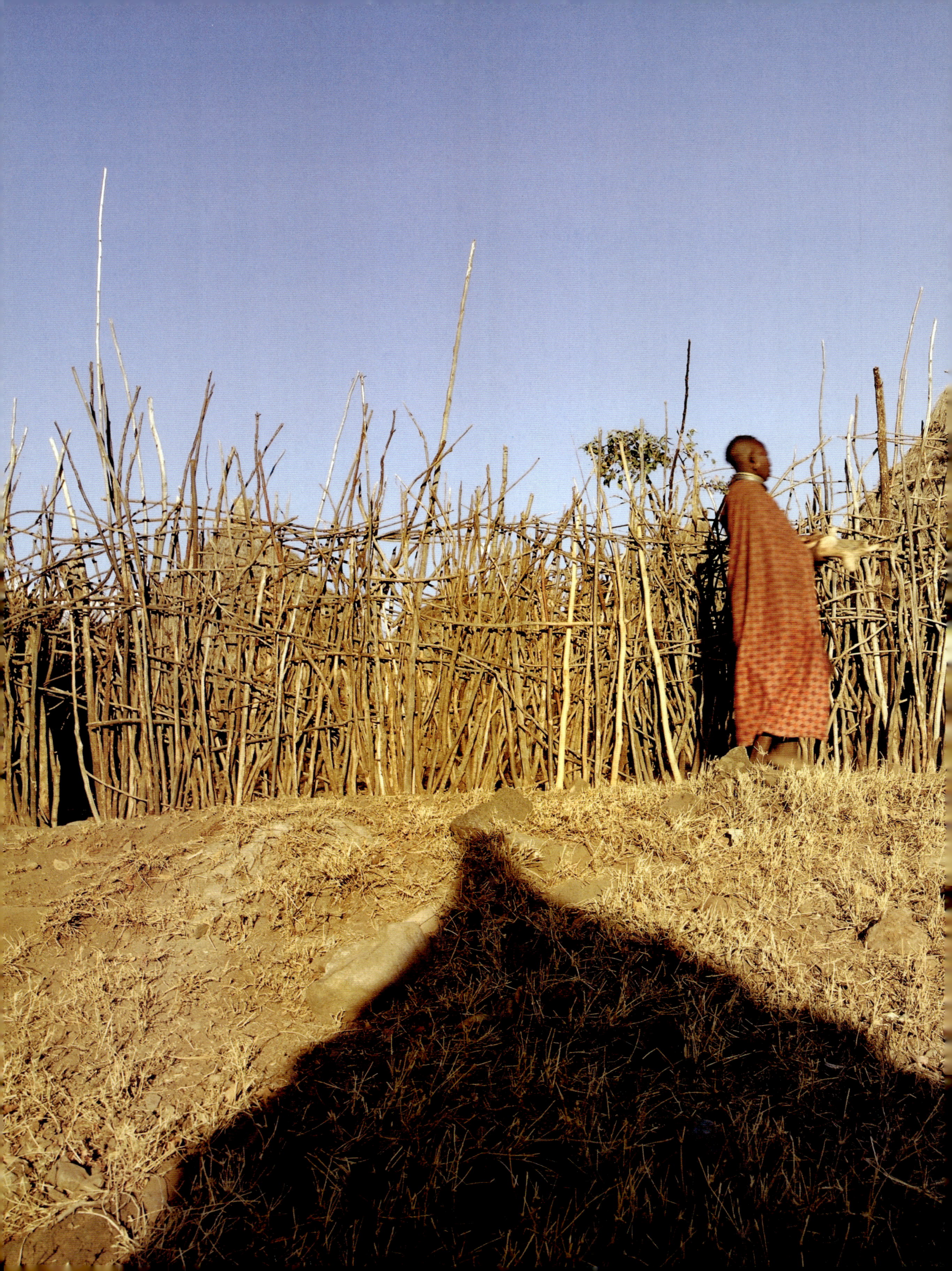

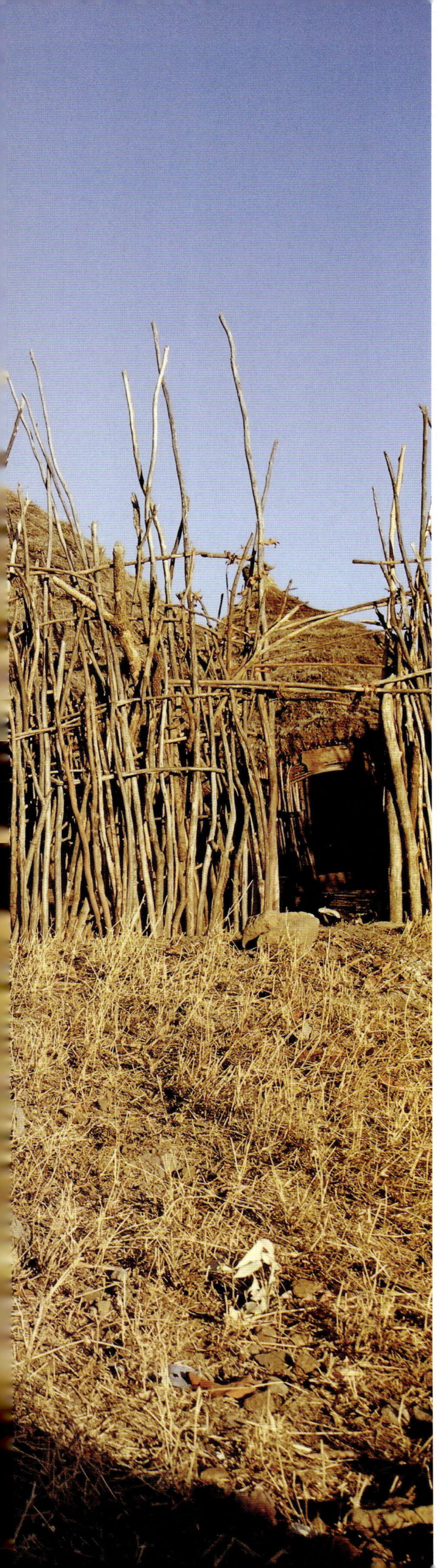

Further afield, the Nyero rock paintings southwest of Kumi are thought to be about 400 years old, and include some of the finest examples of geometric prehistoric rock art in East Africa. There is another set of paintings, as well as an ancient rock gong, at Kakoro, which lies off the main Kumi-Mbale road.

After Mount Elgon, a trip further north to Uganda's most remote national park is a startling and wonderful contrast. Gazetted in 1962, Kidepo Valley National Park is one of the country's most unsung treasures, set in the vast, semi-arid plains of the wild northeast, bordering Sudan and very near to Kenya. A large part of the park's appeal is its remoteness – guaranteeing that the visitor won't be fighting off minibuses in an attempt to see wildlife – but it is also notable for its spectacular and untrammelled scenery. Extending over 1,442 square kilometres (556 square miles), the park is centred on the low-lying Kidepo and Narus River Valleys, which are enclosed by mountainous country rising to the 2,750-metre (8,937-foot) Mount Morongole on the eastern flank, and the forested 2,797 metres (9,090 feet) Mount Lotuke in Sudan.

This remarkable variation in altitude has created a profusion of habitats, including montane forest, grassy plains, open tree savannah, dry thorn bush, thick woodlands, borassus palm forest, and koppies (rocky outcrops). During the six dry months Kidepo's wildlife is attracted to the perennial water of the Narus Valley in the south-west of the park. There is a great diversity of wildlife here, though the former checklist of 86 species – of which 28 occur in no other Ugandan national park – has had to be been pruned to 77 after a recent rash of local extinctions. Even so, wildlife is abundant, with zebra, elephant, eland, kudu, dik-dik, waterbuck, oribi and buffalo among the more conspicuous species.

Kidepo is also an ornithologist's delight. The official checklist includes nearly 500 species, with the park's koppies and forest patches providing very good habitats for unusual species, including around 60 that are not recorded in other Ugandan national parks, notably the outsized ostrich and kori bustard. There are five species of hornbill, including the giant ground hornbill, while the 56 recorded raptors include Verreaux's eagle, lammergeyer and Egyptian vulture. But while the game viewing and birding can be excellent, it is the thrilling sense of supreme isolation that distinguishes this rare slice of wild Africa, as yet undiscovered by the mass safari market.

Visitors can get a good look at this bountiful wildlife and birdlife from several game-viewing loops close to the main rest camp at Apoka in the Narus Valley, where most of the game is concentrated. Visitors can also take the drive north to the Kanangarok hot springs, crossing the Kidepo River, with its sandy beaches and borassus palm forest. In addition, the

Right: Nyero rock paintings.

Following pages: Kidepo sunset.

park nature exhibit at the Apoka headquarters is open to visitors and contains specimens of lion skins, giraffe skulls, butterflies, scorpions, and photographs of a rare albino buffalo.

Kidepo lies in a region known as Karamoja (although its no longer officially named as such) after the famous Karimojong pastoralists who graze their cattle across the plains. There are actually about six different groups of Karimojong in Uganda: the Jie, Ik, Nyangia, Napore, Teuso, and Dodoth. The Napore and the Nyangia have become more involved in agriculture over recent years, while the Teuso are hunter-gatherers, speaking a different dialect from the other Karimojong. The Dodoth, however, still maintain their strong pastoralist way of life. For a taste of local life, one can arrange to visit Karimojong manyattas (homesteads) in the area to see the traditional clothing, stools, spears, headdresses, knives, bows and arrows, and jewellery. If the visitor is lucky enough to witness one of their traditional dances – such as the *emuya* and *ekaharo* – it will be a memorable experience.

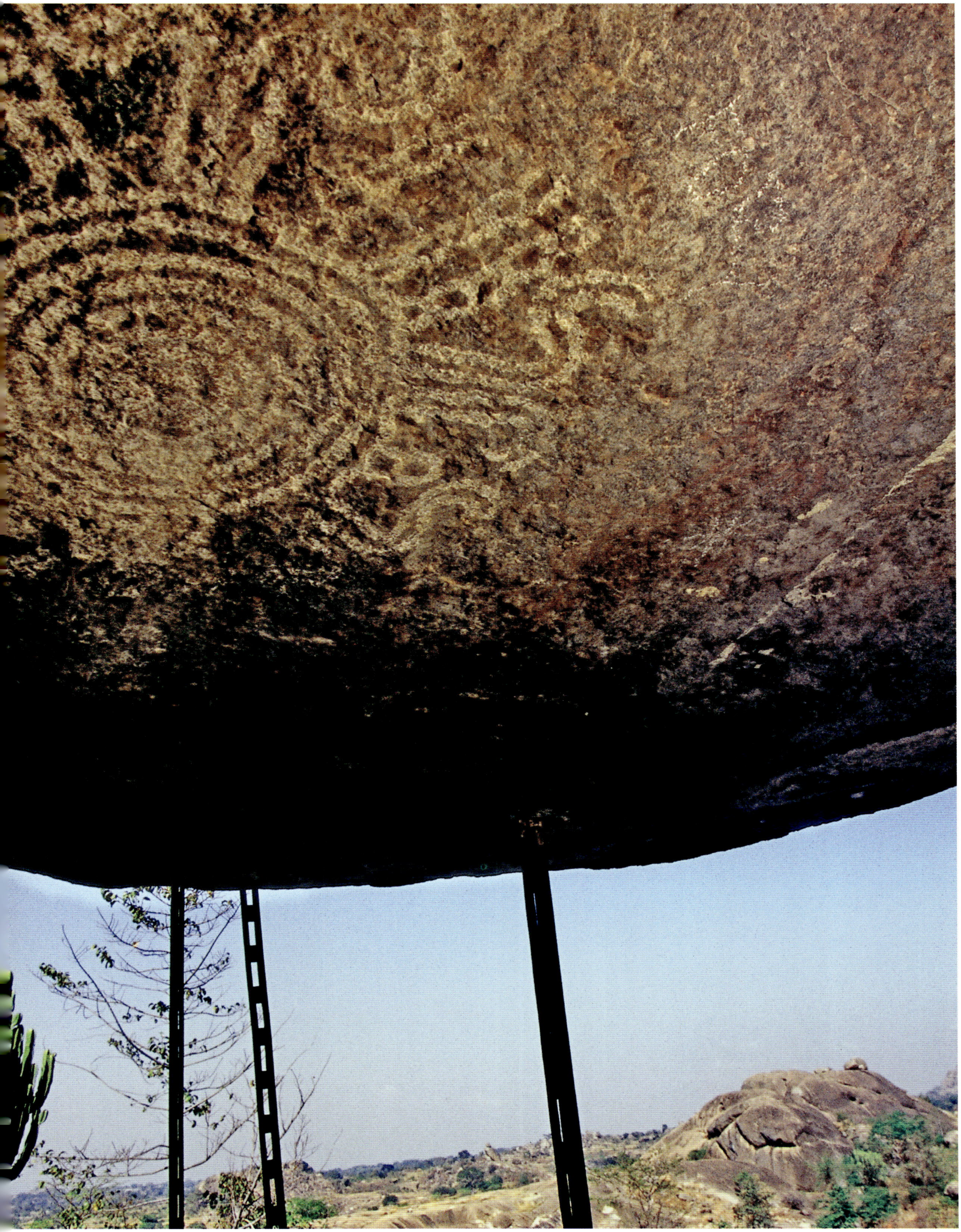

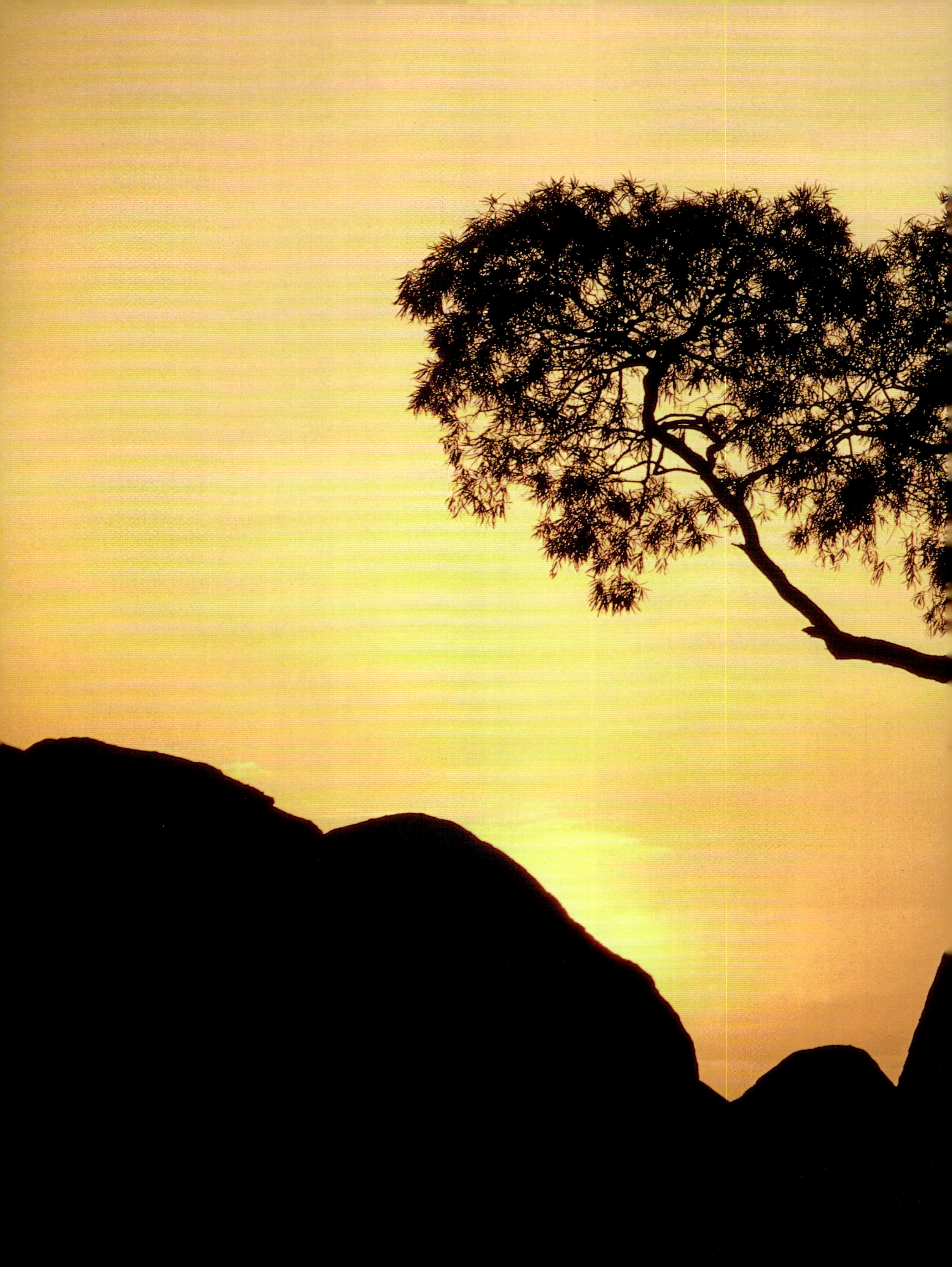

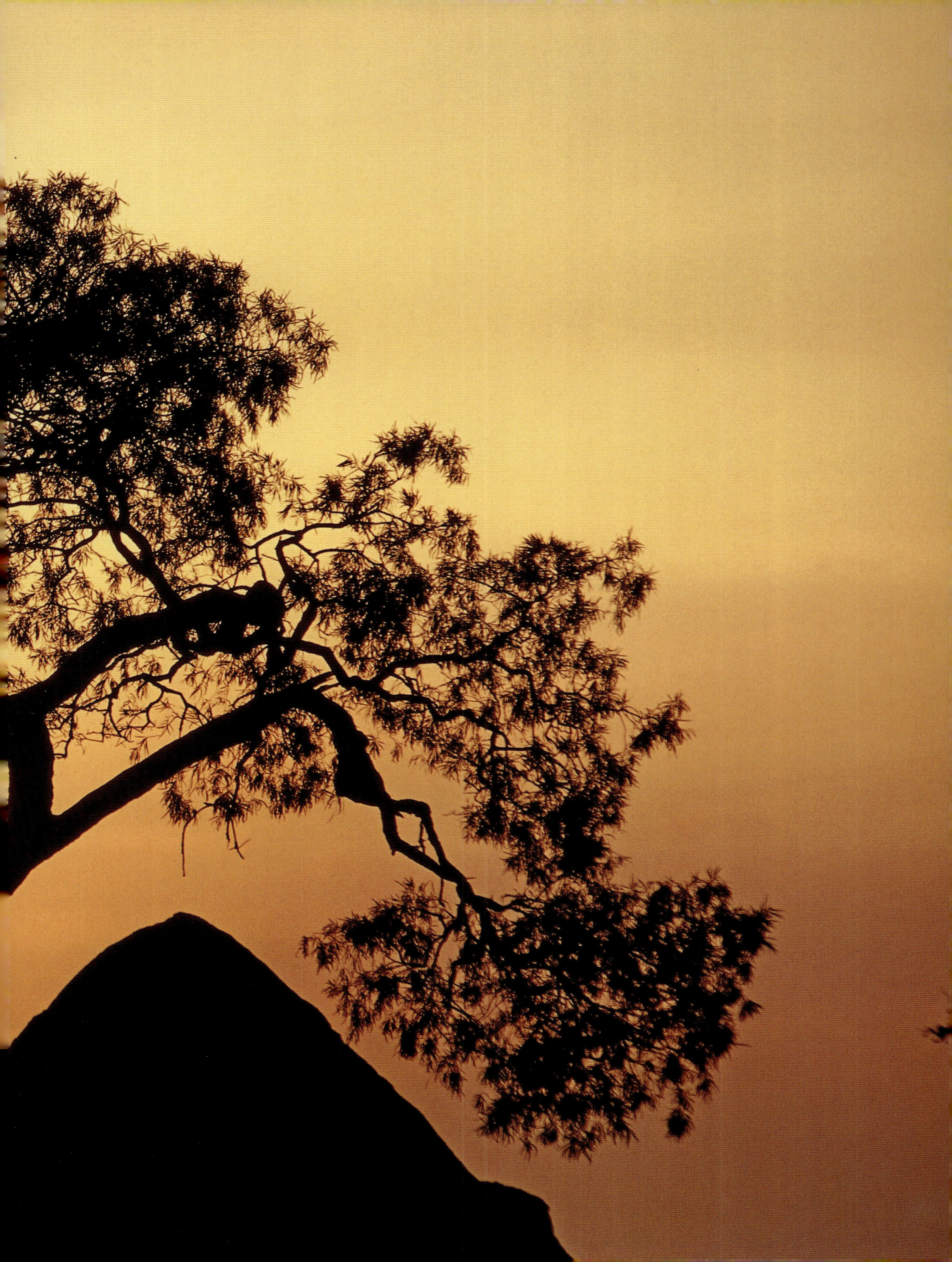

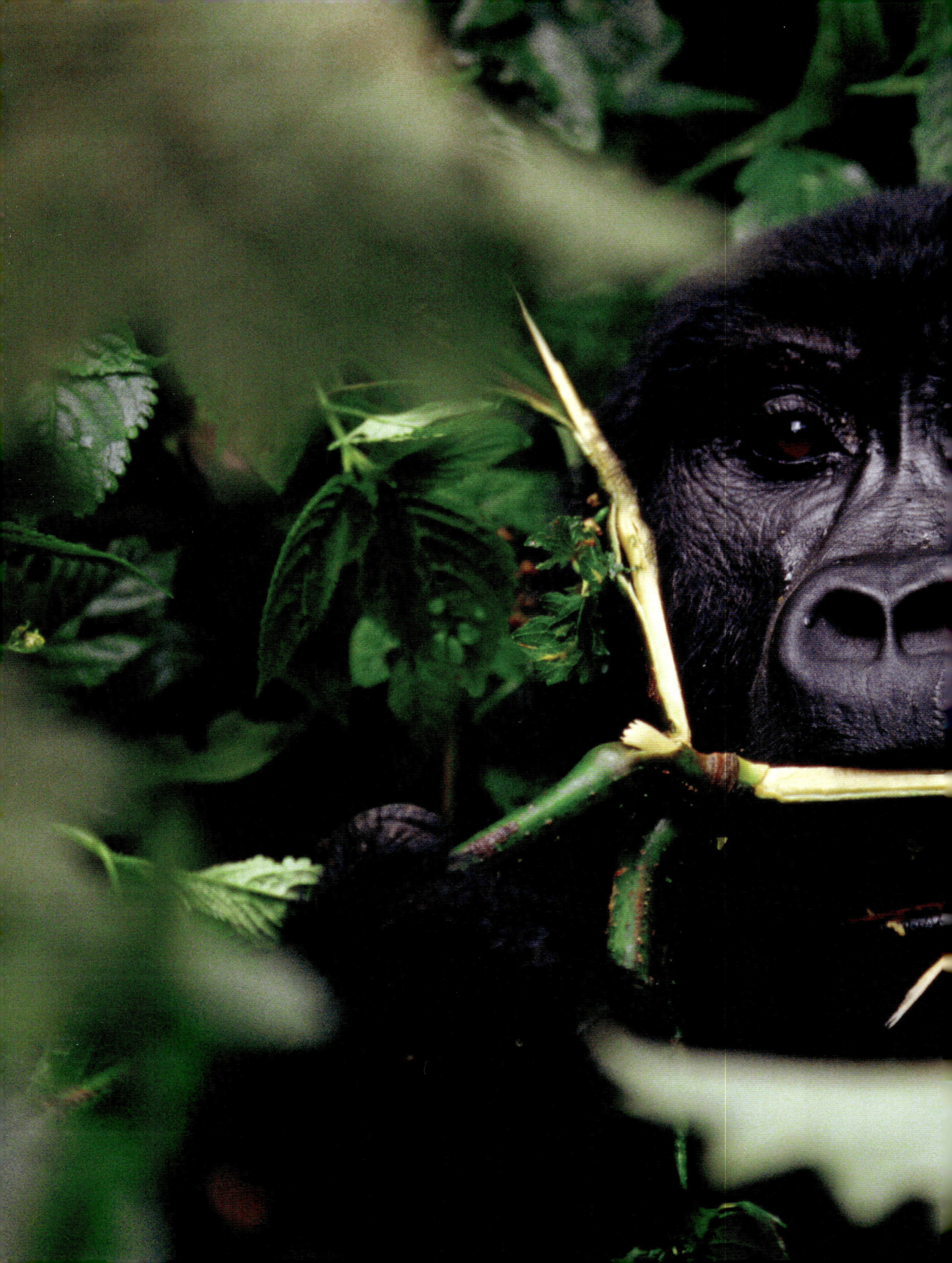

8. Gorillas and other wildlife

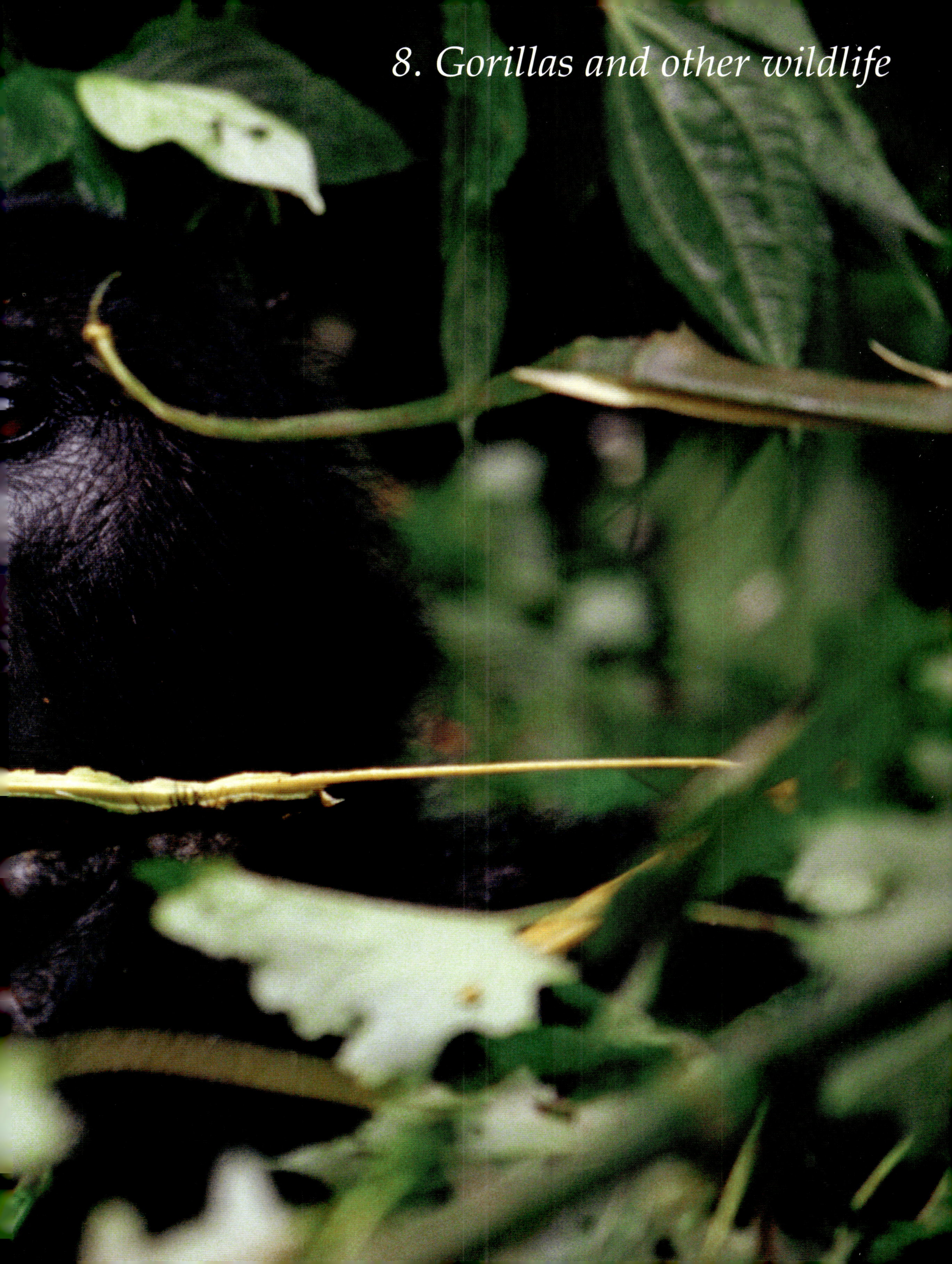

Opposite: Chimpanzee in its forest habitat.

Previous pages: Gorilla in Bwindi Impenetrable National Park.

Uganda is one of the world's most exciting ecotourism destinations. True, it lacks the large herds of grazers associated with neighbouring Kenya and Tanzania, but this is compensated for by the rich biodiversity if its varied savannah, forest and wetlands habitats, where typical plains dwellers such as lion and giraffe rub shoulders with creatures more normally associated with the relatively inaccessible rainforests of Central Africa. Overall, Uganda's wildlife is in remarkably good shape: Bwindi, Budongo, Semliki and Kibale rank among the most pristine forest habitats in East Africa, while savannah reserves such as Queen Elizabeth and Murchison Falls National Park are now largely recovered from the intensive poaching that blighted the Amin era.

Uganda's most important wildlife attraction is its wealth of primates. Specifically, Mgahinga Gorilla and Bwindi Impenetrable National Parks, in the far southwest of the country, are two of only four places in the world where one can see the endangered mountain gorilla. Gorilla tracking permits are expensive and may be hard to come by in peak tourist seasons, and the activity itself sometimes involves some serious trekking on slippery rainforest slopes, but the odds of a sighting in Bwindi are better than 99%. In addition to mountain gorillas, Uganda is also one of the top places in the world to see wild chimpanzees, which are more closely related to humans than to any other ape. Kibale Forest is the country's leading chimp-tracking destination, but these charismatic apes can also be tracked in Budongo Forest and the Chambura River Gorge in Queen Elizabeth National Park. A less authentic option, but one that guarantees close-up sightings, is the sanctuary for orphaned chimps situated on Ngamba Island, which lies in Lake Victoria and can be visited as a day or overnight excursion from Entebbe.

All the monkeys found in the country belong to the family Cercopithecidae (Old World monkeys). The largest species on show is the olive baboon, which has a doglike head, an impressive mane, and occurs in a wide variety of lightly and heavily wooded habitats. Also associated with savannah are the ubiquitous vervet monkey, which is grey with a black face and blue genitals, and russet-coloured patas monkey, which mainly occurs in the arid north. Widespread forest dwellers include blue monkey, red-tailed monkey, black-and-white colobus, while the likes of de Brazza's monkey, L'Hoest's monkey, Wolf's mona monkey, owl-faced monkey, grey-cheeked mangabey and red colobus are more localised. Of special note is the golden monkey, a striking orange bamboo-dweller whose range is practically confined to the Virunga Mountains on the border with Rwanda. Nocturnal primates include the wide-eyed greater bushbaby and its smaller relative, the lesser bushbaby – more often heard than seen.

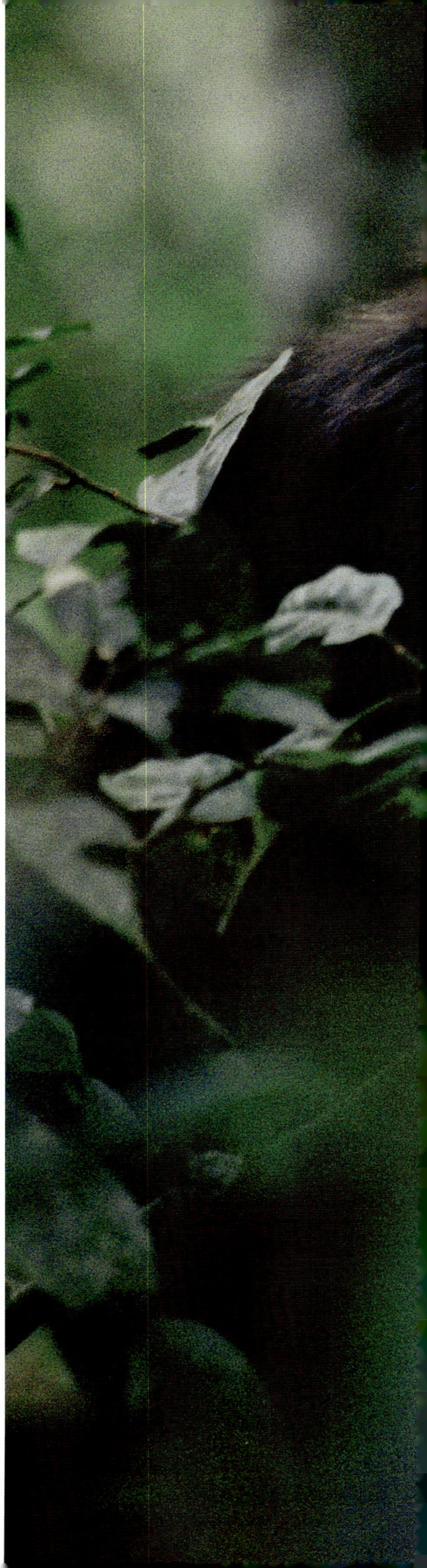

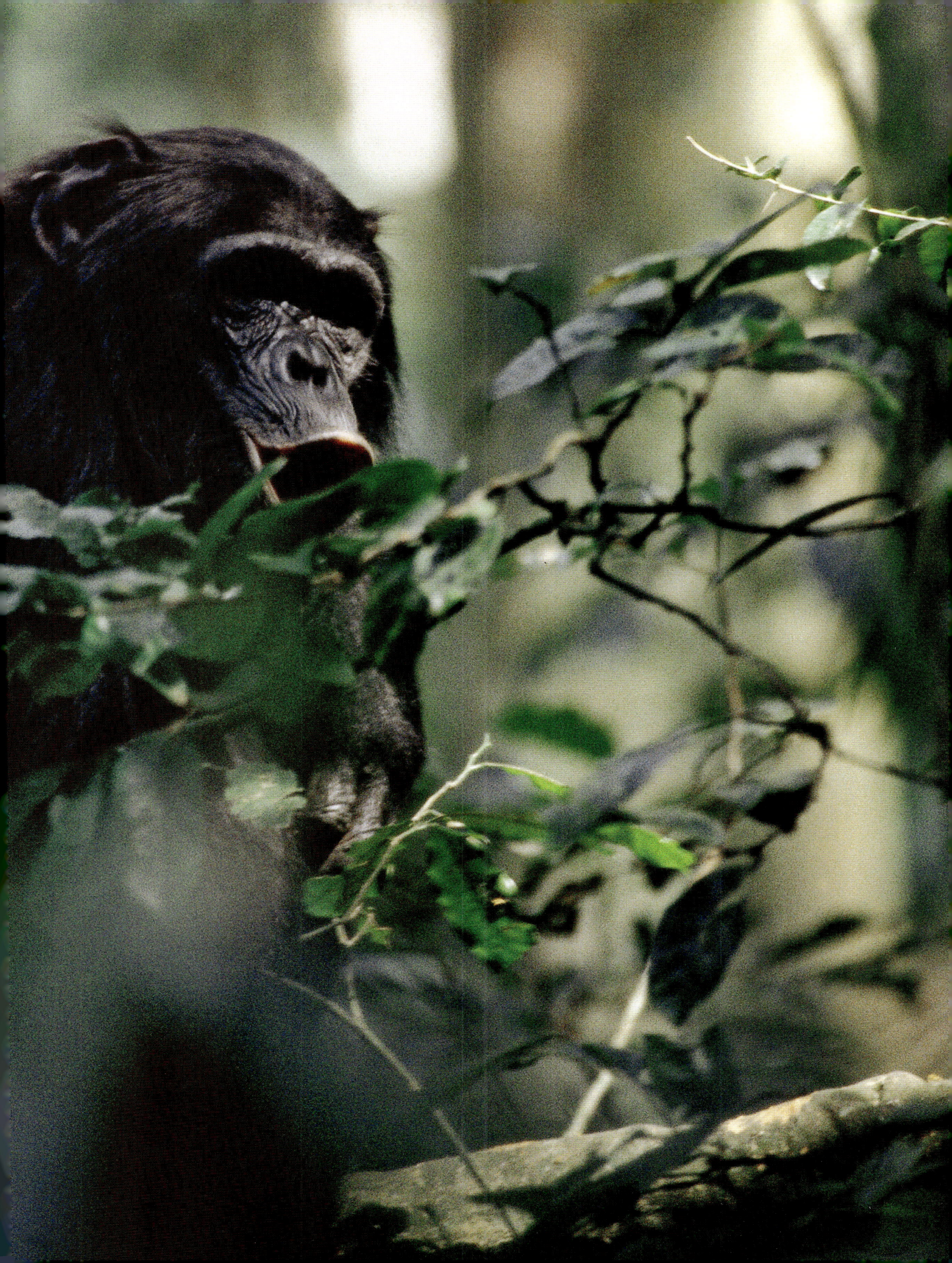

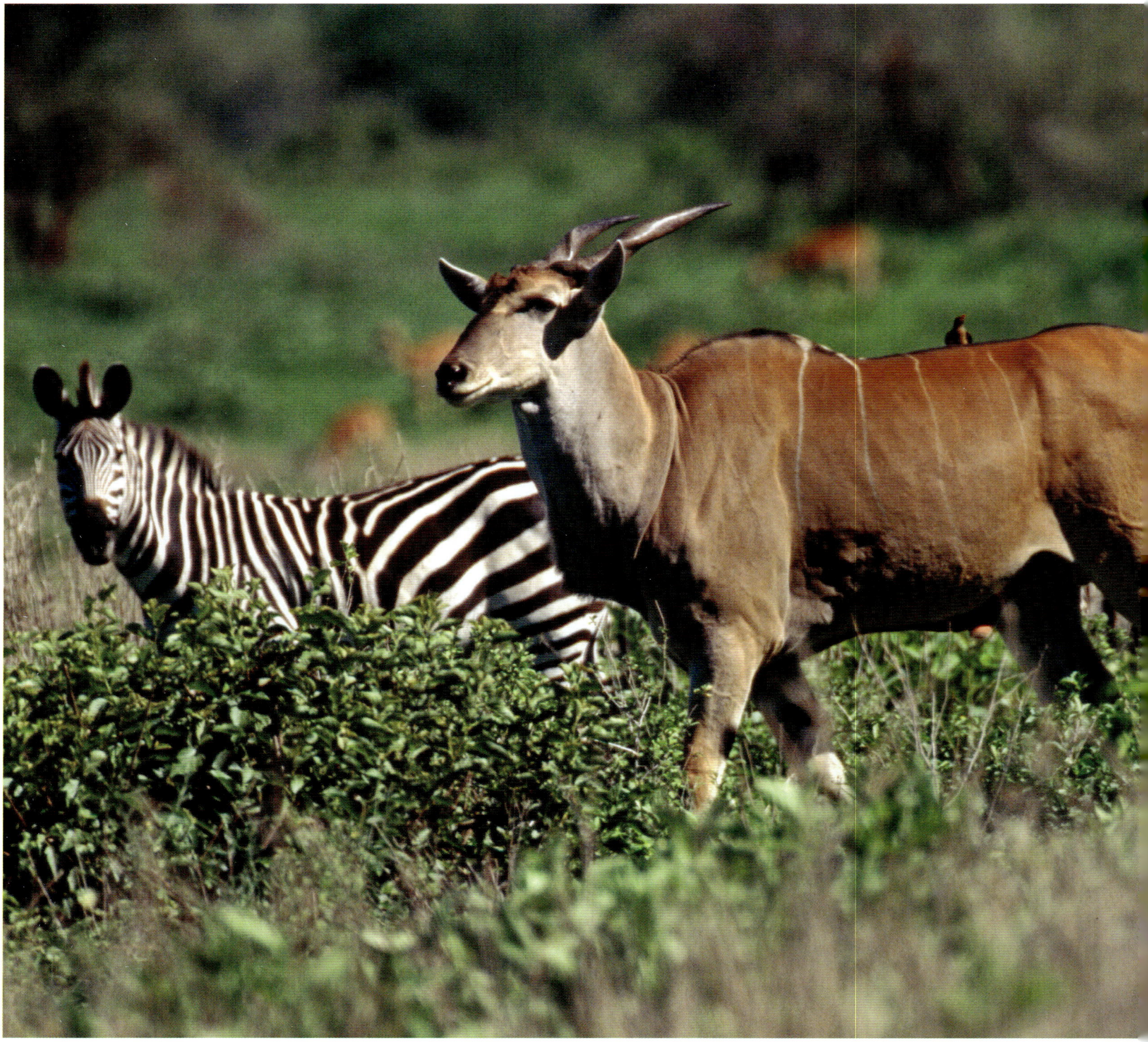

Of the Big Five – elephant, buffalo, lion, leopard, and rhinoceros – the latter were poached to local extinction in the 1980s, but a few recently reintroduced individuals can be tracked in Ziwa Ranch en route between Kampala and Murchison Falls. The world's largest terrestrial creature, the African elephant, has fared rather better, and numbers have recovered strongly over the past two decades. Two races (sometimes regarded to be full species) are recognized in the country: the savannah elephant and the forest elephant, and the two are thought to interbreed in parts of western Uganda. Large herds may be seen in Kidepo Valley, Murchison Falls and Queen Elizabeth National Parks, and smaller numbers are present in several other sites. The African buffalo is found in virtually all the national parks and forests, often in large herds. One may spot a mixed breed of savannah buffalo and the West African red buffalo in several national parks.

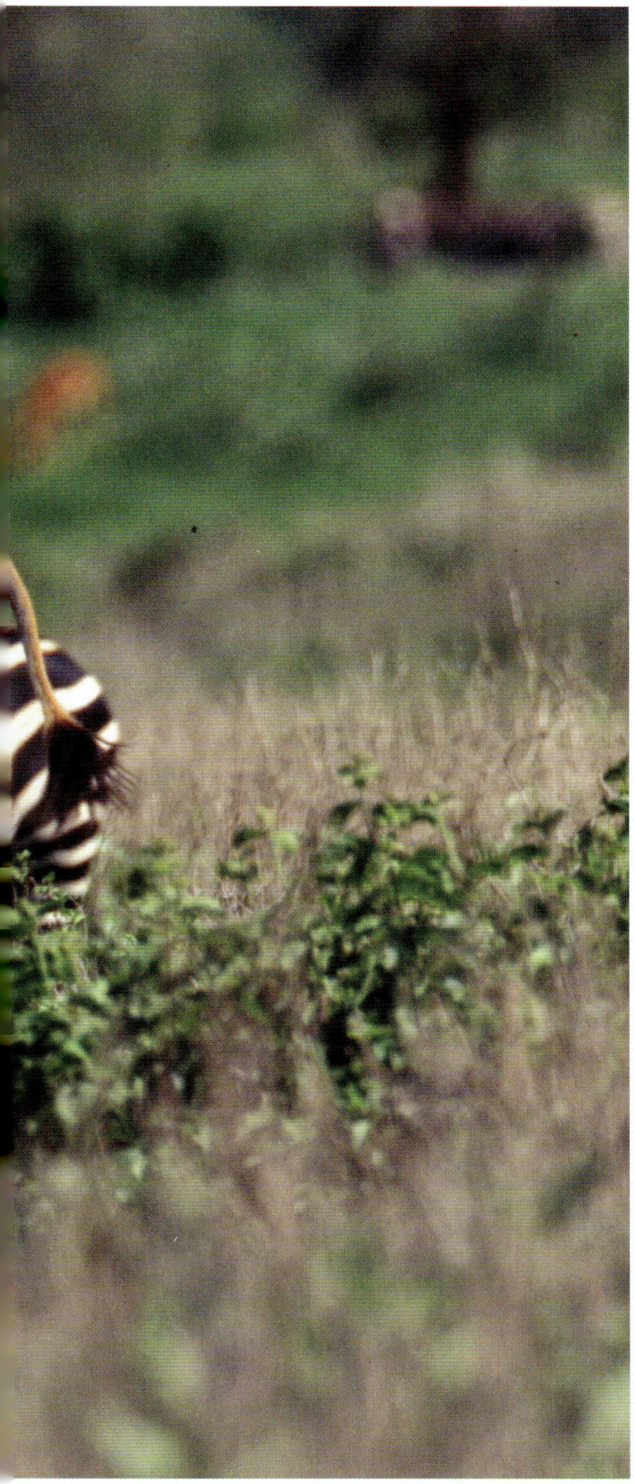

Lions, the most regal of predators, were poached close to extinction in the 1980s, but they have since recovered well and the national population probably exceeds 600 individuals. The most important leonine strongholds are Murchison Falls and Queen Elizabeth National Parks, but they might also be seen in Kidepo Valley or Semliki. Far more common is the leopard, which survives in virtually all Uganda's national parks and forests, and in areas close to human habitation. It has rosette-shaped spots and is stockier than the streamlined cheetah, which in Uganda is found only in Kidepo Valley National Park. The leopard is seldom seen because of its nocturnal ways and secretive nature, though Channel Drive in QENP has a good reputation for sightings. Other members of the cat family present in Uganda are the caracal, golden cat and serval, though they are rarely seen as they are nocturnal.

Of the other predators, the most likely to be seen is the spotted hyena, which is more closely related to mongooses and cats than to the dogs it so closely resembles. Living in clans dominated by females, the hyena is widespread and common throughout the country, although it prefers savannah and woodland habitats. The most widespread dog in Uganda is the side-striped jackal, but it is replaced by the similar black-backed jackal in the northeast. The African hunting dog, a ferocious pack hunter last seen in Queen Elizabeth National Park, is probably extinct in Uganda because of its susceptibility to canine disease. A smaller predator found throughout Uganda – but rarely seen – is the ratel, or honey badger, which has an amazing symbiotic relationship with the greater honeyguide. The bird, wanting honey, will lead the ratel to a beehive. The ratel then obligingly tears the hive open, eating what it wants, leaving the rest for the honeyguide. Also nocturnal, the superficially catlike genet may often be spotted slinking around campsites at night, but the related civet is seldom seen. More likely to be seen are various mongooses, of which the sociable banded mongoose of probably the most common, while Lake Bunyonyi is quite possibly the best site in Africa for seeing otters.

Antelopes of all shapes and sizes exist in Uganda in fairly large numbers. One most often associated with the country (often referred to as its 'national antelope') is the Uganda kob, a stocky, russet-coloured animal about half the size of a waterbuck, to which it is related. Preferring moist, savannah-like habitats, this highly sociable antelope is easily seen in Murchison Falls and Queen Elizabeth National Parks, where it is worth spending time at the kob mating grounds to observe some of the interesting habits of this animal. Kobs are also quite common in the Semliki and Katonga Wildlife Reserves. The smaller Bates's pygmy antelope is a central and west African rainforest endemic whose range extends into a handful of western Uganda's forests. Weighing only three

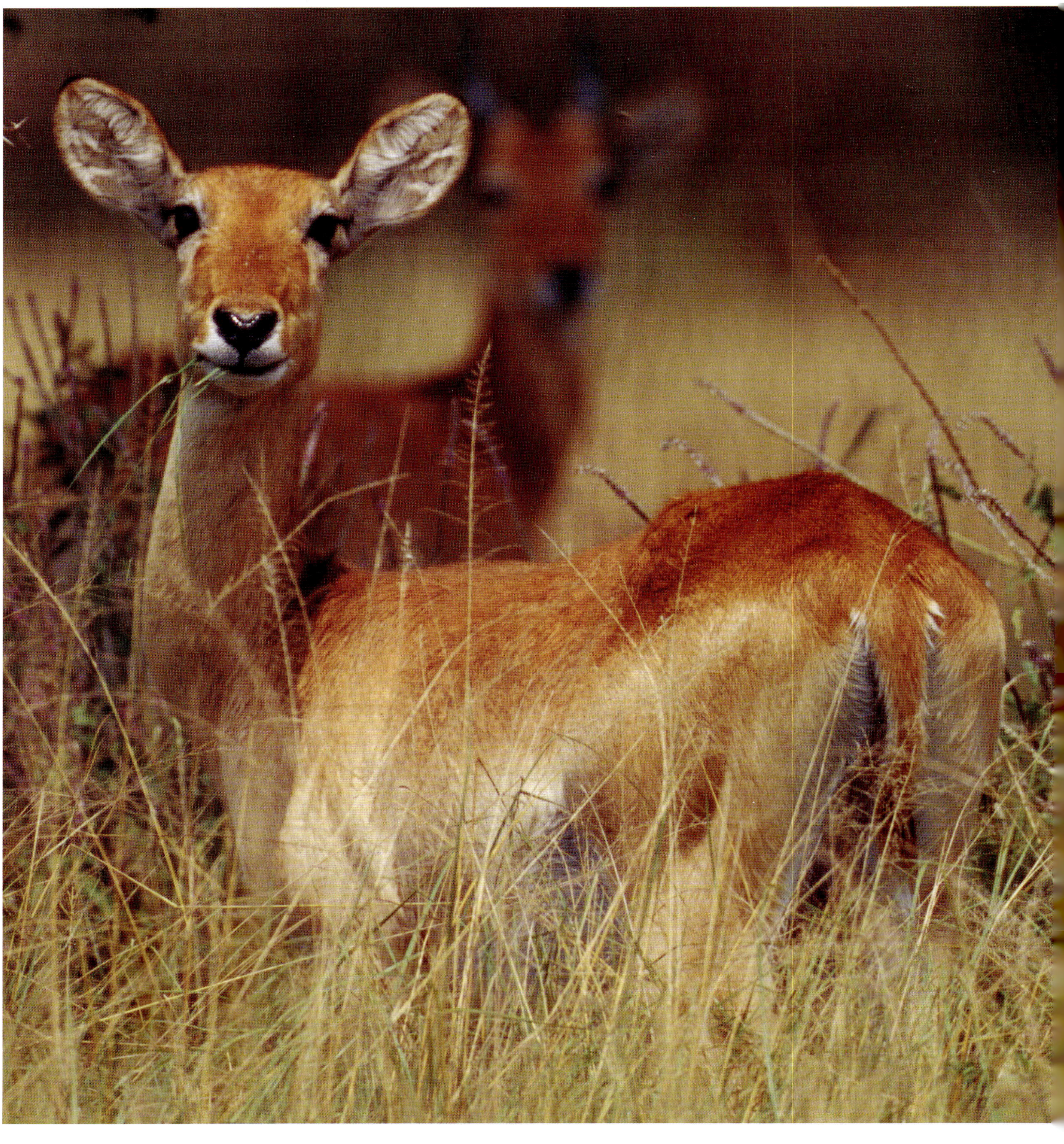

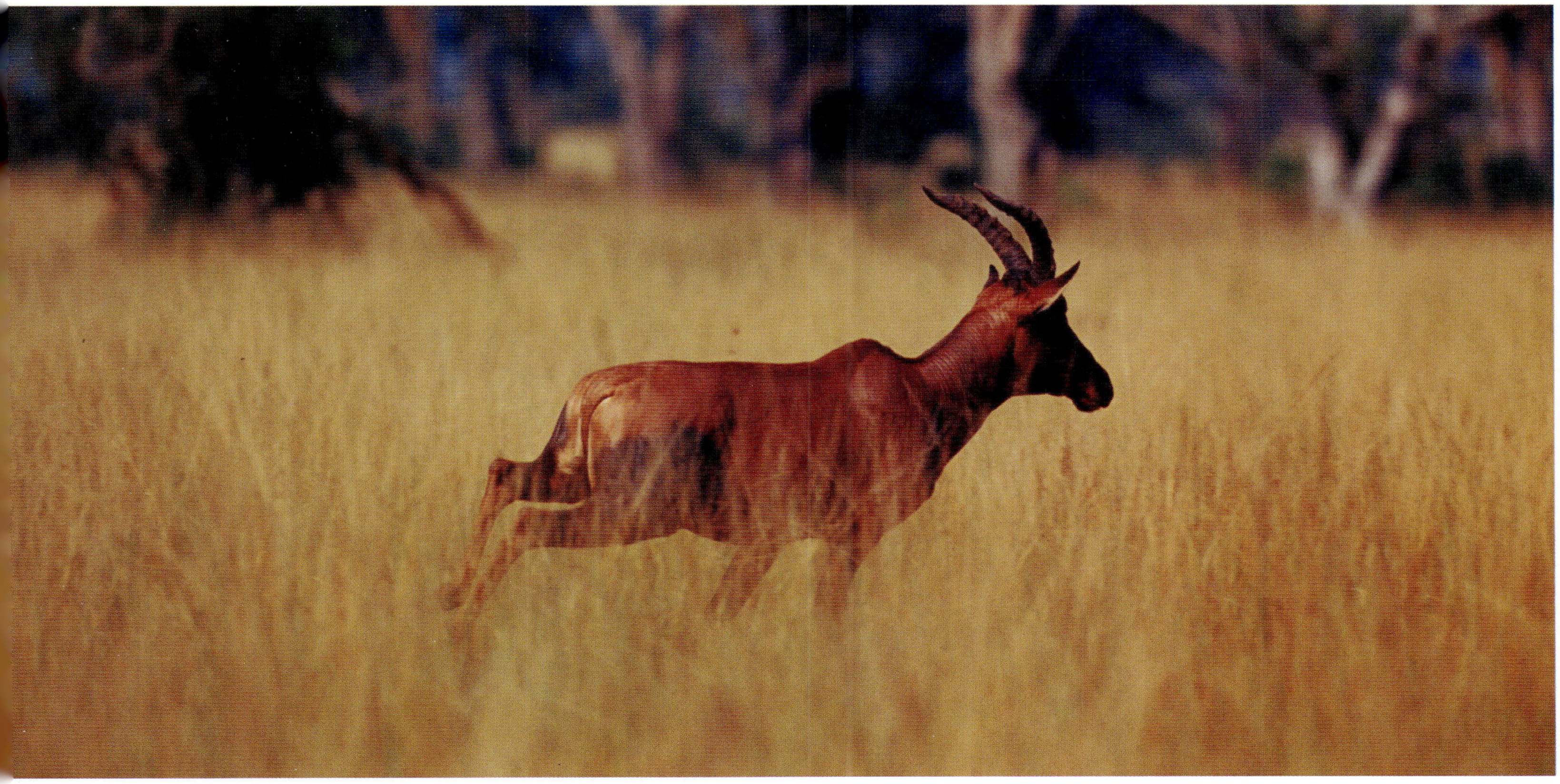

bove: Topi.

pposite: Female kob.

kilogrammes (seven lbs), it is the one of the smallest ungulates in East Africa, and is seldom seen as it prefers thick cover and is very shy.

Africa's largest antelope, the eland, with its long spiralled horns and large dewlaps, is also found in the country. Weighing in at around 700 kilos (1,500 lbs), the eland occurs in Kidepo Valley National Park in the north and Lake Mburo National Park in the south. Kidepo Valley National Park is also home to two other beautiful spiral-horned antelope, the greater kudu and the lesser kudu. Although, true to its name, the lesser kudu is about half the size of the greater, both varieties having light brown coats and delicate white stripes down the sides of their bodies. Only the males have horns. The most widespread spiral-horned antelope is the bushbuck, a common but shy antelope of forest and riverine woodland. In Uganda, it can be found in most forests and national parks and is particularly plentiful in Queen Elizabeth National Park. The most unusual spiral-horned antelope resident in Uganda is the sitatunga, whose greatly elongated hooves enable it to walk on floating vegetation in papyrus swamps. It is very shy and hence difficult to see; when confronted, it dives under the water and hides, with only its nose showing.

Two species of the awkward-looking hartebeest, with its long, mournful face, exist in Uganda. Most common is Jackson's hartebeest, found in Murchison Falls, Kidepo Valley and Lake Mburo National Parks, while

Opposite: Kidepo Waterbuck.

Below: Curious lion emerges from an afternoon siesta.

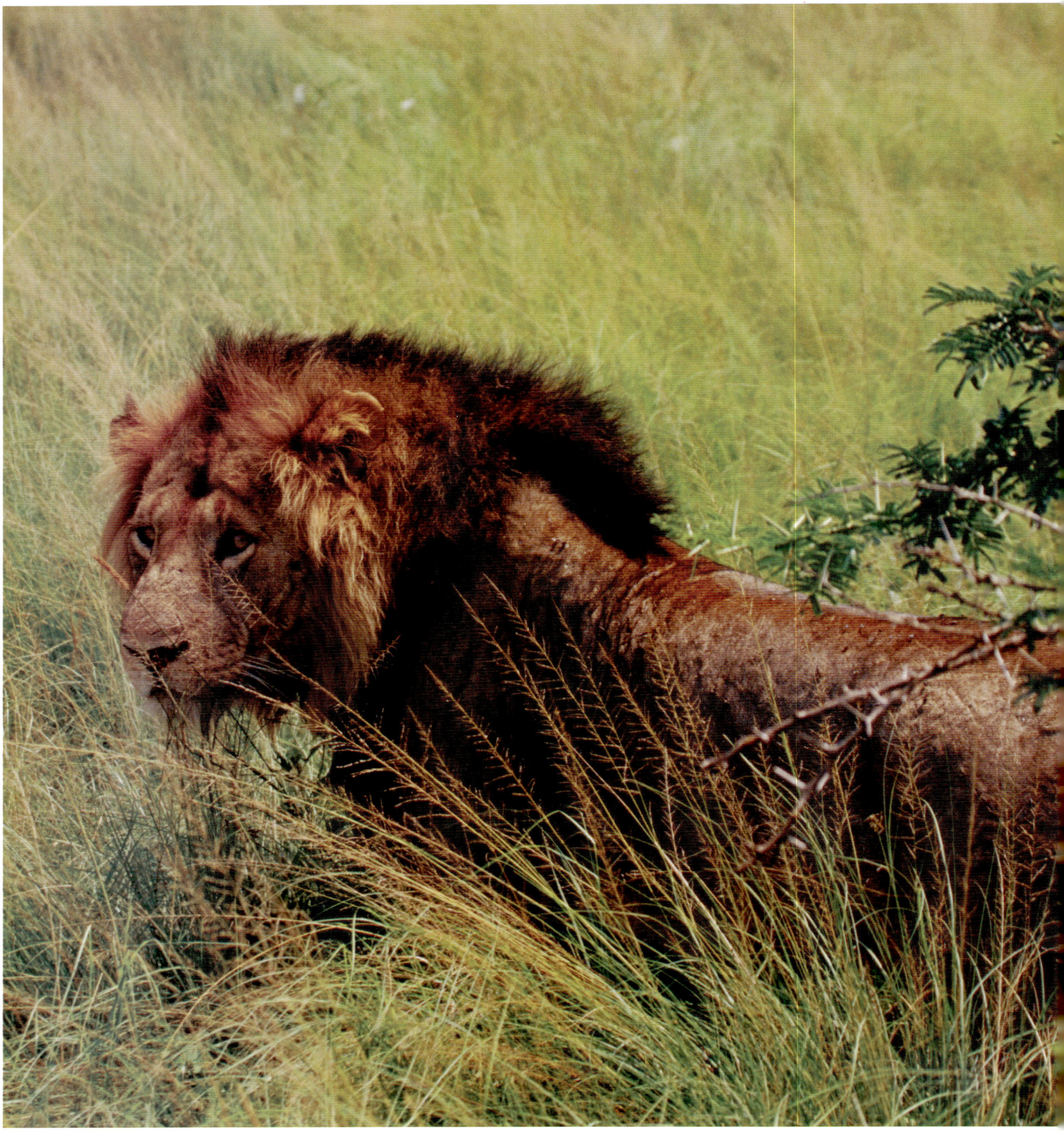

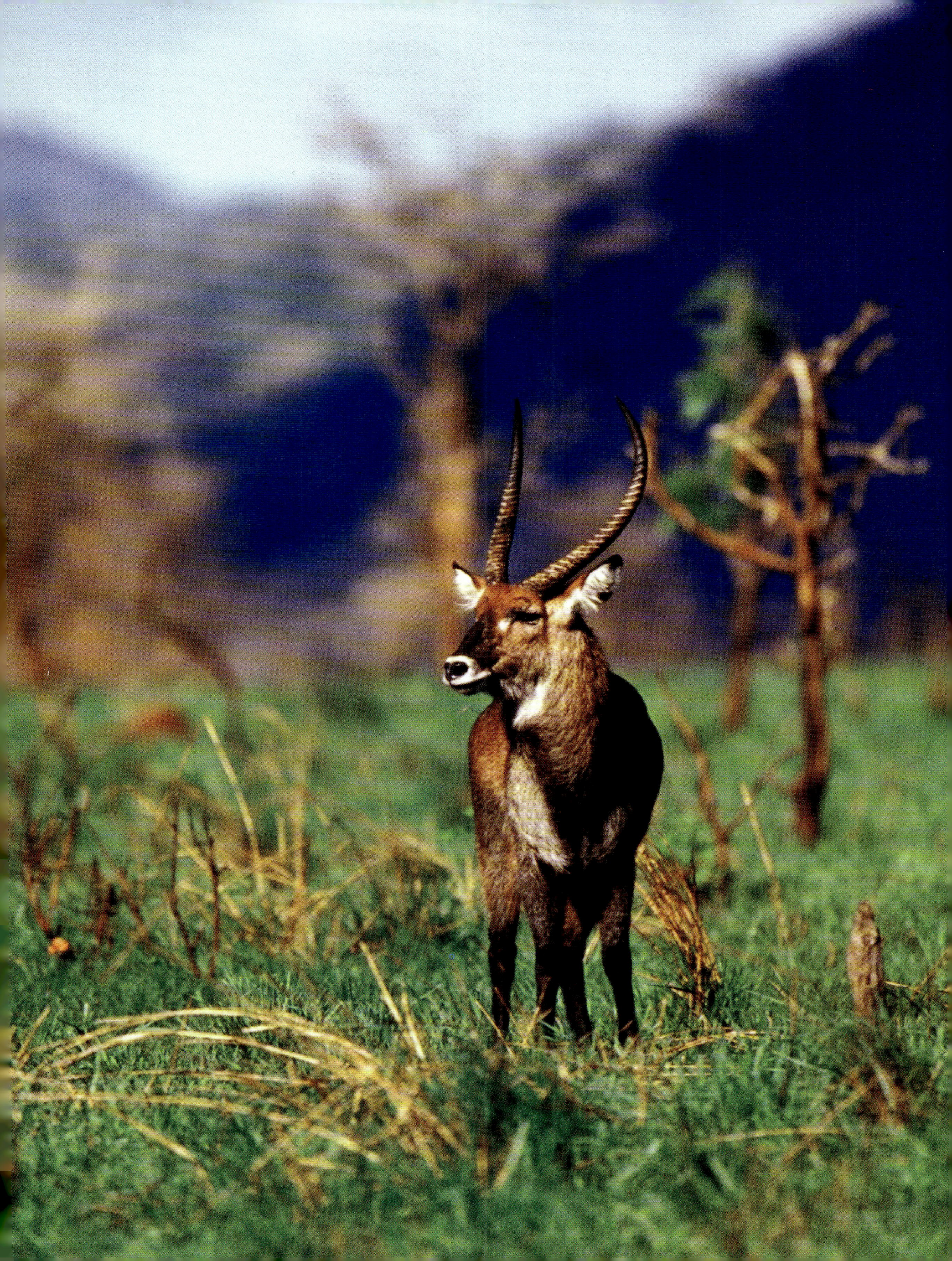

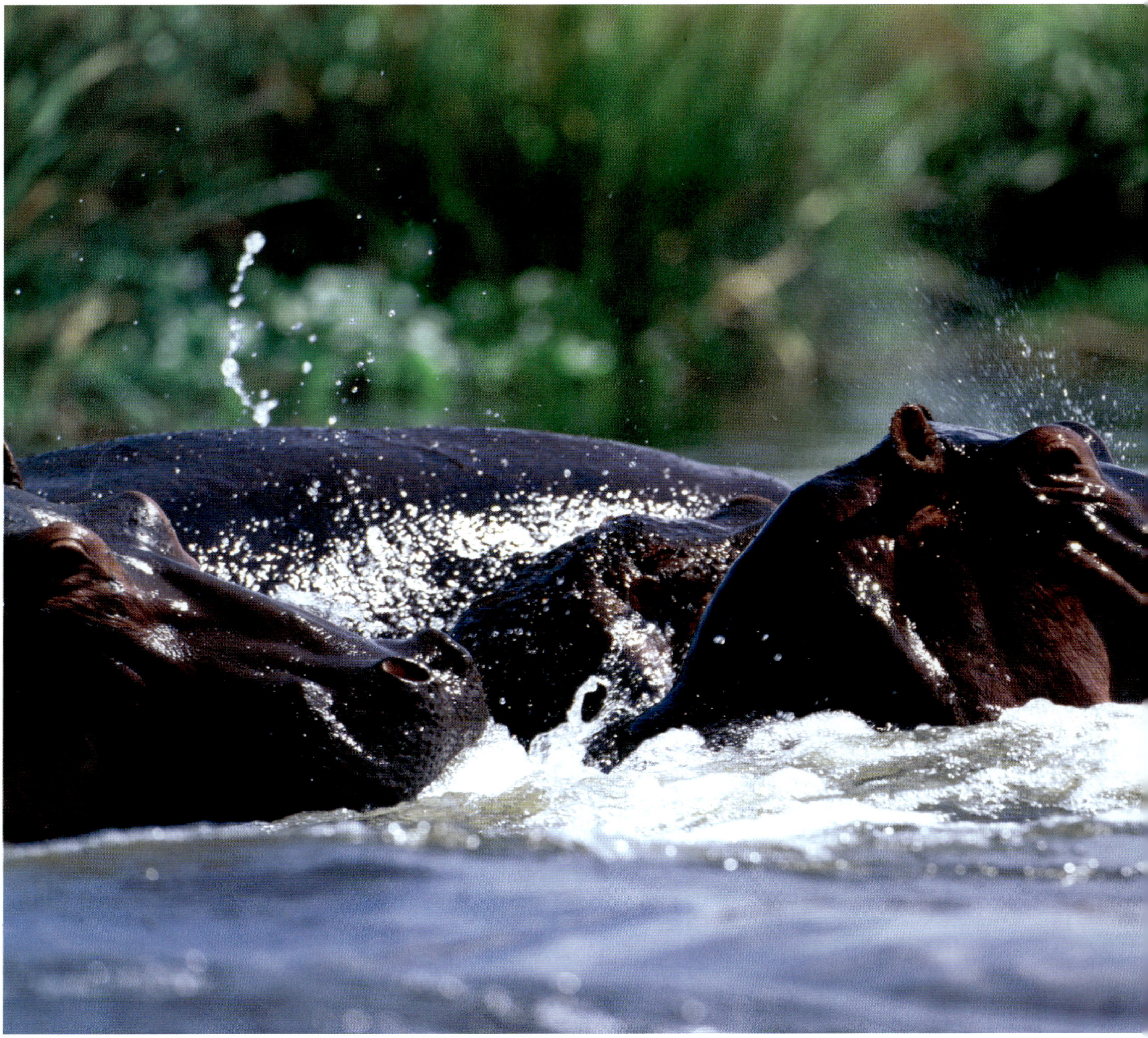

the lelwel hartebeest occurs west of the Nile. The hartebeest's darker cousin, the topi, is frequently seen in the Ishasha sector of Queen Elizabeth National Park. Far more common and widespread is the shaggy-looking waterbuck, which occurs in all protected savannah areas, grazing in small herds close to water. The variety that occurs there is the Defassa waterbuck, which has a solid white rump, as opposed to the white ring on the rump of the extralimital common waterbuck.

The handsome roan antelope is a reddish-brown animal with short backward-curving horns and a small mane on the back of its neck. It no longer occurs in any national park, having recently become extinct in Kidepo Valley and Lake Mburo, but may still occur in small numbers in Pian-Upe Wildlife Reserve. The rapier-horned Beisa oryx, weighing over 200 kilos (440 lbs), is a gregarious desert-adapted species that occurs in the drier parts of Kidepo Valley. Another species preferring the arid lands of Kidepo is the delicate Grant's gazelle, a light brown animal with lyre-

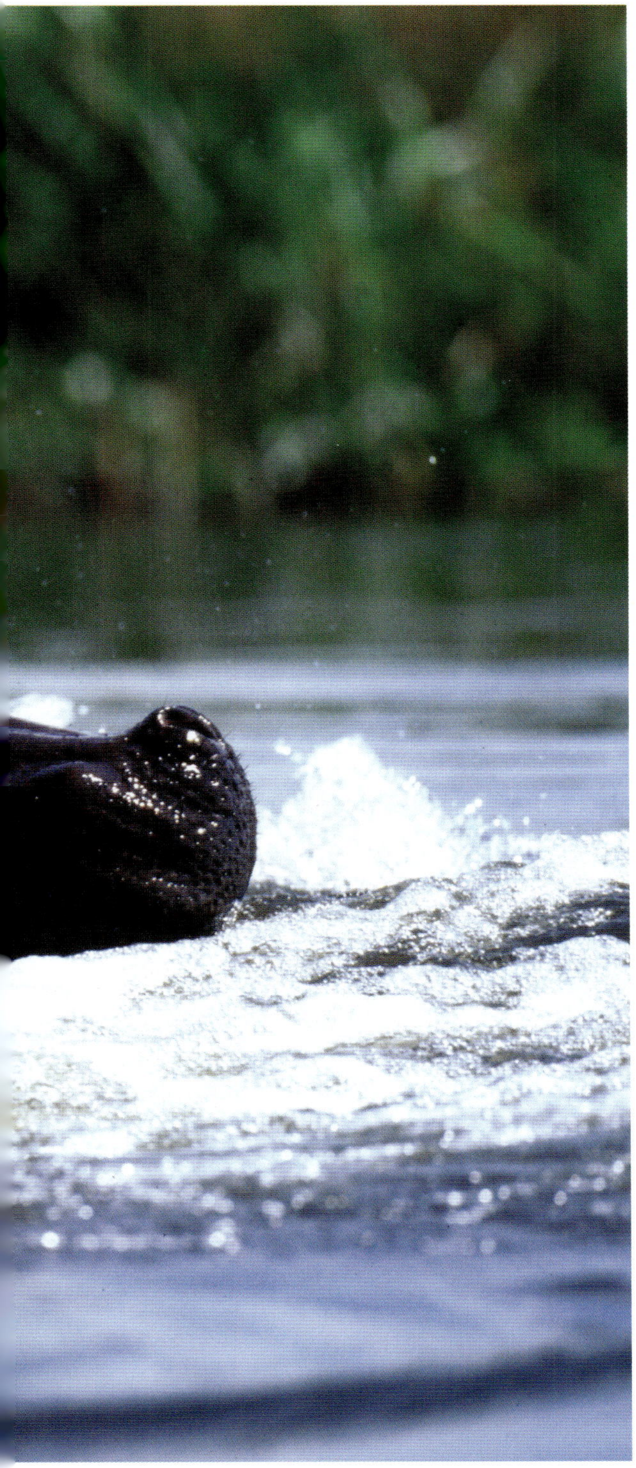

Left: Hippos are regularly seen up the stretch of the historic Nile.

shaped horns. Although herds can number up to 400, it is more common to see 20 to 40 of these gazelles grazing together on the plains. Common elsewhere in East Africa, the impala is a handsome chestnut antelope notable for the male's large horns, but its Ugandan range is limited to Lake Mburo National Park.

The medium-sized yellowish Bohor reedbuck, which prefers rank, medium-height grasslands as its home, may be found in Lake Mburo, Queen Elizabeth, and Murchison Falls National Parks. With small, crescent-shaped horns, it is often seen in pairs in open country near water. The smaller oribi, which has a long slender neck and silky coat, and is readily identified by the large black gland below each ear, is very common north of the Nile in Murchison Falls National Park, where one may see between 50 and 100 in one game drive. The smaller 18-kilogramme (40-lb) klipspringer can be seen prancing about on cliffs, rocky hillsides and mountain screes. It is thought that the klipspringer mates for life; it is often seen in pairs. Uganda is home to several species of duiker, including red, Harvey's, blue, and yellow-backed, all of which are restricted to rainforest interiors, where they tend to be common but very shy and elusive. The aberrant grey duiker is more often seen in woodland and savannah.

In addition to antelope, elephant and buffalo, several other herbivores occur in Uganda. One of these is the giraffe, the world's tallest animal, represented in Uganda by the Rothschild's race, which is intermediate to the blotchy-spotted Maasai giraffe and the more cleanly marked reticulated giraffe. Very common in the north of Murchison Falls National Park, but also present in Kidepo Valley, the giraffe is a creature of open woodland and acacia savannah, but there are curious gaps in its distribution – it has never been recorded in suitable habitat between the Victoria Nile and Kagera River, possibly because it finds large rivers difficult to cross.

The plains (Burchell's) zebra is the only species of wild horse family to occur in Uganda, where it is most common in Lake Mburo National Park. Although always within daily reach of water, the zebra avoids wetter areas where grasses are uniformly higher than one metre (three feet) and too tough and rank. Mature stallions gather small harems of mares and, even when they congregate in their hundreds, it is easy to spot these basic social units.

All three East African members of the pig family – warthog, giant forest hog, and bushpig – are present in Uganda. Most regularly seen is the ubiquitous warthog, a diurnal creature that typically trots busily across the savannah in small family parties with tail held upright. As a rule, the other two species are less readily located, because they forage nocturnally in thicket and forest interiors, but the giant forest hog can be seen in daylight on QENP's Channel Drive with unusual ease.

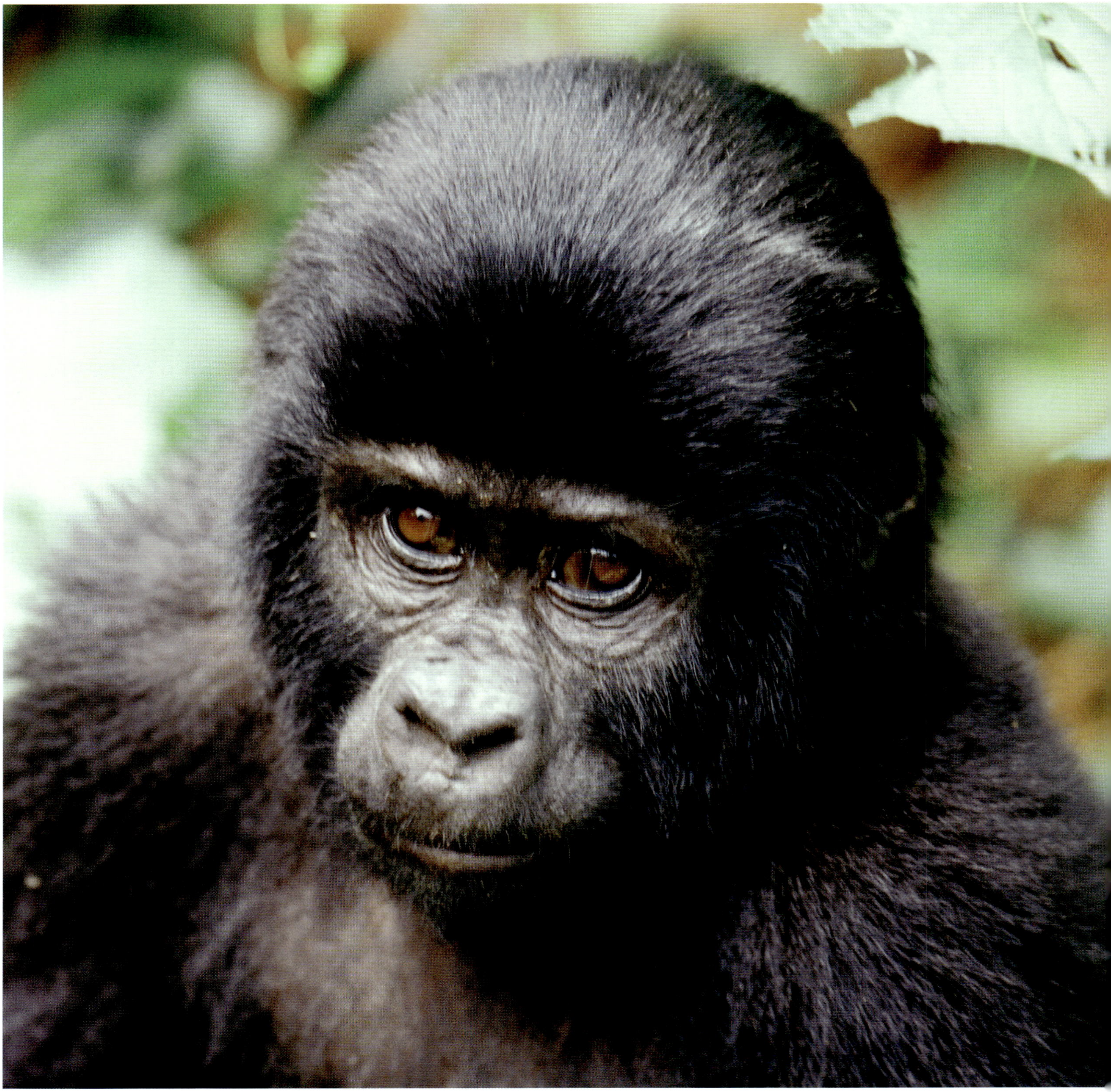

Despite appearances, the hippopotamus is more closely related to cetaceans (whales and dolphins) than to pigs. It is the most characteristic creature of many African waterways and Uganda is no exception, with the boat trips in Lake Mburo, Queen Elizabeth, and Murchison Falls National Parks offering a good opportunity for close-up views (and audios) of strongly territorial and highly vocal small family groups. Hippos forage out of the water, mostly at night, and normally spend their non-grazing hours partially submerged, but they do also sometimes walk a long way from water by day in cool moist weather. Because water is a separate habitat from that of humans, the two often live close together, and hippo persist in the midst of human settlement in many parts of Uganda where no other large mammals remain.

Above: Young gorilla.

Opposite: Adult gorilla at Bwindi.

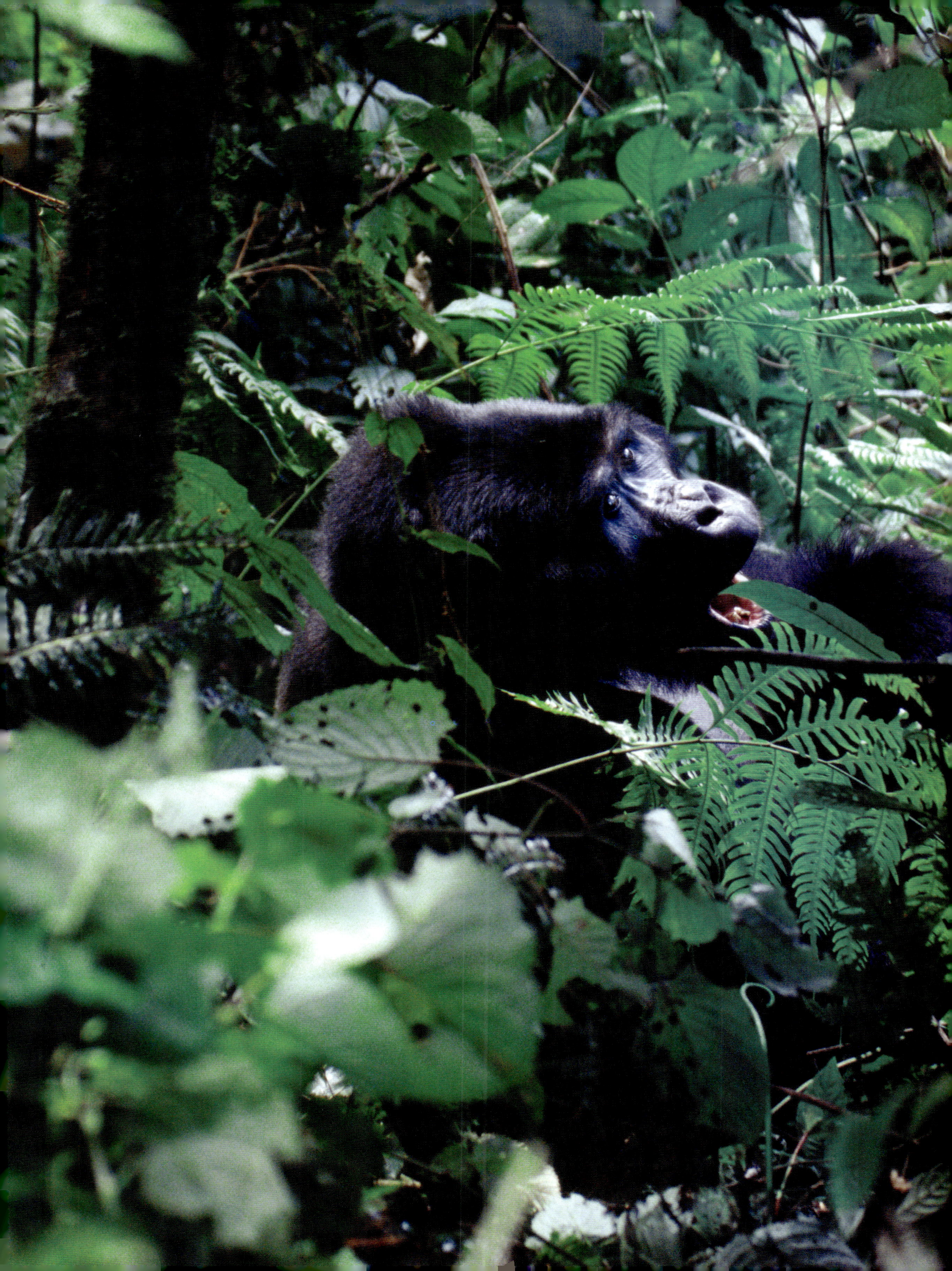

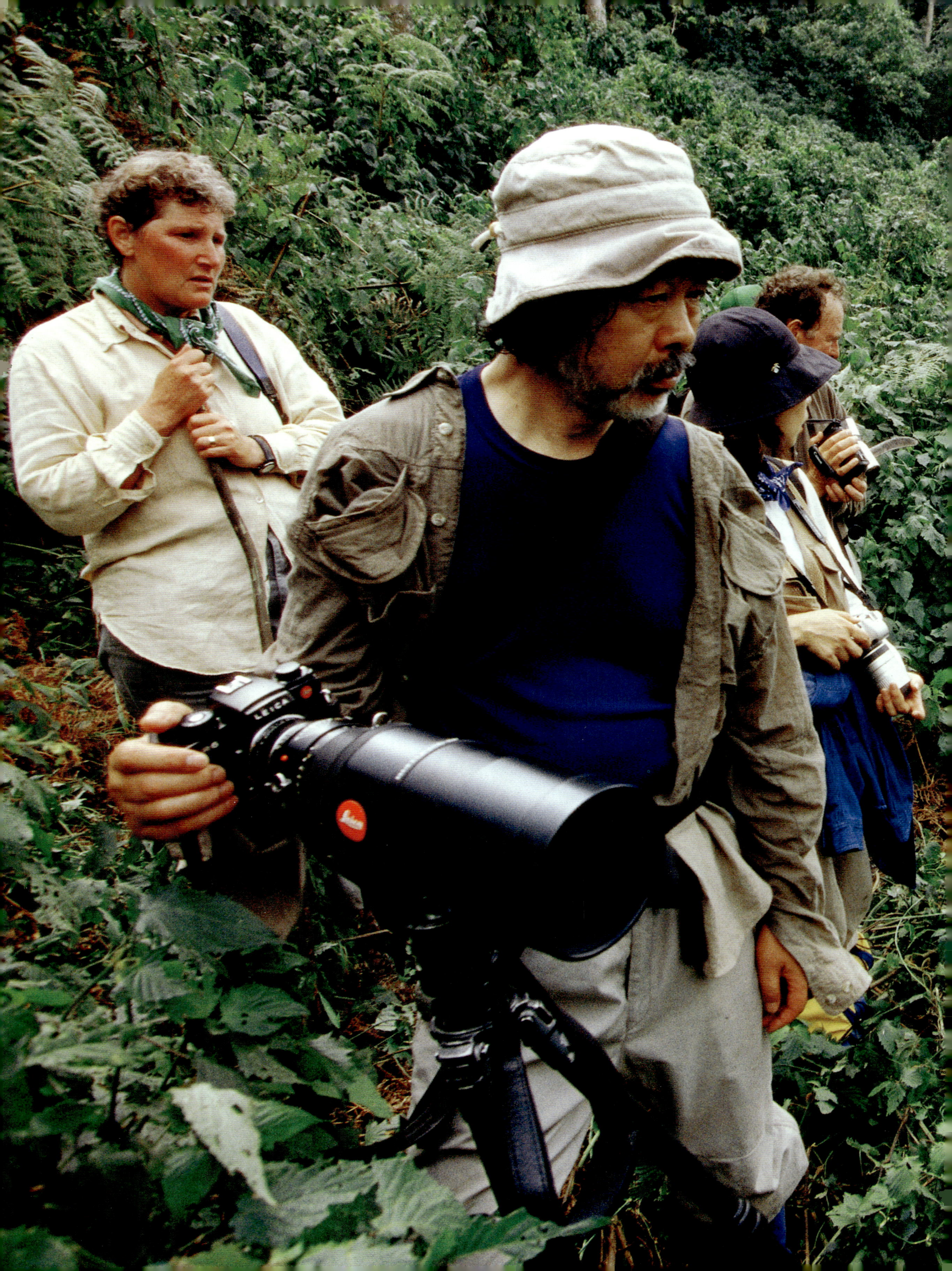
LEICA

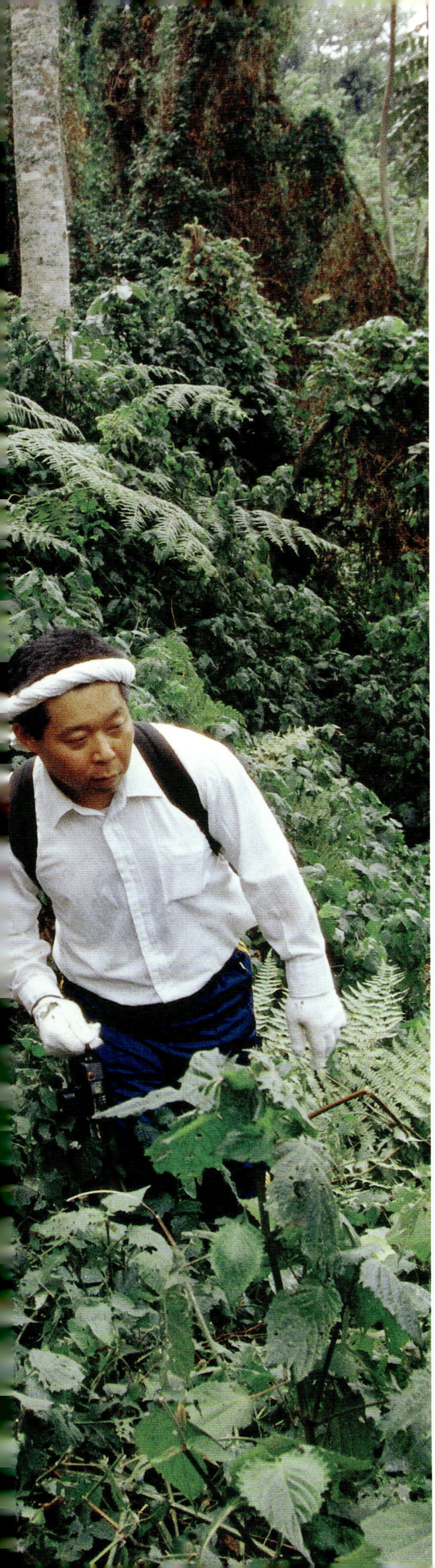

Uganda's Mountain Gorillas

Few creatures have captured humankind's attention like the gorilla. Although maligned for decades as one of the world's most ferocious and dangerous beasts, gorillas are now more often – and more accurately – portrayed as gentle giants teetering on the brink of extinction. Anatomically, socially, and behaviourally, humans recognize components of themselves in our largest primate cousin's physique and lifestyle. In-depth scientific field studies and comprehensive conservation programmes have increased our knowledge of the gorilla, and today individuals and governments are battling to preserve the species and its threatened forest homes.

Gorillas occur only in Africa and until 2001 they were all assigned to the same species, with three species being recognised, of which the mountain gorillas was the scarcest. More recent DNA testing and morphological studies suggest that the western and eastern gorilla populations, whose ranges lie more than 1,000 kilometres apart, are separate species. As things stand, the status of the western gorilla is relatively secure, though the population of 80,000 is undoubtedly in rapid decline. The situation with the eastern gorilla is far less certain: the estimated population of 17,000 lowland gorillas in the early 1990s is thought to have halved as a result of the Congolese civil war, while the mountain gorilla is listed as Critically Endangered, with perhaps 700 surviving individuals split more-or-less evenly between the Virunga Volcanoes (on the DRC/Rwanda/Uganda border) and Bwindi National Park – allowing Uganda 'boasting rights' to more than half the world's mountain gorillas.

Mountain gorillas are essentially terrestrial quadrupeds, walking on the soles of their hind limbs, but pivoting on the knuckles of their forelimbs, and (except when young) they seldom leave the ground or move much more than 1 kilometre in the course of a day. They are predominantly herbivorous, feeding mainly on the leaves, stems, and roots of specific plants.

Of the great apes, the gorilla shows the most stable bonding patterns. The same individuals typically travel together for years at a time, led by an adult male or 'silverback'. All males, as they mature, become silverbacks, developing very distinct characteristics, including an impressive silver saddle extending across their back from shoulders to rump. However, not all silverbacks are successful enough to ultimately gain leadership of a group. The size of a gorilla group varies from two to as many as 35 individuals. Average group size is about nine. In addition to a dominant silverback and occasionally one or two subordinates, the group consists of several adult females, sub-adults (who will most likely transfer out of their natal group upon reaching sexual maturity), juveniles, and infants.

Right: Male silverback gorilla.

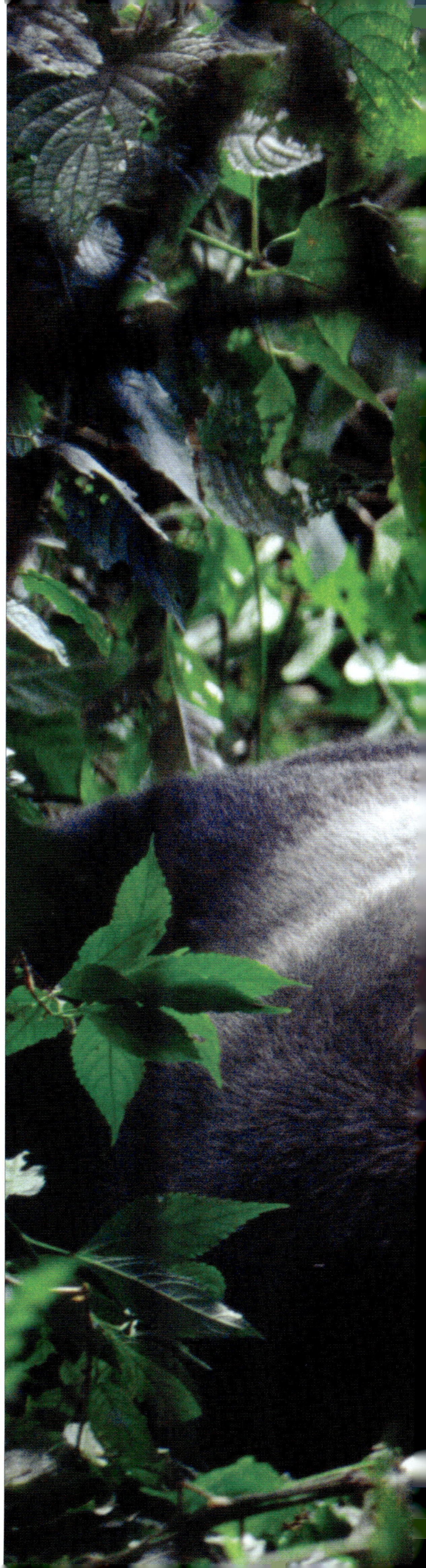

Male gorillas mature at 10 to 12 years, but because of competition for mates, few will start to breed before 15 years. Female gorillas mature sexually at about nine years. Gorillas do not have a distinct breeding season; females cycle about every 28 days (comparable to a human female). Gestation is about eight-and-a-half to nine months. Newborn infants weigh 1.8 to 2.2 kilos (four to five pounds) and are totally dependent on their mother. Infants are weaned at about three-and-a-half years of age and females, who mature at six to nine years, typically give birth at four- to five-year intervals.

Group daily activity patterns follow a relatively simple routine. Awaking in their night nests after daybreak, gorillas begin foraging and continue to feed slowly and selectively until a mid-morning rest period, during which individuals sleep, groom each other and, if younger, play. The rest period may last more than an hour, after which feeding once again begins. An afternoon rest period follows several additional hours of feeding. The group wraps up the day with another feeding bout, and just before dusk, each gorilla – excluding infants – begins constructing a nest in which it will sleep throughout the night. Unweaned infants sleep with their mothers.

Mountain gorillas are protected in two parts of Uganda: the Bwindi Impenetrable National Park (formerly known as the Impenetrable Forest) and Mgahinga Gorilla National Park on the northern slopes of the Virunga volcanoes adjacent to Volcano National Park in Rwanda and Virunga National Park in DRC. The Ugandan gorilla conservation programmes are modelled after Rwanda's innovative Mountain Gorilla Project and have received monetary and technical assistance from the International Gorilla Conservation Programme, a consortium funded by the African Wildlife Foundation, the World Wide Fund for Nature, and the Fauna and Flora Preservation Society. The programme integrates sound park management policy, anti-poaching patrols, conservation education programming, gorilla tourism, and community revenue sharing to produce a product of improved forest and gorilla protection.

Bwindi Impenetrable National Park is Uganda's most accessible and dependable gorilla viewing park. The gorilla tourism programme that has become such an integral component of mountain gorilla conservation complements the daily activity patterns of the gorillas. Beginning in the early morning, trackers hike to the point in the forest where the gorilla group was last seen on the previous day. Following a trail through dense forest and over rough terrain, the previous night's nests are discovered and a fresh trail is pursued. With luck, the gorilla group will be found quickly, during the mid-morning or early afternoon rest period, and visitors will be able to observe a wide variety of social interaction and

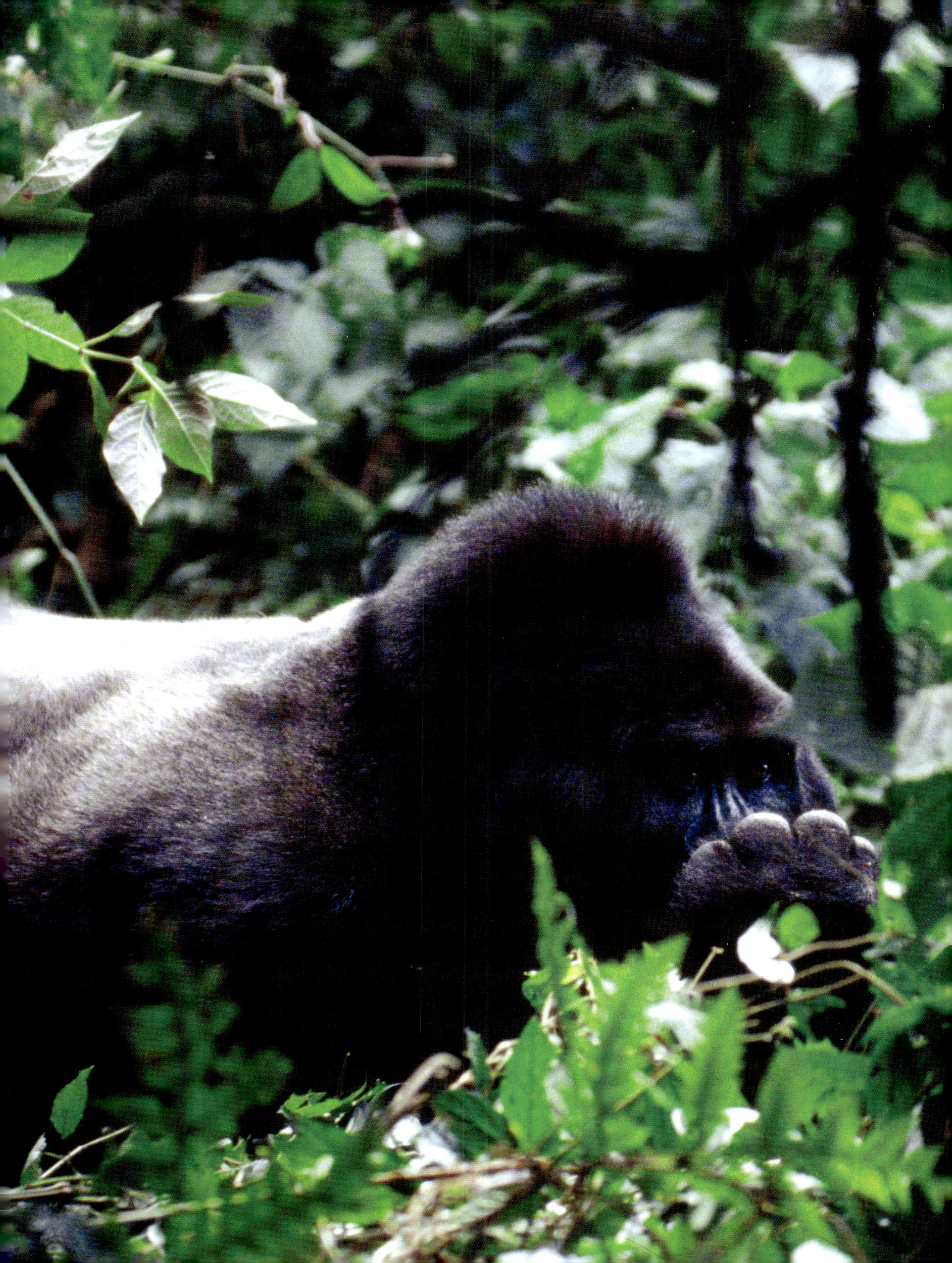

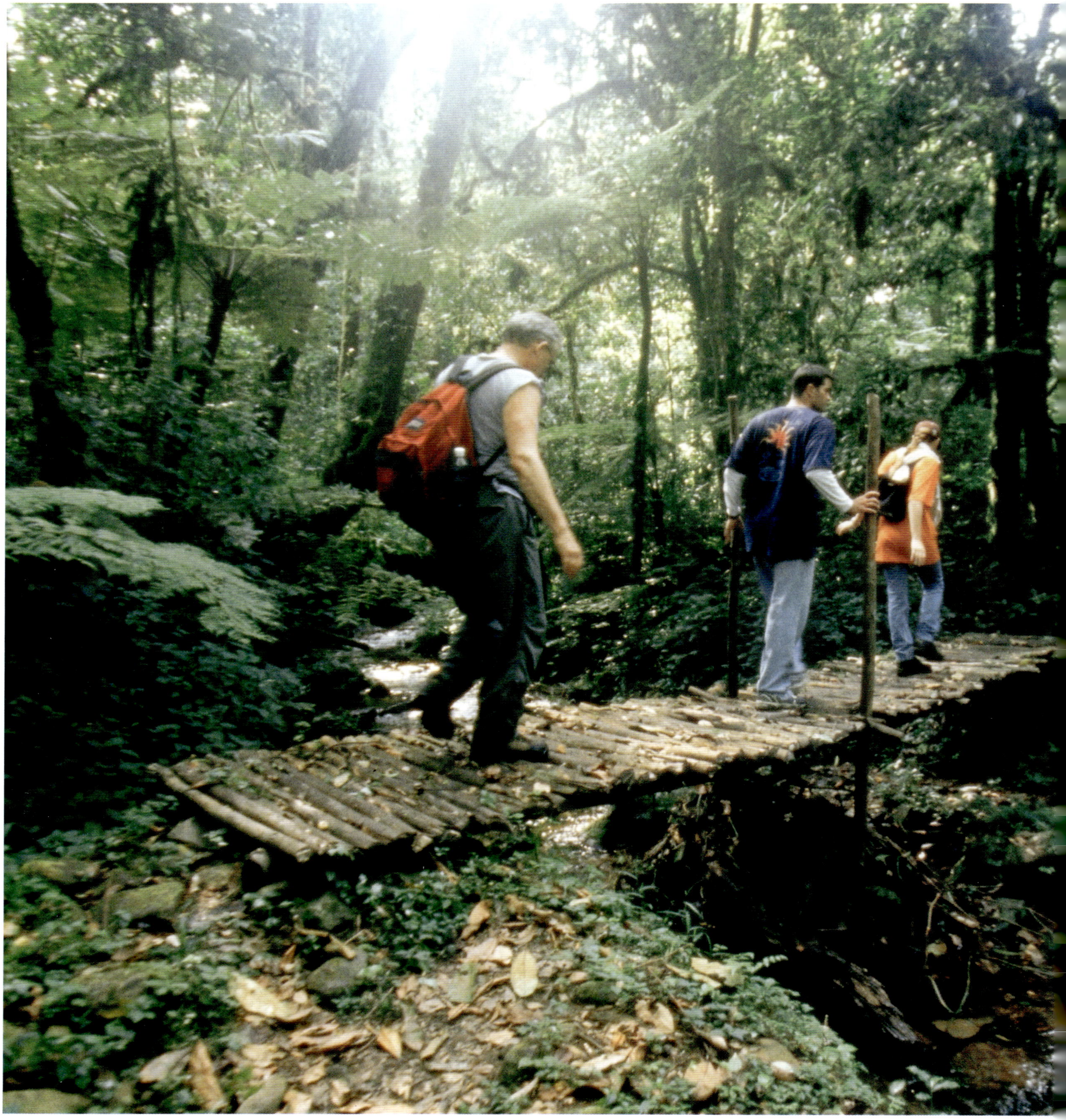

Below: Tourists cross wooden bridge on floor of Bwindi National Park.

Following pages: The thick rainforest of Bwindi Impenetrable National Park.

Mwamba Crater Lake towards Kasese with the Rwenzoris rising on the right.

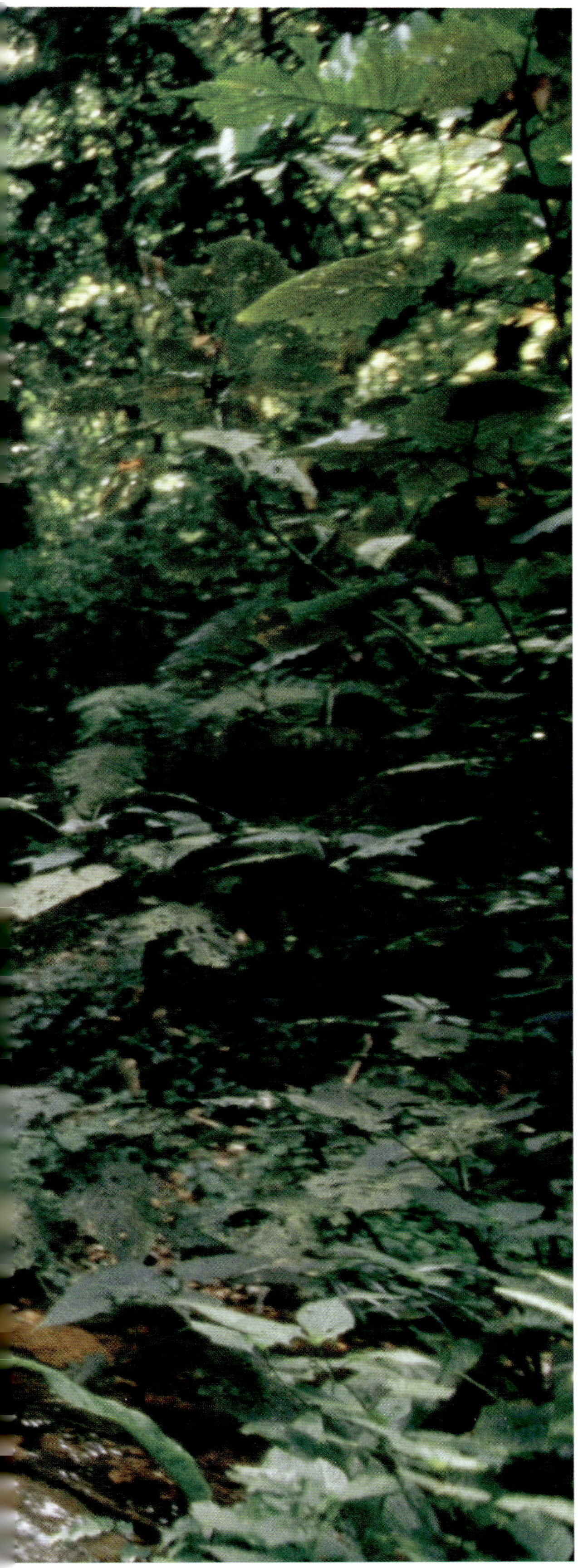

behaviour. Tourists stay only one hour with a gorilla group; the gorillas are then left to pursue their lifestyle within their established home range, which averages 10 to 15 square kilometres (four to six square miles).

This limited, well-regulated, expensive, and relatively non-intrusive natural history tourist activity has become a key ingredient in protecting the mountain gorilla. By allowing national governments and local communities to perceive gorillas and their forested homes as important national resources, it is hoped that the future of this extremely endangered species may be ensured. Indeed, despite several incidents of poaching in recent years, the global mountain gorilla population has increased by around 15% since gorilla tourism was initiated in the 1980s.

Birdlife: Beautiful and Bounteous

As with most of eastern Africa, Uganda has a large and diverse avifauna, some species of which are found nowhere else. More than 1,000 species, including many migratory species from Europe or Asia, have been recorded. Given the relatively small size of the country, this number is exceptionally high – in Africa, only the DRC, Kenya and Tanzania have longer national checklists, and all are much larger countries. Uganda is of particular interest for the presence of at least 100 species whose range is otherwise limited to inaccessible parts of central Africa, and it's the best place in Africa to see the eagerly sought shoebill.

Flora: A Rich Diversity

Despite the strong human impact, botanically Uganda remains a rich country. Because of its geographical position, astride the equator between east and central Africa, it is a real melting pot of influences.

The vegetation of Uganda can be divided into six principal belts. Four are mainly dependent on the quantity of available moisture: forest and its derivatives; moist savannah, including evergreen woodlands, open, bushed or wooded grasslands; dry savannah, including mainly thorn bushland; and semi-desert vegetation with mainly dwarf shrub grassland. A fifth belt includes aquatic vegetation and permanent swamps. A sixth one, the afro-alpine moorland and grassland, is influenced more by temperature than by rainfall.

If Uganda had not been deeply marked by human activity in the last 3,000 years, a continuous belt of dense rainforest would stretch from the hot Semliki lowlands and the ice-topped Rwenzoris to the shores of Lake Victoria and the slopes of Mount Elgon. A few thousands of years ago these forests probably covered about 20 per cent of the country. Today only a few isolated blocks remain, more or less protected in national parks and forest reserves.

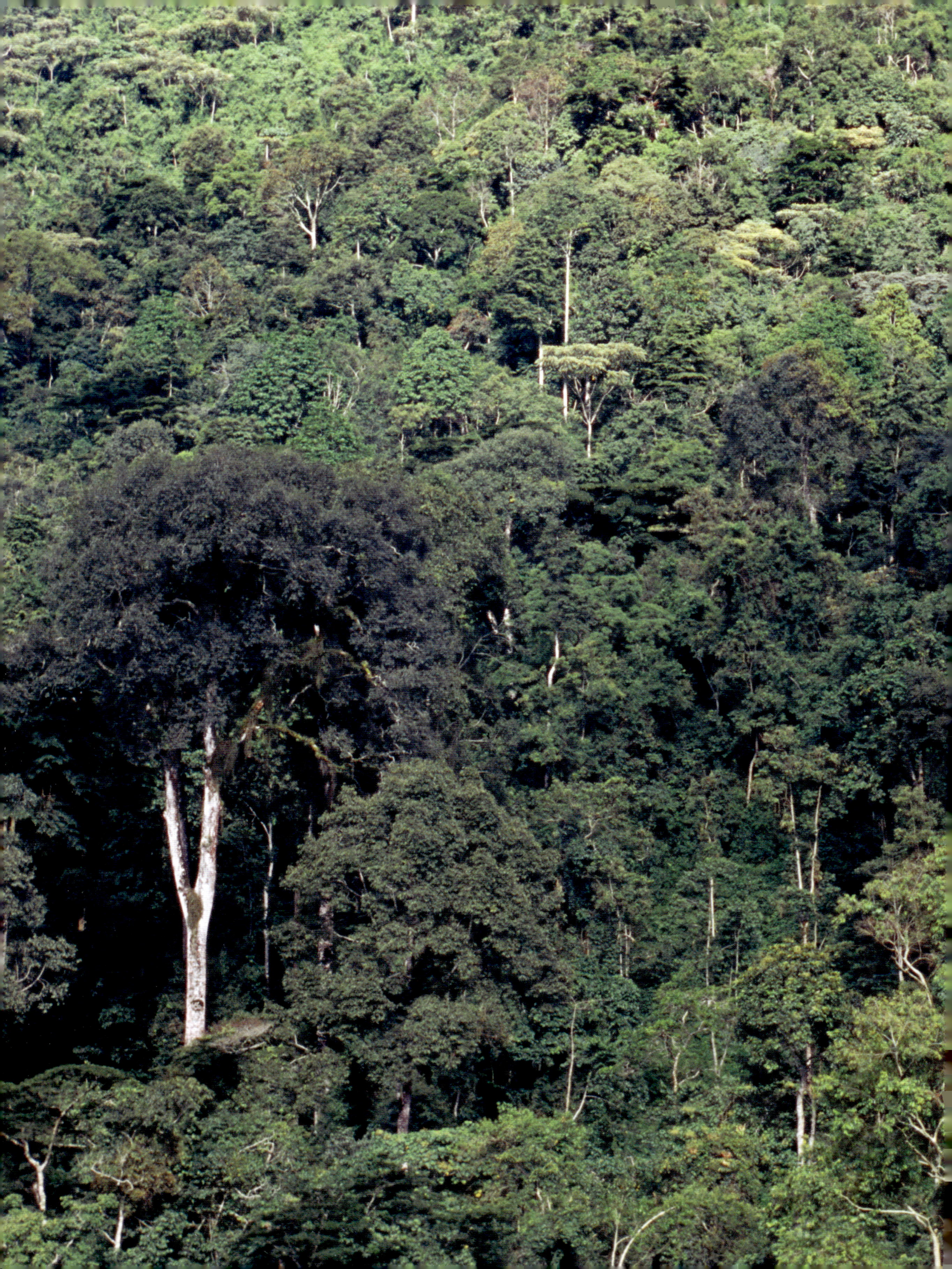

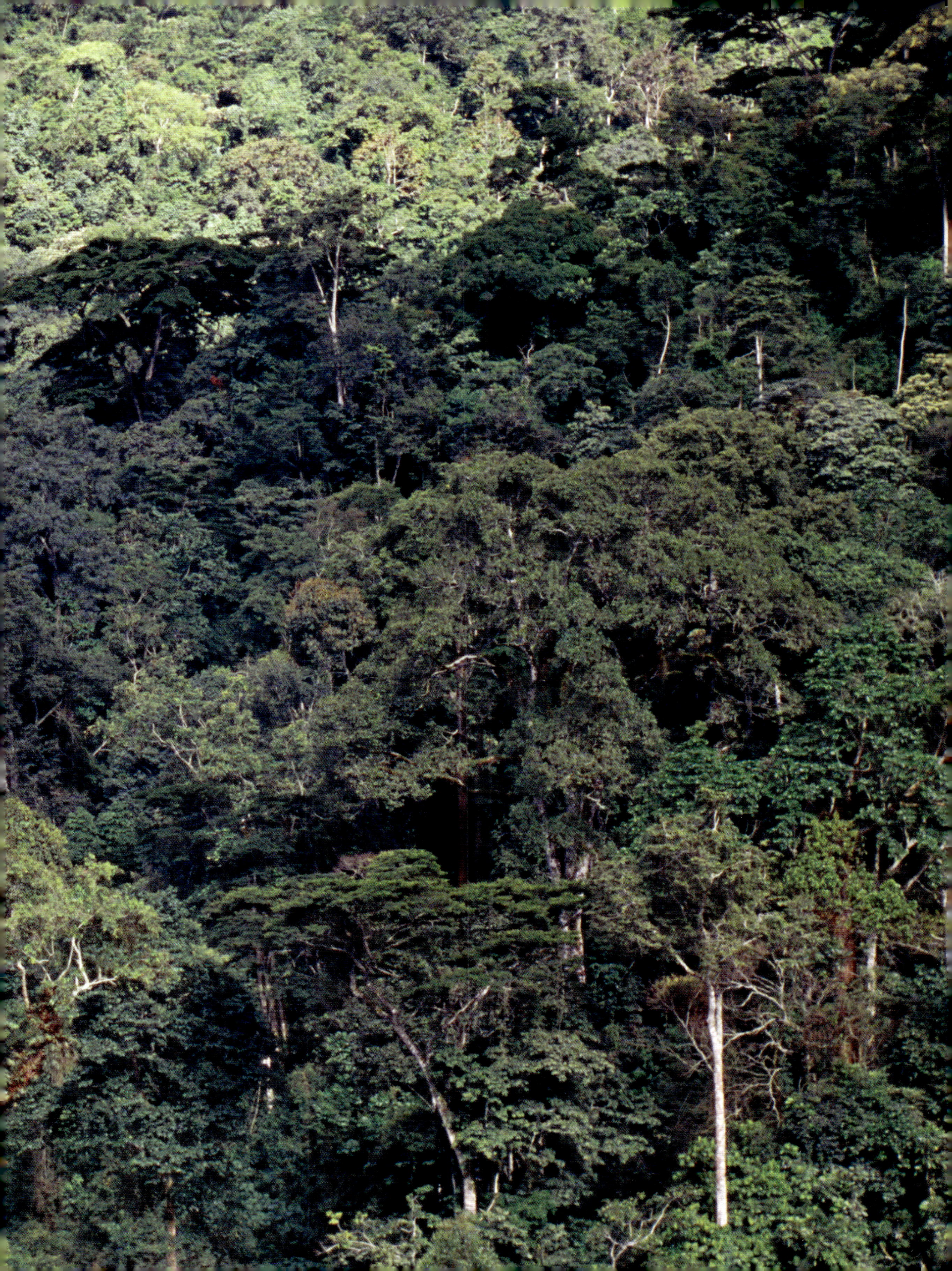

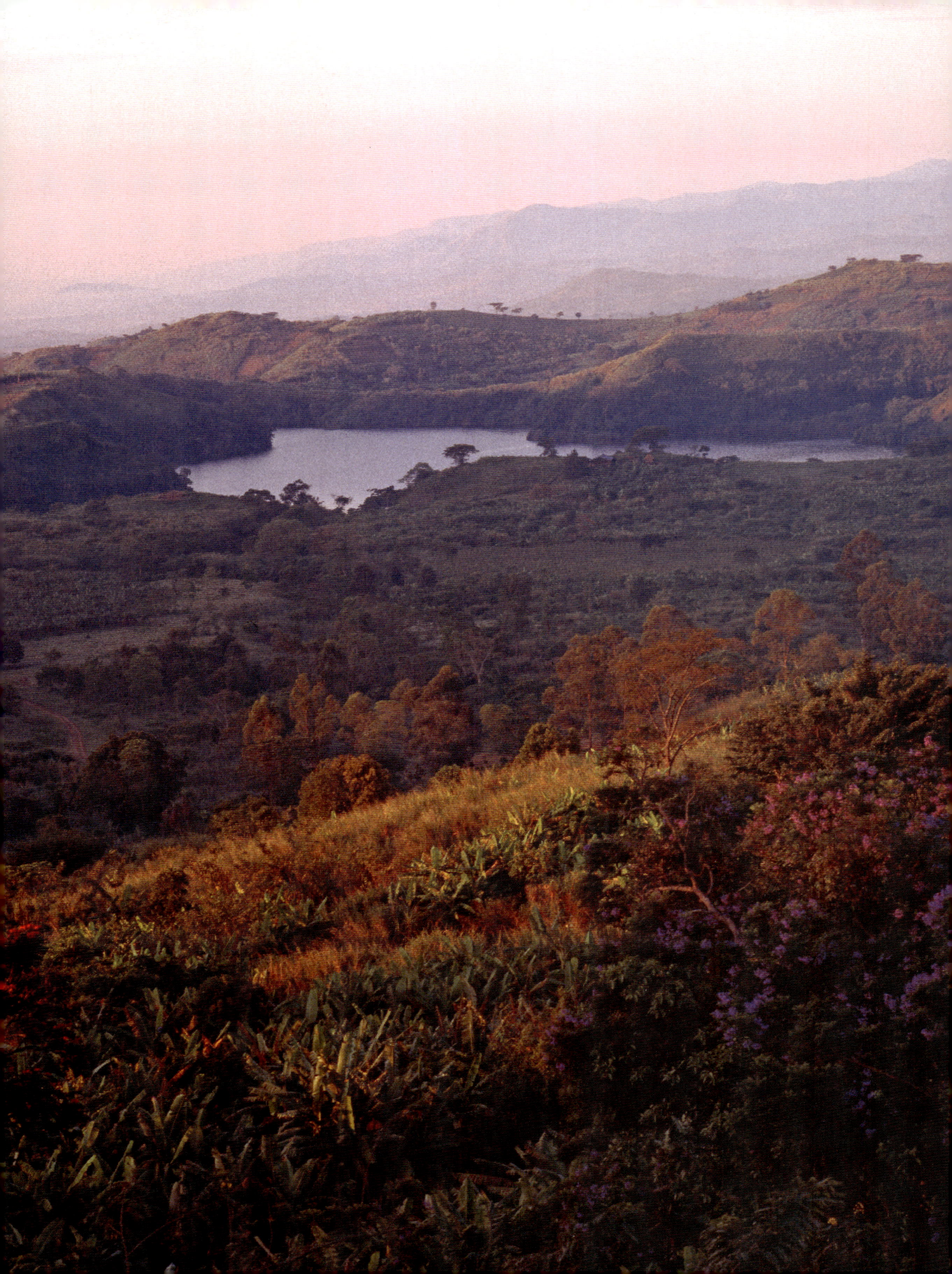

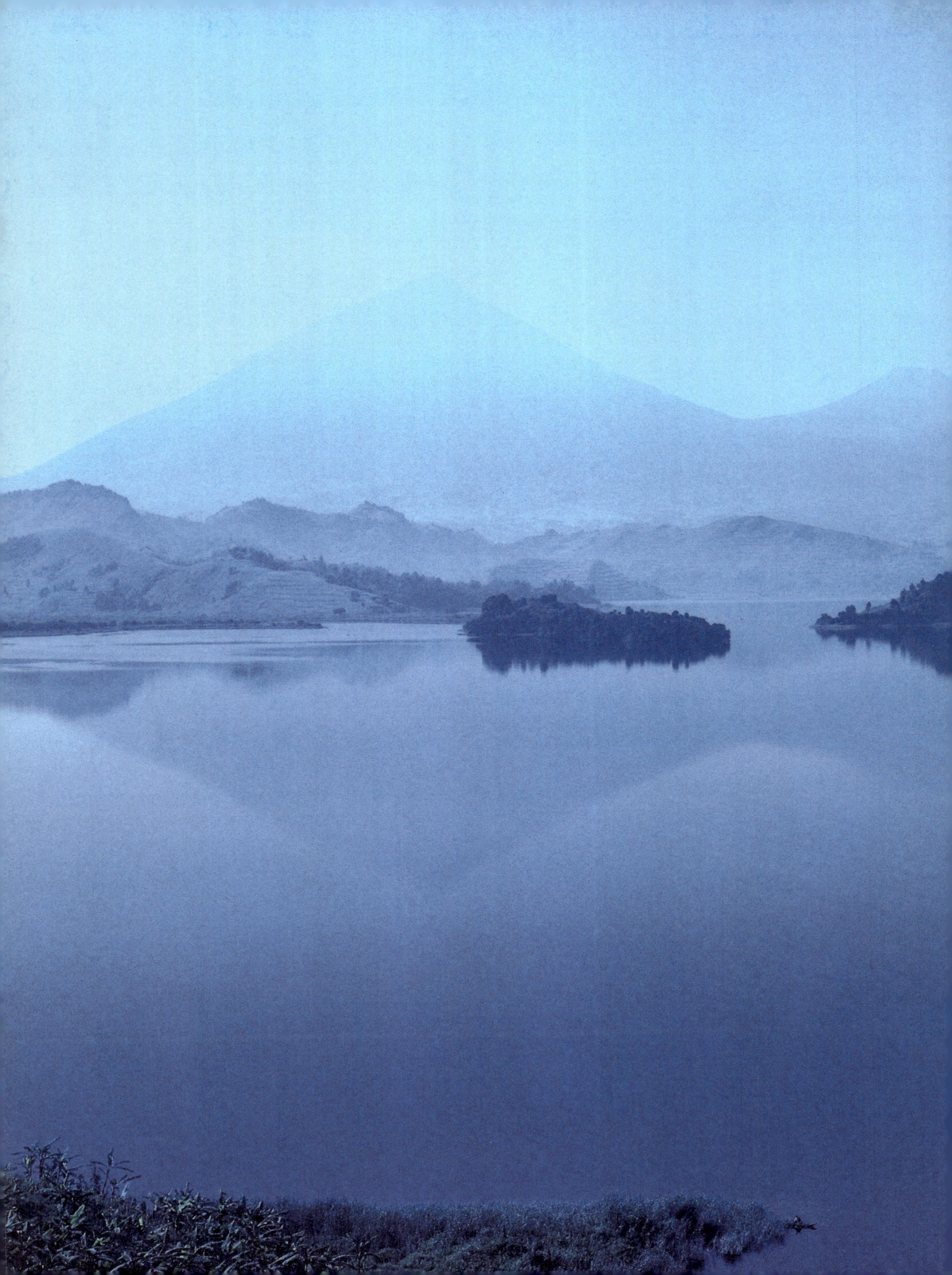